# Networking Fundan

Develop the networking skills required to pass the Microsoft
MTA Networking Fundamentals Exam 98-366

**Gordon Davies**

BIRMINGHAM - MUMBAI

# Networking Fundamentals

**Commissioning Editor:** Amey Varangaonkar
**Acquisition Editor:** Rohit Rajkumar
**Content Development Editor:** Carlton Borges
**Senior Editor:** Rahul Dsouza
**Technical Editor:** Komal Karne
**Copy Editor:** Safis Editing
**Project Coordinator:** Anish Daniel
**Proofreader:** Safis Editing
**Indexer:** Manju Arasan
**Production Designer:** Arvindkumar Gupta

First published: December 2019

Production reference: 1171219

Published by Packt Publishing Ltd.
Livery Place
35 Livery Street
Birmingham
B3 2PB, UK.

ISBN 978-1-83864-350-8

www.packt.com

Subscribe to our online digital library for full access to over 7,000 books and videos, as well as industry leading tools to help you plan your personal development and advance your career. For more information, please visit our website.

# Why subscribe?

- Spend less time learning and more time coding with practical eBooks and Videos from over 4,000 industry professionals

- Improve your learning with Skill Plans built especially for you

- Get a free eBook or video every month

- Fully searchable for easy access to vital information

- Copy and paste, print, and bookmark content

Did you know that Packt offers eBook versions of every book published, with PDF and ePub files available? You can upgrade to the eBook version at www.packt.com and as a print book customer, you are entitled to a discount on the eBook copy. Get in touch with us at customercare@packtpub.com for more details.

At www.packt.com, you can also read a collection of free technical articles, sign up for a range of free newsletters, and receive exclusive discounts and offers on Packt books and eBooks.

# Contributors

## About the author

**Gordon Davies** has been in the IT industry for 18 years. He has worked for a number of high profile UK national and global organizations with a particular focus on networking and infrastructure. More recently, Gordon has provided IT training to IT apprentices in the UK undertaking infrastructure, networking, and cybersecurity apprenticeships. Gordon has recently joined an international cybersecurity service provider as a cybersecurity analyst.

*I want to thank Summer, for her support and patience and for putting up with me, especially each time I've had to spend yet another weekend working on this book.*

# About the reviewer

**Richard Price** has been a Cisco certified instructor trainer and academy instructor since 2006, following on from a career in the IT industry working for larger UK and international companies.

Richard is a qualified teacher and taught networking in both higher and further education. He was instrumental in developing FdSc and BSc programs for The Manchester College and supervising graduate projects. Richard has several years of experience as a lead technical trainer on apprenticeship courses within apprenticeship provisions at leading UK training providers, specializing in infrastructure, networking, and cybersecurity.

# Packt is searching for authors like you

If you're interested in becoming an author for Packt, please visit authors.packtpub.com and apply today. We have worked with thousands of developers and tech professionals, just like you, to help them share their insight with the global tech community. You can make a general application, apply for a specific hot topic that we are recruiting an author for, or submit your own idea.

# Table of Contents

# Preface

As the world becomes ever more connected, the demand for networking engineers will only increase. In *Networking Fundamentals*, we focus on the objectives of Microsoft's MTA: Networking Fundamentals Exam 98-366. This will not only help you prepare in terms of sitting the exam, but will also provide you with a basic knowledge of networking to build upon throughout your networking career.

## Who this book is for

This book is intended for those individuals wishing to gain an introductory understanding of networking or those wishing to undertake the MTA: Networking Fundamentals Exam 98-366.

## What this book covers

Chapter 1, *Differentiating between Internets, Intranets, and Extranets*, provides you with an understanding of what a network is, before going into the details of internets, intranets, and extranets, describing each of these in turn. The chapter also introduces a number of basic security mechanisms, including firewalls and demilitarized zones. It goes on to explain how to configure internet security zones on a Windows client.

Chapter 2, *Understanding Local Area Networks*, gives you an overview of what the author describes as *scales of networks*, defining the differences between LANs, WANs, PANs, MANs, and CANs. In this chapter, we focus on local area networking, and explain the use of IP addresses, hostnames, and MAC addresses to identify devices on a network. Following on from this, it describes the key characteristics of wired and wireless networks, before concluding with a discussion of **virtual local area networks (VLANs)**.

Chapter 3, *Understanding Wide Area Networks*, introduces the concept of WANs, and explains the steps required to set up and configure a broadband connection. It goes on to discuss the various WAN technologies, including circuit switching, packet switching, frame relay, and leased lines. It looks at dial-up and takes you through the process of setting this up. The chapter also focuses on carrier standards, and looks at those in use, including ISDN, xDSL, SONET, satellite, and cellular.

Chapter 4, *Understanding Wireless Networking*, focuses on the ever-developing technology of wireless, specifically Wi-Fi. The chapter begins by exploring the various IEEE 802.11 standards, discussing the attributes of each, and the CSMA/CA access method. We then move on to discuss wireless topologies, before concluding the chapter by covering wireless security methods.

Chapter 5, *Network Topologies – Mapping It All Out*, looks at various topologies in use in modern networks, beginning with differentiating between logical and physical topologies. The chapter then moves on to cover bus, ring, star, mesh, and hybrid topologies, discussing the attributes of each.

Chapter 6, *Switches and Switching – Forwarding Traffic on a Local Network*, looks at how data moves around a local network. It begins by explaining the purpose of switching and how frame-forwarding decisions are made, before focusing on the use of spanning-tree protocols to combat broadcast storms. The chapter then covers the characteristics of switches, such as managed versus unmanaged, connectivity, ports, and VLANs, and finishes with a discussion of switch security.

Chapter 7, *Routers and Routing – Beyond a Single Network*, moves us into the realm of moving data between networks, and begins by looking at how routing decisions are made, and discusses static and default routes. The chapter then moves on to provide an overview of distance vector, link-state, and hybrid protocols. It then explains the steps required to implement routing on a Windows Server, before concluding the chapter with a discussion of network address translation and quality of service.

Chapter 8, *Media Types – Connecting Everything Together*, discusses the various means of physically connecting networking devices. The chapter looks at the attributes of each cable type – coaxial, twisted pair, and fiber optic – and a use case of each.

Chapter 9, *Understanding the OSI Model*, introduces the concept of network models before focusing on the OSI model. We take each of the seven layers of the OSI model in turn, discussing the functionality of each, and, where applicable, discuss the use of ports and highlight common protocols for the layers.

Chapter 10, *Understanding TCP/IP*, looks at the second of the two common network models. It provides a comparison between this and the OSI model, and explains the functionality of each layer.

Chapter 11, *Understanding IPv4*, discusses the most common of the addressing schemes in use today. The chapter begins by providing an overview of IPv4, in particular, the structure of an IPv4 address. It then moves on to discuss the five classes of IPv4 available, including, where appropriate, providing a distinction between public and private address ranges. Following on from this, subnet masks and their purposes are covered, before moving on to classless inter-domain routing. Finally, the chapter explains the steps in assigning IPv4 addresses to hosts.

Chapter 12, *Understanding IPv6*, introduces you to the successor to IPv4, namely, IPv6. An overview of IPv6 is provided, including the syntax of an IPv6 address, and the rules for representing an IPv6 address in a shortened format. The chapter then moves on to discuss the various address types and prefixes, and how IPv6 addresses are assigned. The chapter concludes by covering methods of interoperability between IPv4 and IPv6.

Chapter 13, *Understanding Name Resolution*, discusses the purpose of name resolution in modern networks. We cover the most prevalent method, **Domain Name Service (DNS)**, explaining the use of fully qualified domain names, and how they link to DNS records to provide resolution. The chapter then explains how host files are used to provide a localized static name resolution methodology, before looking at the relative legacy name resolution provided by **Windows Internet Name Service (WINS)**.

Chapter 14, *Network Services*, rounds up a number of common network services. The chapter begins by disusing **Dynamic Host Configuration Protocol (DHCP)**, including how it operates, and explains the steps to setting this up on a server. We then move on to covering firewalls, providing differentiation between how each type of firewall operates. Next, an overview of proxy servers is provided, before we move on to remote desktop services and explain the steps for connecting to such a service. The chapter then explains the difference between active and passive file transfer protocols. Following this, the chapter covers file servers, and introduces the concepts of share and NTFS permissions. The chapter concludes by discussing print servers and domain controllers.

Chapter 15, *Mock Exam 1*, provides you with an opportunity to test the knowledge that you have acquired throughout this book by means of a 40-question mock exam.

Chapter 16, *Mock Exam 2*, provides a second mock exam of 40 questions to test your knowledge even further.

# To get the most out of this book

You should have a basic understanding of how to navigate round a Windows operating system, including how you navigate to the control panel of your particular system, and also how to open Command Prompt.

While the majority of the activities in this book can be carried out on your standard operating system, it is recommended that you install a version of your operating system on a virtual machine. This will ensure that any changes you may make do not impact your normal system.

Some examples utilize a Windows Server operating system. If you would like to attempt those examples yourself, you can do so by downloading an evaluation copy of the operating system from Microsoft's Evaluation Center: `https://www.microsoft.com/en-gb/evalcenter/`.

Undertake all of the end-of-chapter quizzes, and address any wrong answers before moving on to the next chapter. It is important that you know why something is the answer, rather than just knowing that it is the answer.

Read Chapter 11, *Understanding IPv4*, and then re-read it. This is arguably the one topic everyone struggles with. Make sure you understand it before moving on.

# Download the color images

We also provide a PDF file that has color images of the screenshots/diagrams used in this book. You can download it here: `https://static.packt-cdn.com/downloads/9781838643508_ColorImages.pdf`.

# Conventions used

There are a number of text conventions used throughout this book.

`CodeInText`: Indicates code words in text, database table names, folder names, filenames, file extensions, pathnames, dummy URLs, user input, and Twitter handles. Here is an example: "In Command Prompt, type `hostname` and press the *Enter* key."

**Bold**: Indicates a new term, an important word, or words that you see on screen. For example, words in menus or dialog boxes appear in the text like this. Here is an example: "Select **Properties** from the context menu."

Warnings or important notes appear like this.

 Tips and tricks appear like this.

# Get in touch

Feedback from our readers is always welcome.

**General feedback**: If you have questions about any aspect of this book, mention the book title in the subject of your message and email us at customercare@packtpub.com.

**Errata**: Although we have taken every care to ensure the accuracy of our content, mistakes do happen. If you have found a mistake in this book, we would be grateful if you would report this to us. Please visit www.packtpub.com/support/errata, selecting your book, clicking on the Errata Submission Form link, and entering the details.

**Piracy**: If you come across any illegal copies of our works in any form on the internet, we would be grateful if you would provide us with the location address or website name. Please contact us at copyright@packt.com with a link to the material.

**If you are interested in becoming an author**: If there is a topic that you have expertise in, and you are interested in either writing or contributing to a book, please visit authors.packtpub.com.

# Reviews

Please leave a review. Once you have read and used this book, why not leave a review on the site that you purchased it from? Potential readers can then see and use your unbiased opinion to make purchase decisions, we at Packt can understand what you think about our products, and our authors can see your feedback on their book. Thank you!

For more information about Packt, please visit packt.com.

# Section 1: Network Infrastructure

In this section, you will be able to describe the difference between internets, intranets, and extranets, and identify the characteristics and technologies in use in local and wide area networks. You will also gain an understanding of the various wireless technologies available to us. Finally, you will learn about the common network topologies and the benefits and disadvantages of each.

This section comprises the following chapters:

- Chapter 1, *Differentiating between Internets, Intranets, and Extranets*
- Chapter 2, *Understanding Local Area Networks*
- Chapter 3, *Understanding Wide Area Networks*
- Chapter 4, *Understanding Wireless Networking*
- Chapter 5, *Network Topologies - Mapping It All Out*

# 1
# Differentiating between Internets, Intranets, and Extranets

As technology moves more and more toward providing us with a completely interconnected world, there is an ever-increasing demand for IT professionals who are skilled in networking to plan, implement, and maintain these networks. The world of networking is vast and ever-evolving, meaning that IT professionals need to keep their skill set up to date. By understanding the fundamentals of networking, you will be forming a solid foundation that you can build your skills upon and will be in a better position to support your infrastructure.

This chapter focuses on identifying the key characteristics of internets, intranets, and extranets, allowing you to differentiate between each of them. It will also serve as an introduction to security mechanisms such as **Virtual Private Networks** (**VPN**), security zones, and firewalls.

The following topics will be covered in this chapter:

- Understanding a network
- Introduction to basic security features
- Microsoft security zones

## Technical requirements

To complete the exercises in this chapter, you will need a PC or virtual machine running Windows 7 or above (preferably Windows 10) with a working network connection.

# Understanding a network

Before we dive into this subject in detail, I think it is important to actually define what actually constitutes a network. *Network* is one of those terms that is used often but when you ask someone to describe it, they can't without being vague.

For the purpose of this book, I will define a network as a set of two or more endpoint devices that communicate with each other through a shared medium. You will notice that I refer to *endpoint devices* and avoid the use of the terms *computer* and *servers*. While it would not truly be incorrect to describe them as such, these terms tend to narrow down an individual's train of thought. We'll look at this in the following activity.

 **Activity 1**: Make a list of all the devices you can think of that are networked in some way.

I would envisage that your list included at least PCs, servers, and laptops. At one point in time, this would have been a fairly accurate summarization, but nowadays, we need to move away from what I would dub as *traditional* computers and realize that the ability to connect to a network is ubiquitous in so many devices. Here's my list:

- Phones
- Mobile/cell phones
- Games consoles
- Smart TVs
- Fridges
- Heating systems
- Speakers
- Headphones
- Cars
- CCTV
- Toys

The list goes on in this age of the **Internet of Things (IoT)**, where it seems that anything and everything will be given the opportunity to connect to a network in some way.

What do all these devices have in common? They all possess at least one **network interface card (NIC)**, they are running a **network operating system (NOS)**, and have been coded in a way that takes advantage of one or more of the networking protocols that are available. We have liberated the term protocol from politics, where it means a strict code of etiquette and precedence, for utilization in computing. In computing, it refers to a set of rules or standards that have to be adhered to. Some of the most common networking protocols will be discussed throughout this book.

Another definition of a network is that it's a shared *medium,* and I have found that this term often confuses people, so I feel it is worth clarifying it early on. When referring to a network medium or to network media, we are talking about the channel that the data is being transferred across. This could be a cable or through airwaves in the case of wireless networks. It should be noted that the use of the terms *medium* and *media* in computing are not restricted to networking, and you will also hear them being used in reference to storage and hard drives, floppy disks, CDs, DVDs, Blu-rays, and USB flash drives. Network cables and wireless standards will be discussed in Chapter 7, *Routers and Routing – Beyond a Single Network,* and Chapter 4, *Understanding Wireless Networking,* respectively.

We need to have some means of identifying devices on a network. To achieve this, we can use hostnames, IP addresses, and MAC addresses. None of these are mutually exclusive, and most networks will utilize all three. We will discuss these in more detail later in this book. Next, we will try to understand what an internet is all about.

# Understanding internet

Although they're often used synonymously, there is a subtle difference between an internet and the Internet. When spelled with a lowercase *i*, internet is derived from inter-network and refers to the connectivity between different networks. When capitalized, the Internet refers to the services that are publicly available outside of our own networks and the supporting infrastructure.

Let me clarify this with two examples. Company A's infrastructure connecting directly to company B's infrastructure would be classed as an inter-network. In this instance, the connections are not publicly available. However, when you connect to a web page such as Facebook or Hotmail, or to a **File Transfer Protocol (FTP)** server, this is classed as the Internet as they are publicly available.

We have also come to treat the Internet and the **World Wide Web (WWW)** as the same entity, whereas this is not the case. As we mentioned previously, the Internet refers to services and infrastructure. In contrast, the WWW is only a portion of the services that the Internet provides, albeit a large portion, and refers to servers that provide websites to end users.

For the purposes of this book, unless specifically mentioned, I will use the terms internet, Internet, and WWW interchangeably.

# Understanding intranets

The prefix *intra-* means on the inside. From that, we can deduce that an intranet relates to network communication within our network. Any services that are provided within an intranet are restricted to your network. Access to these services will be controlled through user/device authentication to ensure that they remain private and inaccessible from the Internet.

You will find that some organizations host internal web pages, such as the collaborative tool SharePoint from Microsoft, or a Human Resources self-service portal, to name just two. It is often the case that these are also referred to as the company intranet.

 **Exam tip:** If you can remember that *intra-* means inside, then an internet must be outside your network.

# Understanding the extranets

As more and more organizations rely on network connectivity, it makes sense to utilize this technology to make business more efficient. How can we do that? By allowing access to our intranet to organizations other than our own. This raises obvious security concerns. Therefore, access is only permitted to trusted (or authorized) organizations such as our business partners or our larger customers. Furthermore, this access is limited only to the resources that they need for their normal interaction with us.

Let's assume that company A sells specialist circuit boards; company B uses these circuit boards as key components for a product they sell. Before company B takes any orders for their product, they need to ensure company A has the circuit boards in stock. They could call company A over the phone, but this means they may have to call multiple times a day. Wouldn't it be easier to allow them to check stock availability themselves and then place an order? You can facilitate this by creating an extranet.

 **Exam tip**: Do not confuse an extranet with a **demilitarized zone (DMZ)**, otherwise known as a perimeter network, which we will discuss shortly. For an extranet, the words to look for are *trusted* or *authorized*.

The following diagram is a visual representation of how these three areas fit together:

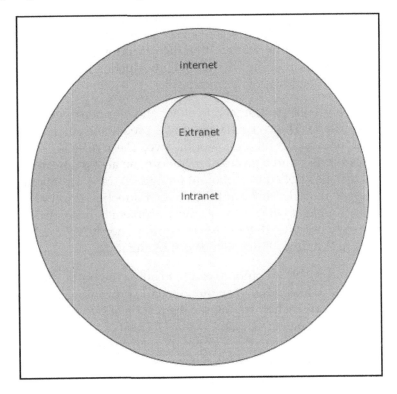

Figure 1.1: The internet, intranet, and extranet

Now that we have understood what internets, intranets, and extranets are, we will now look into the basic security features of a network.

# Introduction to basic security features

With all of this interconnectivity, it is important that we protect our networks and the data held within them. At this stage, I would like to introduce you to some of the following basic security technologies that we can utilize to protect our networks:

- Firewalls
- DMZ
- VPN

# Firewalls

Firewalls are arguably one of the best methods of protecting your computer, yet very few people understand them. I would suggest the reason for this is because Microsoft does a pretty good job of implementing firewalls within their Windows **operating systems (OSes)**. Windows Firewall has been part of the OS since its introduction in Windows XP Service Pack 2, and over time, its functionality has increased.

As a basic description, a firewall is designed to either allow or deny network traffic based upon a set of defined criteria. These criteria could be a predefined set of default rules or could be user-created, or even a combination of the two. These rules are often referred to as **access control entries (ACEs)**, and a group of them form an **access control list (ACL)**. These criteria could then be applied to outbound (or egress) traffic or inbound (or ingress) traffic. Understanding that a rule can be applied in each direction is important to know. For example, you may be troubleshooting a connectivity problem between two devices, so you would use the commonly used ICMP tool known as ping since ICMP can be used for malicious purposes and Windows Firewall blocks it by default.

You are aware of this and enable an outbound rule to allow the traffic out, but you get no responses back. This is very likely due to an inbound rule preventing ICMP traffic back into your PC. In the following screenshot, we can see the results of two attempts to ping the IP address 8.8.8.8, which belongs to Google's public DNS server, and is commonly used by IT support staff to test connectivity to the Internet. We can see that the ping command at the beginning of the screenshot is successful. Before running the command a second time, I enabled an outbound firewall rule that blocks ICMP traffic. As you can see, the second command does not elicit the same results as the first one:

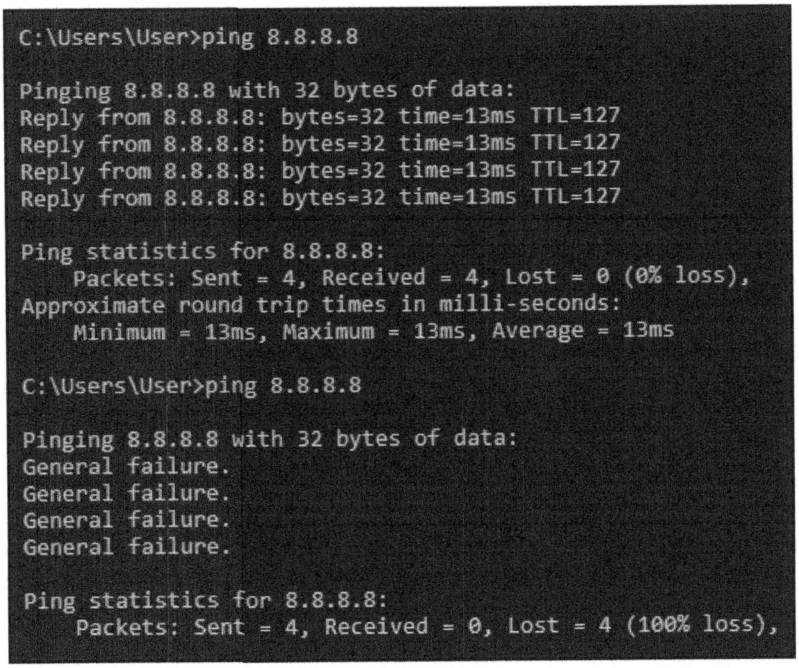

```
C:\Users\User>ping 8.8.8.8

Pinging 8.8.8.8 with 32 bytes of data:
Reply from 8.8.8.8: bytes=32 time=13ms TTL=127
Reply from 8.8.8.8: bytes=32 time=13ms TTL=127
Reply from 8.8.8.8: bytes=32 time=13ms TTL=127
Reply from 8.8.8.8: bytes=32 time=13ms TTL=127

Ping statistics for 8.8.8.8:
    Packets: Sent = 4, Received = 4, Lost = 0 (0% loss),
Approximate round trip times in milli-seconds:
    Minimum = 13ms, Maximum = 13ms, Average = 13ms

C:\Users\User>ping 8.8.8.8

Pinging 8.8.8.8 with 32 bytes of data:
General failure.
General failure.
General failure.
General failure.

Ping statistics for 8.8.8.8:
    Packets: Sent = 4, Received = 0, Lost = 4 (100% loss),
```

Figure 1.2: Ping results

A number of firewalls read through their rules in a sequential manner. They read the rules in order until they find one that matches, and then apply that rule and doesn't carry out any further processing. So, what problems could arise from this? Let's look at the following pseudo-firewall rules:

1. Block all inbound traffic from an IP address between 10.0.0.1 and 10.0.0.10.
2. Allow all inbound traffic from IP address 10.0.0.5.

The firewall would look for a match for rule 1 first, and if no match was found, it would then move on to check rule 2. If a match was found against rule 1, then it would block the traffic, and not even look at rule 2. That's all well and good, but what happens to any inbound traffic from 10.0.0.5? Despite that address explicitly being allowed at rule 2, it matches the criteria at rule 1, so it would be blocked. A better way of doing this would be to reverse the order of the rules:

1. Allow all inbound traffic from IP address 10.0.0.5.
2. Block all inbound traffic from an IP address between 10.0.0.1 and 10.0.0.10.

By reversing the rules, any inbound traffic from 10.0.0.5 would be received by the firewall and compared against rule 1. In this case, rule 1 is a match. The traffic is allowed and rule 2 never gets checked.

Windows Firewall is an example of a host-based firewall. A host-based firewall is one that is either built into the OS or installed on the device. The limitation of this is that you need to configure the firewall on each device and it only protects that device. One saving grace if you are in a domain environment is that you can deploy these settings to each machine using a group policy object. A network-based firewall, on the other hand, provides protection to all of your networks and monitors traffic going in and out of the network. This may be through a dedicated hardware device or as a feature on another network device, such as a router. In an organization, you may find network-based firewalls are in operation between your own networks, and not just between your internal network and the outside world.

Reading the preceding content, you may be thinking that a network-based firewall is the better of the two as it protects the entire network. However, look at the following diagram and pay particular attention to the placement of the firewall. It's only inspecting traffic that transits through it. But what would happen if **Computer A** was compromised? If we only had a network-based firewall in place, there is nothing preventing **Computer A** from attacking **Computer B**:

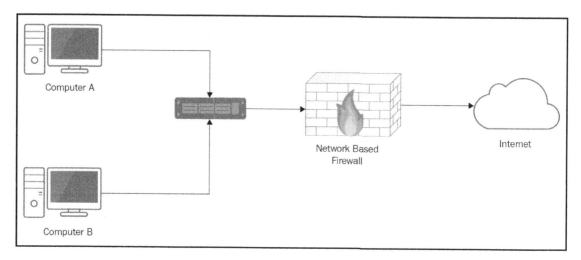

Figure 1.3: Network-based firewall

So, is a host-based firewall better? It would certainly prevent the preceding issue where **Computer A** attacks **Computer B**, but it leaves your network susceptible to an attack from outside. You may be thinking, *that's OK, because the host-based firewalls would protect the systems*. That may be correct for some systems, but not all network devices have the capability to have a host-based firewall. A lot of IoT devices are prime examples of this. Because of this, it is recommended that any network you run has both host-based and network-based firewalls to provide what is known as defense in depth.

Careful consideration needs to take place in respect of positioning the network-based firewalls to ensure there are no gaps, and to allow you to plan your rules out adequately.

We will cover the various different types of firewalls in more detail later in Chapter 14, *Network Services*, but for now, I would like to look at the built-in Windows Firewall.

Windows Defender Firewall is accessible via **Control Panel | System and Security | Windows Defender Firewall**. We can see how my firewalls have been configured in the following screenshot:

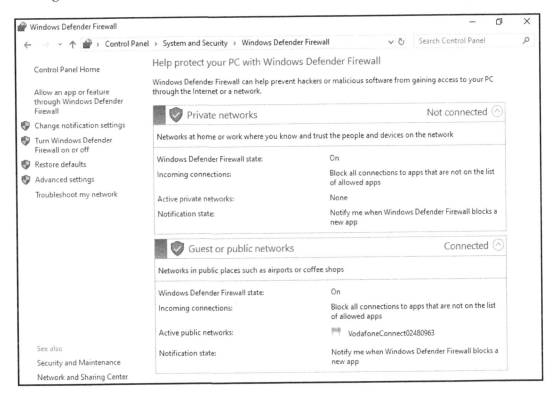

Figure 1.4: Windows Defender Firewall settings

Notice that it details the configuration for private networks and public networks. When you connect to a new network, you are prompted to specify what sort of network location you are connecting to. Home or work networks are classed as private networks; Wi-Fi hotspots in bars, libraries, coffee shops, and so on would be classed as guest or public networks. When you select one of these options, a set of preconfigured firewall rules are applied to that connection. A connection type that is not displayed in the preceding screenshot is domain. This option is only available if the device is connected to a domain. Notice that these are read-only settings. To change them, we need to click on **Turn Windows Defender Firewall on or off** on the left-hand side of the page. This will take us to the following screen:

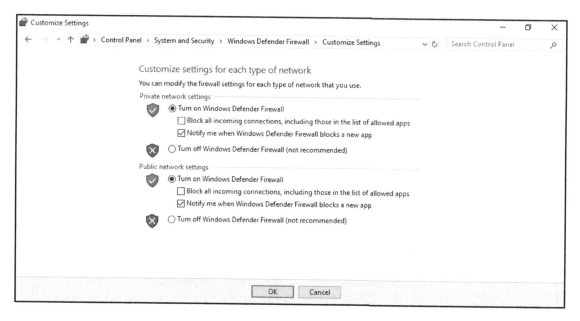

Figure 1.5: Basic Windows Defender Firewall settings

As you can see, if the firewall is turned on, we have two further options we can configure: **Block all incoming connections, including those in the list of allowed apps** and **Notify me when Windows Defender Firewall blocks a new app**. The latter option is useful if you don't know what applications are trying to use your network connection since you can allow or deny on a case-by-case basis.

The preceding screenshots just show basic configuration. We can go into the **Advanced settings** by clicking on that option on the left-hand side of the Windows Defender Firewall pop-up screen. This will open a new window, as shown in the following screenshot:

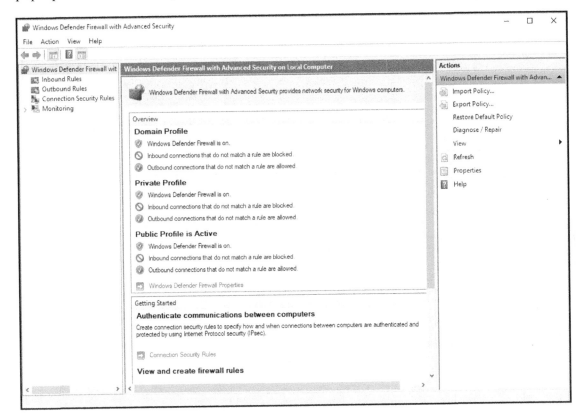

Figure 1.6: Windows Defender Firewall advanced settings

The initial screen provides you with an overview of the firewall and, on the right-hand side, allows you to import and export firewall policies. Clicking on **Inbound Rules** takes you to a list of current inbound rules, as shown in the following screenshot:

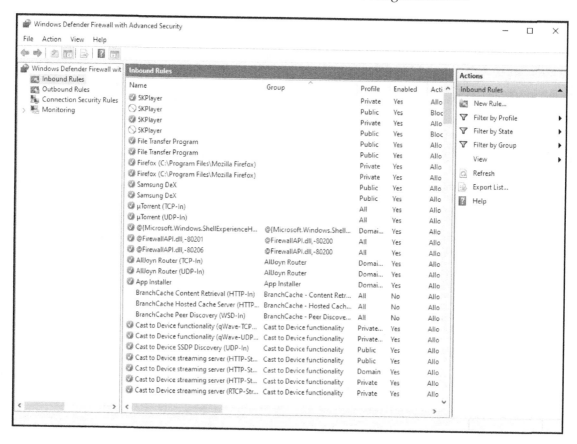

Figure 1.7: Inbound Rules

Likewise, clicking on **Outbound Rules** provides you with a list of current outbound rules, as shown in the following screenshot:

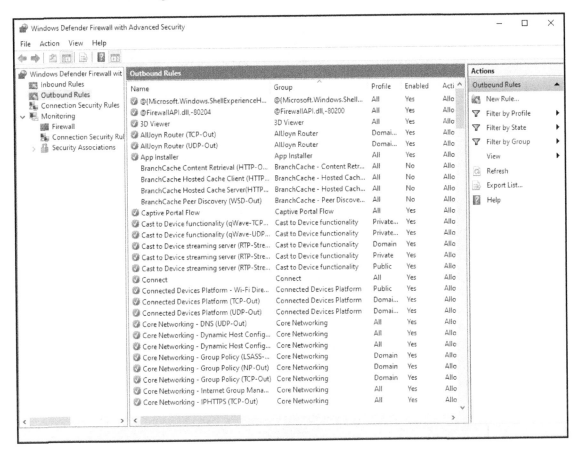

Figure 1.8: Outbound Rules

By double-clicking on an existing rule, you can see the properties of that rule and edit the configuration accordingly:

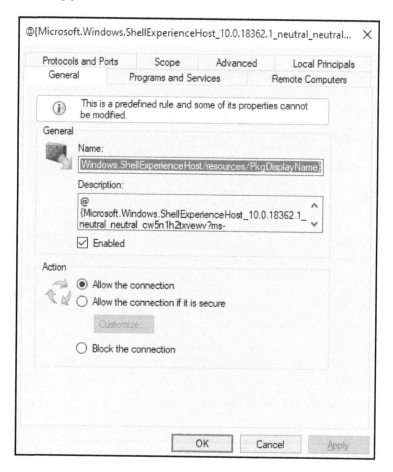

Figure 1.9: Rule properties

A new rule can be created by selecting the appropriate direction, that is, inbound or outbound, and then clicking on **New Rule...** on the right-hand side. As shown in the following screenshot, I have chosen an outbound rule:

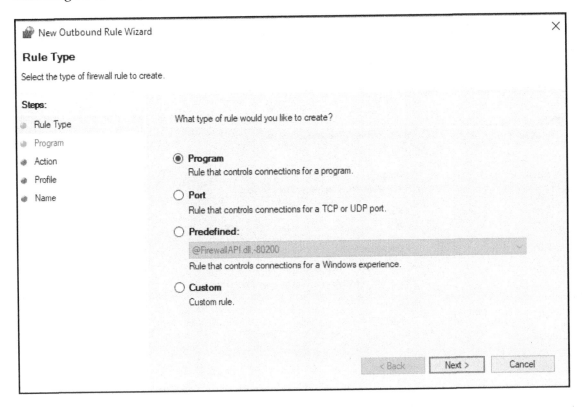

Figure 1.10: Creating a new rule

Note that we can create program, port, predefined, and custom rules. Look at the steps on the left-hand side. The **Program** and **Port** options have five steps. **Predefined** only has two steps since the action is predefined. Choosing **Custom**, however, gives us seven steps, as shown in the following screenshot:

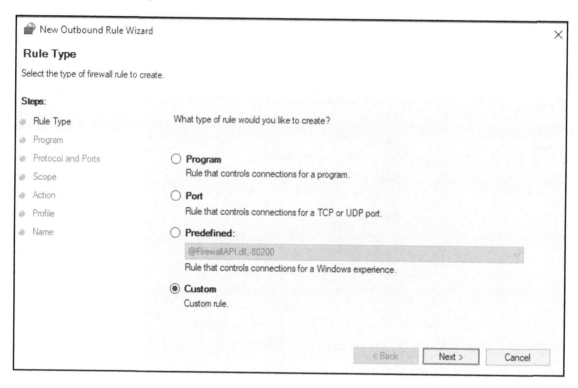

Figure 1.11: Custom rules

Going through each of the rule types and configuring each would drastically increase the length of this book; however, I would like to just highlight one of the steps of the custom rule, namely **Protocols and Ports**:

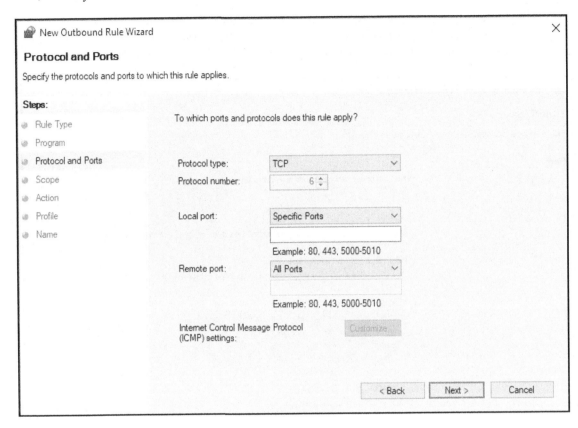

Figure 1.12: Protocols and Ports

On this particular screen, we are only able to define local and remote ports if our chosen protocol is either **TCP** or **UDP**. All the others will use the specific port for the protocol that's been selected.

Another rule type you can configure is **Connection Security Rules**, which allow or deny traffic based on what security mechanism is in place on the connection. The following screenshot shows some of the options that are available when you configure a rule here:

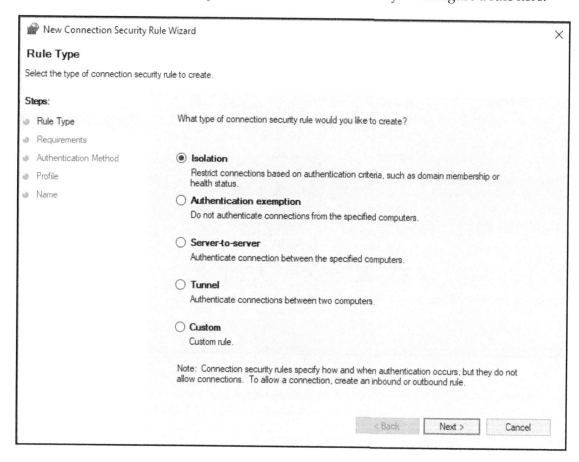

Figure 1.13: Connection Security Rule

One final area I would like to mention is firewall logging. As network engineers, we may be required to troubleshoot network connectivity where firewalls are involved. Therefore, it is important to know where the firewall logs are stored. On Windows devices, this is located at `%systemroot%\system32\LogFiles\Firewall\pfirewall.log`.

We need to enable logging in the properties of Windows Firewall with advanced security, as shown in the following screenshot:

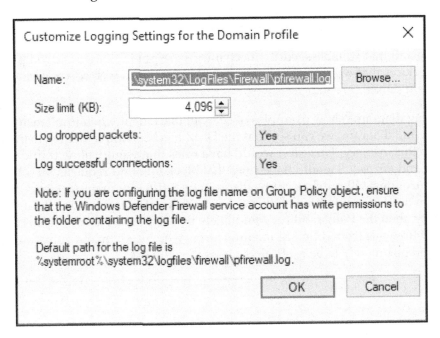

Figure 1.14: Firewall logging settings

Whenever you configure a new firewall rule, it is imperative to test that rule has been applied correctly. Is it allowing/denying the traffic we want it to? Is it allowing/denying traffic that we don't want it to? A scenario I have come across a number of times is when an engineer only tests to see if the firewall is allowing/denying the traffic it is intended to, without testing if it has affected anything else.

# DMZ

A DMZ, or a perimeter network, is a means of allowing the public to access certain network services while still maintaining the security of your internal devices. At this point, you may be thinking, *that's what an extranet does.* Yes, there are some similarities between them, but, remember, an extranet provides access to those services to trusted organizations, whereas a DMZ allows access to the public. No trust or authorization is required.

Obviously, making anything accessible to the public brings with it inherent security risks, so it is important that only services that are deemed as public-facing and necessary are placed there and that suitable security mechanisms are put in place as added protection. Common services that would be placed in the DMZ include a web server and a **Domain Name System (DNS)** server.

The following diagrams show examples of firewall placement when implementing a DMZ. In the following diagram, we can see that the DMZ has been implemented using two firewalls. In this instance, *Firewall A* would have rules that would allow traffic requesting web traffic, and *Firewall B* would have rules that block inbound requests for web traffic. Some organizations will purchase firewalls from two different manufacturers. If an organization used the same firewall throughout its infrastructure, and that firewall had a vulnerability, then the vulnerability would likely be reproduced across the network. However, if firewalls from different manufacturers were used, then a vulnerability in one model would be unlikely to be replicated across the network:

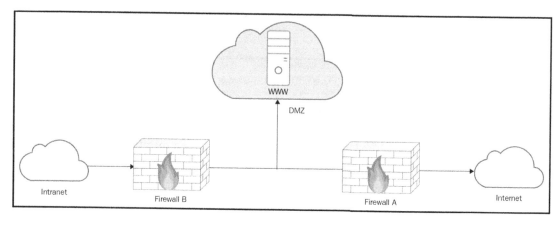

Figure 1.15: Using two firewalls

A more common implementation of firewalls is the three-homed firewall shown in the following diagram:

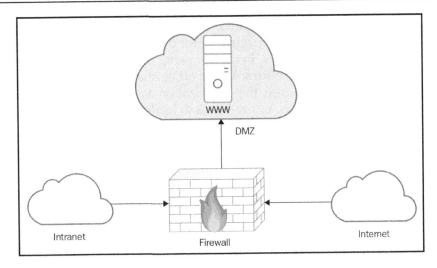

Figure 1.16: Three-homed firewall

This implementation is sometimes also referred to as triple-homed or a screened subnet. Each home on the firewall refers to a different network: the external network, the DMZ, and the internal network. Although a single firewall is being utilized, each port can have different rules assigned to it. For example, port 2 can allow inbound web request traffic and port 3 can block this traffic. While it obviously saves the cost of only requiring one firewall, it increases the risk. If that one firewall is breached, then both the DMZ and the internal network could be compromised.

# VPNs

Recently, more people have become aware of the existence of VPNs and have begun to use them in their personal lives. There are a number of legitimate reasons for people to do this, such as protecting their privacy when using an open network, and a number of illegitimate reasons, such as circumventing regional locks on streamed media. In this book, I will focus on the use of VPNs in a business environment.

A virtual private network can be defined as a means of transmitting private data securely from one network across an unsecured network to a third network. Generally speaking, the unsecured network we are referring to is the Internet, which, due to the nature of its design, has a number of potential security risks. However, this is not always going to be the case. I worked for one organization that required the use of VPNs within their own infrastructure. In this case, the network being transmitted was not insecure – we just needed to ensure any data that was transmitted across it was not visible to other users, even though they were from the same company. We often refer to the use of VPNs as using a VPN tunnel.

You may be wondering why companies would need to use a VPN, and that is a good question. First, let's look at a very common reason for doing so, and that is when an organization is located on multiple sites. In the following diagram, we can see a site-to-site VPN, where the organization has two sites: a head office and a branch site (sometimes referred to as satellite sites). In this case, the organization wants to ensure that all the traffic between the sites is protected, so they utilize VPNs to facilitate this. All the traffic from the branch offices passes through a device known as a VPN concentrator. The VPN concentrator at each site will directly connect to the VPN concentrator at the head office. The transmission of data across the VPN is transparent to most users, that is, they are unaware that this takes place:

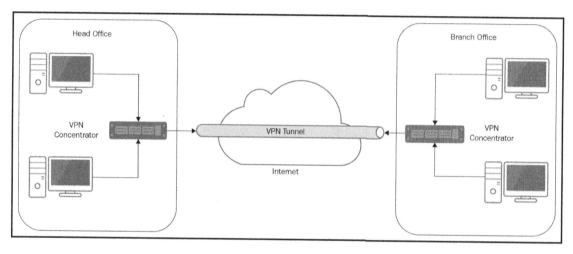

Figure 1.17: Site-to-site VPN connectivity

Another common form of implementation is through the installation of a VPN client on each device, also known as a remote access VPN. When a user wants to connect to the head office, they need to open up the VPN client application on their device and then authenticate via the application before they can gain access to the head office network. This implementation is usually reserved for telecommuters or mobile users, such as sales staff or field engineers, or home-based users, since the administrative overhead becomes too great.

On the user's end, they have to deploy and configure the application on each device and run the application. You also have to rely on the user remembering their VPN credentials, which may not be the same as their domain credentials. Users who are connecting remotely will be required to authenticate against some form of remote authentication server before access is granted. The following screenshot shows how this may be implemented:

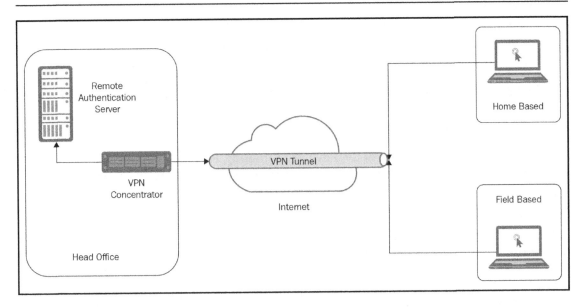

Figure 1.18: Device-based VPN

A VPN may also be used with an extranet to provide limited secure communication to our infrastructure for our trusted partners. In all the preceding implementations, the user's device will appear as if it is on the head office network.

VPN tunnels provide data security through the use of encryption and authentication. The methods that are used vary, depending on the tunneling protocol that's used. Microsoft has used the following three different VPN protocols in recent years:

- **Point to Point Tunneling Protocol (PPTP)**
- **Point to Point Protocol (PPP)**
- **Secure Socket Tunneling Protocol (SSTP)**

The now obsolete PPTP was designed to transmit PPP traffic through a VPN. In this case, PPTP creates a communication channel to the recipient, and that channel would then be used to create a **Generic Routing Encapsulation (GRE)** tunnel for the data to be transmitted across. Encryption was provided by **Microsoft Point-to-Point Encryption (MPEE)**, and authentication was by **Password Authentication Protocol (PAP)**, **Challenge Handshake Authentication Protocol (CHAP)**, or Microsoft's version, MS-CHAP.

**Exam tip:** It is very easy to confuse the acronyms PPTP and PPP. Remember that the **T** stands for **Tunneling**.

SSTP was implemented in Windows Vista. Like PPTP, SSTP was designed to securely transmit PPP traffic. However, SSTP uses **Secure Socket Layer/Transport Layer Security (SSL/TLS)** to provide encryption. It also utilizes the same network port as HTTPS traffic, that is, port 443. Since this port is usually open on firewalls for secure web browsing, this means that network administrators didn't need to open another port to allow the traffic through. Authentication of SSTP traffic was provided by MS-CHAP and **Extensible Authentication Protocol-TLS (EAP-TLS)**.

Windows 7 saw the introduction of the **Layer 2 Tunneling Protocol (L2TP)**. While L2TP provided the tunnel, it did not provide any form of encryption, so it was usually deployed alongside **Internet Protocol Security (IPSec)**, which does. Authentication is conducted using the **Internet Key Exchange (IKE)**.

To try and overcome the issues with users forgetting to start their VPN connections, Microsoft released support for DirectAccess in Windows 7. When a user started up their device, the DirectAccess service running on it would check to see if it was on the same network as the DirectAccess server. If it discovered it was on the same network, then it knew not to use DirectAccess as a form of VPN. However, if it was not on the same network as the DirectAccess server, then the device would use the DirectAccess service to make a connection to your organization's DirectAccess server. Again, this was transparent to the user. The additional benefit of using DirectAccess was that administrators could manage those remote devices as if they were on the local network.

With the release of Windows 10, Microsoft provided users with a service called **Always On VPN**, which was designed to replace DirectAccess. **Always On VPN** could be configured to create a device tunnel that would connect through the VPN once the device had booted up, or could be configured to use a user tunnel that connects once a user logs in. These two options are not mutually exclusive and both can be implemented at the same time. However, to utilize a device tunnel, you have to use either an Enterprise edition of Windows 10 or an Education edition.

With this, we have finished looking at the basic security features of a network. Now, we will move on to study Microsoft Security Zones.

# Microsoft security zones

Despite its name, the **Internet Options** settings within the Windows OS also applies to the intranet. These options are accessible through the control panels of all the recent versions of Windows:

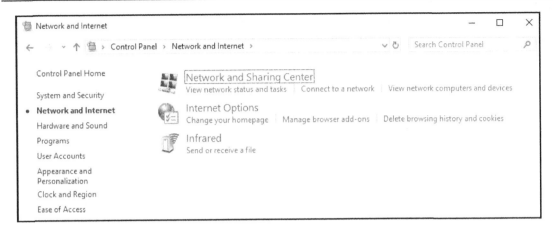

Figure 1.19: Internet Options in Windows 10

Alternatively, we can access them through the settings of the Internet Explorer browser, as shown in the following screenshot. Oddly, its successor, Microsoft Edge, doesn't have the same functionality. Regardless of the version of Windows being used, the options we will discuss are the same:

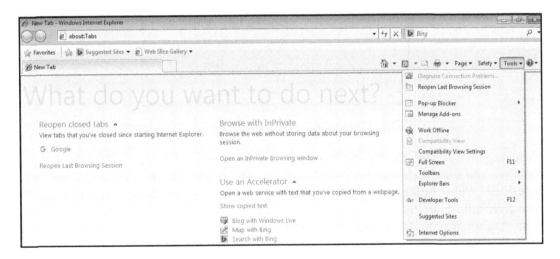

Figure 1.20: Internet Options via Internet Explorer

 **Exam tip**: Be familiar with both methods of accessing these options. Any questions around this topic may have either or both in the answer set.

The **Internet Options** settings allow you to configure security levels separately for each of the four zones: **Internet**, **Local intranet**, **Trusted sites**, and **Restricted sites**. These can be seen in the following screenshot:

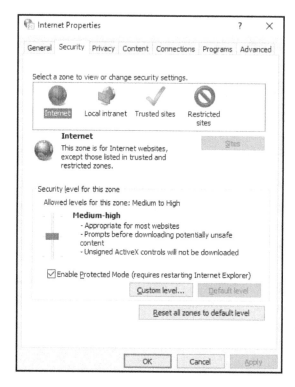

Figure 1.21: Windows Internet zones and security

By clicking on a zone in the top box, you will be presented with its default settings. If you do not wish to use the default settings, you may use the slider to choose one of the other predefined levels – or templates, as Microsoft calls them. As you change the slider, the text to the right adjusts to describe the level. These templates are listed as follows and refer to the level of security that's applied. For example, **High** refers to high security and **Low** refers to low security:

- **High**
- **Medium-high**
- **Medium**
- **Medium-low**
- **Low**

If the predefined templates do not fulfill your requirements, you can choose the option to configure a **Custom level...** by clicking on that option. The custom levels are configured separately for each zone, as shown in the following screenshot. When configuring custom levels for a zone, you have the ability to adjust the settings to a very granular level. Be warned that this is not for the faint-hearted as there are a lot of options. Fortunately, you don't get tested on these options in the exam. If you incorrectly adjust the custom level for a zone, you have the option to reset it to one of the predefined levels, and Microsoft helpfully highlights which was the default level for that zone. On the main **Security** tab, there is also the option to reset all the zones to their default levels:

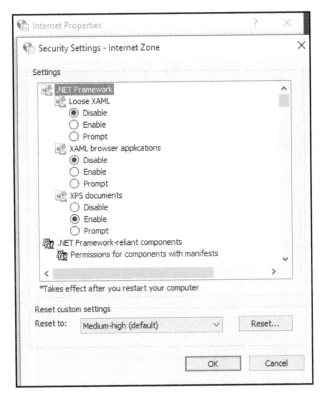

Figure 1.22: Custom levels for the Internet zone

Although it isn't mentioned in the exam objectives, I would like to briefly mention *enable protected mode*, in case you think I have omitted it. This option refers to how the browser application itself works. When this option is selected, the browser runs with restricted privileges, thus reducing the chances of a malicious website compromising the system.

Now, we will discuss each of the zones.

# Internet

As the name implies, this security zone relates to any website outside of your infrastructure, or more accurately, any website outside of your infrastructure that does not fall under any of the other zones. By default, this zone will use the **Medium** template. Note that when using the predefined templates, you are unable to adjust the level to anything lower than **Medium**.

# Local intranet zone

This zone applies to all the websites deemed to be inside of your infrastructure. By default, this zone will use the **Medium-low** template. You may be wondering how the browser determines whether the site is on the Internet or on an intranet. This is a very good question, and there are two methods of doing so. First, you can add a site manually by clicking on the **Sites** button, as shown in the following screenshot, and then clicking **Advanced** on the next screen:

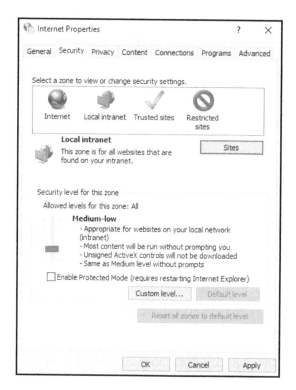

Figure 1.23: Local intranet zone

As shown in the following screenshot, when you're adding a site to the local intranet zone, it is simply a case of entering the URL and clicking **Add**. You may also specify that sites that have been secured with the HTTPS protocol can be added. You may also use a wildcard to represent any host on the named domain; for example, `http://*.mydomain.local` would implicitly add `myserver.mydomain.local` and `anotherserver.mydomain.local` to the local intranet zone:

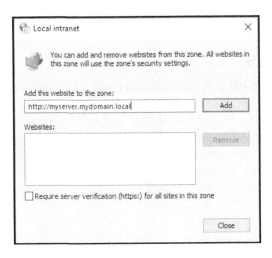

Figure 1.24: Adding a site to the local intranet zone

The other option is for the OS to perform this check automatically, as shown in the following screenshot, but this is beyond the scope of the exam. However, if you are interested in knowing how this happens behind the scenes, Microsoft has provided a good explanation at `https://blogs.msdn.microsoft.com/ieinternals/2012/06/05/the-intranet-zone/`:

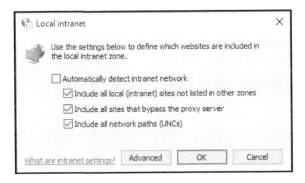

Figure 1.25: Automatically detect intranet network option

# Trusted sites

If you firmly believe that a website that you are visiting can be trusted, and thus want to reduce the level of security on the website, you can add it to the **Trusted sites** zone. Again, this is done by clicking on the **Sites** button. Unlike local intranet, sites in this zone have to be added manually. The default template that's used is **Low**, but there is a requirement for all the sites to require HTTPS. However, this can be disabled.

# Restricted sites

This zone uses the **High** template by default and cannot be lowered using the slider, although custom levels can be applied. If you apply a custom level in Windows 10, you will receive a warning notification. Any website that you believe may cause harm, or has done so in the past, should be added to this zone. As well as preventing potentially malicious functions to run on the website, this zone will also warn users if they are downloading potentially malicious content. This zone doesn't have an option that allows you to enforce the use of HTTPS.

# Local machine zone

This zone is not available on the **Security** tab of **Internet Options**, but it still applies. This is an implied zone that assumes that anything that's stored and retrieved by the browser from the local machine, with the exception of cached web pages, can be trusted, and therefore applies the **Low** template.

In the following activities, you will explore a number of the **Internet Options** that are available on a Windows OS:

**Activity 2: Accessing Internet Options in Windows 10:**

1. On the desktop, click in the **Type here** box to search.
2. Type in `Internet Options`.
3. Select **Internet Options** from the suggested list.
4. Click on the **Security** tab.

**Activity 3: Investigating the predefined levels and custom levels:**

1. For each zone, adjust the security level slider.
2. Note the differences in each level.
3. Note the available predefined level for each zone.
4. Click on **Custom level...** and explore the various options there.
5. Click on **Restore all zones to default levels** on the **Security** tab to revoke any changes you may have made.

**Activity 4: Adding sites to zones:**

1. Click on **Trusted sites**.
2. Click on the **Sites** button.
3. In the **Add this website to this zone** box, enter `https://www.google.com` and click **Add**.
4. Repeat *step 3* with `http://www.google.com` open and click **Add**. What happens?
5. Click **Close**.
6. Click on **Restricted sites**.
7. Click on the **Sites** button.
8. In the **Add this website to this zone** box, enter `http://www.google.com` and click **Add**.
9. Repeat *step 8* with `https://www.google.com` open and click **Add**. What happens?
10. Click **No**.
11. Click **Close**.
12. Click **OK** to close down the **Internet Options** dialog box.

As you can see, Windows allows us to have some control over the level of security that is applied to websites, though this is dependent on the zone they are located in. Most websites will be within the Internet zone; however, you may find that you are required to explicitly add sites to either the local intranet zone or trusted sites zone. Any sites you add here should be added with caution. Sites in the restricted zone may not run with their full functionality and so you will have to balance this with your security requirements. While there is the option to custom configure each of these zones, it is unlikely that you will do this unless doing so resolves a particular issue.

# Summary

In this chapter, we discussed the minimal requirements that are needed to form a network. We highlighted how networks had grown away from the traditional idea of connecting personal computers together and moved toward the interconnectivity of a whole range of items. We introduced the concept of internets, intranets, and extranets while highlighting the subtle difference between internets and the Internet. Then, we went on to describe some of the basic security concepts involved in a network. Firewalls were discussed as a means of regulating traffic in and out of our network. Then, we covered demilitarized zones, or perimeter networks, and their use of providing public access to a subset of an organization's infrastructure. Next, VPNs and their implementation were introduced. Finally, we listed the security zones that are available in Windows operating systems and how to add sites to restricted and trusted zones.

Now that we have covered some of the foundation elements of networking, we will move on to discuss the methods of implementing what I would describe as the two major versions of networks, namely **local area networks** (**LANs**), which we will cover in the next chapter, and **wide area networks** (**WANs**), which we will cover in `Chapter 3`, *Understanding Wide Area Networks*.

# Questions

1. Which of these refers to the connectivity between different external networks?

(A) VPN
(B) Intranet
(C) Internet
(D) DMZ

2. Which of these does not allow us to identify a device on the network?

(A) Virtual port number
(B) IP address
(C) MAC address
(D) Hostname

3. Replace the underlined word in the following statement with the correct word(s). If you believe the statement is already correct, then select *No change is required*:
A <u>DMZ</u> allows or denies network traffic based on a set of rules.

(A) VPN
(B) Internet
(C) Firewall
(D) No change is required

4. Which of these technologies allows you to securely connect to a private network over an insecure network?

(A) Extranet
(B) DMZ
(C) Firewall
(D) VPN

5. Which of the following devices would you most likely position within a DMZ?

(A) Domain controller
(B) DHCP server
(C) Print server
(D) Web server

6. What is the default security level for **Restricted sites**?

(A) Low
(B) Medium-Low
(C) Medium-High
(D) High

7. What network protocol is used by the ping utility?

(A) DHCP
(B) ICMP
(C) ARP
(D) PPTP

8. When would you use a VPN concentrator at both ends of the VPN tunnel?

(A) When home-based users are connecting to the head office
(B) When field-based engineers are connecting to the head office
(C) When a branch office is connecting to the head office
(D) None of the above

9. Which of the following would you implement to allow trusted third parties to gain limited access to your internal network?

(A) Extranet
(B) DMZ
(C) Firewall
(D) Internet

# Further reading

To find out more about remote access VPN, visit `https://docs.microsoft.com/en-us/windows-server/remote/remote-access/vpn/always-on-vpn/`.

# Understanding Local Area Networks

# 2

Most network engineers will *cut their teeth* supporting an organization's internal network infrastructure. This internal infrastructure will normally take the form of a **local area network (LAN)**. Therefore, it is important to have a good understanding of LAN technologies to provide this support and ensure that the organization can continue to function effectively and efficiently. Any network failures can have results ranging from inconvenience to financial loss.

This chapter focuses on the implementation of LANs in a small office/home office environment. We will discuss the differences between a LAN and a WAN, as well as the use of private IP address ranges. We will identify the key components in both wired and wireless networks, and finish by discussing **virtual local area networks (VLANs)**.

The following topics will be covered in this chapter:

- Scales of networks
- Introduction to LANs
- Local addressing
- Wired and wireless LANs
- VLANs
- MANs
- CANs
- PANs

Let's get started!

# Technical requirements

To complete the exercises in this chapter, you will need a PC or virtual machine running Windows 7 or above (preferably Windows 10) with a working network connection.

This chapter also includes an optional activity for which you will need to install Wireshark (available from `https://www.wireshark.org/download.html`).

# Scales of networks

Networks can be described in terms of their scale of deployment according to how much of an area they cover or what type of area they cover. The exam objectives specifically call out LANs and **wide area networks (WANs)**. LANs and WANs will be discussed in this and the following chapters. I will round off this chapter with a brief explanation of **metropolitan area networks (MANs)**, **campus area networks (CANs)**, and **Personal Area Networks (PANs)**. The following diagram is a visual representation of where each of these fits in the scale of networks:

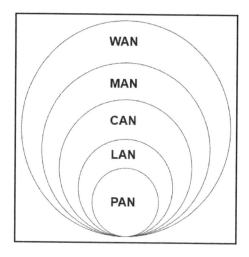

Figure 2.1: Scale of networks

It should be noted that you may see the acronyms prefixed with the letter *W*; for example, WLAN, WWAN, and so on. This usually indicates that it is a wireless variant of the network.

# Introduction to LANs

I'm going to start this section by asking you to complete an activity. The reason for this is that I feel that if you can understand how your home network is connected, you will understand the concepts we will discuss here better.

**Activity 1**: Sketch out your home network. Don't worry about artistic quality; this is not the aim here. Draw any device you have on your network and how they connect together. If they are wired together, draw a solid line between the devices; if they are wireless, draw a lightning bolt between them.

Congratulations! You have just drawn out a LAN. My home network is as follows:

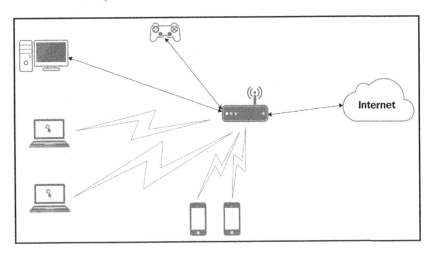

Figure 2.2: My home network

So, what is a LAN? A LAN can be described as something that covers a *small geographical area* that's small enough that the devices can be classed as being local to each other. When you sketched your home network, all of the devices were in the vicinity of each other, that, is, all of them were within your house. However, LANs are not restricted to home use, and they are prevalent in most organizations. Most modern LANs will usually be a combination of wired and wireless devices, and we will discuss these shortly. Another way of thinking about LANs is that, usually, all of the devices that make up the infrastructure are owned by you or your organization.

When communication takes place between devices on a LAN, there is a requirement to identify and thus differentiate between the devices on the network. The methods of doing so are covered in the next section.

# Local addressing

As we mentioned briefly in the previous chapter, identifying devices on a local network can be done using hostnames, MAC addresses, and IP addresses. All of these must be unique within the LAN. Let's have a look at each of them.

# Hostnames

A computer's hostname is an easy-to-read (for humans) method of identifying a device on the network. Each device's hostname is configured by the system administrator. The hostname may be reflective of the role that the device is performing; for example, MXServer for a mail exchange server, DC1 for a domain controller, and so on. They may follow a set naming convention; I have worked in organizations that name file servers after Star Wars characters, and print servers after Star Trek characters. This is useful if everyone is a fan of these two movie and TV franchises. Alternatively, you can let Windows provide a hostname during the installation phase. While this method makes things a little easier during the installation phase, it can cause you headaches later on since the names aren't easy to type out. For servers, I would recommend naming the device before installing any services, to avoid complications later.

When referring to a destination device by its hostname, the sending device will need to resolve it to an IP address. This process will be discussed in more detail in `Chapter 14`, *Network Services*. The following two activities explain the most common ways we can find our hostname.

**Activity 2**: Find your hostname from Command Prompt:

1. While on your desktop, press the Windows key + *R* to open the run command.
2. Type `cmd` and press the *Enter* key.
3. In the Command Prompt, type `hostname` and press the *Enter* key.

4. Your output will look similar to mine:

Figure 2.3: Output of the hostname command

**Activity 3**: Find your hostname from system properties:

1. On your desktop, open up a Windows Explorer window.
2. Right-click on either **This Computer** (Windows 10) or **Computer** (Windows 7).
3. Select **Properties** from the context menu.
4. Your output should look similar to mine:

Figure 2.4: System properties window

Although hostnames make identifying devices a little more human-friendly, often, we tend to think of IP addresses as the main means of identifying a device on a network. We will cover IP addresses in the next section.

# IP addresses

While hostnames are human-friendly, they are not that friendly for devices since their syntax doesn't provide a means of identifying whether a device called *Gordons-PC* is on a local or remote network. On its own, a hostname would generally be thought of as being local, but this may not always be the case. Therefore, we need to resolve hostnames to an IP address. We will cover IP addresses in more detail in `Chapter 11`, *Understanding IPv4* and `Chapter 12`, *Understanding IPv6*, but for the purposes of understanding LANs, I would like to touch upon IPv4 here. An IPv4 address is broken down into two sections:

- A network element
- A host element

The network element is used as a means of identifying the network a device is on, while the host element identifies the device itself on the network. This provides a hierarchical approach to addressing. A common analogy that is used is that the network element is like your street name, and the host element is like your house number. Just like your house number needs to be unique on your street, lest your neighbor receives your mail and vice versa, a host element needs to be unique on a network.

Since there are limits on the number of IPv4 addresses that are available globally, we can reuse IP addresses in different LANs by following the **Request for Comments (RFC)** 1918. The RFC allocates three ranges of IP addresses that can be used in LANs. These addresses are known as **private IP addresses** and are deemed non-routable outside of your network. An address can be used in multiple LANs without any issue as long as it is used only once within each LAN.

These address ranges are as follows:

- **Class A**: `10.0.0.0 -> 10.255.255.255`
- **Class B**: `172.16.0.0 -> 172.31.255.255`
- **Class C**: `192.168.0.0 -> 192.168.255.255`

Don't worry about the references to the classes at this point. Arguably, you could use other public IP addresses within your network, but this would cause numerous issues.

In the following diagram, we can see that the same private IP address is used in each of the three LANs. This is perfectly acceptable and demonstrates the reuse of such addresses:

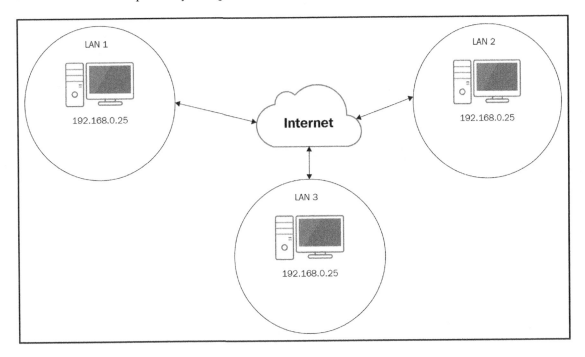

Figure 2.5: Reuse of private IP addresses

While the preceding diagram shows permissible reuse of private IP addresses, the following diagram shows the reuse of private IP addresses within a single LAN. This is not permissible and would cause you to receive numerous IP address conflicts or duplicate IP address error messages:

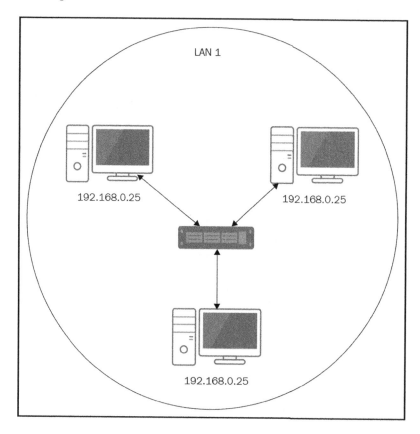

Figure 2.6: Incorrect reuse of a private IP address

When a transmitting device has identified the IP address of a recipient device, it asks itself, *is the recipient on the same network as me, or is it on a remote network?*.

It does this by comparing the network element of its own IP address with the network element of the recipient's IP address. If the network element matches, it assumes that the devices are on the same network; if they differ, it assumes that the recipient is on a remote network. An example of this can be seen in the following diagram. **Server A** is using a public IP address since it represents a public-facing server on the internet:

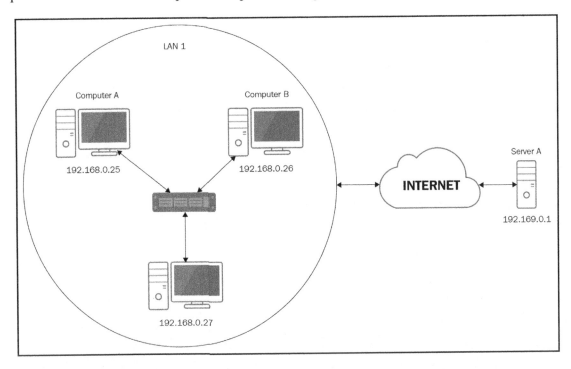

Figure 2.7: Local versus remote addresses

For this example, the network element of the IP addresses in **LAN 1** will be 192.168.0 and the host elements will be .25, .26, and .27. For **Server A**, the network element will be 192.169.0 and the host element will be .1.

If **Computer A** wants to talk to **Computer B**, it compares the network elements of both addresses and sees that they are both 192.168.0. **Computer A** can reasonably assume that **Computer B** is on the same local network as itself. However, if **Computer A** wants to talk to **Server A**, it carries out a similar comparison and notices that **Server A** has a network element of 192.169.0, which differs from its own network element. **Computer A** can reasonably assume that **Server A** is on a remote network.

This comparison is important to make since any network traffic destined for a remote network has to be sent via a default gateway for onward transmission.

In this section, we have focused on IPv4, and you may be wondering whether there is an IPv6 equivalent. The simple answer is yes, but in reality, it is a little more complex. IPv6 uses what is known as **unique local addresses**, which have the prefix `fc00::/7`. However, because IPv6 has so many addresses available compared to IPv4, these are not generally configured as there are enough public IPv6 addresses for every device in the world. We will discuss IPv6 in more detail in `Chapter 12`, *Understanding IPv6*.

# MAC addresses

A MAC address is a means of identifying a device on the local network. It is an address that has many names. As well as being referred to as a MAC address, it is also referred to as a physical address, a hardware address, or a **burnt-in address (BIA)**. These three variations refer to the fact that the MAC address is on the physical network card, or *burnt into* the network card.

A MAC address is represented as a 48-bit hexadecimal number. Hexadecimal is referred to as a base-16 numbering system. How hexadecimal works is beyond the scope of this book, but it is important that you are able to identify a MAC address. The following screenshot shows the output of the `ipconfig /all` command and shows the MAC address (listed as a physical address) of this network card as `08-00-27-F5-50-3F`. It should be noted that if you have multiple network cards, you will see multiple MAC addresses:

```
Select Command Prompt
C:\Users\User>ipconfig /all

Windows IP Configuration

    Host Name . . . . . . . . . . . . : Windows10-Test
    Primary Dns Suffix  . . . . . . . :
    Node Type . . . . . . . . . . . . : Mixed
    IP Routing Enabled. . . . . . . . : No
    WINS Proxy Enabled. . . . . . . . : No
    DNS Suffix Search List. . . . . . : broadband

Ethernet adapter Ethernet 2:

    Connection-specific DNS Suffix  . : broadband
    Description . . . . . . . . . . . : Intel(R) PRO/1000 MT Desktop Adapter
    Physical Address. . . . . . . . . : 08-00-27-F5-50-3F
```

Figure 2.8: Output of ipconfig /all

In Linux, the equivalent to `ipconfig` is `ifconfig`. Although `ifconfig` is not mentioned in the exam objectives, it may appear in the answers as a distractor, and you might select it by accident under exam pressure.

Another method of listing your MAC addresses is by using the `getmac` command from the Command Prompt. However, the output is not as user-friendly, as shown in the following screenshot:

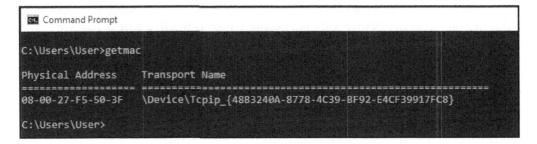

Figure 2.9: Output of getmac command

Here, we can see that the MAC address is comprised of 12 characters broken into 6 pairs. Each of these characters uses 4 bits (12 characters * 4 bits = 48 bits). As you can see, each pair is separated by a –. This is specific to Windows, and you may see :, _, or even no separator, depending on the system you are looking at.

You may be asked to identify a MAC address from an answer set. There are three things to look for: first, whether there are 12 characters, second, whether each individual character is either a number between 0-9 or a letter between A-F, and third, whether there are no double colons, for example, : :. The latter is a legitimate character set in IPv6 addresses and may mislead you.

MAC addresses are not randomly generated. They should be globally unique and no two network cards should have the same MAC address. To facilitate this, each network card manufacturer is issued an **Organizationally Unique Identifier (OUI)**. The OUI is the first six characters of the MAC address. Using the MAC address shown in the preceding screenshots, my OUI is `08-00-27`. Using an online OUI lookup website, I can see that my network card is from PCS Computer Systems GmbH. The last six characters should only be allocated to one network card by the manufacturer.

**Activity 4**: Identify your MAC address using any of the methods described previously. Then, using an online OUI lookup site, identify the manufacturer of your network card.

 Although MAC addresses are supposed to be globally unique, they can be spoofed using software.

To find a MAC address related to a particular IP address, our computer will use the **Address Resolution Protocol** (**ARP**). When using the ARP, your computer shouts out to all the devices on the network (broadcasts), asking who has the IP address you are communicating with. All the devices on the network will receive that ARP request and will look at the IP address that was requested. If the IP address doesn't belong to that device, it will ignore the request. If the IP address does belong to the device, it will send an ARP reply saying that IP address ABC belongs to MAC address XYZ. The following screenshot shows a Wireshark capture of an ARP request, while the screenshot after that shows the ARP response.

In the following screenshot, we can see that, at *line 48*, the ARP request where the source MAC address 58:ba:d4:9c:10:80, with a source IP address of 192.168.1.1, is asking who has 192.168.1.15. Note that the destination MAC address is ff:ff:ff:ff:ff:ff, which is a broadcast MAC address that's used when you want to speak to all the devices on the network:

| No. | Time | Source | Destination | Protocol | Length | Info |
|---|---|---|---|---|---|---|
| 48 | 4.817668709 | 58:ba:d4:9c:10:80 | ff:ff:ff:ff:ff:ff | ARP | 60 | Who has 192.168.1.15? Tell 192.168.1.1 |
| 49 | 4.817684703 | 6c:88:14:02:b4:90 | 58:ba:d4:9c:10:80 | ARP | 42 | 192.168.1.15 is at 6c:88:14:02:b4:90 |

```
› Frame 48: 60 bytes on wire (480 bits), 60 bytes captured (480 bits) on interface 0
› Ethernet II, Src: HuaweiTe_9c:10:80 (58:ba:d4:9c:10:80), Dst: Broadcast (ff:ff:ff:ff:ff:ff)
▾ Address Resolution Protocol (request)
    Hardware type: Ethernet (1)
    Protocol type: IPv4 (0x0800)
    Hardware size: 6
    Protocol size: 4
    Opcode: request (1)
    Sender MAC address: 58:ba:d4:9c:10:80
    Sender IP address: 192.168.1.1
    Target MAC address: 00:00:00:00:00:00
    Target IP address: 192.168.1.15
```

Figure 2.10: ARP request

In the following screenshot, we can see the ARP reply where the source MAC address is `6c:88:14:02:b4:90` is responding to the ARP request and saying it has the IP address `192.168.1.15`:

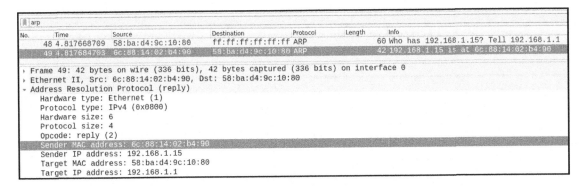

Figure 2.11: ARP reply

Once the MAC address is known for its IP address, the Windows device will store the address resolution in its ARP cache. The ARP cache is checked before an ARP request is sent. If there is a corresponding entry in the cache, no ARP request is sent. It should be noted that cache entries have a *reachable time* that stipulates how long the address resolution is stored for, before being removed from the cache. By default, this is between 15 and 45 seconds, but this can be adjusted.

> You can view your ARP cache by going into a Command Prompt and typing `arp -a`.
>
> It should be noted that the title of the left-hand column, that is, **Internet Address**, is slightly misleading since these are the IP addresses on your local network or special-purpose IP addresses.

**Activity 5**: Looking at the output from the `arp -a` command, identify any IP addresses that are mapped to the broadcast MAC address. We will discuss why there are multiple entries for this in `Chapter 11`, *Understanding IPv4*.

**Optional activity**: The preceding screenshots showed ARP requests in a Wireshark packet capture. If you would like to see this in action on your own device, perform the following steps:

1. Install and run Wireshark.
2. Click **Edit** | **Preferences** | **Name Resolution**. Clear the checkmark for **Resolve MAC Addresses**:

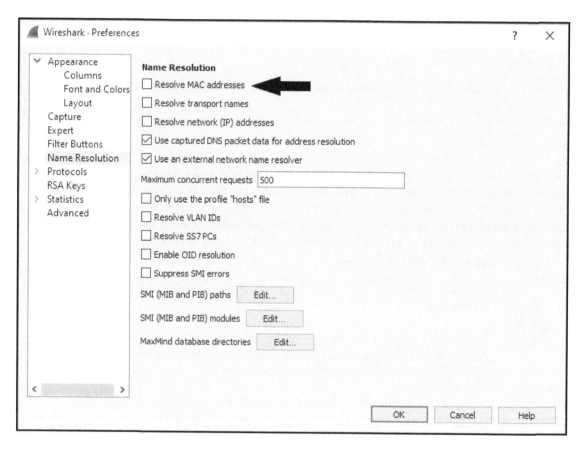

Figure 2.12: Name Resolution tab in Wireshark

3. Click on the shark fin in the menu bar to start the capture:

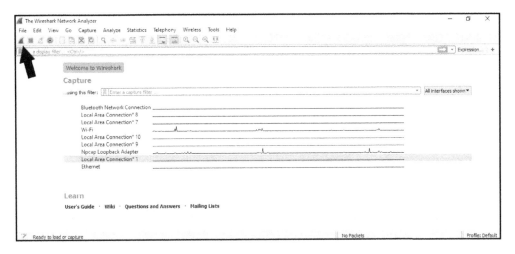

Figure 2.13: Shark fin on the Wireshark menu bar

4. Leave the capture running for a few minutes.
5. Click on the red stop button:

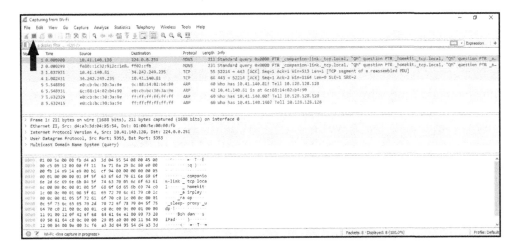

Figure 2.14: Red stop button on the Wireshark menu bar

6. In the display filter bar, type `arp`:

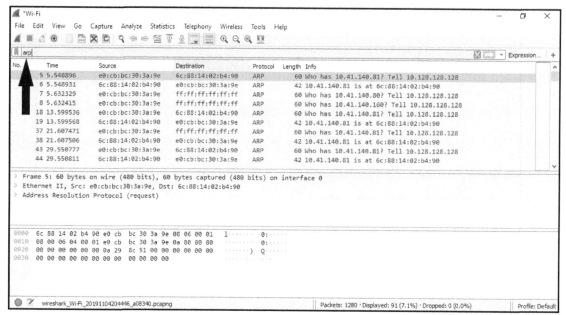

Figure 2.15: Display filter bar in Wireshark

7. Hit *Enter*.
8. Investigate the ARP requests and replies.

You may be wondering why you use MAC addresses and IP addresses. Remember, MAC addresses are used for local communication only, whereas IP addresses are used for local and remote communication. If we only use MAC addresses, we won't be able to communicate with remote devices. If we only use IP addresses, then we would have to send all the data to every device on the network. Yes, we do send an ARP request to all devices, but that is a small amount of data, and it's only sent once in a while.

Let's take a look at a high-level view of communication taking place locally and remotely. It should be noted that this is a simplified version of the process:

- Local device to local device:
    1. Get the recipient hostname.
    2. Resolve the recipient hostname to an IP address.
    3. The sender checks to see if the IP address is on the local network. In this case, it is local.

4. The sender checks the ARP cache for an IP | MAC mapping. None are found.
5. The sender broadcasts an ARP request.
6. The recipient machine sends an ARP reply.
7. The sender updates its ARP Cache.
8. The sender packages the data to be transferred and sends it out.
9. The recipient machine receives the data and checks that the destination MAC address belongs to it. It does.
10. The recipient machine checks that the destination IP address belongs to it. It does.
11. The recipient machine processes the data that's dependent on the service/application it is for.

- Local device to remote device:
    1. Get the recipient hostname.
    2. Resolve the recipient hostname to an IP address.
    3. The sender checks to see if the IP address is on the local network. In this case, it is remote, and any data that's transmitted needs to be sent via the default gateway.
    4. The sender looks up the IP address of the default gateway.
    5. The sender checks the ARP cache for an IP | MAC mapping for the default gateway. None are found.
    6. The sender broadcasts an ARP request, asking for the MAC address of the IP address linked to the default gateway.
    7. The default gateway sends an ARP reply.
    8. The sender updates its ARP cache.
    9. The sender packages the data to be transferred. It stipulates that the destination MAC is that of the default gateway, but the destination IP address is that of the remote device.
    10. The sender transmits the data to the default gateway.
    11. The default gateway receives the data and checks that the destination MAC address belongs to it. It does.
    12. The default gateway checks that the destination IP address belongs to it. In this case, it does not.
    13. The default gateway forwards the data, as per its *rules*, to the destination device. The source and destination MAC addresses are altered at each router they transit, but the IP addresses remain the same.

14. The recipient machine receives the data and checks that the destination MAC address belongs to it. It does.

15. The recipient machine checks that the destination IP address belongs to it. It does.

16. The recipient machine processes the data that's dependent on the service/application it is for.

Now that we have looked at how devices are identified on a LAN, we will shift our focus to factors that should be considered when creating a LAN.

# Wired and wireless LANs

When creating a LAN, we generally have three options available to us: implement a wired network, implement a wireless network, or, more commonly, implement a hybrid of both types. In this section, we will discuss the implementation of wired and wireless networks and briefly introduce the devices that are utilized in each.

 For connectivity to remote networks, a routing device or default gateway would be required, with the exception of *Figure 2.22* (*Wireless routers* section). I have omitted these from the images for clarity.

# Considerations

When implementing any network, it is important to take a number of factors into consideration to ensure your network runs efficiently. A non-exhaustive list is as follows:

- **Budget**: This constraint will dictate how much you can spend on equipment, any third-party support you receive, time frames, and so on.
- **Skill set**: Do you have staff with the necessary skill set to implement and maintain the network?
- **Existing infrastructure**: Do you want to integrate with the existing infrastructure or replace it?
- **Hardware**: What equipment do you want to use for end users, network devices, and so on? Are they compatible with each other?

- **Environment**: Do you have sufficient power to support all the network devices? What coverage do you need to provide? Is there anything that could cause interference in the transmission of data? Is it a listed building with restrictions on laying cables?
- **The number of users**: How many users will you need to support? Can you support them and still provide a quality service? Do you need to balance the network load across a number of devices to provide that quality?
- **Security**: How are you going to protect your data in transit? Can it be eavesdropped, either digitally or physically? How are you going to protect your network devices from physical attacks?
- **Network model**: Are you going to implement a peer-to-peer network or client-server network model?

Let's look at that last point in more detail.

# Network models

When discussing network models, we are really focusing on the software side of implementing the network. The type of network operating system you are using, the number of users, and the skill set of supporting staff are usually the key deciding factors as to which model you implement.

## Peer-to-peer networks

When raising the topic of **peer-to-peer** (**P2P**) networks in recent years, you may have found people mentioning torrents or other file-sharing technologies. While there is some overlap, it is the original use of the term peer-to-peer that Microsoft will include in the exam.

A P2P network (sometimes referred to as a workgroup) is one where there is no one device that has complete control of the network and the files, services, and so on that are used on the network. The term *peer* refers to individuals with the same status, and that applies here. All the endpoints on the network have the same status. Every device is responsible for authenticating users and holds a security database it needs to check. This means that any user wishing to log on to that computer needs to have an account on it. This is referred to as a local user account. The device is also responsible for controlling access to the files, services, and so on that it provides.

As shown in the following diagram, we can see that we have four PCs, and we have four users listed. If each of those users needs the ability to log on to each of those PCs, we would need to create four accounts on **Computer A**, four on **Computer B**, four on **Computer C**, and four on **Computer D**. A total of 16 accounts need to be created. If **Bill** is sitting at **Computer A** and he changes his password, he is only changing his password on **Computer A**. The passwords on the other computers don't change. This is referred to as decentralized administration:

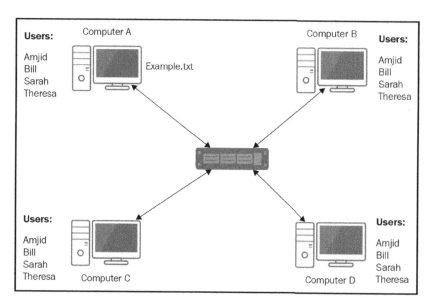

Figure 2.16: P2P network

Likewise, **Computer A** has a file called Example.txt that other users may wish to access over the network. To do so, they need to have an account on **Computer A**. When accessing the file over the network, they may be prompted to enter their credentials for **Computer A**. However, if the credentials (username and password) are the same on both **Computer A** and the computer they are sitting on, Windows will implement what is known as pass-through authentication, and no credentials will be asked for.

The benefit of using this model is that it doesn't require a server and therefore there is no demand on the support staff (if they even exist) to have a higher-level skill set. Due to the addition of homegroup in Windows 7, sharing resources has become even simpler, which makes a peer-to-peer network an attractive option for smaller environments. However, because of the administrative overhead involved in using a decentralized model such as this, it is recommended that you only use this model when you have 10 or fewer users/devices.

# Client-server networks

Unlike P2P networks, client-server networks have some form of hierarchy. The most common form of this is a domain model that utilizes some form of directory service, such as Microsoft's Active Directory, for authentication and control when it comes to accessing resources. In contrast to P2P networks, this provides centralized administration and is geared toward a network that contains servers and has skilled support staff, and more than 10 users/devices.

The following diagram shows a client-server model. If **Amjid** wants to log on to **Computer A**, his credentials are sent from **Computer A** to the domain controller that authenticated him and he is able to log on. Likewise, if he jumps over to **Computer B**, a similar process happens. Any time **Amjid** changes his password, the change is stored on the domain controller, which affects all the computers he logs on to. Similarly, if he wants to access **Example.txt**, which is stored on **Server A**, his credentials will allow him to (as long as the permissions on the file allow him to):

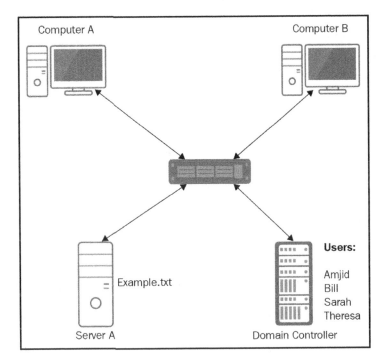

Figure 2.17: Client-server model

Remember that P2P is for 10 or fewer users and offers decentralized administration. The client-server model is for 10+ users and offers centralized administration.

Regardless of the model that's used, we can describe networks as being wired or wireless. We will discuss each of these in the following sections.

# Wired networks

With the introduction of the OSI and TCP/IP models as network standards, as discussed in Chapter 9, *Understanding the OSI Model*, and Chapter 10, *Understanding TCP/IP*, the implementation of wired networks has become such a simple process that they have become prevalent in both home and business environments. In this section and the section after, we will focus on their implementation in a business environment, but will briefly talk about home networks at the end.

As we mentioned in the previous chapter, the minimum number of devices we need to form a network is two, and we also need some form of medium to connect them. Therefore, we could connect two PCs together using, for example, a crossover cable or a Firewire cable, but the limitations due to the size of this network mean that it is unlikely to be implemented. Most LANs will have more than two devices and will need some form of interconnectivity device to link them together. Interconnectivity devices are those that are not deemed endpoints (PCs, laptops, phones, servers, and so on), and include hubs, bridges, switches, and routers. Let's have a look into LANs using different interconnectivity devices.

# LANs using a hub

It is unlikely that you will see a LAN that utilizes a hub device, but I have included it here (and bridges, later) to provide you with a better understanding of the benefits of a switched network. A hub is a dumb device. It acts as an interconnectivity device that applies no logic to the transmission of data. It just forwards the data out of all of its ports, which means the data is sent to all the connected devices, each of which will have to process the data marginally to see if the data is for it or not. This is shown in the following diagram:

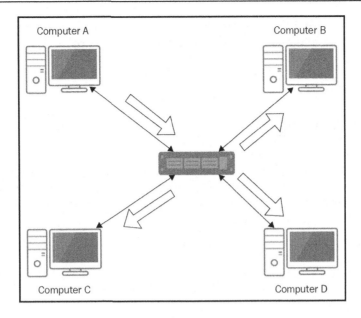

Figure 2.18: A hub network

When **Computer A** sends data to **Computer B**, the hub receives the data and sends it out to all devices, including **Computer C** and **Computer D**. One of the other downfalls of using a hub in the network is that it provides two types of transmission, as follows:

- Half-duplex transmission
- Full-duplex transmission

Half-duplex means that although data is able to flow in both directions, it can only flow in one direction at a time. On the other hand, in a full-duplex transmission, data can flow in both directions at the same time. Because of this half-duplex limitation, and the flooding of data to all devices, a hubbed network will only allow one device to communicate at any one time. If more than one device communicates at the same time, a *collision* occurs, and the data doesn't go through. Because of this, all the devices connected to a hub are said to be in the same *collision domain*.

**Activity 6**: Think about the security of this type of network. How much data would an attacker be able to capture if they plugged a sniffing device into one of the ports on the hub?

Some **Internet Service Providers (ISPs)** will provide you with a device they may refer to as a home hub or something similar. This is usually just a name. They are unlikely to be the same as the hubs described in this section and will offer more functionality.

# LANs using a bridge

To improve the efficiency of hubbed networks, bridges were introduced to segment the network. Bridges learn the MAC addresses on each side of the bridge, and will only forward data it knows is destined for a device on the opposite side of the bridge. Usually, a bridged network would also include hubs. The following diagram shows a simplified bridged network:

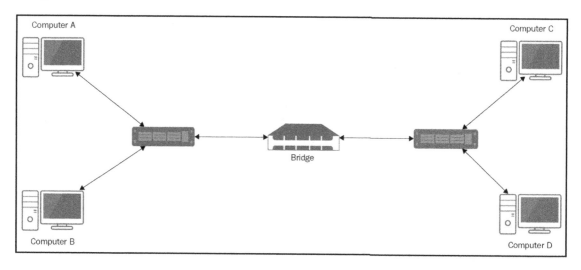

Figure 2.19: A bridged network

When **Computer A** wants to talk to **Computer B**, the data is sent to the hub. The hub sends the data to **Computer B** and also to the bridge. When the data is received at the bridge, it checks the destination MAC address and sees that it belongs to a device on the same side as **Computer A**. The bridge discards this traffic and doesn't forward it. However, if **Computer A** wants to talk to **Computer C**, the data is received by the hub and sent to **Computer B** and the bridge. **Computer B** will ignore the data, but the bridge will see that the destination MAC address is on the other side of the bridge and will forward it on. The data is then received by the hub on the opposite side, which forwards it out of all the ports to **Computer C** and **Computer D**. **Computer C** will process the data while **Computer D** will ignore it.

As you can see, bridges, while not perfect, will reduce the amount of contention on the network and make them more efficient.

# LANs using switches

Switches have become the backbone of most organizations' networks, and having an understanding of their functionality is an important skill for any IT support member. Not only do switches allow for greater network segmentation, but they also offer full-duplex communication, making them more efficient.

The following diagram shows a simplified switched network:

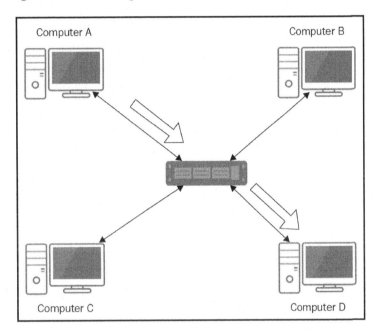

Figure 2.20: Switched network

Switches operate by learning which of its ports a particular MAC address is connected to and base their forwarding decisions on this knowledge. We will talk about this learning process in more detail in `Chapter 6`, *Switches and Switching – Forwarding Traffic on a Local Network*. Looking at the preceding diagram, we can see that **Computer A** wants to communicate with **Computer D**. It sends the data to the switch, the switch looks up which port **Computer D**'s MAC address is linked to, and it sends the data through that port to **Computer D**. In essence, the switch is creating a virtual connection between the two devices.

One of the benefits of using a switch is that all the devices can communicate at the same time. If **Computer C** wants to talk to **Computer B** while **Computer A** is talking to **Computer D**, it can. The switch will form a virtual connection between **Computer C** and **Computer B**. But what happens if **Computer C** wants to talk to **Computer D** while **Computer A** is talking to **Computer D**? Here, the switch buffers (or stores) the data until there is a *gap* in the traffic, and then it forwards it on. This means that every port on a switch is in its own collision domain. A collision will only occur if there is more than one device connected to the switch port, which is very unlikely as it would involve the use of legacy devices such as hubs or bridges.

The following is an example of an enterprise switched network. As the size of the organization increases, you will start to see a tiered approach being adopted:

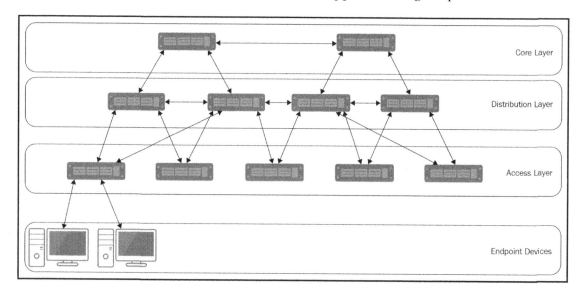

Figure 2.21: Tiered switches

Access switches allow endpoint devices to connect to the network. Traffic that's sent to and from the endpoints is transmitted through these switches. Switches on the **distribution layer** allow traffic to passed between the access switches. Finally, core switches allow traffic to passed between distribution switches. Looking at the preceding diagram, you may be wondering why we need the core switches if the distribution layer switches are connected either directly or via another switch on the same layer. The simplest reason is speed. Distribution switches and their links have a higher capacity and speed than access switches, and in turn, the core switches have a higher capacity and speed than the distribution switches. If the leftmost access switch wanted to send data to the rightmost access switch by going via a core switch, it goes through one less link than if it were connected via distribution layer only, and the links up to and between the core switches will be of a higher bandwidth than the links on the **distribution layer**.

# Wireless networks

With the increasing presence of wireless devices, it is highly unusual to find a LAN that doesn't provide some form of wireless connectivity. When was the last time you went into a coffee shop that didn't offer Wi-Fi? When implementing a wireless network, special consideration needs to be made in terms of coverage, security, and possible sources of interference. It is recommended that we carry out a site survey to ensure that full coverage is obtained.

Wireless networks can be classed as either ad hoc or infrastructure. An ad hoc wireless network is one where devices connect directly to each other without going through any interconnectivity device, whereas wireless infrastructures do go through one. In either of these cases, some form of wireless NIC is required in the endpoint devices. Each wireless NIC will meet certain IEEE 802.11 standards, which dictate their performance abilities. These standards will be discussed in more detail in Chapter 4, *Understanding Wireless Networking*, but it is important to know that any standards that are implemented are compatible with each other.

When implementing an infrastructure mode wireless network in a business environment, you will need **Wireless Access Points (WAPs)**. WAPs allow wireless devices to connect to the wired LAN. The WAP will be configured so that it has a **service set identifier (SSID)**. The SSID is a means of identifying the wireless network using a human-readable name. Once associated with the WAP, the wireless device can communicate with other devices, regardless of whether they are wired or wireless. In the case of communicating with other wireless devices, the traffic is forwarded to the WAP the recipient device is associated with. The following diagram shows a small wireless LAN with a WAP attached to a switch. A laptop and mobile phone are connected to the WAP:

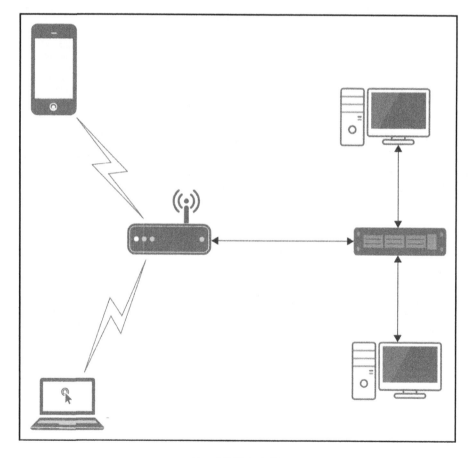

Figure 2.22: Wireless LAN

You may be thinking that the preceding wireless LAN is not quite the same as the one you have at home, and you would most likely be right. The reason for this is that, in a home network, it is unusual to have a WAP and a switch. It's likely that you have a single device that functions as a WAP, a switch, and a router. These devices are known as wireless routers and allow endpoint devices to connect directly to it. Most wireless routers will also have the ability to connect wired devices as well. A wireless router will have separate circuitry for each function that allows for one circuit to pass data to another as and when it is required. The following diagram shows a simple network utilizing a wireless router:

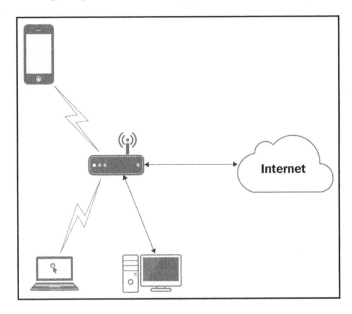

Figure 2.23: Wireless router

In the preceding sections, we have discussed the physical means of creating networks. However, we can use software to create virtual networks by configuring switches.

# Virtual LANs

While switches allowed us to make our networks more efficient through segmentation, they can allow us to segment the network down even further through the use of VLANs. Before we discuss the use of VLANs, I would like to introduce you to the idea of broadcast domains so that you have a better understanding of one of the benefits of implementing VLANs.

When a device sends out a broadcast transmission, it is sent to every device on the local network. All of the devices receiving that broadcast transmission are said to be on the same *broadcast domain*. Routers aren't designed to forward broadcast transmissions, thereby limiting them to your local network. You may be thinking that broadcasts don't happen that frequently, but if you look at the Wireshark capture in the following screenshot, you will see that a number of them are being used for ARP requests on my home network. ARP is just one use of broadcasts, and there are numerous other legitimate purposes. If you scale this up to 1,000 endpoint devices, you will start to understand how much traffic is actually sent as a broadcast. When we implement VLANs, each VLAN is said to be in its own broadcast domain:

| No. | Time | Source | Destination | Protocol | Length | Info |
|-----|------|--------|-------------|----------|--------|------|
| 957 | 29.175594938 | HuaweiTe_9c:10:80 | Broadcast | ARP | 60 | Who has 192.168.1.7? Tell 192.168.1.1 |
| 958 | 29.175762390 | HuaweiTe_9c:10:80 | Broadcast | ARP | 60 | Who has 192.168.1.3? Tell 192.168.1.1 |
| 959 | 29.175953801 | HuaweiTe_9c:10:80 | Broadcast | ARP | 60 | Who has 192.168.1.2? Tell 192.168.1.1 |
| 960 | 29.176239476 | HuaweiTe_9c:10:80 | Broadcast | ARP | 60 | Who has 192.168.1.4? Tell 192.168.1.1 |
| 961 | 29.176461770 | HuaweiTe_9c:10:80 | Broadcast | ARP | 60 | Who has 192.168.1.5? Tell 192.168.1.1 |
| 962 | 29.176634775 | HuaweiTe_9c:10:80 | Broadcast | ARP | 60 | Who has 192.168.1.14? Tell 192.168.1.1 |
| 963 | 29.176815282 | HuaweiTe_9c:10:80 | Broadcast | ARP | 60 | Who has 192.168.1.6? Tell 192.168.1.1 |
| 964 | 29.177050552 | HuaweiTe_9c:10:80 | Broadcast | ARP | 60 | Who has 192.168.1.8? Tell 192.168.1.1 |
| 965 | 29.177247790 | HuaweiTe_9c:10:80 | Broadcast | ARP | 60 | Who has 192.168.1.9? Tell 192.168.1.1 |
| 966 | 29.177423065 | HuaweiTe_9c:10:80 | Broadcast | ARP | 60 | Who has 192.168.1.10? Tell 192.168.1.1 |
| 967 | 29.177619020 | HuaweiTe_9c:10:80 | Broadcast | ARP | 60 | Who has 192.168.1.11? Tell 192.168.1.1 |
| 968 | 29.177836704 | HuaweiTe_9c:10:80 | Broadcast | ARP | 60 | Who has 192.168.1.15? Tell 192.168.1.1 |
| 970 | 29.178056824 | HuaweiTe_9c:10:80 | Broadcast | ARP | 60 | Who has 192.168.1.12? Tell 192.168.1.1 |
| 971 | 29.178282975 | HuaweiTe_9c:10:80 | Broadcast | ARP | 60 | Who has 192.168.1.13? Tell 192.168.1.1 |

Figure 2.24: Packet capture of broadcast transmissions

In *Figure 2.23*, you may notice that the source MAC address is represented differently than in *Figure 2.9* and *Figure 2.10*. This is because I have asked Wireshark to resolve the first six characters (the OUI) to the manufacturer.

VLANs allow us to break the network down further. Rather than doing this physically, this is done virtually by configuring the switch. How you break down the network into the VLANs will vary from organization to organization. Some examples of how you may want to break down the LAN into VLANs are as follows:

- One for each floor of a building
- One for each department
- One for each classroom in a school
- One for different levels of security
- One for data and one for voice communications

Think for a moment about a hospital. In a hospital, you may find that there are a number of devices that fall under the remit of the radiology department. These devices may be used in A&E for X-rays, in maternity for ultrasound, in oncology for mammography, and in MRI machines in neurology, to name just a few. Each of these devices may need to communicate to some central point such as a **radiology information system** (**RIS**); however, they are likely physically spread out across the hospital. This is where VLANs come into play. We can tell the switches that the switch port each of these belongs to is part of the same VLAN. VLANs are usually identified by a number.

The following diagram shows the hospital scenario we detailed previously. We can see that the radiology devices I have listed are all in VLAN 10, whereas **Computer A**, **Computer B**, and **Computer C** are in **VLAN 20**. If **Computer A** sends out a broadcast transmission, only other devices in **VLAN 20** will receive it. The device in oncology will not receive it, despite being physically connected to the same switch, since it is on a different VLAN. In fact, for any communication to take place between the two VLANs, we need a device that's capable of routing traffic between the two. This may be the switch itself, that is, a layer 3 switch that's capable of IP addressing (switches without this capability are referred to as layer 2 switches, or just switches), or a router somewhere in the network.

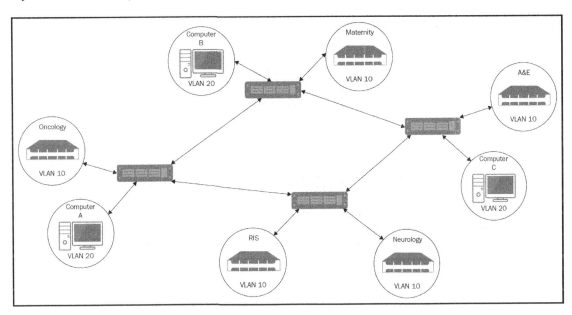

Figure 2.25: Example VLAN in a hospital

While implementing VLANs requires some administrative overhead, they provide great benefits in terms of security and performance. We can segment the network into areas of varying degrees of data sensitivity; for example, all of the human resources devices will be on a dedicated VLAN, as would all the finance department devices. Because each VLAN is in its own broadcast domain, the network becomes more efficient, thereby increasing performance.

# Metropolitan area networks

A MAN is a network that spans across a city. This may be used by organizations such as property management companies that may have numerous properties that they are managing across the city. Other uses of MANs include providing mobile customers with a continuous network service across the city. For example, in Manchester, UK, the tram provider, Metrolink, offer free Wi-Fi on all their trams. To be able to provide this, they need to implement a MAN.

# Campus area networks

When we think of a campus, we usually think of a university campus or a high school campus. However, large organizations such as Google and Microsoft refer to each of their physical locations as a campus. Both uses of the term are correct when discussing a CAN. A CAN is a network that connects multiple LANs within a defined geographical area, such as a university site.

# Personal Area Networks

A PAN refers to the interconnection of devices around a person. An example will help clarify what I mean here. I am a keen runner, and I track all my runs using a Garmin Forerunner 920XT watch. When I finish my run, my watch synchronizes with the Garmin Connect application that's running on my phone. It does this via a Bluetooth connection, and no data that's transmitted between the two traverses my LAN. Another example that's becoming more prominent is Bluetooth headphones that are connected to your phone. While both of these examples use Bluetooth, other technologies that can be used include infrared, Wi-Fi, USB, and Firewire.

# Summary

In this chapter, we learned how to differentiate between the different scales of networks. Then, we moved on to methods of identifying devices, including how each method was used. Then, we looked at the implementation of wired and wireless networks. While we primarily focused on physical networks, we finished this chapter by looking at using VLANs to further segment our network.

Now, you will be able to identify private IP address ranges that you will use extensively throughout your career. You have learned how to identify the MAC address of a Windows device, as well as the manufacturer from the OUI, which can help pinpoint what sort of device is communicating. You also gained an understanding of factors to consider when planning LANs. While this may not be something you will do in the early stages of your career, having an understanding of it will be beneficial. We also looked at the different network devices in a LAN and gained a basic understanding of how these functioned, which will prove invaluable when troubleshooting networks.

In the next chapter, we will look at moving outside of our local networks and discuss the technologies behind WANs. From this, you will start to understand how the infrastructure of the internet is formed and gain knowledge of how to troubleshoot issues across different networks.

# Questions

1. What protocol is used to map an IP address to a MAC address?

(A) DHCP
(B) ICMP
(C) HTTP
(D) ARP

2. Which of the following is a valid MAC address format?

(A) AA:AA:12:34::AA:AA
(B) AB:F1:1B:FE:12:D1:65:91
(C) AB:12:12:CA:1F
(D) AG:CA:1F:AA:11:DA

3. What type of data transmission allows traffic to flow in both directions at the same time?

(A) Unidirectional
(B) Simplex
(C) Half-duplex
(D) Full-duplex

4. Which of the following describes a network that spans a city?

(A) CAN
(B) LAN
(C) MAN
(D) WAN

5. An IP address that can be used locally within your network and is not routable across the internet is known as what?

(A) An alternate private IP address
(B) Private IP address
(C) Public IP address
(D) ARP

6. Which of these commands will display the MAC addresses of your interfaces?

(A) `ipconfig /all`
(B) `show mac`
(C) `display mac`
(D) `ifconfig /all`

7. What identifier does a switch use when making a forwarding decision?

(A) Destination IP address
(B) Source IP address
(C) Destination MAC address
(D) Source MAC address

8. A network that covers a small geographical area is known as a _____. Fill in the blank:

(A) CAN
(B) LAN
(C) MAN
(D) WAN

9. Which of the following is the broadcast MAC address?

(A) `aa:aa:aa:aa:aa:aa`
(B) `ff:ff:ff:ff:ff:ff`
(C) `11:11:11:11:11:11`
(D) `99:99:99:99:99:99`

10. Looking at the following diagram, if **Computer A** sent a broadcast transmission, which devices would receive the data? Do not include **Computer A** in the count.

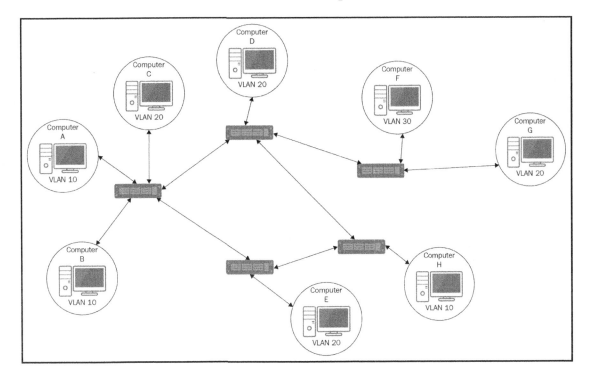

(A) 2
(B) 3
(C) 7
(D) 8

# Further reading

- To find out more about RFC 1918—address allocation for private internets, visit `https://tools.ietf.org/html/rfc1918`.
- To find out more about RFC 5494—IANA allocation guidelines for the ARP, visit `https://tools.ietf.org/html/rfc5494`.

# 3
# Understanding Wide Area Networks

Historically, organizations in the early days of networking were concerned with the sharing of information and data internally. However, as more organizations began to own their own computer systems, it became increasingly evident that it would be beneficial to share information between organizations, such as universities. From this, the idea of wide area networking began to take shape to become what it is today. There are very few organizations in the developed world that have not taken to the internet. Gaining a good foundation knowledge of how some of the basic **wide area network (WAN)** infrastructure works will give you a good grounding to be able to support your organization and troubleshoot any issues as they arise.

This chapter moves out of your own networks and discusses the principles behind WANs. It focuses on the services offered by service providers, discussing the characteristics of each of the different methods, including use cases.

The following topics will be covered in this chapter:

- Introduction to WANs
- Setting up a broadband connection
- Leased lines
- Dial-up
- Carrier standards

# Technical requirements

To complete the exercises in this chapter, you will require a PC or virtual machine running Windows 7 or above (preferably Windows 10) with a working internet connection.

# Introducing WANs

In the previous chapter, we defined a LAN as a network that covered a small geographical area. In contrast, a WAN is one that covers a large geographical area. We can further define this by saying that a WAN is also used to link LANs, and a prime example of this is the internet. Pretty much every resource we access on the internet is located within someone's LAN. Because of the size of the network involved in a WAN, we will usually find parts of the infrastructure are hosted and controlled by third-party service providers.

For the purposes of the MTA exam, the definitions I have used for LAN and WAN should be adhered to. However, in the real world, you will likely find that uses of the terms LAN and WAN are used incorrectly. For example, I once worked for a global company with offices across the world. You can't get much larger. Resources we accessed could be in the UK, Japan, the United States, or anywhere the company was based. Yet we referred to the network as a LAN, and not a WAN.

Pretty much every organization will connect to a WAN via a third-party service provider, and your service provider will have some form of reciprocal agreement with other service providers to allow each other's traffic across their respective infrastructure. Which service provider you use for that initial connection will depend on a number of factors, which are beyond the scope of this book and the exam, however, ultimately you will need to choose a provider that can meet your requirements. One of the key considerations, though, will be the choice of whether you want a dedicated connection or a shared connection. We will discuss these in the following sections.

# Setting up a broadband connection

In the 1990s, when I got my first computer, most ISPs would provide you with a CD that included software that configured your home connection to their service. These usually would configure your dial-up modem, and in some cases also gave you a graphical user interface to navigate the internet. However, the use of CDs has pretty much faded with the demise of modems. Nowadays, our ISP will provide us with some form of preconfigured home router that will connect directly to the ISP, and all you have to do is connect your devices to the router.

While we can usually connect directly to our ISP-provided hub/router, there may be times when we need to manually configure this broadband connection. In the following activity, we will manually set up a broadband connection.

 Because in the real world this requires an account with a service provider, we will set up the connection, but it will not connect. Your screens may differ slightly depending on the OS used.

# Setting up a broadband connection

**Activity 1**: Setting up a broadband connection is relatively straightforward, and in the real world the ISP would provide you with some of the configuration values that we use in the following process:

1. Open **Network and Sharing Center** on your PC.
2. Select **Set up a new connection or network**:

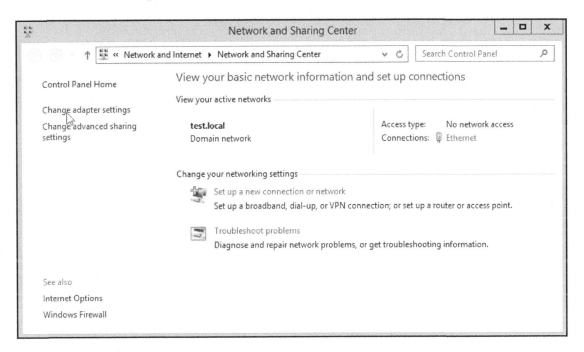

Figure 3.1: Network and Sharing Center

3. Select **Connect to the Internet** and click **Next**:

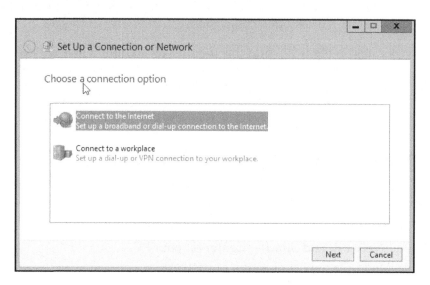

Figure 3.2: Setting up a connection or network

4. Choose the appropriate option to connect. In this case, you can see that I only have one option:

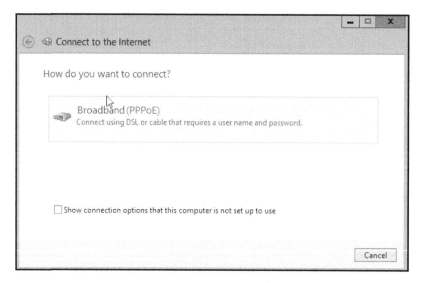

Figure 3.3: Connecting to the internet

5. Enter the credentials provided by your ISP, provide a **Connection name**, and, if appropriate, check the box to allow other users of the device to use the connection. Then, click **Connect**:

Figure 3.4: Inserting your credentials

6. The device will now try to connect. As we do not have a connection, you can either click **Skip** here, or wait for it to time out, then click **Set up connection anyway**, followed by **Close**:

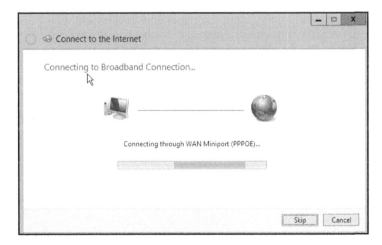

Figure 3.5: Trying to connect

In the preceding activity, we configured the initial setup of a broadband connection. Now we have an internet connection set up, let's look at some of the properties.

# Configuring connection properties

**Activity 2**: There are a number of properties that we can configure for each connection. We cover a number of these in the following activity:

1. Click on **Internet Options**:

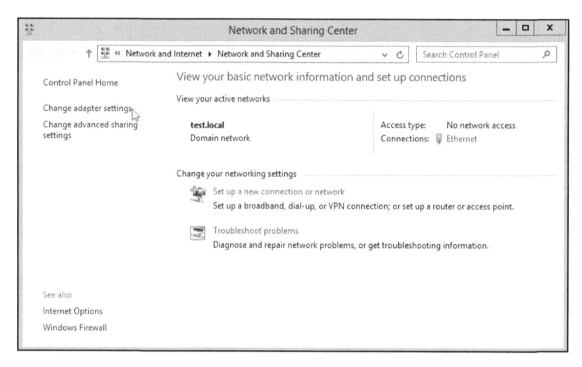

Figure 3.6: Network and Sharing Center

2. Select the **Connections** tab on the **Internet Properties** dialog box:

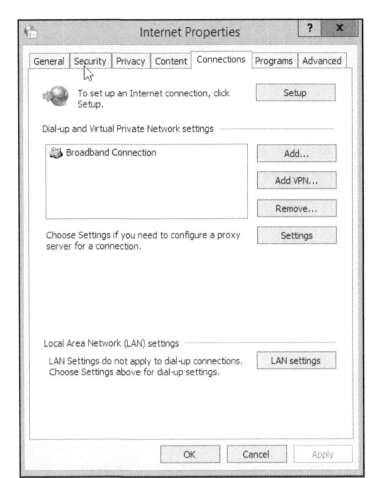

Figure 3.7: Internet Properties dialog box

3. The **Setup** option allows you to repeat the previous activity, but also allows you to select an existing connection. The **Add...** option allows you to create a new connection.
4. Select the connection you created in the previous activity and click **Settings**.

5.  Investigate the options available to you here. You will not need to know these for the exam but it is worthwhile knowing they exist for the real world. Of the options shown in this dialog box, I will draw your attention to the **Proxy server** option, which we will discuss in more detail in Chapter 14, *Network Services*:

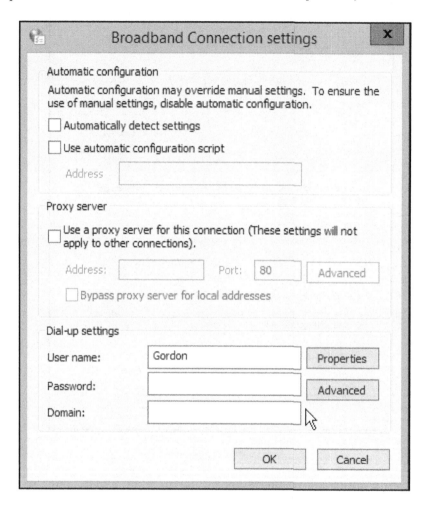

Figure 3.8: Broadband Connection settings

6. Click on **Properties** and investigate the options there. In the **Sharing** tab, you will see that you can share the device's internet connection. This is seldom used nowadays and is a throwback to the days when you only had one modem and wanted to share it in a household. You would connect the PCs to a hub, and one of the PCs would be connected to the modem. This allowed the other devices to share the modem-connected PC's internet connection:

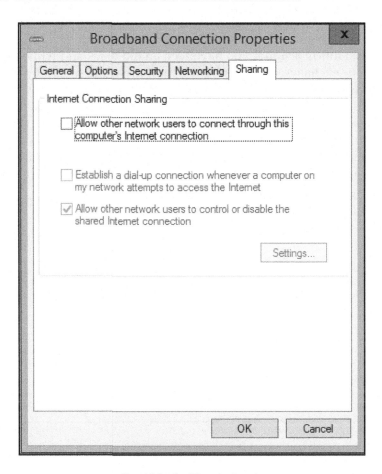

Figure 3.9: Broadband Connection Properties

Once the data has been received on the WAN, it has to be moved around to get to its destination. To do this, we use some form of packet switching technology; usually, this will be either X.25 or Frame Relay. Before these technologies came along, when the only means of connection was via dial-up, we used circuit switching.

# Circuit switching

With circuit switching, the telephone system created a physical connection from the person initiating the call to the person receiving the call. This is not to say there was a cable that ran my house to my friend's house. There would be a cable that connected my house to the telephone exchange, and from there another cable was then connected to create a connection to another exchange where the process was repeated until the final exchange would connect me to my friend's house.

You may have seen this in action if you have seen an old black and white movie with a scene at a telephone exchange. The telephone operators would manually plug and unplug the cables to make or end the physical connection. Because it would only be my call on this connection, the bandwidth was dedicated to me, and thus the quality of the call was guaranteed. However, circuit switching was not without its drawbacks. If there was a break in the connection, there was no redundancy in place, and a new connection had to be initiated. If it failed during a data transfer, you would have to re-transmit. *Figure 3.10* shows an example of how a circuit switching connection may have been made:

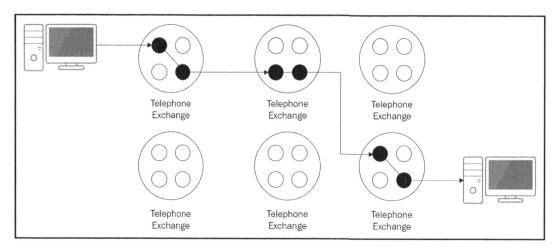

Figure 3.10 Circuit switching example

As circuit switching was not without its faults, an alternative was required to address them. Packet switching was the solution, and we will cover this next.

# Packet switching

Packet switching was introduced to alleviate some of the issues that were found in circuit switching. Using this method, the data being transferred is broken down into smaller chunks of data called **packets**. A virtual connection is made between the devices. One of the key differences between packet switching and circuit switching is that there is no fixed path between the devices, and each packet may take a different route. As you can see in *Figure 3.11*, the first packet (single black line) and the second packet (double black line) have gone different paths. Note that, for clarity, I have not added the double black line for the connection between the devices and the central offices:

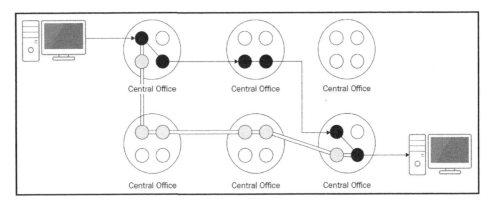

Figure 3.11: Packet switching network

Each of these packets includes a portion of the original data (payload), a header, and a trailer. As the header and trailer are additional to the data being transmitted, they are classed as management overhead. The header will include information such as the source and destination addresses, and a segmentation number, as well as other details. The segmentation number is used to rebuild the segmented data at the recipient's end and as a means of accounting for all the data. Has it all been received? The trailer contains a **cyclic redundancy check (CRC)** for error checking. When sending data, the following process is followed:

1. The sending device performs a mathematical calculation on the data being sent.
2. The output of that calculation is added to the trailer.
3. On receipt of any data, the receiving device performs the same calculation.
4. The receiving device then compares its result with the value stored in the trailer.
5. If the two values match, then the data has been transmitted correctly.
6. If they do not match, then the data is deemed to be corrupted, and some form of correction or re-transmission is required.

How large these packets are is dependent on the network itself. We'll look at an example scenario and identify how many packets need to be transmitted.

Joe wants to send a file that is 4 Kb in size, across a network that supports a fixed packet size of 512 bits. Each packet has 124 bits of overhead (92 bits for the header and 32 bits for the trailer). We can see just from comparing the file size and fixed packet size that the original data needs to broken down into packets. But how many? To work this out, we need to know how big the payload can be in each packet. We can find this using the following calculation:

- *Payload size = fixed packet size - overhead:*

  *Payload size = 512 bits - 124 bits*

  *Payload size = 388 bits*

- With this information, we can find out how many packets we would send:

  *Number of packets = original file size/Payload size*

  *Number of packets = 4096 bits/388 bits*

  *Number of packets = 10.55*

Obviously, we cannot send .55 of a packet, so this would be 10 packets with a payload of *388 bits* each, and an 11th packet with a payload of 216 bits.

# X.25 packet switching

While X.25 packet switching is one of the oldest packet-switching technologies, it is still in use today even though frame relay is available. Through the use of X.25 technology, an organization can take advantage of a 64 Kb WAN connection that is *called up* whenever there is data to be transmitted. X.25 provides an end-to-end connection that is digital throughout, thus removing the requirement to convert data from digital to analog and back again. While all data being transmitted across any network will have some form of management overhead included in the transmission, X.25 has a greatly reduced overhead compared to that used in circuit switching. This leads to more efficient use of available bandwidth.

There are a number of components you need to be familiar with to understand how X.25 packet switching works, and I would like to define them before providing an overview of how communication takes place.

- **Packet Assembler Disassembler (PAD)**: This is likely to be the router on the sending device's network. It takes the original data and breaks it down into packets. On arrival at the destination network's router, the packets are re-assembled back into their original form.

- **Data Terminating Equipment (DTE)**: This is the device where the data being transmitted on a packet-switched network terminates. In most modern iterations, this would be the router, but may actually be a terminal device. The DTE is owned by the client.

- **Data Circuit-Terminating Equipment (DCE)**: This device connects your network to the medium that links you to the packet switching network. In a packet-switching network, this would be a device called a **Channel Service Unit/Data Service Unit (CSU/DSU)**. One of the important functions these devices provide is that of clocking. Clocking is a function that allows synchronous transmission of data, that is, all devices are working on the same timings and thus avoid collisions.

- **Central Office (CO)**: This is the building owned by your service provider where all the digital connections go to.

- **Packet Switching Exchange (PSE)**: A device located in the CO that is used for routing the data. Each PSE contains thousands of circuits, and it will choose one of these circuits to transmit the data through. (This is represented by the small circles in *Figure 3.2.*)

- **Virtual circuit**: The collection of circuits selected for the transmission of a set of data.

- **Demarcation point (Demarc)**: This is the point where services from your service provider interface with your own services. This will mark the boundaries of responsibilities, and is quite important to know when troubleshooting. Is it a problem in your devices or with the providers, or possibly subsequent providers, that your data is transiting through. A demarcation point may be an interface on a device or something as simple as a network jack.

*Figure 3.12* shows the connection from the end device to the internet, where the CO will be located. The routing that takes place within the internet is shown in *Figure 3.12*:

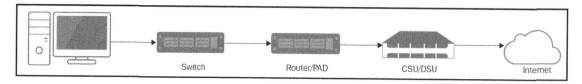

Figure 3.12: X.25 setup

Now you know the components, let's put this all together and discuss the process:

1. Your device sends the data to a router.
2. The router (PAD) disassembles the data into packets.
3. The PAD forwards the packets to the CSU/DSU.
4. The CSU/DSU then forwards the packets via the Demarc to the CO.
5. Once received at the CO, a PSE may disassemble the packets further if they are too big for onward transmission. The PSE will then view the destination information within the packet, and decide which circuit to forward it through. There is no requirement for all of the packets from one set of original data to be sent through the same circuit/path.
6. The PSE sends the data on to the next hop in the path. This may be another PSE or may be the recipient's PAD.
7. Once the data arrives at the recipient's PAD, it is checked (using the CRC) and reassembled.
8. The PAD finally forwards the data to the intended recipient.

X.25 allows for devices on the LAN to share the WAN connection. As you can see from *Figure 3.12*, the end devices connect to the router via a switch, meaning they can all transmit data to the router. The PSEs have the capacity to store data in their buffers for onward transmission later (store and forward). Because they are storing the data before transmitting it, there is an element of fault tolerance here. If the data being transmitted fails for whatever reason, the PSE still holds it in its buffer and can therefore attempt to forward it on again. This may mean forwarding it via a different circuit if the original one is no longer available.

It is possible to identify the path that the data takes using the `tracert` command. `tracert` traces the route your data takes to reach a destination. The following activity will demonstrate this command in action:

**Activity 3**:

1. Open Command Prompt on a Windows PC.
2. `tracert` to Google's public DNS server using this command: `tracert 8.8.8.8`.
3. Review the output.

Your output should look similar to mine (*Figure 3.13*). If you receive a `General failure` message, it is likely that the ICMP packets being used by `tracert` are being blocked by the firewall:

```
C:\Users\User>tracert 8.8.8.8

Tracing route to google-public-dns-a.google.com [8.8.8.8]
over a maximum of 30 hops:

  1     1 ms     1 ms     1 ms  vodafone.broadband [192.168.1.1]
  2    19 ms    21 ms    26 ms  host-212-158-250-32.dslgb.com [212.158.250.32]
  3    13 ms    13 ms    12 ms  63.130.105.130
  4    12 ms    12 ms    12 ms  72.14.216.237
  5     *        *        *     Request timed out.
  6    13 ms    13 ms    13 ms  216.239.63.136
  7    30 ms    31 ms    30 ms  216.239.50.73
  8    13 ms    13 ms    13 ms  google-public-dns-a.google.com [8.8.8.8]

Trace complete.
```

Figure 3.13: tracert output

Looking at my output, we can see a number of things. Firstly, we can see that `tracert` has resolved the IP address of `8.8.8.8` to what is known as a **fully qualified domain name (FQDN)** of `google-public-dns-a.google.com`. We can see that it allowed the route to be a maximum of 30 hops (routers). If the destination was any further than this, it would not have completed the trace. Then, the output provides us with the details of the 8 hops to get to `8.8.8.8`. Hop #1 is my home router (default gateway). There are three sets of timings for each hop. `tracert` sends three packets of data to each hop (basically sends a ping) and records the latency (how long it takes for a reply to come back). Then, I am informed of the IP address of the hop, and, where available, its name. Look at hop #5.

Notice there are no timings, just an asterix, `*`, and it says `Request timed out`. This is most likely due to the device at hop #5 being configured not to respond to ICMP requests. It is not unusual to see multiple entries similar to hop #5. However, I would suggest that if you have no connectivity to the end device (in this case `8.8.8.8`) and from hop #5 onward you have just received `Request timed out` messages, that there is a problem between hop #4 and hop #5.

**Exam tip**: I would encourage you to refer to `tracert` as **trace route.** A lot of people refer to it as *trace R T*, and then forget what it is used for. By referring to it in full, you can easily recognize its function. I would, however, be remiss not to include a caveat to this. In Linux, the command is `traceroute`, not `tracert`. If you follow my recommendation of referring to `tracert` as *trace route*, be careful as the Linux variant may be in the answer set as a distractor.

# Frame relay

We discussed previously how X.25 segmented the original data being transmitted by breaking it down into packets. Frame relay utilizes a similar technique, but breaks the original data into chunks of data known as **frames**. However, confusingly, it is still referred to as packet-switching technology. Devices in a frame relay network are similar to those used in an X.25 network, except the former uses a **Frame Relay Access Device (FRAD)** instead of a PAD, and the DCE is a device known as **frame relay switch** instead of the CSU/DSU (*Figure 3.14*):

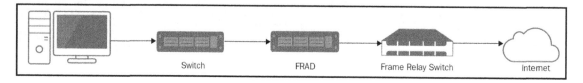

Figure 3.14: Frame relay

With frame relay, the virtual circuits created are not dedicated to just you and are shared with other organizations. This raises some obvious concerns regarding privacy, and also leads to decreased transmission speeds as you share the connection. This doesn't sound too appealing, so why use frame relay? Quite simply, it is cheaper and uses fewer devices. To try and help alleviate the issue of decreased speed, frame relay does not attempt to correct any errors it detects during the transit of the data. If a frame is detected as having an error, it is simply discarded. Error correction is left to the relevant endpoint devices. They will identify that data is missing and attempt to correct the issue, usually by re-transmission.

Unlike X.25, which is needed to *call up* to transmit data, frame relay uses **permanent virtual circuits (PVCs)**. As the name implies, these are permanently connected and do not need to *call up* to transmit data. These PVCs connect to PSEs sitting in a frame relay cloud and are likely to be paired. One PVC will be for transmission, and the other for receiving, giving you a full-duplex connection.

Organizations will need to decide on what bandwidth they are likely to use and agree this with the service provider. The normal bandwidth you select is known as the **committed information rate (CIR)**. There may be instances when this is not quite enough, and frame relay allows for burst transmissions of up to two seconds. This provides you with additional bandwidth, with two additional rates, **burst rate (BR)** and **burst excess (BE)**. The BR is double the CIR, and the BE is BR plus half the CIR. There are lots of abbreviations there, so let me clarify that:

*Burst rate (BR) = 2 x committed information rate (CIR)*

*Burst excess = Burst rate + (committed information rate/2)*

Both frame relay and packet switching utilize a shared infrastructure. Although this means it is a cheaper option compared to alternatives, it is not without issues. In the next section, we will look at a more costly alternative.

# Leased lines

I find people struggle a little with differentiating leased lines from other forms of connectivity, purely due to the use of the term *leased*. All of these connections require you to lease some form of service from your provider, and that's what confuses people. What I would ask you to do to combat this is to prefix leased lines with the word *dedicated*.

Unlike other forms of connection discussed here, a leased line is a dedicated link between you and another location. It's dedicated in that it is only you using it, and, unlike the others we will discuss, it is not shared with other subscribers. You may have noticed that I refer to *another location* rather than specifically mentioning the connection is to your service provider. This is deliberate, because although most leased lines will connect you to your service provider, you may also have a dedicated connection between company sites. Because the lines are dedicated to you, the service providers can guarantee a level of quality. They also tend to offer full-duplex connectivity with the same speed for uploads as that available for downloads.

Leased lines offer *always-on* communication. They are permanently connected and ready to send and receive data at any time of day, and there is no requirement to initiate the connection. Because of this, leased lines are a more expensive option, and potentially you are paying for the connection when it is not being used, such as night time or weekends. It is unlikely, therefore, that a leased line will be used to connect a residential home to a service provider. In fact, in 18 years of working in IT, I have only once come across a home user that had a dedicated lease line.

# Dial-up connectivity

You may be looking at the title of this section and wondering why are we covering such an old technology. The simple answer to this is that, despite its age, dial-up is still used. However, unless you're living in rural areas where faster methods are not available, it is unlikely that it would be used as a primary means of connection to a WAN. In most instances, dial-up would be used as a backup means of connectivity, used for allowing support staff to connect and rectify any issues with the primary means of connection. Imagine that you are an on-call network engineer, and someone calls you up in the middle of the night to report that there is no internet access. You try to connect to the router from home, but there is no connectivity. You then use a dial-up connection to dial into the network, connect to the router via its internal interface, and rectify the fault.

Dial-up connections utilize the traditional telephone network. You may hear this referred to as **public switched telephone network (PSTN)** or more informally, **plain old telephone service (POTS)**. The telephone network was designed to carry voice communications, and its use for carrying data was piggy-backed on to the existing infrastructure. The performance of dial-up can vary significantly depending on a number of factors. For example, distance can impact the quality of the signal, likewise the environments where the telephone line is shared, such as a workplace or a hotel, will suffer from degradation.

To connect using dial-up, a user needs to use a device called a **modulator/de-modulator (modem)**. A modem may be a standalone device, maybe on an expansion card added to the computer, or embedded on the motherboard, although this is unlikely on modern PCs. If using a standalone device, you will need to connect it to the PC. The modem is then connected to the telephone socket in your building. The purpose of the modem is to convert the digital signals from your PC into analog signals for transfer across the telephone lines. The destination modem reverses this process, taking the analog signal, and converting them back into a digital format that can be understood by the recipient PC. *Figure 3.15* shows a simplified dial-up network. In reality, the modem connects to a telephone socket at the wall, and does not connect directly to the telephone pole:

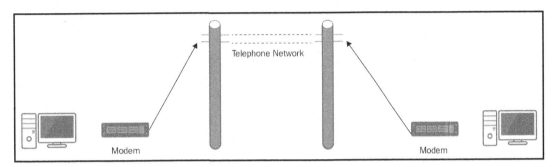

Figure 3.15: Dial-up connection

Compared to modern technologies, dial-up offers a very slow service. Although the telephone lines can transmit 64 Kb/s, only 54 Kb/s is used for data, and the remaining 8 Kb/s is used for signaling purposes. As modem technology advanced, compression was used to transfer data at a higher rate. For example, V.44 would boost the speed up to the equivalent of 320 Kb/s. ISPs were able to extend this further by using compression to reduce the size of web page content such as text and images.

**Activity 4: Setting up a dial-up connection**: In this activity, we will go through setting up your computer to use a dial-up connection:

 As it is unlikely that you have access to a modem and a relevant dial-up account with your ISP, this activity will include some steps that you are unlikely to see if you're doing this for real.

1. Open **Network and Sharing Center** on your PC.
2. Select **Set up a new connection or network**:

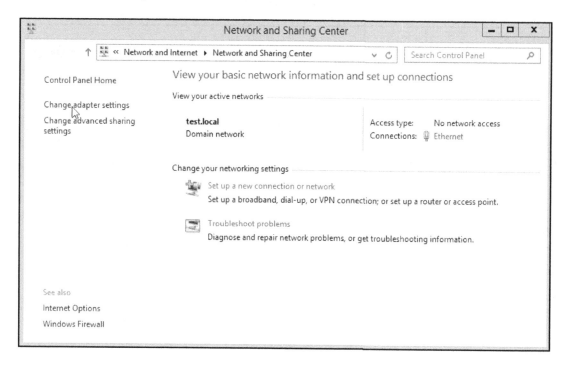

Figure 3.16: Setting up a new connection

3. Select **Connect to the Internet** and click **Next**:

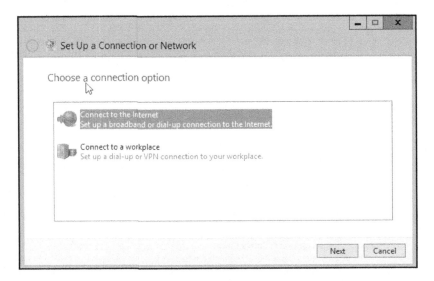

Figure 3.17: Connecting to the internet

4. Choose **Dial-up** (note: as I do not have a modem connected, I had to choose **Show connection options that this computer is not set up to use** for it to show):

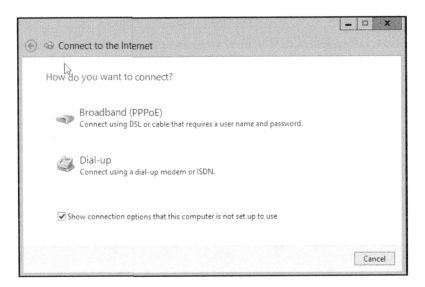

Figure 3.18: The Dial-up option

5. Enter in the details provided by your ISP. Then, click **Dialing Rules**:

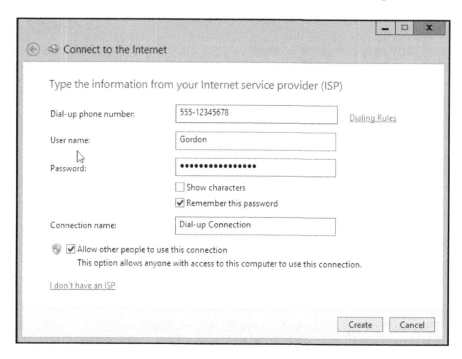

Figure 3.19: Inserting your credentials

6. In the **Dialing Rules** dialog box, you can configure the following options. The option to set a number in the **If you dial a number to access an outside line, what is it?** field is useful for you when you are in a hotel or workplace where you have to dial a **9** to get an outside line. Click **OK** to close this dialog box:

Figure 3.20: Dialing rules dialogue box

7. To use this connection, repeat *steps 1* to *3* again. Then, from the presented connections, choose **Dial-up Connection**, and click **Next** to connect:

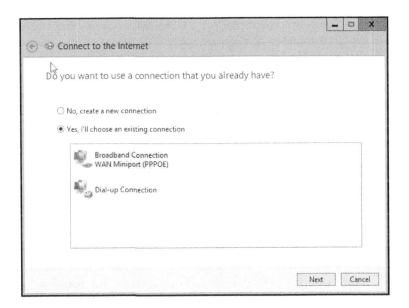

Figure 3.21: Setting up a connection

As you can see from the preceding activity, this is quite a convoluted process and would be difficult for a lot of users, especially at the height of dial-up's popularity when people were not as computer-savvy as they are now. Because of this, most ISPs would provide a setup CD that would do all the donkey work for you. In fact, at one point you could not buy a computer magazine, or go into a supermarket, without being presented with a free CD for a trial with some ISP or other.

Obviously, in a business environment, you don't want just anyone being able to dial in. To avoid this, we need to configure the system to authenticate and authorize the user before allowing them to gain access to the network. Traditionally, this was carried out by a **Remote Authentication Dial In User Service** (**RADIUS**) server, and in modern implementations this role is carried out by a **Network Policy Server** (**NPS**). As can be seen in *Figure 3.22*, the client device connects to the dial-in server, and the server forwards the user's credentials to the RADIUS server for approval. The RADIUS server sends back either an approval or rejection based on credentials and the user's permissions. If approved, the client device is allowed on the network. It should be noted that, despite its name, a RADIUS server provides authentication for more than just dial-in remote users:

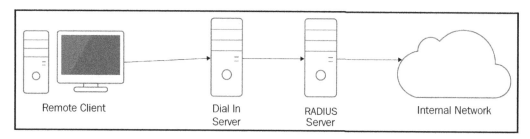

Figure 3.22: RADIUS server setup

The user's dial-in permissions are set in their user profile. *Figure 3.23* shows the options available. At the top, we either allow or block connection, or we can allow the connection based upon the settings in the **Network Policy** (**NP**). This policy simply states what criteria a user or device has to meet to be considered safe to be allowed on the network. The next section is an option to verify caller ID. This only allows calls to come in from a predefined phone number. As companies tend to get cheaper calls due to business rates, it is usually more cost-effective to *call back* the user rather than them calling up from their individual houses (assuming they can claim the calls back on expenses), so there is an option to call the user back on the number they dialed in on. As an added security option, you can specify a number that is called back to. The obvious restriction to this is that the user dialing in is restricted to that one location if it is a landline number. The last options allow the allocation of static IP addresses (as opposed to DHCP-issued ones) and static routing. We cover routing in more detail in Chapter 7, *Routers and Routing - Beyond a Single Network*:

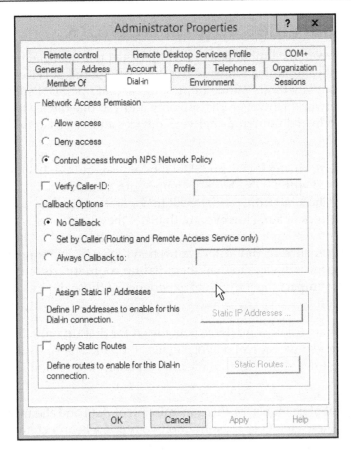

Figure 3.23: User dial-in settings

With the need to provide faster inter-connectivity to accommodate the requirements of more dynamic and demanding services, the days of dial-up were numbered. The following section discusses the various *successors* to this standard.

# Understanding carrier standards

The term *carrier standards* refers to standards that have been agreed upon for the various different carrier technologies. These standards cover a whole range of areas, including coding mechanisms, modulation, voltages, and physical attributes. However, for the exam we only need to have a high-level understanding.

We will now look at some of the common individual carrier standards.

# Integrated Services Digital Network

As technology developed, the limitations of dial-up began to become a hindrance. Faster and better methods of communication were required. **Integrated Services Digital Network (ISDN)** was one of those methods. While improving on dial up, ISDN still utilized the existing telephone network. However, dial-up only allowed one device to use the line at a time, whereas ISDN allowed numerous network devices and voices to utilize the line at the same time.

To connect to the internet using ISDN, an ISDN modem is required. It should be noted that although a modem used with ISDN shares its name with a modem used with dial-up, that is pretty much where the similarities end. Recall that a dial-up modem converts digital signals to analog and back again. However, with ISDN the signal used is digital throughout the journey, and no conversion to/from analog is required. Removal of the conversion step helped improve performance, as did faster connection times. ISDN modems also tend to have more ports to connect devices to than their dial-up counterparts, although connecting too many devices may impact the individual experience of those devices due to having to share a finite bandwidth.

It is easy to think of modems being used for dial-up only. If a question mentions conversion of analog signals, then the answer is definitely leaning toward dial-up, but ensure you read the question and the answer set fully.

ISDN uses the concept of channels for the transmission of data and the management of such transmissions. These channels are split into two types, a bearer channel (B) and a data channel (D). Rather confusingly, the B channel is used to *bear* the data, and the D channel is mainly used to carry the management data for signaling and control. Oddly, because this seems the wrong way round to me, it actually sticks in my mind more. Each B channel is capable of carrying 64 Kb/s, and the D channel is also capable of carrying 64 Kb/s.

There are two types of access available in ISDN, **Basic Rate Interface (BRI)** and **Primary Rate Interface (PRI)**. BRI utilizes two B channels and a single D channel. This provides 128 Kb/s for data. In contrast, PRI varies depending on the region. In North America, it uses what is known as a T1 connection (one of a number of T-Carriers discussed later), Japan uses a J1 connection, and Europe and the majority of the world uses an E1 connection. A T1 and J1 connection utilizes 24 B channels providing a bandwidth of 1,544 Kb/s (or 1.544 Mb/s), whereas E1 uses 32 B channels providing a bandwidth of 2,048 Kb/s (or 2.048 Mb/s).

# Asynchronous Transfer Mode

**Asynchronous Transfer Mode (ATM)** is another method that allows the integration of data and voice communications, and is used within PSTN and ISDN networks. ATM splits the data into fixed-size *cells* of data, and requires a connection to be made between endpoints before any data is transferred. This helps make the network more efficient. If no connection can be established, then no data is transmitted.

# Digital Subscriber Line

Similar to ISDN, **Digital Subscriber Line (DSL)** provides a means of transmitting digital signals across the existing telephone network. Again a modem is required, but unlike ISDN a digital to analog conversion does take place. Although the data being transmitted is now an analog signal, both data and voice communications can take place simultaneously as the data is being transmitted at a higher frequency than the voice communications. Common forms of DSL are **Asymmetric DSL (ADSL)** and **Symmetric DSL (SDSL)**:

- **ADSL**: Most homes utilized ADSL, so this became synonymous with the term DSL. ADSL offers a faster download speed than upload speed. This made sense at the time. Most home users would only be downloading from the internet, even if this was just web pages, and the only uploads they would be doing were the commands from their devices to pull those websites down.
- **SDSL**: SDSL was more the domain of organizations, as this was a dedicated line, and therefore more expensive. As can probably be deduced from its name, SDSL could upload and download at the same speed.

There are a number of other variations of DSL, and you may see the acronym xDSL to represent DSL; however, ADSL and SDSL are the two main ones. ADSL can provide around about 24 Mb/s download and 1 Mb/s upload, and SDSL provides a speed of about 2 Mb/s. The speeds mentioned here are dependent on the distance from the central office. As the distance increased, the speed would reduce due to attenuation (degradation of the signal).

# Synchronous Optical Network

**Synchronous Optical Network (SONET)** is a means of sending digital data down a high-speed optical connection. One of the benefits of SONET was the ability to send multiple data streams through a single connection. The following table shows the details of the speeds of each level:

| Level | Transmission speeds |
| --- | --- |
| OC-1 | 51.84 Mb/s |
| OC-3 | 155.52 Mb/s |
| OC-12 | 622.08 Mb/s |
| OC-24 | 1.244 Gb/s |
| OC-48 | 2.488 Gb/s |
| OC-192 | 9.953 Gb/s |

If you can remember the speed of OC-1, then to find the other speeds you just multiply that value by the OC level number.

While SONET utilized optical cabling, other technologies utilized copper cabling and T-carriers, which we will discuss in the next subsection.

# T-carriers

T-carriers or Transmission carriers are utilized by some of the technologies listed previously to transmit data at high speed. In addition, they may be used as a link between LANs to provide a high-speed connection with the added benefit of privacy. The following table shows the details of the relevant speeds per standard:

| Europe | | Japan | | North America | |
| --- | --- | --- | --- | --- | --- |
| Level | Speed | Level | Speed | Level | Speed |
| E1 | 2.048 Mb/s | J1 | 1.544 Mb/s | T1 | 1.544 Mb/s |
| E3 | 34.368 Mb/s | J3 | 32.064 Mb/s | T2 | 44.736 Mb/s |
| E4 | 139.264 Mb/s | J4 | 97.728 Mb/s | T3 | 274.176 Mb/s |

SONET and T-carriers will usually be used in organizations where the additional bandwidth offered by these technologies prevents any performance issues. Let's look at an option for the home environment.

# Broadband cable

At this point, you may have read through all of the preceding sections and are now thinking, my home network does not use any of these. If this is true for you, it is likely you use some form of broadband cable, especially if your TV and internet is provided by the same supplier, for example, Sky in the UK. This one connection probably uses a single RG-6 coaxial cable.

# Fiber to the X

While not specifically mentioned in the exam objectives, I would like to discuss other WAN technologies that I feel it is worth knowing exist, namely **Fiber to the X** (FTTx), satellite, and cellular.

FTTx is a term that will crop up in the real world. FTTx is a generic term referring to the varying levels of **Next Generation Access** (**NGA**) that fiber optic connections and services provide. The following sums up the common versions of FTTx:

- **Fiber to the home (FTTH)**: A form of **Fiber to the Premises** (**FTTP**). It provides a fiber connection to your house. It should be noted the fiber connection usually ends at some form of junction box attached to your outside wall, and the connection from that box to devices inside, such as the modem, will not be fiber.
- **Fiber to the building/business (FTTB)**: Another form of FTTP. This is similar to FTTH but is geared towards either business or multi-tenancy buildings such as apartment blocks. Fiber is used to the building but from that point to the offices or different apartments a different medium is used.
- **Fiber to the curb/kerb (FTTC/K)**: In this instance, the service provider lays fiber connections to the communications cabinet at the end of the road (realistically this could be anywhere within 300 m of your premises).

In Chapter 8, *Media Types - Connecting Everything Together*, we discuss the characteristics of various cabling technologies including fiber. In that chapter, we will discuss the speeds of fiber. It is important to note that although the various FTTx implementations provide fast speeds to the various endpoints (home, business, curb, and so on) the onward connection from there to your end devices is likely to be slower, and you will not be able to take the full advantage of the speeds fiber offers.

# Satellite

Satellite WAN is an ideal connectivity solution in areas where the laying of cables is problematic, such as rural locations, hazardous terrain, on board ships, and so on. Laying cables to each of the aforementioned locations would be either prohibitively expensive or impossible. Although still a relatively expensive option, satellite avoids the problem of laying cables to these areas by utilizing satellites in a geo-stationary orbit above the equator. Geo-stationary means the satellite orbits the earth at the same speed the earth is rotating, thus allowing the satellite to be easily located. End user devices will connect to a modem-like device, which in turn is connected to a satellite dish. For communication to take place, the dish needs to have a clear line of sight to the satellite for the signal to get through. When installing and aligning a satellite dish, an engineer will have to take into consideration potential environmental factors. An example of this is trees. An engineer may have obtained a perfect signal during a wintertime installation, but come spring, leaves return to the tree and block the line of sight.

Satellite communication is known to have high latency. The signal has to go from earth to the satellite, and from the satellite to your provider's **Network Operations Center (NOC)** back on earth, from the NOC to the destination device. The data sent back in response follows that route in reverse. In ideal conditions, this can take about half a second to complete, but in reality is usually going to be slower due to internet traffic, heavy rain, snow, solar interference, and so on. In early satellite implementations, this latency resulted in maximum speeds of approximate 2 Mbp/s, which limited you to either web browsing or file downloading. Video conferencing, streaming, and online gaming was a definite non-starter. However, speeds have now increased dramatically, and at the time of writing (2019), Viasat offers a connection of 100 Mbp/s. *Figure 3.24* gives an overview of a satellite network:

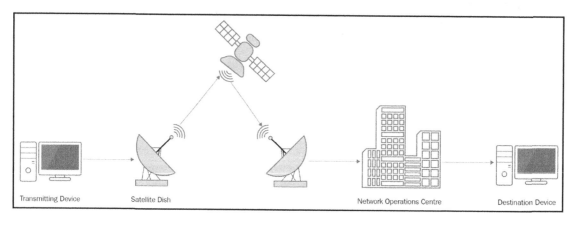

Figure 3.24: Satellite network

Interestingly, until recently I had a mindset that the use of satellite was few and far between and performance was relatively poor in comparison to wired connections. However, having just purchased a cave house in an area of Spain (trust me – Google them), I realized most of the village does not have the ability to have wired connections physically laid down and satellite is the only viable option. In addition, the quality of streaming video seemed to be better than my wired broadband connection in the UK.

As the price of cellular connections has started to drop or the data allowance per dollar has increased, the use of cellular connectivity as a means of sole connectivity has started to grow. My latest cellular contract offers me 100 GB of data per month for a reasonable price. This is more than enough for most people and moves us away from the need to have a fixed base station. In the next section, we discuss this technology in a little more detail.

# Cellular

Cellular technology has improved in leaps and bounds since its inception, and has become one of the main methods of accessing a **wireless WAN (WWAN)**. The majority of modern cell phones have the ability to connect through either 3G or 4G to provide information at our fingertips. A number of tablet devices and laptops also have cellular data connectivity functionality. This technology, along with cloud services, has allowed businesses to truly embrace the concept of having a mobile workforce.

To be able to utilize 3G or 4G, as with the other technologies, you need to have a subscription with a service provider and a mobile device. The mobile device will use either **Global System for Mobile (GSM)** or **Code Division Multiple Access (CDMA)** technology. GSM devices require a **Subscriber Identity Module (SIM)** card, whereas CDMA doesn't and providers use the device's **Electronic Serial Number (ESN)** to identify and authorize it on their network. CDMA is the prominent technology in the USA, and GSM elsewhere.

3G and 4G are the third and fourth generations (the G) of mobile data technology. As no formal standards have been agreed on as to what constitutes each of these technologies, it is difficult to state a maximum speed possible. 3G using HPSA+ can, theoretically, reach 21.6 Mb/s, and 4G can achieve 300 Mb/s. The caveat to these speeds is that they are achievable under ideal conditions rarely seen in the real world. There is also an impact on the speed obtained if the user is moving, as there is slowdown as they switch between cell towers.

# Summary

In this chapter, we moved away from our own infrastructure and looked further afield into WAN. We defined a WAN, before we covered the two packet-switching technologies of X.25 and frame relays. We then discussed the benefits of using a dedicated lease line. Dial-up, and other networking methodologies that used the POTS/PSTN, such as ISDN, ATM, and xDSL, were then covered. We also discussed some characteristics of the T-carriers and their equivalents, and the OC-levels used in SONET. Finally, we finished off this chapter by covering broadband and fiber connections, satellite, and cellular.

Going through this chapter, you learned how to create broadband connections on a Windows computer, before going on to learn how to configure network properties. While the former is becoming less common, you will still come across this; the latter you will be required to configure on a more regular basis. You also learned how to use the `tracert` command to identify the path data takes to the destination. This is a command you will use on a regular basis to identify points of failure on a route. We also saw how to configure dial-up connections, and while this may seem like legacy technology, large organizations will use this as part of their disaster recovery.

In the next chapter, we will look at wireless networking, and discuss the various standards and topologies before talking about wireless security. You will begin to gain an understanding of some of the factors that influence and impact wireless deployments, and from this, mitigate against them.

# Questions

1. What type of network medium is used by SONET?

(A) UTP
(B) Coaxial
(C) Wireless
(D) Optical

2. What is the speed of an E3 connection?

(A) 1.544 Mb/s
(B) 2.048 Mb/s
(C) 34.368 Mb/s
(D) 44.736 Mb/s

3. Which devices convert digital signals to analog signals for transmission over the telephone network?

(A) Modem
(B) Switch
(C) Router
(D) Telnet

4. Which device in a packet-switching network is most likely to function as a PAD?

(A) Modem
(B) Switch
(C) Router
(D) Telnet

5. How many B channels does an ISDN Basic Rate Interface have?

(A) 1
(B) 2
(C) 3
(D) 4

6. Which WAN technology used fixed-size cells to transfer data?

(A) Frame relay
(B) Packet switching
(C) ATM
(D) 3G

7. Which of the following is used for error checking in X.25 networks?

(A) CRC
(B) ATM
(C) ECC
(D) PSE

8. If you had a committed information rate (CIR) of 128 Kb/s, what would the burst excess be?

(A) 128 Kb/s
(B) 192 Kb/s
(C) 224 Kb/s
(D) 320 Kb/s

9. What device routes traffic around a packet-switched network?

(A) PSE
(B) PAD
(C) CSU/DSU
(D) DTE

# Further reading

Learn more about the various types of cables here:

- *Difference Between Circuit Switching and Packet Switching*: `https://techdifferences.com/difference-between-circuit-switching-and-packet-switching.html`
- *ADSL vs Fibre broadband: what do they mean and which do I need?*: `https://www.techradar.com/uk/broadband/adsl-vs-fibre-broadband`

# 4

# Understanding Wireless Networking

Looking around my bedroom right now, I can see several devices that can connect to wireless networks: mobile phone, laptop, tablet, fitness watch, games console, and television. It seems each month some hitherto non-smart device develops wireless connectivity. As we move toward the ubiquitous use of wireless technologies, the ability to understand how to implement and configure a wireless network is a skill that is in greater demand.

This chapter will introduce you to current technologies in use, covering the various standards that are in common use today. We'll discuss topologies in use in wireless networks, allowing you to identify which best suits your needs. Given the broadcast nature of wireless, we'll finish this chapter by highlighting the importance of security to maintain data protection.

The following topics will be covered in this chapter:

- Wireless standards
- Wireless topologies
- Wireless security

## Technical requirements

To complete the exercises in this chapter, you will require a computing device with access to the internet.

# Understanding wireless standards

As networked technology has developed, it appears to have thrown off the shackles of cables to a great extent. Most endpoint user devices now come shipped with some form of wireless connectivity already built in, offering us information at our fingertips as we connect to various wireless hotspots on our travels, uttering our mantra to the waiter in the coffee shop, *what's the Wi-Fi password?* As these devices are from different manufacturers, there was a requirement for a specification to be created that all network devices would adhere to.

Wireless standards are a set of standards that allows devices from different manufacturers to communicate with each other. My focus in this section will be on the IEEE 802.11 wireless standards (or Wi-Fi). Although there are other wireless standards, such as IEEE 802.15 (Bluetooth) and IEEE 802.16 (WiMAX), these are not covered in the exam objectives.

In July 1990, the **Institute of Electrical and Electronics Engineers (IEEE)**, announced that their 802 project was forming a working group to investigate and develop wireless standards. This working group was named 802.11. Over the years, the working group has created several wireless standards that are in operation in various environments, but we will only look at five of these.

I would like to discuss some terminology common to all of these standards before going into their various characteristics.

# CSMA/CA

Wi-Fi is classed as a contention-based technology. All devices on the network are vying for the attention of the access point. The access method used in Wi-Fi networks is called **Carrier Sense Multiple Access/Collision Avoidance (CSMA/CA)**. Let's break that down a bit to understand it better:

- **Carrier sense** means it *listens* to what is happening on the carrier, in this case, the airwaves.
- **Multiple access** simply means that the carrier is available to multiple devices.
- **Collision avoidance** means that there is a mechanism in place to avoid collisions.

With a wired connection, you can detect a collision; in a wireless network, you cannot, so you need to avoid it.

As can be seen in *Figure 4.1*, CSMA/CA follows a simple process of **Ready To Send/Clear To Send (RTS/CTS)**:

1. The sending device listens out for any transmissions (carrier sense).
2. If no transmissions are heard, it sends an RTS message to the access point advising it has data that it wants to transmit.
3. If the access point is free, it will send a CTS message to the device. All other devices hear it and do not attempt to transmit for a period of time.
4. The sending device transmits the data:

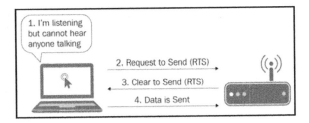

Figure 4.1: CSMA/CA process

You may be thinking, if the sender is listening to make sure the network is clear, why do we need to send an RTS message? I would like to draw your attention to *Figure 4.2*, which demonstrates what is known as the hidden station problem or hidden node problem:

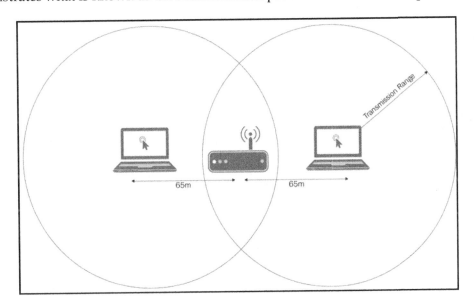

Figure 4.2: The hidden station problem

As you will read in the following sections, wireless networks can only transmit over a limited distance. In the preceding diagram, we can see that both laptops are 60 meters away from the wireless access point. Both devices are within range of the access point but are so far away from each other that they cannot hear when the other is talking to the access point. Because of this, when the device are listening to hear any device talking (*step 1* of CSMA/CA), they do not hear each other, and therefore send an RTS message. The access point will receive this but will not send a CTS message.

# Radio waves

For this chapter, we will look at wireless communication through the use of radio waves, as opposed to light waves. Radio waves form part of the electromagnetic spectrum, and appear, as the name would suggest, in the radio frequency zone of the spectrum. These waves are generated by passing an alternating current through a conductor and transmitted out of an antenna as a waveform (*Figure 4.3*) or sine wave. Data is transmitted through these radio waves:

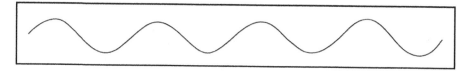

Figure 4.3: Waveform

How close each of the peaks of the waves are is dictated by the frequency, which is discussed in the following subsection.

# Frequency

Frequency can be defined as the number of times a specific event occurs in a specified period of time. Looking at *Figure 4.4*, we can see that when the wave signal has returned to its starting point, it has completed a single RF signal cycle. Each cycle is measured in **hertz** (**Hz**):

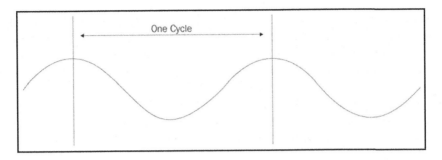

Figure 4.4: RF signal cycle

Frequency is defined by the number of cycles it completes in one second. One cycle per second is 1 Hz. *Figure 4.5* shows radio waves at two different frequencies. The top wave has a lower frequency (2 Hz) than the bottom wave, which is ~9 Hz. The higher the frequency, the more data can be transmitted per second. However, higher frequencies tend to have a shorter wavelength, which means that, over distance, the signal becomes too weak to be received:

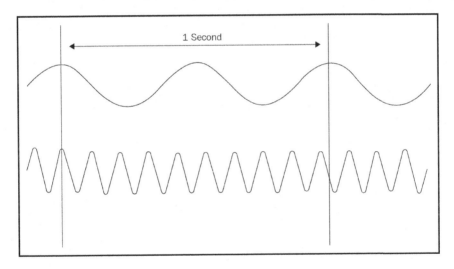

Figure 4.5: Two different frequencies

For ease of reference, as the number of hertz increases, we use a set of prefixes to identify the frequency:

- 1,000 Hz = 1 Kilohertz (1 KHz)
- 1,000 KHz = 1 Megahertz (1 MHz)
- 1,000 MHz = 1 Gigahertz (1 GHz)

The two most common frequencies used in Wi-Fi communication are the 2.4 GHz and 5 GHz ranges. Both of these are classed as unlicensed frequency ranges. Unlicensed means that anyone can use them without requiring a permit. The obvious advantage of this is avoiding every user of a wireless computing device seeking a license, but that advantage is a double-edged sword. Because anybody can use devices working within these ranges, there is an abundance of them out there, which can lead to unexpected **Radio Frequency Interference (RFI)**. The 2.4 GHz range is particularly affected by this as baby monitors, microwave ovens, Bluetooth, radio-controlled toys, and so on all use this range.

The 2.4 GHz frequency band is broken down into up to 14 overlapping channels (*Figure 4.6*), each with a width of 22 MHz. In the US and Canada, there are 11 channels available; most of Europe has 13; and Japan has 14 channels available. These differences are due to regional legislation. Whenever you implement a wireless network, you ideally want to perform a site survey, in part, to see what channels are already in use by you or surrounding organizations.

You will look to see what channels are available to use and, where possible, spot an unused channel that does not overlap with any channels in use. Just looking at the channels available in *Figure 4.6*, you can see that channels **1**, **6**, and **11** do not overlap:

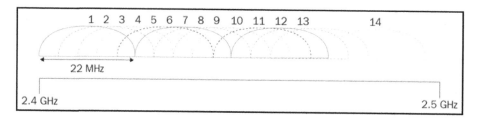

Figure 4.6: 2.4 GHz channels

However, if you look at the quick survey I have carried out on my laptop at home (*Figure 4.7*), you will see, in the bottom graph, that there is a lot of overlap going on. There are a couple of reasons for this.

First, I have no control over the wireless access points, so I am reliant on my neighbors being tech-savvy enough to check and configure the channels they are using. Second, most modern wireless access points will configure the channel used automatically, and select the channel least used:

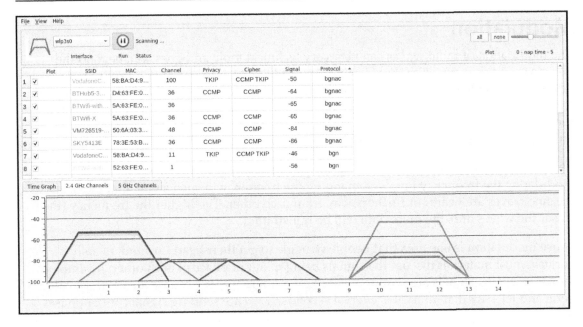

Figure 4.7: Overlapping 2.4 GHz channels

 Although channels **2**, **7**, and **12** do not overlap either, it is unlikely you will need to think about these as channel **12** is not available in the US and Canada.

The 5 GHz frequency range, at one point, was less saturated with devices than its 2.4 GHz counterpart. However, as more devices embraced standards that supported this range, this is becoming less the case. Like the 2.4 Hz range, the 5 GHz range is split into channels, however, they are non-overlapping and there are 23 of them of 20 MHz each. Any devices that support both frequencies are referred to as dual-band.

The realms of frequencies can easily become quite complex, however, the exam does not go into any great detail. Remember that, for two devices to communicate, they need to be on the same frequency, and for better performance with 2.4 GHz devices, you utilize non-overlapping channels.

# Modulation

The modulation of radio waves can be a very technical topic and goes well beyond the objectives of the exam. With that in mind, I would like to summarize its purpose here, and briefly mention it as we go through the various standards, as I feel it is relevant in the real world. Modulation can be simplified to mean a method of modifying the transmission of radio waves to increase efficiency. This modification can be applied to either the power (amplitude), frequency, or phase.

By modulating the power, you are increasing or decreasing the height of the sine wave; modulating the frequency involves changing the frequency in such a way that the peaks of the sine waves are nearer or further away from each other. The higher the frequency (the closer the waves are), the more data will be transmitted.

Phase modulation is one area that people struggle to get their heads around, usually because most materials discuss the signals being $n°$ out of phase of each other. In simpler terms, normally, signals are sent down at regular intervals; let's choose an arbitrary value here, and let's say that interval is every 4 seconds. If we are sending signals out of phase, we might send signal 1 at 0 seconds, signal 2 at 2 seconds, signal 3 at 4 seconds, and so on. If you have ever sung the song *row, row, row your boat*, where other people start the song when you are part of the way through it, those other singers are out of phase with you.

By modulating the signal, we are making more efficient use of the available bandwidth offered by the channel.

# IEEE 802.11a

The 802.11a standard was released in September 1999 and supported devices using the 5 GHz range. In ideal conditions, this standard had a speed of 54 Mbps and had an indoor range of 35 m.

To make more efficient use of the available bandwidth, 802.11a utilized a modulation technology called **Orthogonal Frequency Distribution Multiplexing (OFDM)**. This technique broke the 20 MHz channels used by this frequency range into 52 sub-carriers per channel. Each sub-carrier had a bandwidth of 312.5 KHz, and therefore had a lower data rate than a full channel. While this may seem counter-intuitive, it actually worked quite efficiently as the number of sub-carriers meant the overall data rate was better. An analogy may be beneficial here. Imagine you are driving a single car down a three-lane motorway, and no other cars are allowed to use it. The motorway itself is the channel. The single car is only using part of that channel. The other two lanes are sitting there unused and redundant. If, however, we split that motorway into lanes (the sub-carriers) and let other cars use the motorway, we can see that we are using it more efficiently. In essence, this is what OFDM facilitates.

# IEEE 802.11b

Like IEEE 802.11a, the 802.11b standard was released in September 1999. However, this standard utilized the 2.4 GHz frequency range and therefore is not compatible with 802.11a. This disparity in frequency between the two standards meant that there was no compatibility between the devices in each of the standards. 802.11b has a maximum indoor range of 35 m.

For modulation, 802.11 uses a technique called **Direct Sequence Spread Spectrum (DSSS)**. If a radio signal is corrupted in transit between devices for any reason, such as interference or a weak signal, then it would likely be discarded and the original transmission would have to be re-sent. This becomes more of an issue over distance or in areas of higher RFI. To overcome this obstacle, additional data would be transmitted that would allow for errors occurring in the transmission. On any network, data is transferred at a base level in bits. Each bit can be one of two values, 0 or 1. When DSSS is used, rather than sending the data over as a single bit, a representative set of bit values is sent (known as **chips**). An example of this is as follows:

- `1 = 10101101`
- `0 = 01010010`

So, every time a device wants to send a bit with a value of `1`, it actually sends over a stream of bits: `10101101`. Again, this may seem counter-intuitive, however, if one of the bits in the stream is corrupted, then we can still calculate the original value of the bit being transmitted, hence avoiding having to re-transmit and use up bandwidth.

# IEEE 802.11g

IEEE 802.11g was released in 2003 and was designed to enhance the technical capabilities of 802.11b and provide a speed of up to 54 Mbps. Like 802.11b, a frequency of 2.4 GHz was used, which meant that devices from both standards were able to communicate on the same network. This meant in the early days of 802.11g implementation, organizations did not necessarily have to replace all of their hardware at the same time. However, the downfall of mixing standards on a network was that the network could only go as fast as the slowest device. Therefore, a mixed network would likely reach 11 Mbps, which really defeated the object of having a faster standard. IEEE 802.11g had a maximum indoor range of 38 m.

For modulation, this standard uses a derivative of OFDM.

# IEEE 802.11n

While previous iterations of the Wi-Fi standards marginally improved with each release, IEEE 802.11n really leaped forward. To begin with, it supported both 2.4 GHz and 5 GHz, therefore, devices supporting it were usually dual-band. It also introduced the concept of **Multiple-Input Multiple-Output (MIMO)** antennas. Simply put, 802.11n devices usually had multiple antennas. Of those, all of them could send or all of them could receive, or most likely you would have some antennas transmitting or some receiving. All of these antennas could be used for communication with one or other or multiple devices, and you could even have some antennas working on one frequency, while the remainder worked on the other frequency.

In addition to MIMO, 802.11n had a couple of other tricks up its sleeve. Firstly, it could combine two adjacent 20 MHz channels into one 40 MHz channel, in a process called **channel bonding,** effectively more than doubling the bandwidth (more than double due to less management overhead). Secondly, it could use a technique called **beamforming**. When an antenna transmits, the signal goes out equally in all directions (technically, it's more of a doughnut shape than a ball). However, with beamforming, the signal is more focused in a particular direction and therefore provides a stronger signal, reaching up to 70 m. By combining all of these techniques, 802.11n provides speeds of up to 600 Mbps (in total).

For modulation, this standard uses a derivative of OFDM.

# IEEE 802.11ac

The final Wi-Fi standard I will cover is IEEE 802.11ac. This more recent standard returned to using a single frequency, namely, 5 GHz, but improved on the MIMO beamforming and channel bonding that we first saw in 802.11n. In fact, it utilized 40 MHz channels that could be bonded to make 80 MHz and 160 MHz channels. It also used a very efficient modulation technique called **Quadrature Amplitude Modulation (QAM)**. These improvements allowed 802.11ac to have a staggering overall speed of 1.3 Gbps. However, the indoor range dropped back down to 35 m.

## Summarizing the standards

I've given you a lot of facts and figures in the preceding sections, so I feel it would be beneficial to summarize them in a table. You will notice in the table I have not put the standards in alphabetical order. This is deliberate, as I find people remember them better this way as you generally start low (frequency, speed, and so on) and work up. And it spells B(e)GAN AC. I have to admit before AC came along, it was a little tidier:

| Category | Speed | Frequency | Indoor distance | Modulation |
|----------|-------|-----------|-----------------|------------|
| B | 11 Mbps | 2.4 GHz | 35 m | DSSS |
| G | 54 Mbps | 2.4 GHz | 38 m | OFDM |
| A | 54 Mbps | 5 GHz | 35 m | OFDM |
| N | Up to 600 Mbps | 2.4 GHz & 5 GHz | 70 m | OFDM |
| AC | 1.3 Gbps | 5 GHz | 35 m | QAM |

Now we have talked about the standards, we will look at the topologies we can implement to take advantage of them.

# Implementing wireless topologies

Wireless networks can fall into general topographic groups, ad hoc and infrastructure. We will discuss both of these in this section, as well as some peripheral information pertinent to wireless networks, such as planning a network.

In Chapter 2, *Understanding Local Area Networks*, we discussed various areas that we needed to consider when planning our LAN. All of these are still valid in a wireless network, but I would like to specifically highlight some that have a major impact on the performance of a wireless network:

- **Hardware**: Recall that in the preceding section, we discussed the different wireless standards, and how they needed to support the same frequency to be compatible.

- **Environment**: One of the reasons we would implement a wireless network is to support devices in locations where we do not have the capacity to lay cables. This may cause us some issues in a large warehouse-like environment where the distance from the device to WAP may hit the limits, or the equipment within the warehouse may interfere with the signal. In those instances, we may want to locate a WAP in the center of the warehouse. But what if there is no power there? In that case, we would use a network cable to provide power to the device. This is referred to as **Power over Ethernet (PoE)** and has to be supported on the device.

- **The number of users**: The number of users efficiently supported by a WAP varies depending on whether it is a consumer-grade or business-grade device. Remember that Wi-Fi is a contention-based technology. The more users, the less efficient the network will be for an individual user.

- **Site surveys**: Planning a wireless network should include conducting a site survey. A survey will help you to identify the best positioning for your WAPs and identify any wireless black spots or dead zones where there is no signal. Ideally, you will want the coverage area of the WAPs to overlap to a degree to allow users to roam the building and have a continuous signal.

A Wi-Fi network is identified by its **Service Set Identifier (SSID)**. This is a human-readable name usually created by the network administrator and broadcast out by the WAPs.

# Ad hoc mode

An ad hoc mode network (or peer-to-peer) is geared toward connecting devices together without the need for any intermediary devices such as WAPs. The devices quite simply talk to each other, in what is referred to as an **Independent Basic Service Set (IBSS)**. The IBSSID is a pseudorandom identifier similar to a MAC address generated by the device creating the ad hoc network.

# Infrastructure mode

In an infrastructure mode wireless network, wireless clients must connect to an intermediary wireless network device, such as a WAP or wireless router, to be able to communicate to other devices on the network. This network may involve just one WAP or multiple WAPs and usually connects to a wired backbone network. Regardless of which method you implement, the SSID will be the same for all WAPs. A single WAP and its associated devices are referred to as a **Basic Service Set (BSS)** and are identified by a **Basic Service Set Identifier (BSSID)**, which is the MAC address of the WAP. A collection of BSSes using the same SSID form an **Extended Service Set (ESS)** and are identified by an **Extended Service Set Identifier (ESSID)**, which is usually the SSID of the network.

The implementation of a wireless network using an extended service set allows users to roam around the building and maintain connectivity as they do so. We can see, in *Figure 4.8*, that this network is made up of three separate BSSes that share the same SSID, hence forming an ESS:

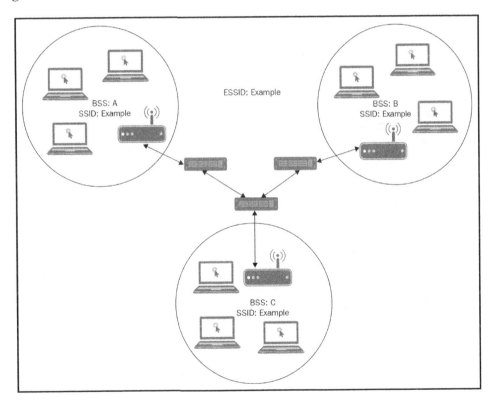

Figure 4.8: Service sets in operation

An infrastructure mode wireless network will be the main type of wireless network implemented within an organization and at home. I will now discuss a few variations of the infrastructure mode network.

## Point-to-point wireless including wireless bridge

Traditionally, a wireless bridge allows you to connect a wired network to a wireless network, and that still holds true. However, we can also think of a wireless bridge as connecting two wireless networks together, such as when you want to connect one building to another building but cannot lay cables (*Figure 4.9*):

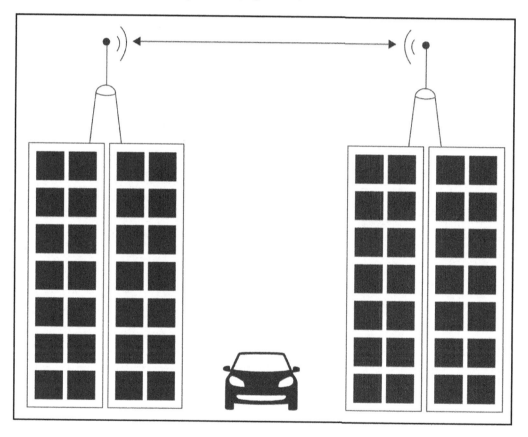

Figure 4.9: Wireless bridge connecting between two buildings

In this sort of implementation, you will most likely use a unidirectional antenna, such as a Yagi. I would also like to mention that, although the preceding diagram shows a straight line connecting the two antennae, this is for simplicity, and the transmission is, in reality, more of a flattened oval shape, known as a Fresnel zone.

A wireless bridge is a form of point-to-point network. When we use a wireless access point, this is point-to-multipoint communication. That is, the one device (point) connects to multiple clients (multipoint). As you saw earlier with the wireless bridge, one antenna (point) is talking to only one other antenna (point). Wireless point-to-point communication can reach up to around 15 km at the time of writing, and therefore avoids the costs associated with laying cable in most cases. An important consideration is that the two devices have *line-of-sight* of each other so the signal be transmitted clearly. In some instances, this may require elevating the antenna so it avoids any obstacles.

We have already discussed the attrition suffered by wireless communication, and point-to-point is no exception. Of course, over these greater distances, this can be more of an issue, and the signal can be affected by things such as solids (for example, buildings and trees), dust, and water. You may think water is an odd thing to affect a wireless signal, but it is worth bearing in mind that there is moisture in the atmosphere, and of course, these connections are outside, and there is the potential for rain.

# Wireless Distribution System

A **Wireless Distribution System (WDS)** is a wireless network where the majority of the networks do not connect to a wired network but connect to each other. Any WAP that connects to the wired network is referred to as a main base station. A remote base station is one that receives data from wireless clients and forwards them to a main base station or relay base station. A relay base station receives data from main and remote base stations and forwards it to another base station.

By creating a wireless mesh network (*Figure 4.10*), we allow for redundancy in our network. If a base station fails, there are mechanisms in place to route the data to another relay base station for onward transmission:

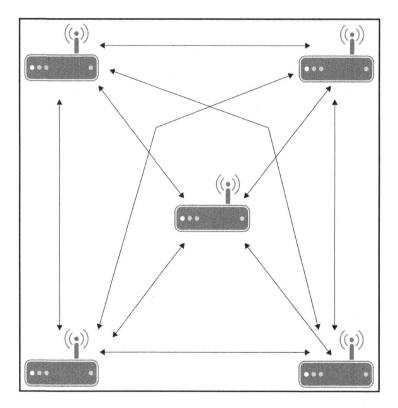

Figure 4.10: Wireless mesh topology

With all of this data flowing across the airwaves, we need to think about how we are going to protect it. In the next section, we will discuss the security methods available to do just that.

# Understanding wireless security

Wireless communication could be described as a broadcast technology. Anything that is transmitted is available for all to hear or eavesdrop on. Can you spot what issues this may bring? If you said this leaves the data unsecure, you would be correct. Therefore any wireless deployment needs to ensure that appropriate measures are taken to protect the data.

There are three principles of data security that we need to bear in mind. These are classed as the **CIA triad** (sometimes the IAC triad) and form the basis of any security plan. CIA is an acronym for **Confidentiality, Integrity, Availability**:

- **Confidentiality**: This refers to protecting data in such a way that only the people who are authorized to see it can do so.
- **Integrity**: This is the trustworthiness of the data. Has the data been changed in any way? This may be through accidental corruption or malicious actions.
- **Availability**: This is ensuring that the data is there and ready to use to those who are authorized to see it.

People tend to confuse the description of confidentiality and availability so I would like to provide you with an example. Let's say you are a member of a web forum and to access the forum and read the posts, you have to sign in with a user account. This maintains confidentiality. One day, the web server crashes, but it fails over to a backup server and the data is there for you to use. This ensures availability.

The following sub-sections describe some of the methods for securing your data on a wireless network. The important thing to note is that relying on only one of these methods is not best practice. It is important to have multiple security mechanisms in place. This layered approach is referred to as defense in depth.

# Encryption

Encryption is the mechanism of taking data that is readable (clear text) and putting it through a mathematical calculation (algorithm) to produce data that is not readable (cipher text). The data is encrypted with what is known as a key and is deciphered using a key. The longer the key, the harder the encryption should be to crack. If the data is encrypted and decrypted using the same key, this is known as **symmetric encryption**. If you use one key to encrypt the data and it can only be decrypted by a second, mathematically-linked key, then you are using asymmetric encryption. For this exam, you do not need to know anything more than that as far as the background of encryption is concerned. Let's discuss the encryption techniques used for security.

# Wired Equivalent Privacy

**Wired Equivalent Privacy (WEP)** was the first form of wireless encryption and, as the name implies, was supposed to give the same level of privacy as a wired connection. However, to be honest, it's misleading as wired connections don't necessarily provide privacy. I want to make one thing clear from the outset. If someone suggests using WEP, don't use it. It is inherently insecure.

WEP uses a form of encryption called **RC4** and uses either a 64-bit or 128-bit **pre-shared key (PSK)**. A PSK is, in essence, a password that you use to connect to the network, and the same password is configured on each device. It should be noted that the effective strength of these is actually 40-bit and 104-bit, as they use 24-bits for a number known as the **Initialization Vector (IV)**, which is different on every frame sent. The problem with the IV is twofold. Firstly, it is sent across in the clear, and secondly, after 16 million frames have been sent (pretty quickly on a busy network), the IV is repeated. This greatly reduces the effectiveness of WEP encryption and it can be cracked in a matter of minutes on even a low-performance device.

At this stage, you may now be thinking why am I telling you about this. If it's that bad, surely no one would use it, would they? You would think so, but I know one of my neighbors is using it, and when on holiday last year (2018), I saw numerous locations with it still.

# Wireless Protected Access

When WEP was cracked, we needed a quick fix to protect networks. This came in the form of **Wireless Protected Access (WPA)** and was essentially a firmware update the network devices. It still used the RC4 encryption cipher but also introduced the **Temporal Key Integrity Protocol (TKIP)**. TKIP uses a genuine 128-bit key and a 48-bit IV and throws into the encryption mix the source and destination MAC addresses. One of the issues with WEP is the repetition of the IV, and TKIP includes a mechanism to avoid this.

WPA is available in two formats, WPA-Personal (or WPA-PSK) and WPA-Enterprise. In a home or small business environment, you will likely use WPA-Personal. You share the key with everyone who needs to know it, and they connect to the network using it. This works well as long as you can securely share the key with the users, such as telling them face-to-face. If someone leaves the organization, you change the PSK and let everyone know the new key. Admittedly, I would be amazed if organizations change the PSK when someone leaves.

PSKs are easy to administer when you have a small number of users and/or devices, but what about an organization with thousands of employees, and possibly a high turnover of staff? As soon as you've told everyone the new key, another member of staff leaves, and you have to repeat the process. In these environments, you would implement WPA-Enterprise. Using this method, users are authenticated using their user credentials against an authentication server (usually RADIUS) using a protocol called 802.1x/**Extensible Authentication Protocol (EAP)**. The process is described in the following steps:

1. The client (known as a supplicant) sends the user's credentials to the access point.
2. The access point (authenticator) forwards the credentials to the authentication server.
3. The authentication server confirms the credentials are permitted to allow wireless access or not, and either an allow or deny response is sent back to the access point.
4. The access point receives the response and forwards it to the client.
5. If an allow response is received by the client it communicates on the network.

*Figure 4.11* shows an example of WPA-Enterprise topology:

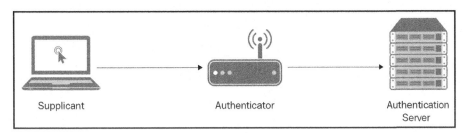

| Supplicant | Authenticator | Authentication Server |

Figure 4.11: WPA-Enterprise using 802.1x authentication

 Don't get confused that EAP uses 802.1x not some derivative of 802.11. This is because it is used in more than wireless in what is known as **Port-Based Network Access Control (PNAC)**.

# WPA2

The original WPA was only intended to be an interim measure following WEP being cracked, while a more permanent solution was identified and has been cracked itself. This (at the time) permanent solution came in the form of WPA2. WPA2 required devices to install new devices that supported the standard and therefore was a total replacement for WEP and WPA.

Whilst WPA2 supported Personal and Enterprise implementations and TKIP, the encryption algorithm used was the 128-bit **Advanced Encryption Standard (AES)**. This stronger encryption standard has stood the test of time well. You may be thinking that WPA2 is safe then. Unfortunately not. Whilst AES is still very secure, the mechanics behind WPA2 itself led to it being cracked last year (2018), and manufacturers have released patches.

# WPA3

I just want to tip my hat to WPA3, although it is unlikely to appear in the exam. Once WPA2 was cracked, there was a rush to bring out a more secure standard that offered better security at the handshake point between devices. Sadly, WPA3-Personal has already been found to include flaws that can be leveraged.

In brief, WPA3 offers enhanced security features such as longer encryption of up to 192 bits; it replaces PSK with *Simultaneous Authentication of Equal*, which allows better key exchange; it also offers forward secrecy. This odd term means that, should an attacker capture encrypted data in the hope that they will subsequently capture the network key and decrypt this captured data, there are mechanisms in place that prevent this. A network key no longer means you can decrypt historically captured data.

# Other wireless security techniques

Encrypting your traffic is arguably the best way to protect your wireless data. In this subsection, I will cover several other methods that are available but will only protect you against a casual attacker. Whether you implement them or not would most likely be based on whether it is worth the hassle of implementing them over any benefits you may reap from having them.

# Disabling SSID broadcast

We discussed the purpose of the SSID in the *Implementing wireless topologies* section previously. There is a train of thought that disabling the SSID being broadcast is a great method for hiding your network, and on the surface, this seems to make sense. If they don't know it's there, they cannot attack it, right?

Remember, we discussed that when connecting to a wireless network for the first time, it is simply a case of looking down the list provided to you by the device and selecting the appropriate one. If we disabled the SSID broadcast, the network would not be on the list and we would have to go through some additional steps to connect to it. Let's say we disabled SSID broadcasts and our network is hidden. How does our device connect to a hidden network? Quite simply, it shouts out for every single wireless network it has ever been associated with and been told to remember, via a probe request.

The following screenshot (*Figure 4.12*) is the output of a Linux tool called Airodump-ng (part of Aircrack-ng), which sniffs the network for any SSIDs and any probe requests. The top table shows information about the SSIDs it has discovered, and the bottom table shows devices that it has detected and the MAC address of any access point that device is currently associated with, and/or any probe requests the devices are sending out. You can see in the screenshot that the device (referred to as STATION) at the bottom is probing for a Wi-Fi connection called Sky10270:

```
CH 10 ][ Elapsed: 6 s ][ 2019-04-27 21:03

BSSID              PWR  Beacons    #Data, #/s   CH  MB     ENC   CIPHER AUTH ESSID

E8:65:D4:CD:C4:31  -82      1         0    0     6  54e    WPA2  CCMP   PSK  Nova booster
00:00:00:00:00:00  -1       0         6    0     1  -1     OPN                <length:  0>
C0:05:C2:08:2C:C1  -41     16         1    0    13  54e.   WPA2  CCMP   PSK  VM4140176-2.4
D2:05:C2:08:2C:C1  -40     14         0    0    13  54e.   WPA2  CCMP   MGT  Virgin Media
E6:CB:BC:49:36:27  -55      6         0    0     1  54e.   WPA2  CCMP   PSK  MA8EXT001
E0:CB:BC:49:36:27  -55      5         0    0     1  54e.   WPA2  CCMP   PSK  m489o5
EA:CB:BC:49:36:27  -54      7        28   11     1  54e.   OPN                O2 Wifi
E6:CB:BC:30:3A:9E  -57      5         0    0     6  54e.   WPA2  CCMP   PSK  <length:  0>
E0:CB:BC:30:3A:9E  -57      5         0    0     6  54e.   WPA2  CCMP   PSK  <length:  0>
EA:CB:BC:30:3A:9E  -57      5         1    0     6  54e.   OPN                O2 Wifi
CA:3A:6B:34:25:B3  -62      8         0    0    13  54e    WPA2  CCMP   PSK  <length:  0>
0A:8D:DB:68:C7:E7  -80      3         0    0    11  54e.   WPA2  CCMP   PSK  <length:  0>
0C:8D:DB:68:C7:E7  -81      4         0    0    11  54e.   WPA2  CCMP   PSK  <length:  0>
E8:65:D4:CD:C4:32  -82      3         0    0     6  54e    WPA2  CCMP   PSK  NOVA VIP
06:8D:DB:68:C7:E7  -81      3         0    0    11  54e.   OPN                O2 Wifi
90:21:06:53:17:9A  -82     10         2    0     6  54e    WPA2  CCMP   PSK  SKYC0FF0
78:3E:53:E6:BA:9E  -84      0         3    0    11  54e    WPA2  CCMP   PSK  SKYC0FF0
20:0C:C8:85:9C:68  -81      7         0    0    11  54e    WPA2  CCMP   PSK  VM880374-2G
F6:9F:C2:03:0D:4E  -85      2         0    0     1  54e.   WPA2  CCMP   PSK  <length:  0>
52:0D:10:1F:F2:89  -85      4         0    0     6  54e.   WPA2  CCMP   MGT  Virgin Media
40:0D:10:1F:F2:89  -85      3         0    0     6  54e.   WPA2  CCMP   PSK  VM0603656
00:03:D8:EA:1F:CE  -86      3         0    0    11  54e.   WPA2  CCMP   PSK  BTHub3-KFF9
02:03:D8:EA:1F:CE  -86      3         0    0    11  54e.   OPN                BTWifi-with-FON

BSSID              STATION            PWR   Rate     Lost    Frames  Probe

00:00:00:00:00:00  DE:CB:BC:30:3A:9E  -75   0 - 1      0        1
00:00:00:00:00:00  DE:CB:BC:49:36:27  -54   0 -24      7        3
00:00:00:00:00:00  32:8D:DB:68:C7:E7  -83   0 - 1      6        2
(not associated)   D6:64:65:1B:AA:1F  -82   0 - 1     11        3
(not associated)   7A:6A:07:00:2C:FA  -74   0 - 1      0        1
(not associated)   DA:A1:19:B4:45:FF  -80   0 - 1     43        3  SKY10270
```

Figure 4.12: Airodump-ng output

Please do not worry about remembering the different sections of the output shown in the preceding screenshot. It will not appear in your exam, and I have only used it here as I feel it really helps to illustrate how ineffective disabling SSID broadcasts is.

# MAC filtering

MAC filtering is another often suggested way of protecting wireless networks. MAC filtering is the process of identifying devices that are permitted on your network by their MAC address. If you don't recognize the MAC address, they are not coming onto your network. This is relatively simple to set up on a small network, but on a larger network where there may be thousands of wireless devices, it is unlikely to be as simple.

The other downfall to this method is that it is relatively simple for an attacker to identify the authorized MAC addresses on a network, de-authenticate a device, and spoof its MAC address.

# Disabling Wi-Fi Protected Setup

**Wi-Fi Protected Setup** (WPS) was implemented to make connecting to networks even easier. What could be simpler than pressing a button on the wireless router and a couple of clicks on your computer? None of that confusing choosing SSIDs, encryption, PSKs, and so on. The problem was WPS was not implemented very well and works on the principle of sharing an 8-digit PIN. Unfortunately, that PIN is split into two 4 digit sections, and the 8th digit is actually a check-digit to make sure the others are correct. Combined, this makes it easier to brute force, hence some devices only allow several attempts before *locking out* the device for a period of time.

A word of caution, I disabled this on my home router, only for the ISP to re-enable it during a firmware update. As with a lot of things in security, if you do not use it, disable it.

# Reducing transmission power

We tend to leave our wireless devices at the default settings as far as transmission power is concerned. Now is the time to ask yourself, do you need it that strong. If you only need coverage within your building, and not in the parking lot or the cafe across the road, reduce the transmission power. As long as everyone in your organization can still connect, you will be fine, and it avoids an attacker sitting in their car connecting in.

# Changing defaults

Several wireless access points/routers ship with a default username and password. These are easy to find on the internet, and therefore you should change these as soon as you can.

# Network segmentation

Have any wireless networks running on a separate VLAN than your wired network. This helps to reduce how far into your network an attacker can encroach. I would also suggest that you separate any guest Wi-Fi network into its own VLAN.

# Faraday cage

A Faraday cage is a metal cage that blocks wireless transmissions from escaping and is usually found in very sensitive government areas. You may have visions of people literally working in a cage, but rest assured this is not the case. Usually, a Faraday cage used for this purpose will be built into the fabric of the room/building itself.

# Scanning for rogue access points

Because you are not physically connecting a device to a network cable, any wireless network is susceptible to **Man-In-The-Middle** (**MITM**) attacks through the use of rogue access points. A common form of rogue access point is an **evil twin**. An evil twin is an access point that pretends to be a legitimate access point in that it has the same SSID, but usually has a stronger signal, so you are more likely to connect to the rogue one. Once you connect to the illegitimate access point, the attacker can easily sniff your data transiting through. To avoid suspicion, an attacker would forward your data to the original destination, and from the destination back to you.

The only real prevention for this is to scan your network for any rogue access points within your area. Remember, they do not even need to be within your building; they may be sat out on the street. If this is the case, the only recourse you have is to report it to the appropriate legal authorities.

**Activity 1**: In the following activity, I would like to embed some of the principles I have discussed previously by simulating configuring a wireless router:

1. Navigate to `https://emulator.tp-link.com/TL-WR702N/Index.htm`.
2. View the current status of the router.
3. Click on **Working Mode** and select **AP** to configure it as a WAP:

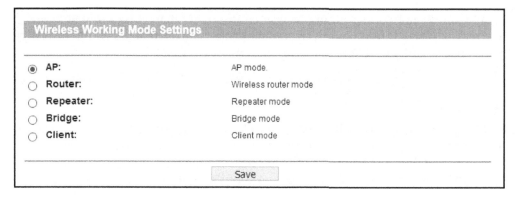

Figure 4.13: Wireless Working Mode Settings

4. Click on **Network**.
5. Provide a suitable private IP address and subnet mask:

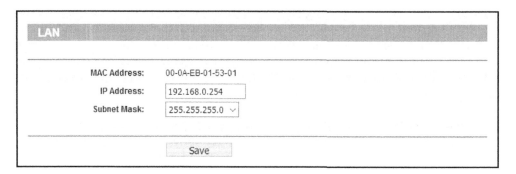

Figure 4.14: LAN settings

6. Change the **SSID** to `<your name> Wi-Fi`:

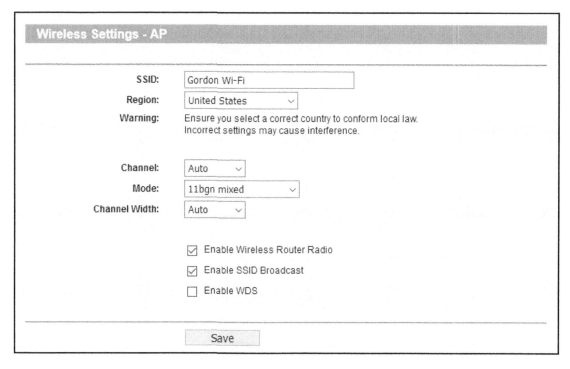

Figure 4.15: Wireless Settings- AP

7. Change the region to your own region.
8. Change the channel to one of the non-overlapping channels.
9. Only allow 802.11n.
10. Click on **Wireless Security**.
11. Configure the latest personal security and encryption.
12. Enter a PSK of your choice.

13. Click on **MAC Filtering**:

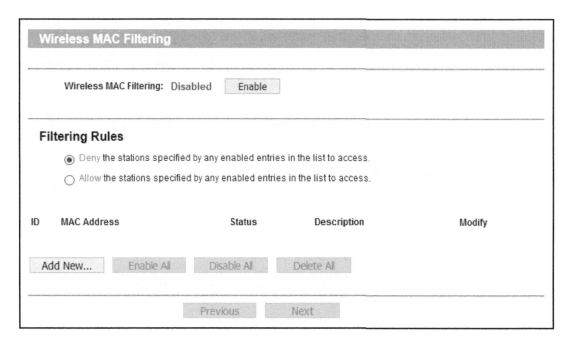

Figure 4.16: Wireless MAC Filtering

14. Allow your own device's MAC address to use this WAP.
15. Click on **Wireless Advanced**.
16. Reduce the transmission power to medium.
17. Click on **Save**.

**Optional Activity**: Log on to your Wi-Fi access point via your web browser but putting the IP address of your default gateway in the address bar. You will need to know the administrator credentials to log on. Investigate the various settings you have configured. Be careful about changing things by accident.

When configuring a Wi-Fi connection in the real world, you will need to apply the appropriate settings for your network.

# Summary

In this chapter, we looked at the various IEEE 802.11 standards pertaining to wireless technologies, including their various attributes and access methods. We discussed factors that would influence our planning of wireless networks, and the two modes available, ad hoc and infrastructure mode. We talked about the configuration of these networks, before moving onto security, emphasizing the main methods for protecting our data.

From this chapter, you will have gained the ability to deploy a basic wireless network, ensuring that you have considered factors that would impact the performance of the network. You also learned how to configure a wireless access point with appropriate security settings for your environment.

In the next chapter, we will look at the various network topologies available to us. We will describe the use cases and highlight the pros and cons of each. Also, we will explain the difference between logical and physical topologies.

# Questions

1. Wi-Fi networks use which access method?

(A) Token ring
(B) CSMA/CD
(C) CSMA/CW
(D) CSMA/CA

2. A junior network technician needs to set up an access point using 802.11g. What frequency will it use?

(A) 2.4 Hz
(B) 2.4 KHz
(C) 2.4 GHz
(D) 2.5 THz

3. Which 802.11 standard has the furthest indoor range?

(A) 802.11g
(B) 802.11a
(C) 802.11n
(D) 802.11ac

4. What type of wireless topology would be used when you want to connect two devices directly together in a peer-to-peer relationship?

(A) WDS
(B) Ad-hoc mode
(C) Infrastructure mode
(D) Wireless bridge

5. Which of these Wi-Fi security standards takes advantage of EAP?

(A) WEP-PSK
(B) WEP-Enterprise
(C) WPA-PSK
(D) WPA2-Enterprise

6. Which of these Wi-Fi standards does not use a 5 GHz frequency?

(A) 802.11b
(B) 802.11a
(C) 802.11n
(D) 802.11ac

7. You have a wireless network that supports 802.11g, but you have noticed that the network seems to be running at 11 Mbps. What is the most likely cause of this?

(A) EMI
(B) Incorrect encryption standard selected
(C) Interference from Bluetooth devices
(D) You have an 802.11b device on the network

8. The EAP falls under which standard?

(A) 802.1a
(B) 802.1x
(C) 802.11b
(D) 802.11x

# Further reading

To find out more about Wi-Fi and wireless security, visit these links:

- *Discover Wi-Fi*: `https://www.wi-fi.org/discover-wi-fi`
- *Wi-Fi security*: `https://ico.org.uk/your-data-matters/online/wifi-security/`

# Network Topologies - Mapping It All Out

# 5

Which network topology should you use for a small business? What about for a large enterprise? Unfortunately, there is no *one-size-fits-all* approach to networks. There is too much disparity between the types of equipment each organization has. A large business may update their hardware on a regular basis, thereby keeping up with newer technology, whereas a smaller business may not update theirs for 5 to 10 years. With the speed at which technology develops, there will be vast differences in that time frame.

This chapter will describe common network topologies in use today and when they can be used. It highlights the advantages and disadvantages of each topology. It is important for all network engineers to understand these differences to ensure that they select the appropriate topology for their purposes, and be able to troubleshoot each.

The following topics will be covered in this chapter:

- Logical topologies versus physical topologies
- Bus topology
- Ring topology
- Star topology
- Mesh topology
- Hybrid topology

# Logical versus physical topology

At this point, you might be wondering what a topology actually is, so I think it is probably best that we clear that up first and foremost. In relation to networks, a topology can be thought of as a map that details how the network fits together and how the data travels. Topologies can be classed as either physical or logical. A physical topology describes how the devices are connected together, whereas a logical topology describes how the data travels from device to device. This can be quite difficult for people to understand, so what I would like you to do is think about getting to work, home, or the local shopping center. My journey is like this:

1. Cycle to the local train station.
2. Train from the local train station to the destination station.
3. Tram from the destination train station to the tram stop close to work.
4. Walk from the tram stop to the office.

In essence, I have summarized my journey into a logical topology. I haven't described the journey in full, by telling you every turn that I take. That would be a physical topology. To confuse things further, quite often the physical and logical topology are the same. Do not worry too much if you are still a little confused; as we go through this chapter I will provide you with a great example that should reinforce this concept fully; however, the following two activities will also be of benefit to your understanding.

**Activity 1**: Choose a destination such as work or college, and create a logical topology of how you would go from home to that destination. This activity works better if you change modes of transport.

**Activity 2**: In this activity, you will create a physical topology for the preceding journey:

1. Go to Google Maps.
2. Search for your destination.
3. Choose **Directions** and plot a route from your home to your destination.
4. The output is your physical topology.

Having a good understanding of topologies will become extremely beneficial to you as you progress through your networking career, particularly when troubleshooting. In the following sections, we will discuss the common topologies in use, and highlight the advantages and disadvantages of each.

# Bus topology

For clarity I'm going to draw the bus topology in a way that in some implementations could be classed as slightly inaccurate, but I will explain why afterward. A bus topology can generally be described as a backbone cable with devices connected directly to it, as shown in *Figure 5.1*:

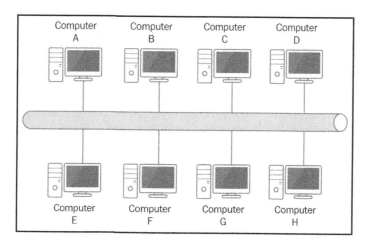

Figure 5.1: Bus topology

In the preceding diagram, I want to draw your attention to two things. Firstly, the backbone is quite clearly one single cable, and in some cases this would be correct, but in some others you might find it is made up of a number of shorter cables. Secondly, the various computers connecting to the backbone are shown as doing so through some form of intermediary cable. Again, in some instances this would be correct, and in others the devices would form part of the backbone and connect those shorter cables I mentioned in the first point.

In Chapter 8, *Media Types - Connecting Everything Together*, I will describe the two types of cable and their connectors that will dictate whether it's one long cable or a number of shorter cables. However, I will mention one characteristic of the cabling here. When the signal reaches the end of the cable, it will *bounce* back along the cable. To avoid this, each end of the cable will be fitted with a device called a terminator, which kills the signal and prevents this bounce.

At this stage, I would like to pause and talk about the access method used in a bus topology. This is deliberate as it will help you understand some of the advantages and disadvantages we will cover shortly. Recall that Wi-Fi uses an access method called **Carrier Sense Multiple Access/Collision Avoidance (CSMA/CA)**; however, the Ethernet standard (IEEE 802.3) uses a similarly named access method called **carrier sense multiple access/collision detection (CSMA/CD)**, which is used for a number of wired connections.

I tend to think of the last **A** in **CSMA/CA** as standing for **airwaves**. It's not a correct interpretation, but it helps me remember that CSMA/CA is used on Wi-Fi as the data travels the airwaves.

The first part of the CSMA/CD process is identical to CSMA/CA in that any device wishing to transmit on the network has to listen out for a gap in the traffic (carrier sense). If no device is talking the device will transmit its data; if a device is already transmitting, the device wishing to send data will wait a random amount of *back off* time, before repeating the process.

Let's revisit *Figure 5.1*, and update it. In the following example (*Figure 5.2*), **Computer B** is wanting to simply send some data to its neighbor **Computer C**. The arrow lines indicate the route of the data sent from **Computer B**. What do you notice about it? If you said that the data goes to all the devices and not just **Computer C**, you would be correct. There is no **Satellite Navigation (SatNav)** on the network that tells the data when it reaches the backbone cable to turn left, turn right, or go straight on. Herein lies one of the problems of a bus topology. It uses half-duplex transmissions and forms one big collision domain. If **Computer B** is transmitting, no one else can transmit, so it is not the most efficient method available.

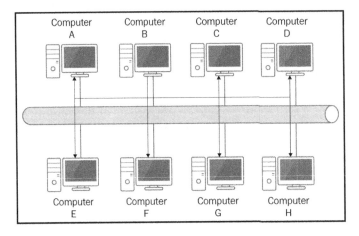

Figure 5.2: Data transmission on a bus topology

I'm going to return to the CSMA/CD process, and talk about what happens when two devices talk at the same time. In this scenario, both devices have listened to the network, and cannot hear anyone talking, so they both decide to send their data at the same time. You have probably had this yourself in normal conversations where no one is talking then all of a sudden two people break the silence at the same time. However, in CSMA/CD there is no polite *you first* option as such.

When two devices transmit at the same time, a collision occurs, and is detected. This detection is picked up through a change in amperage on the cable, and the transmitting devices send a jamming signal that tells all the other devices not to transmit. Both transmitting devices then *back off* for a random period of time, before repeating the transmission process. Once they have transmitted, normal service is resumed on the network.

# Advantages

The relative simplicity of a bus topology means it is well suited for a small network, and can be extended with minimal effort. A bus topology also offers some resilience. As you see later, in some topologies a failure of one node or its connection can bring down a whole network. Look back at *Figure 5.2*: if that connection between **Computer B** and the backbone breaks, it only impacts communications to and from that device. A bus topology is also relatively cheap to implement, as it uses a minimal amount of cabling.

# Disadvantages

I have mentioned already that a bus topology is great for a small network; however, as your network grows it becomes less and less efficient. Therefore, any company growth needs to be factored in when planning a network, particularly if you are leaning toward implementing a bus topology. The more devices you add, the more collisions will occur. I would concede, however, it is unlikely in this day and age that you would implement a bus topology network.

Although this type of network is resilient to a single device failure, the backbone cable serves as a single point of failure. If some break occurs on that one cable, then the whole network is lost. This is further exacerbated by the fact that a bus topology can be quite difficult to troubleshoot.

# Ring topology

In a ring topology, each device is connected to two devices (*Figure 5.3*), and data is transferred by passing it on to the next device in the network. If the data is not for that device, it will forward it on to the next device and so on:

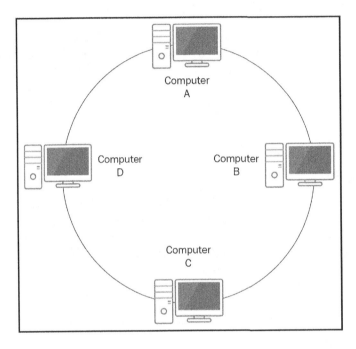

Figure 5.3: Ring topology

Early iterations of the ring topology were unidirectional, and quite often people would draw them as only going clockwise. Yes, they are unidirectional, but the devices do not understand the concept of clockwise and counterclockwise, so devices will transmit in one direction or the other depending on how they are configured. Looking back at *Figure 5.3*, let's imagine **Computer A** wanted to talk to **Computer D**. In a clockwise configuration, the data would pass through **Computer B** and **Computer C** en route to **Computer D**. In a counterclockwise configuration the data would transfer directly to **Computer D**.

In later iterations of this topology, traffic could be transmitted bidirectionally. This could either be *always on* or implemented to happen should a network fault occur. In *Figure 5.4*, we can see there is a fault between **Computer B** and **Computer C**:

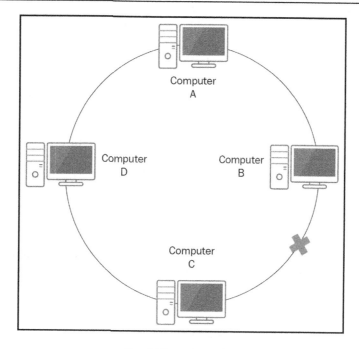

Figure 5.4: Ring topology with fault

However, if a bidirectional implementation was in place, **Computer A** could maintain communication with **Computer B** by sending data clockwise, and with **Computer C** and **Computer D** by sending data counterclockwise. The *reply* traffic would still be able to flow in the reverse direction. An example of a bidirectional ring topology is a **Fiber Distributed Data Interface (FDDI)**, which will send data in both directions.

# Advantages

A ring topology is relatively simple to troubleshoot. Looking back at *Figure 5.4*, if we know that **Computer A** can talk to **Computer B** but not to **Computer C**, then the issue must be somewhere between **Computer B** and **Computer C**, or on the devices themselves.

Additionally, as the devices in a ring topology are not fighting for access to the network media, no collisions take place, making it quite efficient. In addition to this, each device that receives the data will regenerate the signal before passing it on to the next device, thereby reducing signal attrition.

Finally, it is relatively simple to add a new device to a ring network. You disconnect the cable from one of the existing machines, plug that into the new device, and run a new cable between the new device and the device you had previously disconnected.

## Disadvantages

I finished off the last section saying how simple it was to add a new device to a ring topology. While this is indeed the case, to do so will require any unidirectional networks to be brought down. If we are disconnecting a device, albeit temporarily, there is no way for the data to pass through. Likewise, if a device is faulty, it has the capacity to bring down the network, unless a bidirectional implementation is in place.

Another aspect to bear in mind is that, as each device receives the data, it has to perform a check of the data to see if it is for itself, before passing it on if it is not. On a small network, this is not too much of an issue, but as the network scales up, this will start causing considerable delay to the traffic.

## Star topology

I always like to define a star topology as a network where all devices connect to a central point. I have seen numerous materials that refer to a *central hub*, and while this is correct terminology, I find some people get fixated on the word *hub*. That central point could be a hub device, it could be a switch, it could be a router, or it could be a server. Most likely, it will be a switch. You might be puzzled at my inclusion of a server in that list. While it is unusual, it can be done given the right hardware and software. I have also found that some materials draw a star topology with a device that looks like a server in the middle, and that becomes a fixation too.

In *Figure 5.5*, I have placed a switch as the central device, as this is the most common implementation:

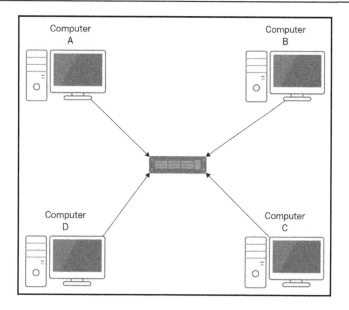

Figure 5.5: Star topology

Quite often you will see star topologies illustrated the way I have done in the preceding diagram, and there is nothing wrong with that. It makes it easier to interpret.

Look at *Figure 5.6*, and ask yourself whether it is a star topology:

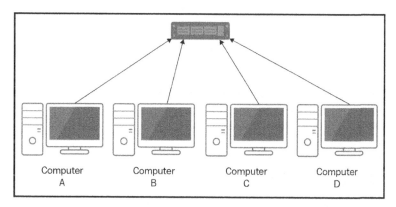

Figure 5.6: Another example for star topology

Remember, a star topology is one where devices connect to a central point. In the image, they all connect to that top switch. All communication must go through that one central device. Therefore, this is a star topology.

# Advantages

There is a reason why the star topology is the most common topology currently in use. It is efficient and fairly resilient. The efficiency is dependent on what central device is in use, but remember that most modern topologies would use a switch as opposed to a hub to reduce collisions. The resilience comes from the fact that the failure of one device or connection generally does not bring down the whole network.

Looking at *Figure 5.7*, we can see that a fault on the cable between the central device and **Computer A** will still allow other devices to communicate:

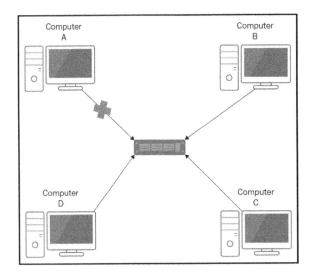

Figure 5.7: Fault on star topology

Other benefits of a star topology include the ability to add devices at will to the network without causing disruption. There is no requirement to take the network down just to add a new device. In addition, this topology scales well to large networks.

# Disadvantages

Although the star topology is resilient to devices or their connections failing, I'd like you to look back at *Figure 5.5* and see if you can identify what could bring down the whole network. If you said the central device, you would be correct. That central device is a **single point of failure** (sometimes referred to as an **SPOF**). If that device goes down, no one is going to be talking. While there is usually some contingency in having spare (redundant) switches, the endpoint devices usually will only connect to one.

The other issue that is common with a star topology is that it can be quite expensive. The images that I have used so far have illustrated a relatively short cable between devices. In reality, in a star topology, your device will be connected to a wall port. That wall port will then be connected to a patch panel in a communications cabinet. Each wall port will have its only cable back to the cabinet. That all starts adding up to a lot of cable. There is no sharing of media here.

# Token ring

At this point, I'm going to link back to logical and physical topologies, and give you the example that I promised at the start of this chapter. First let me explain how a token ring operates, and then I will dive into the topological areas.

In a token ring network (IEEE 802.5), a device can only talk when it is in possession of a *token.* That token is passed from device to device, until someone needs to talk, and they take possession of the token. Once they have finished with the token, they relinquish it for someone else to use.

Judging from its name, you are likely to assume that a token ring is a ring topology. Well, you are right and you are wrong. A token ring network has a physical star topology and a logical ring topology. Physically, the devices connect to a central device called a **media access unit** or **multiple access unit** (**MAU**), hence the physical star (dashed lines). But as far as the data is concerned, it goes from device to device (solid lines), and the MAU is ignored:

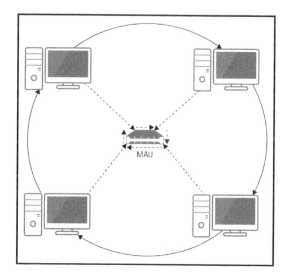

Figure 5.8: Token ring

*Figure 5.8* shows a simplified token ring network. The red straight lines indicate the physical flow of the data. The green curved lines indicate the logical flow of the data. So you can see how this is a physical star and also a logical ring topology. I'd like to finish off this section by just mentioning something about the MAU. Recall that, in a ring network, if a device fails then it can impact on the whole network. Having an MAU in place overcomes that. If it detects that **Computer B** has failed, for example, it will skip that and pass the token to **Computer C**, thereby offering continuity of service.

# Mesh topology

In `Chapter 4`, *Understanding Wireless Networking*, one of the topologies that we covered was a wireless mesh, and we can create a similar topology with a wired network. For ease, when I refer to mesh in this section I will be referring to a wired mesh unless I specify otherwise. A mesh network can take one of two forms, full mesh or partial mesh.

 **Exam tip**: Unless specifically stated, the MTA does not differentiate between a wireless mesh and a wired mesh network. Do not over-think the questions by trying to differentiate between wired and wireless mesh networks yourself.

In a full mesh network, every device is connected to every other device. To be able to do this, devices will need to have a separate interface for each of the other devices. Now, while this is theoretically possible to do with the devices being a computer (if it had enough expansion slots on the motherboard), it is highly unlikely that this would happen. In the majority of mesh networks, the devices we are referring to would be either switches or routers, as they offer multiple available interfaces.

In *Figure 5.9*, I have created a very simple four-device mesh network. As you can see, each device is connected to the others, and therefore each has to have three interfaces available:

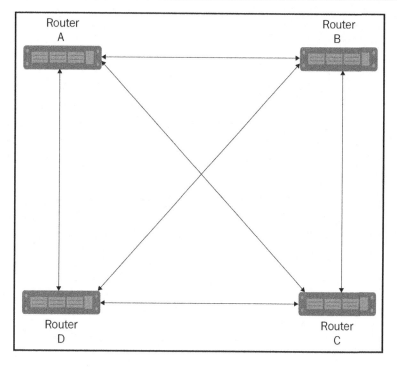

Figure 5.9: Full mesh topology

When planning a mesh network, it is important to be able to calculate how many interfaces you will need and how many cables. Look back at *Figure 5.8*: how many interfaces in total do you think we need, and how many cables? With this small network it is probably relatively easy to calculate just by counting from the image, but what if we have 100 devices? 300? 76,587? Don't worry, there is a pair of fairly simple formulas we can use:

*n = number of nodes/devices*
*Number of interfaces = n(n-1)*
*Number of cables = (n(n-1))/2 or number of interfaces/2*

So how many interfaces did we need for our four-device network?
*Number of interfaces = n(n-1)*
$$= 4(4\text{-}1)$$
$$= 4 \times 3$$
$$= 12$$

*Number of cables = n(n-1)/2*
$$= 4(4\text{-}1)/2$$
$$= (4 \times 3)/2$$
$$= 12/2$$
$$= 6$$

In contrast, a partial mesh network does not connect every device together, but will have some devices that are connected to all of the other devices. Those *fully connected* devices will usually be critical for the running of the infrastructure. *Figure 5.10* shows our four-device network as a partial mesh:

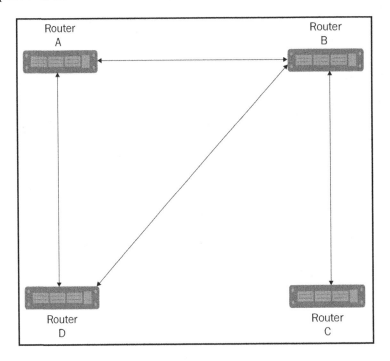

Figure 5.10: Partial mesh topology

As you can see only, **Router B** is connected to all of the other devices, and the remainder are a mixture of connecting to one or two devices.

# Advantages

The key advantage to using a mesh topology is fault tolerance. A full mesh topology offers a high level of redundancy. Should the direct connection between two devices fail, an alternate pathway will be used. This is usually an automatic or dynamic change after the connection is identified as being lost. In *Figure 5.11*, the connection between **Router B** and **Router C** has been lost. Which route could the data from **Router B** take to get to **Router C** now? Let's have a look:

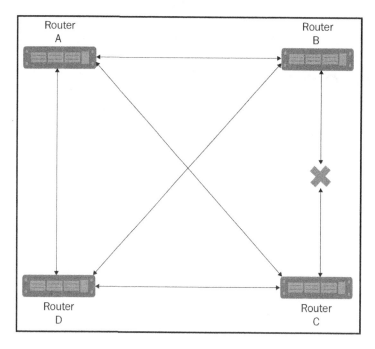

Figure 5.11: Mesh topology with failed connection

There are four possible alternative routes that could be taken in this scenario. The data could go in the following ways:

- **Router B** | **Router A** | **Router C**
- **Router B** | **Router D** | **Router C**
- **Router B** | **Router A** | **Router D** | **Router C**
- **Router B** | **Router D** | **Router A** | **Router C**

As you can see, on such a simple network, a full mesh topology gives quite a lot of redundancy.

# Disadvantages

The obvious disadvantage to implementing this form of network is cost. A full mesh network is expensive to implement due to the number of cables and interfaces required, which is why a partial mesh could be seen as some form of compromise.

The other disadvantage is the skill set required to configure the mesh for redundancy. It is not quite as simple as plug the devices into each other, and it is ready to go. You need to ensure you configure the topology correctly, particularly the routing for failover. Failure to do so, could result in your *super fault tolerant* network crashing to a standstill.

# Hybrid topology

One of the definitions of a hybrid is something consisting of mixed components, and that definition fits our purposes here. A hybrid topology is a network topology that connects two or more different network topologies together. Two such examples are a star-bus (*Figure 5.12*) and a star-ring (*Figure 5.13*):

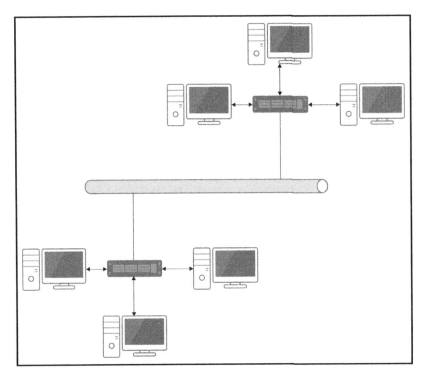

Figure 5.12: Star-bus hybrid topology

Looking at *Figure 5.13*, we can see the bus topology acting almost as a backbone for connecting the two star topologies. Any communications between the two star topology networks will have to abide by the *rules* of the bus topology, that is, follow the CSMA/CD process for access:

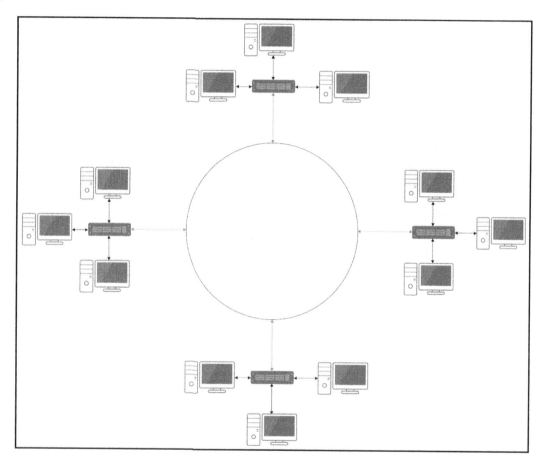

Figure 5.13: Star-ring hybrid topology

As you can see in *Figure 5.13*, the star-ring hybrid topology involves connecting a number of star topologies over a ring topology. Again, the *rules* of the intermediary topology need to be followed.

By using a hybrid topology, you are leveraging the benefits of the component topologies while minimizing the disadvantages. In the preceding two topologies, for example, by using stars as part of the topology, we are still allowing the devices in each star to communicate, even if the connection to the bus is lost.

**Activity 3**: Revisit the network plan that you created in `Chapter 2`, *Understanding Local Area Networks*. Now that you have learned about topologies in this chapter, which topology are you using?

# Summary

We began this chapter by differentiating between logical and physical topologies before looking at the various topologies. The topologies covered included bus, ring, star, mesh, and hybrid, and we highlighted the benefits and disadvantages of each in terms of performance, resiliency, and cost.

You have learned how to understand the flow of the data using logical topologies and from that to understand some of the areas to troubleshoot on each topology in the event of a failure. On bus topologies, you have also learned about the importance of terminators to avoid signal bounce. In addition, you have learned the two calculations needed to identify the number of interfaces and cables in a full mesh topology, which will assist you greatly in planning such a deployment.

In the next chapter, you will be introduced to the first of the two intermediary network devices this book focuses on, namely, switches, with routers being covered in a later chapter. The next chapter discusses the purposes of switches, the benefits of using them over hubs, and how a switch makes a forwarding decision after receiving data.

# Questions

1. In a token ring network, what is the central device known as?

(A) MAU
(B) Switch
(C) Router
(D) Server

2. Which access method is used on a bus topology?

(A) Token
(B) CSMA/CA
(C) Ticket
(D) CSMA/CD

3. All devices in a star topology are unable to communicate with each other. What is most likely at fault?

(A) Operating system
(B) Network card
(C) Switch
(D) Cable

4. FDDI utilizes which form of topology?

(A) Bus
(B) Ring
(C) Star
(D) Mesh

5. In a full mesh network consisting of five devices, how many interfaces are required in total?

(A) 4
(B) 5
(C) 10
(D) 20

6. Which topology offers the best fault tolerance?

(A) Full mesh
(B) Star
(C) Partial mesh
(D) Bus

7. Which IEEE standard covers token ring?

(A) 802.1
(B) 802.3
(C) 802.5
(D) 802.15

8. Which type of topology is shown in the following diagram?

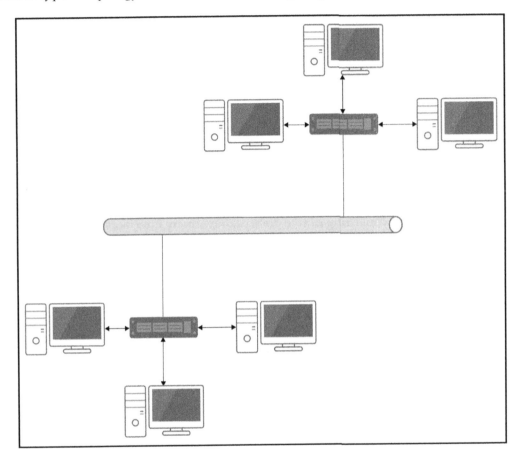

(A) Bus
(B) Partial mesh
(C) Star
(D) Hybrid

# Further reading

To find out more about network topologies, visit https://www.comparitech.com/net-admin/network-topologies-advantages-disadvantages/.

# Section 2: Network Hardware 2

In this section, you will be introduced to the two most common hardware devices, switches and routers, and network cables. You will gain an understanding of the purpose of each device and how they operates. You will also learn about the various physical cables and connectors that are commonly used today.

This section comprises the following chapters:

- Chapter 6, *Switches and Switching – Forwarding Traffic on a Local Network*
- Chapter 7, *Routers and Routing – Beyond a Single Network*
- Chapter 8, *Media Types – Connecting Everything Together*

# 6

# Switches and Switching - Forwarding Traffic on a Local Network

In the introduction to Chapter 2, *Understanding Local Area Networks*, I mentioned how most network engineers *cut their teeth* supporting an organization's internal infrastructure. This will ultimately mean gaining exposure to switches in some form or another. While it isn't likely that you'll be fully configuring switches at the entry-level, it is important that you understand how they function. The abundance of multi-user environments that are used both at home and at work makes it important for traffic to be forwarded quickly and efficiently.

This chapter introduces the concept of switching and provides an explanation of how switching decisions are made. We will discuss the different types of switch, their use cases, and the key attributes of these essential devices.

The following topics will be covered in this chapter:

- The purpose of switches and switching
- Understanding frame forwarding
- Understanding switch characteristics

# Technical requirements

There are no technical requirements for this chapter.

# The purpose of switches and switching

In Chapter 2, *Understanding Local Area Networks*, we introduced the use of switches within a LAN. Recall that a switch is a device that's used to forward traffic from one device to the next within a local network. By introducing a switch to our network, we are providing a means of segmenting the network into smaller, more manageable, and more efficient areas.

At a basic level, this segmentation leads to a reduction in collisions since each port on a switch is classed as its own collision domain. In the following diagram, each computer is connected to a port on the switch in the center and has formed its own collision domain:

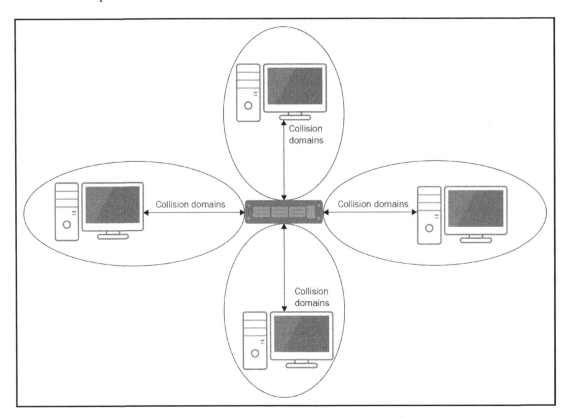

Figure 6.1: Collision domains

Notice that this segmentation reduces collisions but doesn't remove them. The reason for this is that, in most modern switched networks, a switch port is only connected to one device, thus providing zero collisions in a properly configured network. However, if a hub is connected to the switch port or has been incorrectly configured, this would lead to collisions still being detected. Further segmentation can be provided through the use of VLANs.

Now that we know why we should provide our network with a switch, let's look at how frames are forwarded.

# Understanding frame forwarding

Recall that, unlike hubs, switches have intelligence built into them to prevent devices from receiving all the data being sent on the network, even if it isn't destined for them. In this section, I will walk you through the frame forwarding process that a switch undertakes to move data from A to B.

# Methods of frame forwarding

Before I go any further, I would like to briefly mention the two methods of forwarding data. They are as follows:

- Cut-through switching
- Store and forward

## Cut-through switching

In **cut-through switching**, the switch forwards the data almost immediately. It just needs to know the source and destination MAC addresses. As soon as it has this information, it will forward the data, even if the whole frame hasn't been received by the switch. A simplified visualization of this can be seen in the following diagram:

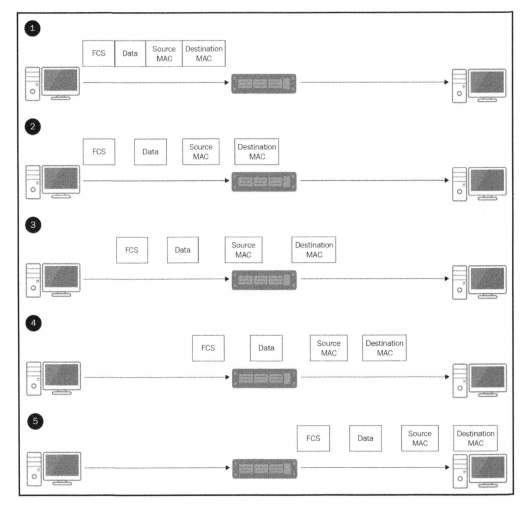

Figure 6.2: Cut-through switching

Let's go through the numbered steps in the preceding diagram so that we can understand this process better:

- In *step 1*, the frame is being sent.
- In *step 2*, the switch receives the destination MAC address.
- In *step 3*, the switch starts to forward the frame, even though it's only received the destination MAC address.
- In *steps 4* and *5*, the switch continues to send the remainder of the frame.

While this is a fast method, it means that frames that containing errors are forwarded. To prevent this, most modern switches will use a process called **store-and-forward** instead of cut-through switching.

# Store and forward

In this process, the switch will store the frame data in its memory buffer until the complete frame has been received. Once the frame has been completely received, the switch will perform error checking on the data before forwarding the frame on. Any corrupt frames are discarded. Store and forward also allows data to be prioritized through **Quality of Service (QoS)**. We can see a simplified visualization of this in the following diagram:

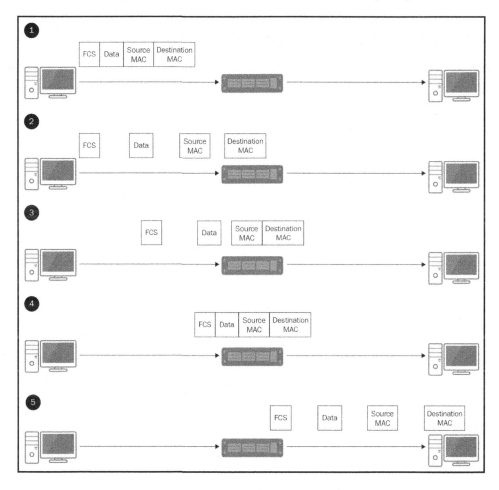

Figure 6.3: Store and forward switching

Let's go through the numbered steps in the preceding diagram so that we can understand this process better:

- In *step 1*, the frame is being sent.
- In *step 2*, the switch receives the destination MAC address.
- In *step 3*, the switch holds on to (stores) the frame.
- In *step 4*, the switch now has all of the frames it will carry out the error check on.
- In *step 5*, the switch forwards the frame(s) on if they passed the error check.

Regardless of which of these two methods you use, the process of frame forwarding will be the same. We'll learn more about this in the next section.

# Frame forwarding process

I will summarize this process here and then walk through an example. When a switch receives data from a device, it follows this process:

1. It checks to see if the source MAC address is in its MAC table (also known as the **Content Addressable Memory (CAM)** table):
   - If it isn't, the switch updates the table by specifying which interface the sender's MAC address is on
2. Then, it looks to see if there is an entry for the destination MAC address:
   - If there is, the frame is forwarded internally to the interface that's listed, which and then transmits it to the destination device.
   - If there is no entry for the destination MAC address, the switch will flood or broadcast the frame from all its interfaces, except the interface the frame came in on.
3. Hopefully, the intended recipient will receive the frame and respond.
4. The switch will repeat this process for the response and should, of course, know the interface that the destination (the original source device) is on.

You may be wondering what happens if the device isn't directly connected to the switch that has received the frame – perhaps the frame has been forwarded from another switch. In this situation, the switch receiving the data doesn't really care. It just cares about what interface the data has been received on. The MAC table will purge entries on a regular basis if they haven't been used for a period of time.

In this walkthrough, we are going to use the topology shown in the following diagram. As an aside, can you recall which topology is shown here?

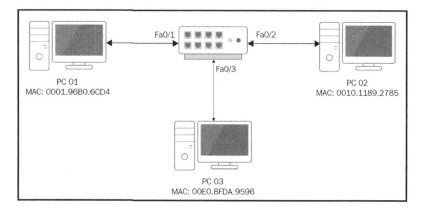

Figure 6.4: Topology walkthrough

In this walkthrough, **PC 01** sends some data to **PC 02**, who will respond:

1. **PC 01** sends data to the switch.
2. The switch receives the data and checks its MAC/CAM table to see if there is an entry for **PC 01**'s MAC address. There is no entry there at the moment:

Figure 6.5: No entry for MAC address

3. Since there is no entry, the switch updates the table with the relevant information:

Figure 6.6: Updated MAC/CAM table

4. Then, the switch looks for the destination MAC address (**PC 02**) in the table.

5. Since there is no entry, the frame is forwarded out of all the interfaces except for the one it came in on (Fa0/1).

6. Both **PC 02** and **PC 03** will receive the frame and check the destination MAC address contained within it. **PC 03** will ignore the frame as it's not intended for it.

7. **PC 02** will process the frame accordingly and, in this case, send a response.

8. On receipt of **PC 02**'s response at the switch, the latter will check the MAC table to see if there is an entry for **PC 02**'s MAC address.

9. Since there is no entry, it will update the MAC table with the relevant information:

```
Switch>show mac-address-table
          Mac Address Table
-------------------------------------------

Vlan    Mac Address       Type        Ports
----    -----------       --------    -----

  10    0001.96b0.6cd4    DYNAMIC     Fa0/1
  10    0010.1189.2785    DYNAMIC     Fa0/2
Switch>
```

Figure 6.7: Updated MAC/CAM table

10. Then, it will look at the destination MAC address (**PC 01**'s) and check whether it's in the MAC table.

11. On this occasion, there is an entry for it, so the switch forwards the frame through Fa0/1. There is no need to flood it out of all the interfaces.

You may have noticed that, in the output shown in the walkthrough screenshots, there is a column for Type, and each of the entries shows DYNAMIC. This indicates that the MAC address/interface mapping has been learned automatically. An administrator may configure static mapping, but this is unlikely.

Here, the switch flooded the frame out of every interface as it didn't know which interface the unicast MAC address was on. It will do the (same for any frame addresses) to broadcast MAC addresses or multicast MAC addresses. When you only have one switch in your network, this will not cause any issues. However, if you have switches that are connected, there are some other things you need to take into considerations. In the following subsection, I will explain one of these main issues and briefly cover a means of preventing it from happening.

# Spanning Tree Protocol

I'd like to start this subsection by talking about the **Spanning Tree Protocol** (**STP**). Look at the simple topology shown in the following diagram. In this topology, I have two switches connected to each other with two links:

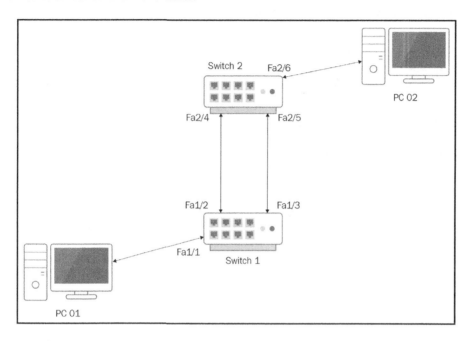

Figure 6.8: Switches connected with redundancy

This is a common practice and offers redundancy. Should one of the links fail, the other is there to allow communication to take place between the two switches. I'd like you to think for a moment about what happens if **PC 01** sends some data to **Switch 1** and **Switch 1** either doesn't know the outbound interface or it's addressed to a broadcast/multicast MAC address. What interface will **Switch 1** send it out of? What will **Switch 2** do when it receives this data and doesn't know the outbound interface, or it's addressed to a broadcast/multicast MAC address? Can you start to visualize what issue might arise?

Let me walk through what's going to happen in this scenario. For simplicity, I have labeled the interfaces so that **Fa1/x** is an interface on **Switch 1** and **Fa2/x** is an interface on **Switch 2**:

1. **Switch 1** receives the data from **PC 01** on **Fa1/1**.
2. It doesn't know the outbound interface, so it sends it out of both **Fa1/2** and **Fa1/3**.

3. **Switch 2** receives the data from **Fa1/2** on its interface: **Fa2/4**. Then, **Switch 2** sends it out of all the interfaces except the one it was received on: **Fa2/5** and **Fa2/6**.

4. Switch 2 also receives the data from **Fa1/3** on its interface, that is, **Fa2/5**, and sends it out of all the interfaces except the one it was received on: **Fa2/4** and **Fa2/6**. **Switch 2** has no way of knowing that the same frame has been received twice.

5. **Switch 1** will receive the data from interface **Fa2/4** on **Fa1/2** and has no way of knowing whether it was the data it forwarded on previously. It sends the data out of all the interfaces except **Fa1/2**.

6. **Switch 1** also receives the data from **Fa2/5** on its interface, **Fa1/3**, and sends it out of all the interfaces except **Fa1/3**.

7. **Switch 2** receives the two lots of data from **Switch 1** and this *looping* continues, with the data going back and forth between the two switches.

This was just one piece of data looping around – imagine what would happen if we had more and more data impacted by this. In the end, this will result in the network failing totally. In this situation, you will have created a **broadcast storm**, and usually the only way of stopping this is by powering off all the switches or unplugging the cables and then taking steps to prevent this from happening again through configuration. On top of this, the end devices will have to process the same piece of data over and over again, possibly resulting in a denial of service. We can't disable broadcasts or multicasts as they are a required function of all networks, so we have to use a protocol such as STP to prevent this.

Fortunately, for the exam, you don't need to know how the STP operates – you only need to know its purpose and the very basics of what it does. You can breathe a sigh of relief knowing that both of these are relatively simple to understand.

The purpose of STP is to prevent looping between switches when redundant links are implemented. To do this, an election takes place between the switches to decide which switch will be classed as the *root bridge*. Once identified, the switches identify which of their interfaces are the closest to the route bridge and dub them **root ports** (**RP**). These ports will always be available. The other ports are referred to as **designated ports** (**DPs**) and **non-designated ports** (**NDPs**). Non-designated ports are prevented from sending data unless something fails on the network that requires them to assume the role of sending data:

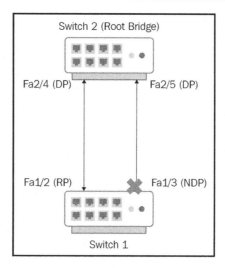

Figure 6.9: STP in operation

In the preceding diagram, we can see that **Switch 2** has been elected as the root bridge, while **Switch 1** has identified **Fa1/2** as the RP. This means it has identified **Fa1/3** as the non-designated port, so no traffic will flow between the two switches through that interface. Behind the scenes, there is a lot of management data going back and forth between the two switches; should the link between **Fa1/2** and **Fa2/4** fail, then this will be identified and **Fa1/3** will be promoted to RP and be allowed to send data.

 **Exam tip**: STP can be used to refer to Spanning Tree Protocol and Shielded Twisted Pair, which is a type of cable. Remember this for the exam. People have been known not to choose it as an answer because they forgot it has two meanings.

Now that we have looked at how a switch functions, let's discuss some of the main characteristics of switches.

# Understanding switch characteristics

While all the switches provide the basic functionality of forwarding frames, not all of them will be equal. In this section, I will provide an overview of some of the main characteristics to be aware of when building a switched network.

# Managed and unmanaged switches

A switch can be classed as either managed or unmanaged. In a business environment, you are more likely to see a managed switch than an unmanaged switch due to the extra functionality the former offers. However, you may see small unmanaged switches being used in offices where there's a shortage of wall ports.

An unmanaged switch is a network device that ships with a preloaded configuration that cannot be changed and is used purely to allow endpoint devices to communicate with each other. Physically, the unmanaged switch will usually be a small box with a small number of ports. The following picture is an example of a NETGEAR unmanaged switch with five ports. Notice the labeling above the port with the red cable. We can see that this switch supports speeds of 10 Mbps and 100 Mbps. The fact that both LEDs below the labels are illuminated indicates that this connection is running at 100 Mbps:

Figure 6.10: Unmanaged switch

 The preceding picture can be found at https://de.wikipedia.org/wiki/ Switch_(Netzwerktechnik)#/media/Datei:Netgear_Gigabit_Switch_5- port.jpg. Figure by Simon A. Eugster. Licensed under Creative Commons CC BY-SA 3.0: https://creativecommons.org/licenses/by-sa/ 3.0/.

In contrast to an unmanaged switch, a managed switch will allow you to configure VLANs, port speeds, security, duplex settings, and so on. To manage the switch, you would either physically connect to the switch's console port or remotely manage the switch using some form of terminal emulator. To be able to connect to the switch remotely, the switch needs to be configured with an IP address. This can only be initially configured through a console port, similar to the one shown in the following picture:

Figure 6.8: Managed switch with a console port

 The preceding picture can be found at `https://upload.wikimedia.org/wikipedia/commons/b/b9/2550T-PWR-Front.jpg`. Licensed under Creative Commons CC BY-SA 3.0.

A laptop or similar device is physically connected to the console port and a connection is made from the operating system using a terminal emulator, such as the popular application PuTTY. This is shown in the following screenshot:

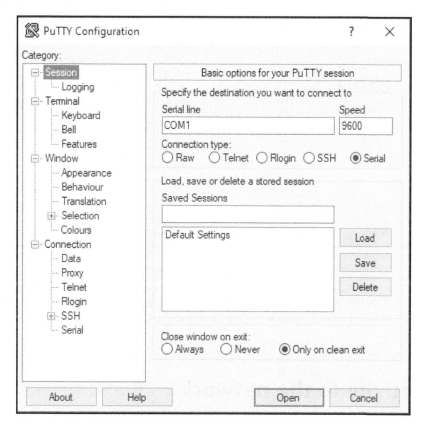

Figure 6.9: PuTTY emulator

As well as selecting **Serial** on the general screen, you also need to ensure that you configure advanced settings, as shown in the following screenshot:

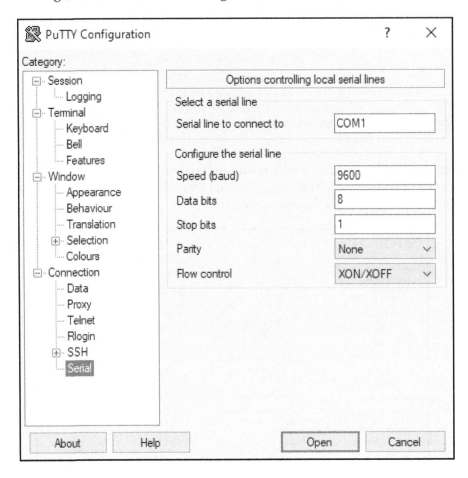

Figure 6.10: PuTTY's additional settings

It is imperative that the settings you select here match those of the device you are trying to configure. If they don't match, you will fail to connect or, if you can connect, you will likely experience issues.

# Connectivity to the network

When using an unmanaged switch, the switch itself will be plugged into an available wall port and the devices will be connected to the switch.

In an enterprise environment, the end devices will be connected to an available wall port. The wall port will be connected to the back of a patch panel, into what is known as a **punch-down block**. The front of the patch panel will be connected to the switch. The following diagram shows how this is laid out. The purpose of using a patch panel is to ease cable management:

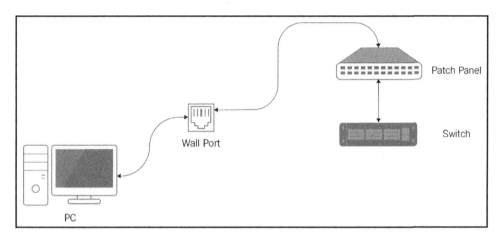

Figure 6.11: Enterprise connectivity

The wall port is wired differently compared to an RJ-45 connector. The connections you can see at the front of the wall port in the following picture are wired directly to the prongs at the rear. The wires from a cable are then connected to these prongs and the cable will be run back to a patch panel:

Figure 6.12: Wall port

The preceding image can be found at `https://en.wikipedia.org/wiki/ Keystone_module#/media/File:Keystone_module_CAT5_orange.jpg`.

The following image shows the back of a patch panel. To connect the cables, you would use a punch-down tool. If you look at the bottom right of this image, you can see that each grouping is broken down into four (there are six sets of four colors: green, orange, brown, and blue). These are color-coded to match the colored pairs of cables being connected:

Figure 6.13: Rear of the patch panel

The preceding image can be found at `https://www.flickr.com/photos/ dbarsky/2261404319`. Figure by Dmitry Barsky. Licensed under Creative Commons CC BY 2.0.

In the following image, you can see how the cables are connected to the front. The patch panels are at the top and the two silver-fronted boxes are the switches:

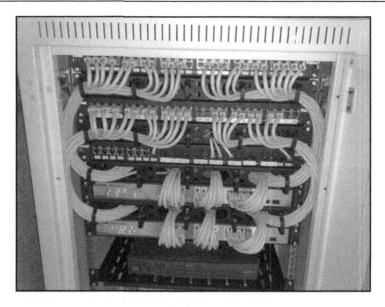

Figure 6.14: Front of the patch panel

 The preceding image can be found at `https://upload.wikimedia.org/` `wikipedia/commons/b/bc/19-inch_rackmount_Ethernet_switches_and_` `patch_panels.jpg`.

The diagram in this section shows all of the ports that are available. We will discuss these now.

# Ports

Once you have decided on whether you want a managed or unmanaged switch, you will likely focus on the number of interfaces or ports the switch can support and the type of port they are. Usually, the options will be 12, 24, or 48 ports. The switch we saw in *Figure 6.8* shows a 48-port switch, where the uplink ports are the four ports to the left of the main interfaces.

In `Chapter 8`, *Media Types – Connecting Everything Together*, we will discuss the various types of cable in detail. For now, though, your port choice will most likely be down to whether you want the switch to support twisted pair cables, fiber optic cables, or both.

Besides the port type, you will also need to focus on the speeds the interfaces can support. Switches can support various speeds, such as Fast Ethernet (10/100 Mbps), Gigabit Ethernet (10/100/1,000 Mbps), Ten Gigabit (10/100/1,000/10,000 Mbps), and even 40/100 Gbps speeds. Obviously, the faster the switch, the more expensive it will be. It's unlikely that the ports that are connected to the end user's computers will need the same connection speed as a port connected to a media streaming server, for example. Another form of speed that you may hear mentioned is backplane speed or fabric bandwidth. These refer to the internal speed of data being moved from one switch port to another.

Since ports can support multiple speeds and duplex settings, they may need to be configured accordingly. Most switches can auto-negotiate these, but it may be more appropriate to configure these manually to avoid any issues that may be caused by failure to successfully negotiate. As a fail-safe, a lot of switches will fall back to the slowest speed and half-duplex. Obviously, this slows down the network, and we would prefer to have the fastest possible speed and, of course, full-duplex to allow for simultaneous two-way communication.

Another characteristic that should be taken into consideration when purchasing an enterprise-level switch is modularity. Modern enterprise switches, such as Cisco's Catalyst range, provide us with the ability to expand the capabilities of a switch through the use of modules that you physically add to the switch. These modules can include support for different cable types, different speeds, and wireless functionality. The use of modules allows an organization to buy a switch at a much lower cost when first starting, but upgrade with minimal disruption as the company grows.

 **Activity**: We have just talked about the modularity of some switches. It is worthwhile having an awareness of what modules are available to organizations so that you understand the device's extensibility. Conduct an online search for Cisco Ethernet switching network modules and investigate the various modules that are available.

In Chapter 2, *Understanding Local Area Networks*, we discussed the use of a tiered approach when it comes to using switches with an access layer, distribution layer, and core layer. To provide suitable speeds when sending data between each of the layers, enterprise-level switches usually include faster uplink ports offering speeds of 10-40 Gbps.

# Layer 3 switches and VLANs

Besides classifying switches as managed or unmanaged, we can also classify them as being a layer 2 or a layer 3 switch. A layer 2 switch only supports the use of forwarding data based on MAC addresses, whereas a layer 3 switch also offers additional support in terms of being able to recognize the IP address of an interface, and also provides traffic routing using an IP address. This is essential when routing traffic between VLANs. In `Chapter 2`, *Understanding Local Area Networks*, we learned how VLANs segment a network into subnets and that no direct communication can take place between them. For them to be able to communicate with each other, you need to implement a router or a layer 3 switch.

When creating a VLAN, you need to configure the relevant interfaces on the switch so that they're a part of that VLAN. By default, all the interfaces on a switch are part of a single default VLAN. That way, the interfaces can communicate with each other. If you want to allocate an interface to a different VLAN, you simply reconfigure it as part of the new VLAN. The following screenshot shows the VLAN configuration of a Cisco switch, with all the interfaces on the default VLAN:

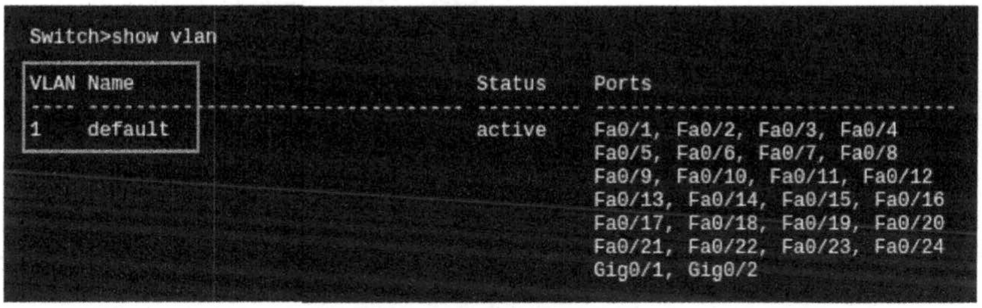

```
Switch>show vlan

VLAN Name                             Status    Ports
---- --------------------------------  --------- -------------------------------
1    default                          active    Fa0/1, Fa0/2, Fa0/3, Fa0/4
                                                Fa0/5, Fa0/6, Fa0/7, Fa0/8
                                                Fa0/9, Fa0/10, Fa0/11, Fa0/12
                                                Fa0/13, Fa0/14, Fa0/15, Fa0/16
                                                Fa0/17, Fa0/18, Fa0/19, Fa0/20
                                                Fa0/21, Fa0/22, Fa0/23, Fa0/24
                                                Gig0/1, Gig0/2
```

Figure 6.15: All the interfaces on the default VLAN

The following screenshot shows a Cisco switch that has been configured so it has multiple VLANs:

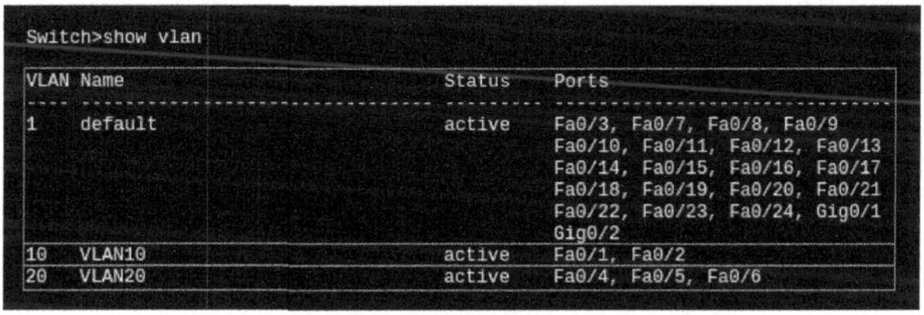

```
Switch>show vlan

VLAN Name                             Status    Ports
---- --------------------------------  --------- -------------------------------
1    default                          active    Fa0/3, Fa0/7, Fa0/8, Fa0/9
                                                Fa0/10, Fa0/11, Fa0/12, Fa0/13
                                                Fa0/14, Fa0/15, Fa0/16, Fa0/17
                                                Fa0/18, Fa0/19, Fa0/20, Fa0/21
                                                Fa0/22, Fa0/23, Fa0/24, Gig0/1
                                                Gig0/2
10   VLAN10                           active    Fa0/1, Fa0/2
20   VLAN20                           active    Fa0/4, Fa0/5, Fa0/6
```

Figure 6.16: Additional VLANs configured

Each interface that's connected to an end device will need to be configured as an access port and either left on the default VLAN or allocated to any VLAN that has been configured. An access port will carry traffic for one VLAN only.

Let's revisit the hospital scenario from Chapter 2, *Understanding Local Area Networks*, as shown in the following diagram:

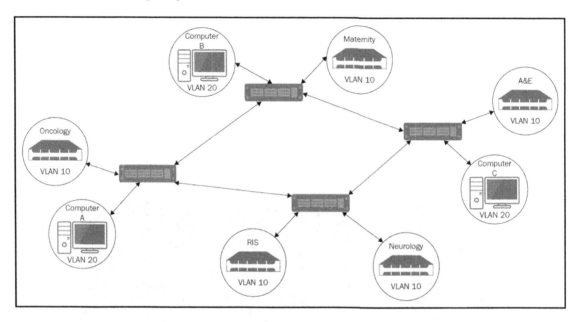

Figure 6.17: Example VLAN configuration

Looking at **Computer A**, **Computer B**, and **Computer C**, the interfaces that each of these is connected to will be classed as access ports. But what about the connections between the switches? Each of those connections will need to carry data from any of the VLANs. Therefore, interfaces connecting a switch to another switch will be configured as *trunk ports*. A trunk port carries data for multiple VLANs and has to be configured to allow the VLANs to transmit data over it.

**Note**: There are switches that work on other layers, but for the exam, it's enough to only understand level 2 and level 3 switches.

# Security

Given the critical functionality of a switch, it is imperative to understand some of the security options that are available in relation to this device. We have already talked about how switches reduce collision domains, thus increasing the efficiency of the network, and we have also discussed how switches forward data out through specific interfaces. This latter functionality contrasts with a hub sending data out of all the available interfaces, potentially allowing data to be sniffed.

Other security options include password-protecting the console connection. Although gaining physical access to the switch is trickier, it is imperative to not risk a possible compromise. If someone can gain physical access to a switch, then it is at risk.

Even if physical access to the port isn't possible, that a rogue device could potentially be plugged into a wall port. There are a few options that could be implemented here. First, any unused switch ports should be disabled in the switch's configuration. The other option is setting port security, which either remembers what MAC addresses should be on that port or can be set to learn a number of MAC addresses that are linked to the port. If an unknown MAC address is connected to the port or the number of MAC addresses is breached, then the port can be configured to send an alert or even shut down.

One final thing about switch security I would like to mention is MAC Flooding. As we've already mentioned, when a switch learns of a new MAC address, it updates its MAC/CAM table. If a switch is receiving too many new MAC addresses (MAC Flooding), it struggles to cope and it fails open. This means it stops trying to forward all the frames properly, and instead sends them out of every port on the switch apart from the ingress port. Port security will help to prevent this since new MAC addresses will need to be authenticated.

# Summary

In this chapter, we explained how switches allow us to segment a network and reduce collision domains. We discussed the various characteristics of switches and highlighted the difference between managed and unmanaged devices. We also talked about cabling between endpoints and switches via patch panels. In addition to this, we walked through the process of frame forwarding and mechanisms to prevent broadcast storms occurring. We finished this chapter by discussing various security processes we can employ on a switch.

This chapter taught you how to identify collision domains on a network. By combining this with the knowledge you have of various different topologies and their access methods, you will be able to implement an efficient network with ease. You also learned how a switch populates its MAC/CAM table during the frame forwarding process. An understanding of this will allow you to troubleshoot issues that arise on a network with switches. In addition, you now have a basic knowledge of the Spanning Tree Protocol. Although going into more detail about this would be beyond the scope of this book, you now have an awareness of what to implement to avoid broadcast storms.

While this chapter focused on the use of switches and their use on internal networks, in the next chapter, we will start to move beyond our own networks and look at communication between networks using routers. We will talk about the various routing protocols that we can use and how a router uses the information from these protocols to make routing decisions.

# Questions

1. What type of switch would you need to support routing between VLANs?

(A) Layer 1
(B) Layer 2
(C) Layer 3
(D) Unmanaged

2. Look at the following diagrams. When **PC 01** sends data to the switch for **PC 02**, what will the switch do with it?

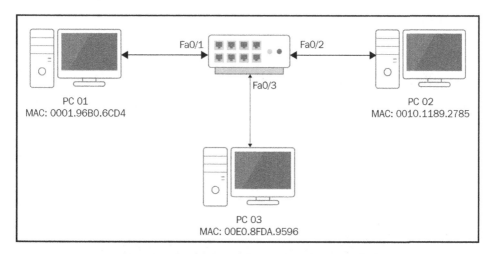

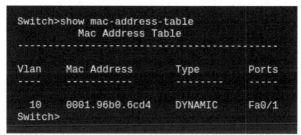

(A) Send it to `Fa0/1` only
(B) Send it to `Fa0/2` only
(C) Send it to `Fa0/2` and `Fa0/3` only
(D) Send it to `Fa0/1`, `Fa0/2`, and `Fa0/3`

3. Which forwarding type waits for all of the data to be received before forwarding it on?

(A) Cut-through
(B) Store and forward
(C) Store and cut-through
(D) Cut-through and forward

4. What type of switch will not allow you to configure VLANs? (Choose the best answer)

(A) Unmanaged switch
(B) Managed switch
(C) Layer 2 switch
(D) Layer 3 switch

5. How many collision domains are in the following diagram?

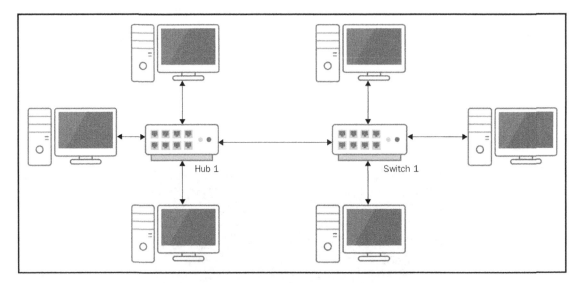

(A) 1
(B) 2
(C) 4
(D) 7

6. What protocol is used to prevent loops in a switched network?

(A) SFTP
(B) UTP
(C) ARP
(D) STP

7. Excessive data caused by loops in a switched network is known as a what?

(A) Broadcast storm
(B) Unicast storm
(C) Multicast storm
(D) Anycast storm

8. What is the speed of the internal connections in a switch known as?

(A) Background Intelligent Transfer Speed
(B) Backplane Speed
(C) STP
(D) Unicast

9. If you wanted to configure simultaneous two-way traffic between a switch port and an end device, what setting would you configure on the interface?

(A) Simplex
(B) Full-Duplex
(C) Half-Duplex
(D) Broadcast

10. By default, how many VLANs are there on a managed switch?

(A) Zero
(B) One
(C) Two
(D) One per interface

# Further reading

To find out more about switches, visit `https://www.cisco.com/c/en/us/solutions/small-business/resource-center/networking/network-switch-what.html#~switches`.

# Routers and Routing - Beyond a Single Network

7

In this age of inter-connectivity and global communication, we must start to look at communicating between networks rather than just between devices on the same subnet. One key component of this communication is the router. This ubiquitous network device allows for efficient communication between networks, whether these are networks internal to our organization or remote networks on the other side of the world. After switches, this is arguably one of the most important network devices for a network engineer to understand.

This chapter introduces the concept of routing and provides you with an explanation of how routing decisions are made. Various routing protocols are explained and the characteristics of each provided. Also, we will introduce you to the concepts of **Network Address Translation (NAT)** and **Quality of Service (QoS)**.

The following topics will be covered in this chapter:

- Making routing decisions
- Understanding static and default routes
- Understanding routing protocols
- Implementing routing using Windows Server
- Understanding NAT
- Understanding QoS

## Technical requirements

To complete the exercises in this chapter, you will require a PC running a Windows OS, preferably Windows 10.

# Making routing decisions

Regardless of which protocol is in use, the premise is the same: the path chosen is the one with the smallest metric. Admittedly, I've oversimplified this, but I wanted to give you an overview before moving on.

All routing devices hold a routing table that contains information about the networks, interfaces, and metrics. Even your Windows PC will have a routing table. And that is where I'm going to start.

# Windows OS routing table

While we tend to consider routing as something that is performed on a router or a server configured for routing, your computer also performs routing functions. The next activity introduces you to the Windows OS routing table.

**Activity 1:**

1. On your Windows PC, open Command Prompt and type `route print`.
2. This will provide details of your routing table. Keep this open to compare as we go through my output (*Figure 7.1*):

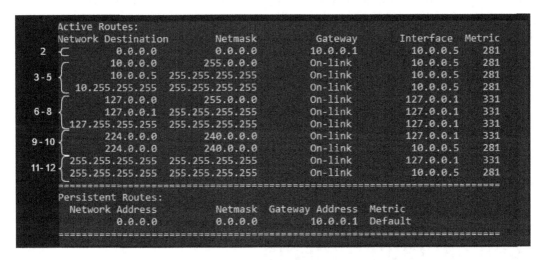

Figure 7.1: Output for route print command

The top row of the output is the headers:

- `Network Destination`: This shows either the network address, a specific IP address, or the broadcast address.
- `Netmask`: This is another term for the subnet mask.
- `Gateway`: If the network is outside of your subnet, this is the default gateway to which the data is sent.
- `Interface`: This lists the IP address of the local interface (that is, the one on the device) from which the data will be sent.
- `Metric`: This is the metric value attributed to that route/interface.

The remaining rows show the network details, and we will examine these in turn:

- Row **2** shows a destination network of `0.0.0.0`. This is a default route and is used as a fallback if no other entry in the routing table can be used. It shows a netmask of `0.0.0.0`, which, in essence, means don't worry about what subnet the destination is on, but, most importantly, it gives you a gateway IP address. This is the address of the default gateway; it then says which interface on the device the data is sent from and refers to it by its IP address. Finally, it gives the metric value.
- Rows **3 - 5** relate to the local network that the device is on. Row **3** shows the address of the network, `10.0.0.0` (we will cover this in more detail in `Chapter 11`, *Understanding IPv4*); it then shows the subnet mask for the network, `255.0.0.0`. The gateway column shows `On-link`. This is just a way of saying that this network is on the same link or subnet as the interface, and it does not have to go to a default gateway. Then, we have the interface and metric columns as before.
- Row **4** shows the IP address of the interface, `10.0.0.5`, and a subnet mask of `255.255.255.255`. This subnet mask means the whole of the IP address has to match, as opposed to row **3**, where it could be anything in the network. In essence, this row is telling the device that any traffic destined for itself is basically routed back into itself. This may seem odd, but some applications will be configured to talk to a service that is running on the device, and this helps it. For example, a DNS server still needs to know which DNS server it needs to query, even if that is itself.
- Row **5** shows the broadcast IP address of the network, `10.255.255.255`, and again a subnet mask of `255.255.255.255`. The remainder is as before. If any traffic is destined for the network's broadcast address, it knows to send it out through the interface the IP address stated sits on.

We generally see a group of three network destinations in a routing table on a Windows device for each normal network. The first row in the group is the network address, the second row is an interface address, and the third row, the broadcast IP address.

- Continuing with our example, the next three rows (**6 - 8**) relate to the loopback network.
- Rows **9 - 10** relate to multicast networks. Notice that row **9** has an interface IP of 127.0.0.1, and row **10** has the IP address of 10.0.0.5—this is telling us that any multicast traffic needs to be sent from both interfaces. Likewise, the last two rows (**11 - 12**) refer to the general broadcast address and have the same interfaces as the multicast group.

You may be wondering why there is a subnet-specific broadcast address, and a general broadcast address. Imagine you had a device that had two network interface cards. They would most likely be on different networks. If we wanted to broadcast from both cards, we would use the general broadcast address, whereas if we wanted to broadcast just to devices on the one subnet, we would use the network-specific address.

Don't worry if you haven't quite grasped broadcast addresses and loopback addresses. We will cover these in more detail in Chapter 11, *Understanding IPv4*.

# Routers

In this section, we are going to look at the routing table on a router. You will be presented with two different topologies with numerous networks within them. We will look at how these networks are represented in the routing table for each of the topologies. Initially, we are going to use the topology shown in *Figure 7.2*:

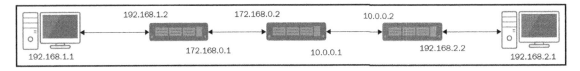

Figure 7.2: Simple routed network

This section contains several screenshots from a Cisco router terminal. These are for illustrative purposes; you do not need to know them for the exam.

In this example, you can see that we have three routers, but initially, we will just focus on one router. *Figure 7.3* shows the routing table of the router on the left before it has been configured to use one of the dynamic routing protocols. We can see in this screenshot that, despite not being configured to use a protocol, there are some entries in it already. Similar to the Windows routing table, the device has learned these by itself, as they are connected to it.

The rows beginning with L refer to the IP address of the router's interfaces. /32 is another way of writing the subnet mask is 255.255.255.255. 32 refers to the number of bits allocated to the subnet mask. We will cover this topic in more detail in Chapter 11, *Understanding IPv4*. These IP addresses would be set as the default gateway on devices within their respective subnets. The rows beginning with C refer to the networks that are directly connected to the router. The first C row shows the network address for the network, 172.16.0.0/16. The /16 notation is another way of writing the subnet mask is 255.255.0.0. The second C row shows the network address, 192.168.1.0/24. This time, the /24 notation refers to a subnet mask of 255.255.255.0:

```
Router#show ip route
Codes: L - local, C - connected, S - static, R - RIP, M - mobile, B - BGP
       D - EIGRP, EX - EIGRP external, O - OSPF, IA - OSPF inter area
       N1 - OSPF NSSA external type 1, N2 - OSPF NSSA external type 2
       E1 - OSPF external type 1, E2 - OSPF external type 2, E - EGP
       i - IS-IS, L1 - IS-IS level-1, L2 - IS-IS level-2, ia - IS-IS inter area
       * - candidate default, U - per-user static route, o - ODR
       P - periodic downloaded static route

Gateway of last resort is not set

      172.16.0.0/16 is variably subnetted, 2 subnets, 2 masks
C        172.16.0.0/16 is directly connected, GigabitEthernet0/0
L        172.16.0.1/32 is directly connected, GigabitEthernet0/0
      192.168.1.0/24 is variably subnetted, 2 subnets, 2 masks
C        192.168.1.0/24 is directly connected, GigabitEthernet0/1
L        192.168.1.2/32 is directly connected, GigabitEthernet0/1
```

Figure 7.3: Basic routing table

Let's look at it now that I have configured a routing protocol, RIP (*Figure 7.4*). The rows beginning with R indicate that these routes have been learned through the use of the RIP routing protocol. We can see that the first R row tells us that the 10.0.0.0/8 network is accessible via the IP address, 172.168.0.2 (the IP address on the connected interface on the adjacent router), which, in turn, can be reached through the internet at GigabitEthernet0/1:

```
Router#show ip route
Codes: L - local, C - connected, S - static, R - RIP, M - mobile, B - BGP
       D - EIGRP, EX - EIGRP external, O - OSPF, IA - OSPF inter area
       N1 - OSPF NSSA external type 1, N2 - OSPF NSSA external type 2
       E1 - OSPF external type 1, E2 - OSPF external type 2, E - EGP
       i - IS-IS, L1 - IS-IS level-1, L2 - IS-IS level-2, ia - IS-IS inter area
       * - candidate default, U - per-user static route, o - ODR
       P - periodic downloaded static route

Gateway of last resort is not set

R    10.0.0.0/8 [120/1] via 172.168.0.2, 00:00:23, GigabitEthernet0/1
     172.168.0.0/16 is variably subnetted, 2 subnets, 2 masks
C       172.168.0.0/16 is directly connected, GigabitEthernet0/1
L       172.168.0.1/32 is directly connected, GigabitEthernet0/1
     192.168.1.0/24 is variably subnetted, 2 subnets, 2 masks
C       192.168.1.0/24 is directly connected, GigabitEthernet0/0
L       192.168.1.2/32 is directly connected, GigabitEthernet0/0
R    192.168.2.0/24 [120/2] via 172.168.0.2, 00:00:23, GigabitEthernet0/1
```

Figure 7.4: Routing table after RIP has been configured

The preceding examples reflect the output on a simple topology. Let's now look at the routing table for the topology shown in *Figure 7.5*:

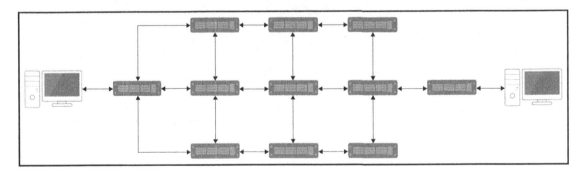

Figure 7.5: Larger routed network

As you can see, this has a few more routers than the previous example. The routing tables for this are in *Figure 7.6*. This screenshot is really for illustrative purposes to show you how the routing table can grow in size. You do not need to be able to interpret this for the exam:

```
Router#show ip route
Codes: C - connected, S - static, I - IGRP, R - RIP, M - mobile, B - BGP
       D - EIGRP, EX - EIGRP external, O - OSPF, IA - OSPF inter area
       N1 - OSPF NSSA external type 1, N2 - OSPF NSSA external type 2
       E1 - OSPF external type 1, E2 - OSPF external type 2, E - EGP
       i - IS-IS, L1 - IS-IS level-1, L2 - IS-IS level-2, ia - IS-IS inter area
       * - candidate default, U - per-user static route, o - ODR
       P - periodic downloaded static route

Gateway of last resort is not set

C    192.168.1.0/24 is directly connected, FastEthernet1/0
C    192.168.2.0/24 is directly connected, FastEthernet4/0
C    192.168.3.0/24 is directly connected, FastEthernet0/0
C    192.168.4.0/24 is directly connected, FastEthernet5/0
R    192.168.5.0/24 [120/1] via 192.168.2.3, 00:00:03, FastEthernet4/0
                    [120/1] via 192.168.3.3, 00:00:16, FastEthernet0/0
R    192.168.6.0/24 [120/1] via 192.168.3.3, 00:00:16, FastEthernet0/0
                    [120/1] via 192.168.4.3, 00:00:21, FastEthernet5/0
R    192.168.7.0/24 [120/1] via 192.168.2.3, 00:00:03, FastEthernet4/0
R    192.168.8.0/24 [120/1] via 192.168.3.3, 00:00:16, FastEthernet0/0
R    192.168.9.0/24 [120/1] via 192.168.4.3, 00:00:21, FastEthernet5/0
R    192.168.10.0/24 [120/2] via 192.168.2.3, 00:00:03, FastEthernet4/0
R    192.168.11.0/24 [120/2] via 192.168.4.3, 00:00:21, FastEthernet5/0
R    192.168.12.0/24 [120/2] via 192.168.2.3, 00:00:03, FastEthernet4/0
R    192.168.13.0/24 [120/3] via 192.168.2.3, 00:00:03, FastEthernet4/0
                     [120/3] via 192.168.4.3, 00:00:21, FastEthernet5/0
R    192.168.14.0/24 [120/2] via 192.168.4.3, 00:00:21, FastEthernet5/0
R    192.168.15.0/24 [120/3] via 192.168.2.3, 00:00:03, FastEthernet4/0
R    192.168.16.0/24 [120/3] via 192.168.4.3, 00:00:21, FastEthernet5/0
R    192.168.17.0/24 [120/4] via 192.168.2.3, 00:00:03, FastEthernet4/0
                     [120/4] via 192.168.4.3, 00:00:21, FastEthernet5/0
R    192.168.18.0/24 [120/5] via 192.168.2.3, 00:00:03, FastEthernet4/0
                     [120/5] via 192.168.4.3, 00:00:21, FastEthernet5/0
```

Figure 7.6: Consolidated routing table

If you look at the first row starting with R (for RIP), you can see there is an entry for 192.168.5.0/24 while the next row does not specify the network. This means that both rows relate to the same network, so in this example, there are two routes from this router to that network. Which other networks have two routes to them?

Each of the routing protocols discussed previously will have some limitations as to how much information it will store in its routing table. It would be unfeasible to know the route to each network in the world.

# Decision making

Although the routing algorithms used by routing devices can be quite complicated, the process they then take to make their routing decisions is relatively simple, as you can see from the following steps:

1. Once a router receives data from another device, it checks the destination IP address.
2. If it is its own address, it will process it internally. If the address is for one of the networks connected to it or a remote network, the router looks it up in its routing table.
3. It then identifies the IP address of the next router (next hop) and the interface the data needs to be sent from.

In *Figures 7.4* and *Figure 7.5* in the previous sub-section, you will notice that both of these values were listed in the routing table in a single entry. Some devices will have to follow a two-step process, that is, find the next hop address, and then look that up in the routing table to identify the interface to send the data through.

If there are two or more possible routes, the routing device chooses the one with the lowest metric.

Now, let's learn how the router uses **Time To Live** (**TTL**) to prevent data being sent in a routing loop.

# TTL

There is the possibility that data could be sent in a massive routing loop. For example, a router may receive some data and route it back to a router that has already seen the data, which then causes a loop. Potentially, data could be on the network forever. One of the ways this is avoided is through the use of TTL.

Every packet of data that is sent out includes a TTL value within the IP packet header. This refers to the number of hops data can go through before it is discarded. The Windows default TTL is 128 hops, though this can be adjusted by applications. To facilitate this, on receiving data, each router decrements the TTL value by 1. When a router receives some data with a TTL value of 1, it decrements it to 0 and sends an *unreachable* message back to the originator.

In this section, we have understood how routing decisions are made. In the next section, we will learn about static and default routes.

# Understanding static and default routes

Because we cannot document every network in a routing table, we need to know what to do with the data if the network is not listed. Quite simply, we have a catch-all route that, in essence, says if you have gone through the routing table and cannot find a match for this destination, then send it from this particular interface to this other router and let them sort it out. If the other router does not know, it will do the same.

Basically, we are playing pass the parcel with the data in the hope that it is finally received by a routing device that actually knows where the destination network is. Remember, the TTL will be counting down at each device. If no default route has been configured, then the data is simply discarded and an error message is sent back to the originating device.

A configured default route is a form of static route. An administrator had to manually enter it into the routing table. As well as the default route, there are possibly other reasons for configuring a static route. Perhaps you are sending sensitive data and need to be assured that it is going through certain routers. Remember, dynamic routing reacts to changes in the network such as failures, so it would not be able to guarantee the route the sensitive data is traversing.

The use of static routes needs to be assessed properly before implementation. If a device on a static route fails, the data will not reach the intended recipient, as the route will not have automatically changed to navigate around the fault. Also, the static route has to be configured on all devices that the data is routed through.

# Understanding routing protocols

A lot of people have this notion that routing involves some form of device that takes your data from your internal network and routes it out on to the internet. In part, this is correct, but for me, it is too specific a description and can be slightly misleading. A better definition would be that routing takes data from a network and forwards it through one or more networks to reach a destination network. These networks could be private to private, private to public, private to public to private, and any combination of any number of networks to get to the final destination.

In this subsection, I will briefly describe routing devices, and then talk about the common routing protocols available to us.

## Routing devices

At this level, we can generally sum routers up into three different categories: dedicated routers, layer 3 switches, and servers configured with routing capabilities. All of these devices have one thing in common: the ability to forward or route data based on the layer 3 address or, as it is popularly known, the IP address.

Besides providing routing capabilities, most routers will provide additional functionality such as NAT, QoS, and the ability to block broadcast transmissions. The first two are covered later in this chapter, but I would like to briefly explain here why routers block broadcast traffic and provide the limits to what is known as a **broadcast domain**. A broadcast domain is a collection of devices that can receive a broadcast transmission from each other. Each interface on a router is classed as its own broadcast domain. Each of these broadcast domains can have multiple collision domains. There is one exception to routers blocking broadcast traffic. If the traffic being transmitted is DHCP traffic, then routers that are RFC 1542-compliant will only forward that broadcast traffic.

Look at *Figure 7.7*: it is a fairly simple topology, made up of four networks connected to the internet. Notice that each network has a router that connects it to the internet or WAN. Inside each network is a switch that acts as an intermediary device allowing communications between the router and the endpoint devices. In this case, the endpoint devices are represented by the laptop:

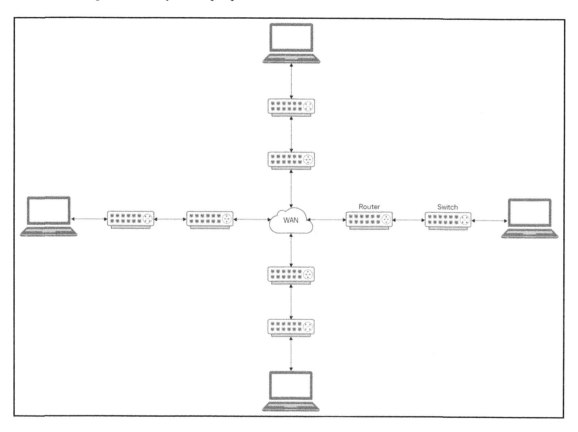

Figure 7.7: Basic topology

If a routing device acted like a switch and forwarded a broadcast transmission, it would be sent from all interfaces and out on to the internet. The internet is connected to lots of routing devices. If each of those routing devices did the same, that one data transmission could potentially keep going until it is finally dropped (more on this later). Now imagine if all devices on every network in the world were broadcasting (which they are). The *noise* of all this data being transmitted would impair any useful data actually being transmitted. Therefore, routers are designed to drop any broadcast traffic.

As the name implies, a dedicated router is a hardware device specifically designed for routing data between networks. In some ways, routers are similar to switches in that they have multiple interfaces, can have modular components, and are configured initially through a console port. Unlike some switches, however, routers are always going to be classed as a managed device, as you will need to configure them. Dedicated routers will also have the ability to support various routing protocols.

A layer 3 switch has the same functionality as a layer 2 switch, with the added ability to route traffic between different VLANs without the need for a further routing device. It is important to remember that a layer 3 switch is not designed to fully replace your routers on a network.

Depending on its operating system, a server can be configured with the capacity to route traffic from one network to another. To do so, the server needs to have at least two network interface cards, one for each network that it will support. Obviously, the physical capacity and processing ability of a device such as this will not be in the same league as a dedicated router.

One important thing to note is that any routing device has to have at least two interfaces. Each of these interfaces on a router or routing server has to be allocated an IP address that is within the same network range as the network that is connected to it. That interface IP address will be the default gateway for the device on that network (*Figure 7.8*):

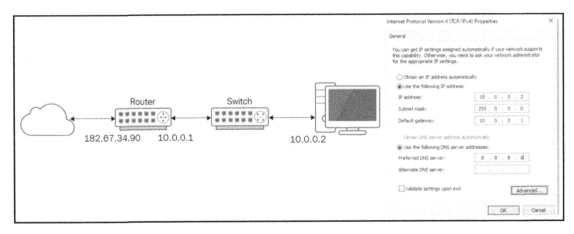

Figure 7.8: Default gateway

I have already mentioned that routers support different routing protocols, and I will discuss these further. A routing protocol is a published standard that developers and engineers follow when creating software/hardware that will carry out routing. One of the key components of these standards is that they each contain an algorithm that calculates the optimal route (or path) to destination networks. These algorithms are re-run regularly, hence, we are creating a network with the ability to adapt to changes. If there is a *break* somewhere on the route between two devices, the network will identify this and re-route traffic accordingly. We refer to these as dynamic routing protocols.

In addition to these, we can also create static routes. Dynamic routing protocols can generally be broken down into a distance vector, link state, or path vector. Understanding how these work in depth is beyond the scope of the exam. Therefore, this chapter merely entails a brief overview.

To enable dynamic routing to work, each router will share its routing table with its neighbors, and by doing so, each router builds up a picture of how the network is configured. Depending on the protocol, this exchange of data may take place at regular intervals, when a change is made, or both. From this exchange of data, the router calculates a metric or a value that helps it to determine the interface from which the data will be sent.

# Distance vector protocols

A distance vector protocol is one that calculates the best route for the data to be transmitted, purely based on how many routers or hops the data has to travel through to get to the final destination. The term can be broken down into two components—distance and vector.

Distance is the metric (that is, the number of hops) it uses to determine the path; vector indicates the direction of travel—that is, which interface the data will be sent through. Routers utilizing a distance vector protocol exchange information about the finished routes only. You can refer to the `tracert` activity that we carried out in Chapter 3, *Understanding Wide Area Networks*, and have reproduced the following for ease:

**Activity 2**:

1. Open Command Prompt on a Windows PC.
2. Trace the route to Google's public DNS server using the `tracert 8.8.8.8` command.
3. Review the output:

```
C:\Users\User>tracert 8.8.8.8

Tracing route to google-public-dns-a.google.com [8.8.8.8]
over a maximum of 30 hops:

  1     1 ms     1 ms     1 ms   vodafone.broadband [192.168.1.1]
  2    19 ms    21 ms    26 ms   host-212-158-250-32.dslgb.com [212.158.250.32]
  3    13 ms    13 ms    12 ms   63.130.105.130
  4    12 ms    12 ms    12 ms   72.14.216.237
  5     *        *        *      Request timed out.
  6    13 ms    13 ms    13 ms   216.239.63.136
  7    30 ms    31 ms    30 ms   216.239.50.73
  8    13 ms    13 ms    13 ms   google-public-dns-a.google.com [8.8.8.8]

Trace complete.
```

Figure 7.9: Output for tracert command

Looking at the first column I have highlighted in the preceding screenshot, you can see the hop count and that the destination was eight hops away. The second highlighted area is the response time—how long it takes for the message to go to each device and receive a reply. Notice that it does this three times per hop. At hop 5, you can see there are no response times, but * instead. This means that the device has not sent a response in a reasonable time (hence, `Request timed out` on the right), which could be indicative of a firewall not permitting `tracert` response traffic. The last highlighted area shows the IP address of the device at each hop, and, where possible, it also resolves the name of the device. Notice, in lines 3 and 4, for example, that there is only an IP address.

Protocols that fall under the guise of distance vector routing protocols include the following:

- **Routing Information Protocol (RIP)** v1, v2, and **ng (next generation)**
- **Interior Gateway Routing Protocol (IGRP)**

Each of these protocols has specific use cases that will help you to determine which one is the best one for your purposes.

The problem with using a distance vector protocol is that they do not take into consideration any other factors, such as the speed of the links. Let's put aside networking for the moment and let's say you want to go and visit your uncle. The most direct route is 120 miles, but this is all small country roads, so you cannot go very fast. If you go down the motorway, it is 125 miles, but you can go much faster (legally of course). A distance vector protocol would send you down the country roads, despite it taking you longer.

We'll go back to networking now. Look at *Figure 7.10*. Notice that the shortest route is that straight line of routers between the two PCs, but that is not the fastest route. Let's look at that a moment with an example. For this example and simplicity, we have a 10 Gb file (note: gigabit not gigabyte) that we want to send from the PC on the left to the PC on the right.

If we were to take the most direct route through the middle, it passes over five routers. To transfer data from the first router to the second, it would take 10 seconds, and likewise between the second and third, and between the third and fourth; from the fourth to the fifth router it would take 1 second. That's a total of 31 seconds.

If we were to take the top route, it passes over six routers. To transfer data from the first router to the second would take 1 second; from the second to the third, it would take 10 seconds, and 1 second for each of the hops between the third and fourth, the fourth and fifth, and the fifth and sixth routers. That's a total of 14 seconds.

Obviously, this has been simplified, but I feel this emphasizes how the shortest route is not necessarily the quickest:

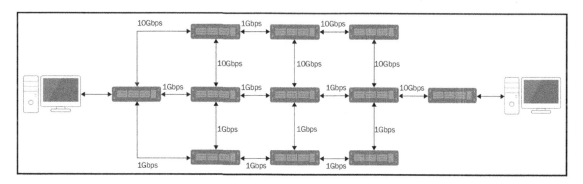

Figure 7.10: Choosing a route based on distance

Surely, it would be better to go the faster route? We'll now look at link state protocols, which actually consider more factors than just the number of hops

# Link state protocols

Link state protocols do not base their routing decisions purely on distance, but can factor in attributes such as the bandwidth of the connection, delay, jitter, and load. Each protocol will use one or more of these values in its routing algorithm to identify the best path. Unlike distance vector protocols, link state protocols exchange everything in terms of the state of each link and form a roadmap of the network to decide routes based on that information.

Protocols that fall under the guise of link state routing protocols include the following:

- **Open Shortest Path First (OSPF)**
- **Intermediate System to Intermediate System (IS-IS)**

Distance vector and link state protocols are the main types of routing protocol. However, we will now briefly look at two other types.

# Hybrid protocols

A protocol that combines the capabilities of both distance vector protocols and link state protocols is known as a **hybrid protocol**. The main hybrid protocol to be aware of is the **Enhanced Interior Gateway Routing Protocol (EIGRP)**. Originally a Cisco proprietary protocol, this routing protocol has since been converted to an open standard. Interestingly, Cisco tends to refer to this protocol as an advanced distance vector protocol rather than a hybrid protocol.

# Path vector protocol

The final routing protocol is path vector. In this protocol, the router knows the IP address of the next router and the actual path that the data will be sent along. This differs from the previous protocol types in that path vector protocols do not know the complete path, just the next router on the path.

The only routing protocol of note that falls under this category is the **Border Gateway Protocol (BGP)**.

Now, let's learn about the **Interior Gateway Protocol (IGP)** and **Exterior Gateway Protocol (EGP)** and compare them.

# IGP versus EGP

To understand these two terms, it is important to understand the **Autonomous System (AS)**. An AS is a collection of networks that fall under the control of one organization. This may be an ISP or any large enterprise organization. An AS number is allocated by the **Internet Assigned Numbers Authority (IANA)**, who delegate the responsibility to local registrars.

IGP is a generic term referring to any protocol responsible for routing within your own AS. Each of the protocols listed in the distance vector and link state sections fall under this umbrella.

In contrast, an EGP refers to any protocol responsible for routing between different autonomous systems. The only protocols this applies to are EGP and BGP.

**Activity 3**: Navigate to this website, `https://www.ultratools.com/tools/asnInfo`, and search for a website. In the top-left of the results box is the AS number. Repeat the same exercise for your public IP address.

**Exam tip**: Do not overthink the different protocols. Just be able to recognize which protocol falls under which category.

# Implementing routing using Windows Server

We previously mentioned in this chapter that a server can be configured to act as a routing device. In this section, we will look at how we can implement this using Windows Server 2019. Recall that any routing device needs to have at least two network interfaces. In the following activity, we will be using a server that has two interfaces configured with IP addresses on different networks (*Figure 7.11*):

```
C:\Users\Administrator>ipconfig

Windows IP Configuration


Ethernet adapter Ethernet:

   Connection-specific DNS Suffix  . :
   Link-local IPv6 Address . . . . . : fe80::3ccb:5a84:ab48:6486%5
   IPv4 Address. . . . . . . . . . . : 10.2.0.1
   Subnet Mask . . . . . . . . . . . : 255.0.0.0
   Default Gateway . . . . . . . . . : 0.0.0.0

Ethernet adapter Ethernet 2:

   Connection-specific DNS Suffix  . :
   Link-local IPv6 Address . . . . . : fe80::c1af:75eb:8086:5538%10
   IPv4 Address. . . . . . . . . . . : 172.16.0.1
   Subnet Mask . . . . . . . . . . . : 255.255.0.0
   Default Gateway . . . . . . . . . : 0.0.0.0
```

Figure 7.11: Output of ipconfig

The following activities assume that you have installed a Windows Server OS already. In some of my screenshots, you may see references to domains. Do not worry if you have not configured a domain; you should be able to follow this activity without this.

# Installing roles and features

**Activity 4**: In this activity, we will install the requisite roles and features:

1. Open Server Manager if it's not already open.
2. Click **Add roles and features**:

Figure 7.12: Server Manager dashboard

3. On the **Before You Begin** screen, click **Next**.
4. On the **Select installation type** screen, choose **Role-based or feature-based installation**:

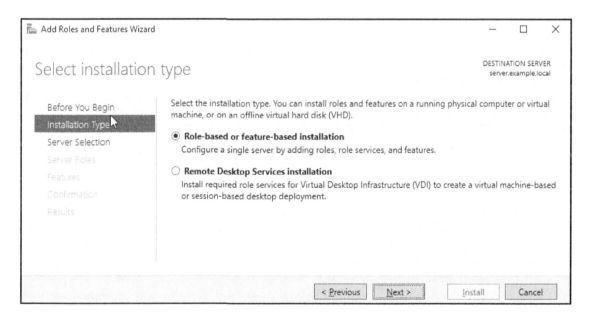

Figure 7.13: Selecting installation type

5. The **Select destination server** screen should automatically have selected your server. Check it has done so, and click **Next**:

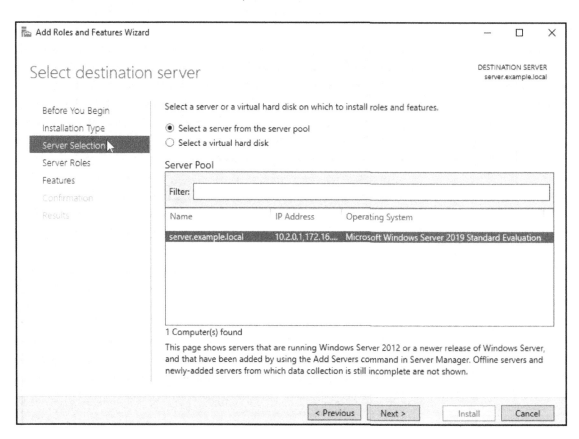

Figure 7.14: Selecting the destination server

6. Select the **Remote Access** role and click **Next**. Note that the options on the left-hand side will appear different to those shown in the following screenshot until you have selected the role:

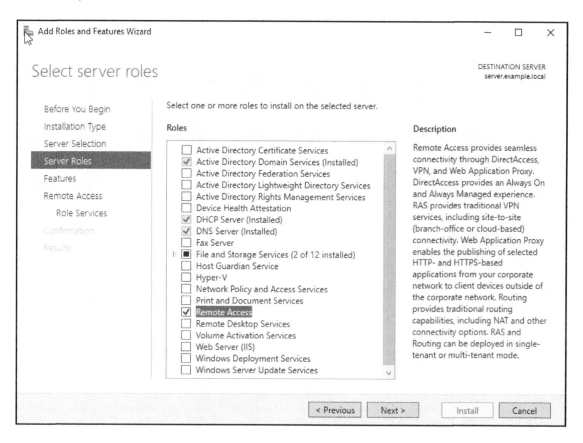

Figure 7.15: Selecting server roles

7. Click **Next** on the **Select features** screen.

8. Click **Next** on the **Remote Access** information screen.

9. Select **Routing** on the **Select role services** screen.

10. You will be prompted to add features. Click on **Add Features**:

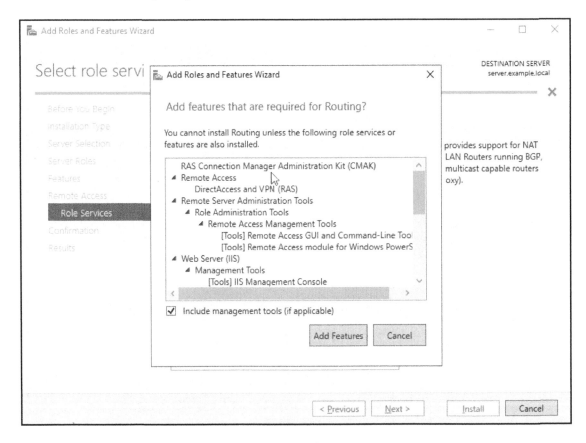

Figure 7.16: Adding features

11. Note that this will also select **DirectAccess and VPN (RAS)**. Click **Next**:

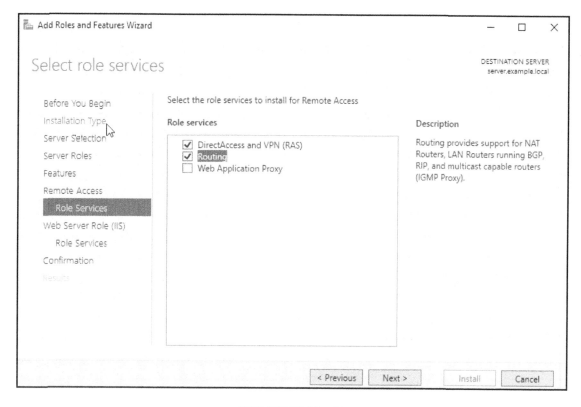

Figure 7.17: Selecting role services

12. Click **Next** until you reach the **Confirm installation selections** screen. Click **Install**:

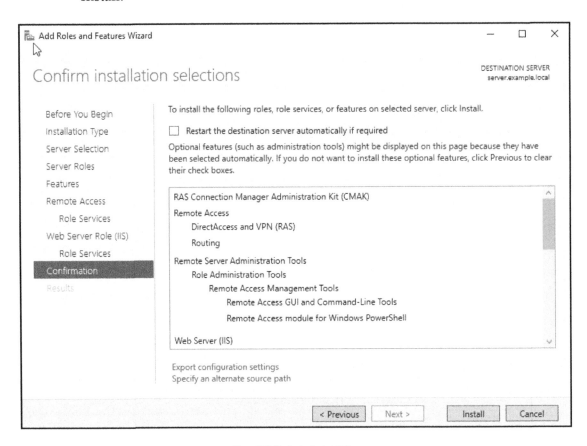

Figure 7.18: Confirming the installation

13. Once the installation has completed, click **Close**.

With this, the selected roles and features will be installed. Moving on, through the next activity, we will now configure the routing component that we have just installed.

# Configuring the routing and remote access component

**Activity 5**: In this activity, we will configure the routing component we have just installed:

1. Open Server Manager if it is not already open.
2. Click **Tools**, and select **Routing and Remote Access** from the drop-down menu:

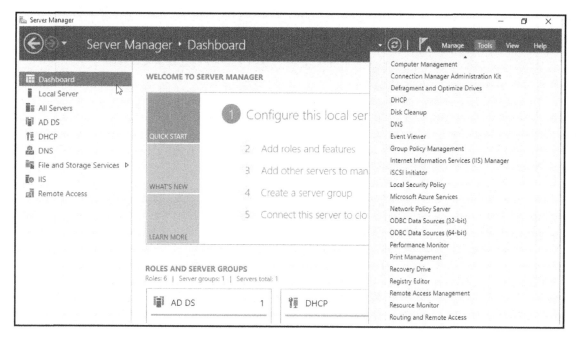

Figure 7.19: Server Manager dashboard

3. This will open the **Routing and Remote Access** management console. Note that **SERVER (local)** has a red down arrow displayed. This indicates that it has not been configured:

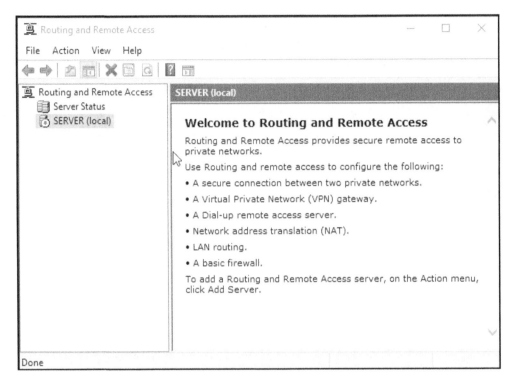

Figure 7.20: Routing and Remote Access console

4. Right-click on **SERVER (local)** and select **Configure and Enable Routing and Remote Access** to open the wizard:

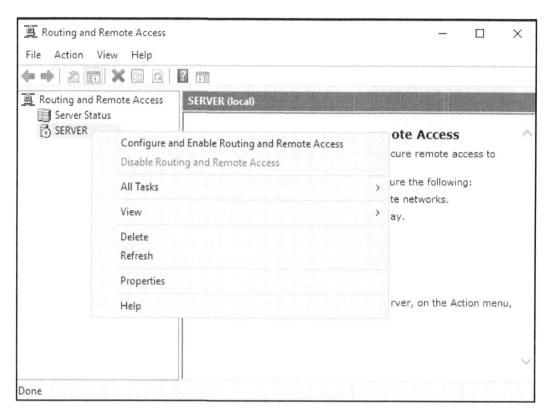

Figure 7.21: Configuring and enabling remote access

5.  At the welcome screen of the wizard, click **Next**:

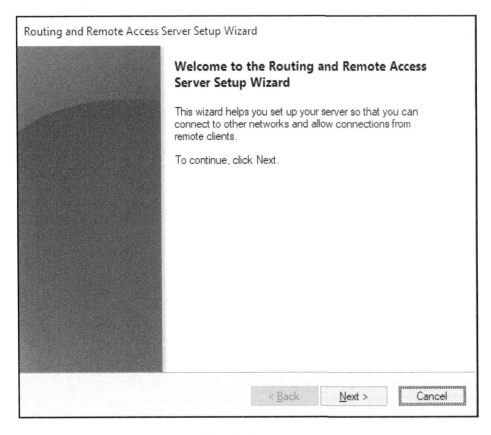

Figure 7.22: Welcome screen

6. On the **Configuration** screen, choose **Custom configuration** and click **Next**:

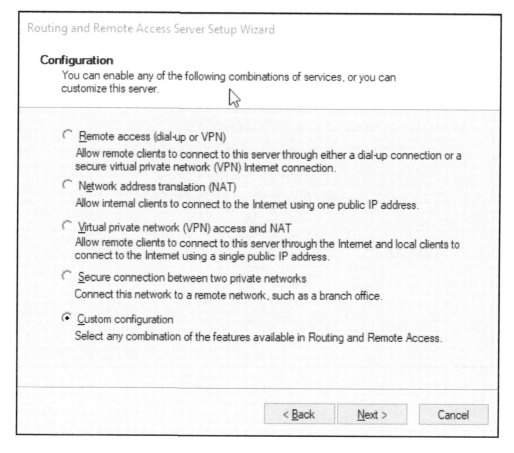

Figure 7.23: Configuration screen

7. Choose **LAN routing** on the **Custom Configuration** screen and click **Next**:

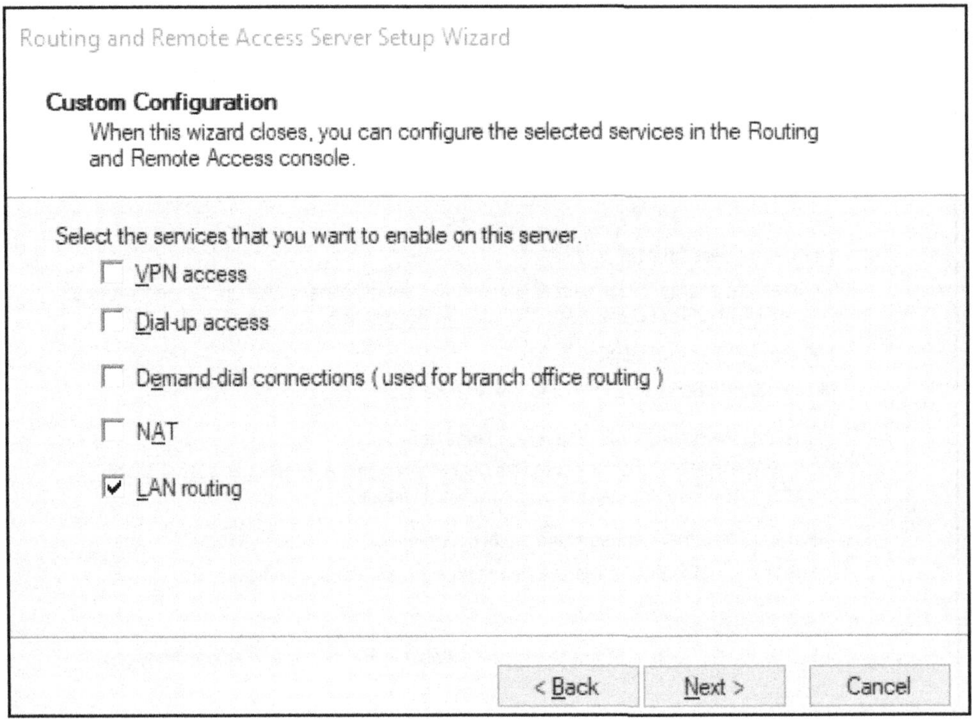

Figure 7.24: Custom Configuration screen

8. Click **Finish** on the summary screen. There will be a short delay as the system processes this.

9. Click **Start service** at the prompt:

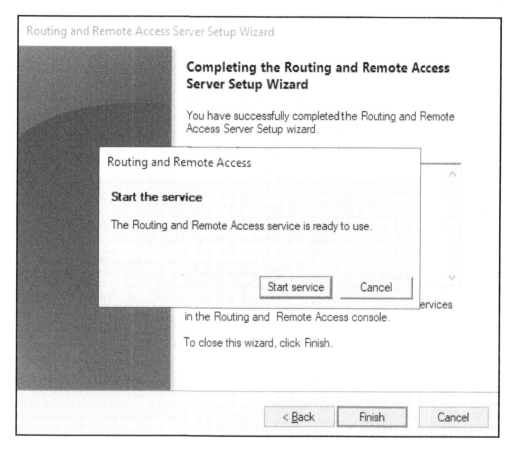

Figure 7.25: Starting the service

10. You will notice that **SERVER (local)** no longer has a red arrow:

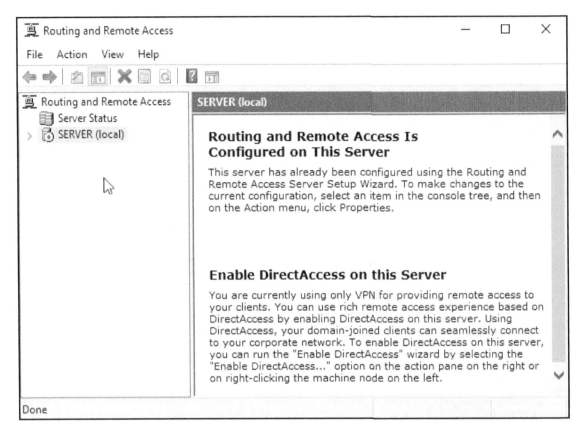

Figure 7.26: Routing and Remote Access console

11. Expand **SERVER (local)** to show the various sub-components:

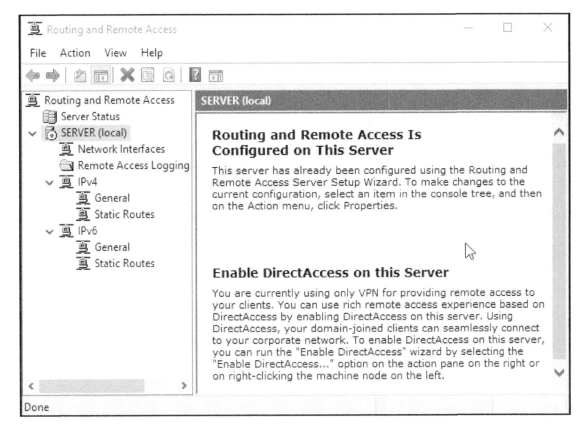

Figure 7.27: Server (local) sub-components

12. Investigate all of the various areas by selecting them and right-clicking.

Note that you are not expected to know this area in any detail for the exam.

While we would prefer to use dynamic routing, there will be occasions when a static route needs to configured. We will see how to do this in the next activity.

# Configuring a static IPv4 route

**Activity 6**: For this final short activity, we will configure a static IPv4 route:

1. Select **Static Routes** in the **IPv4** section:

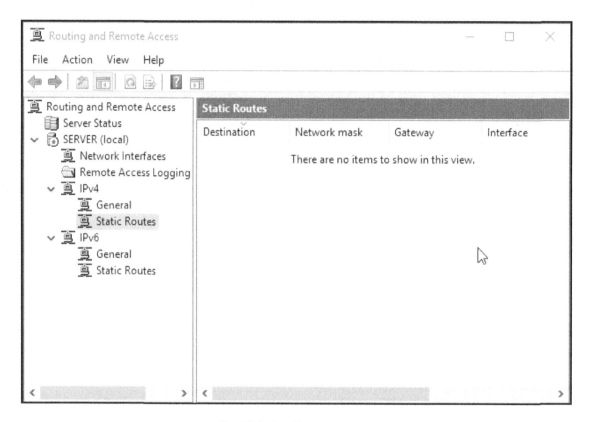

Figure 7.28: Routing and Remote Access console

2. Right-click in the white space in the main window, and choose **New Static Route...**:

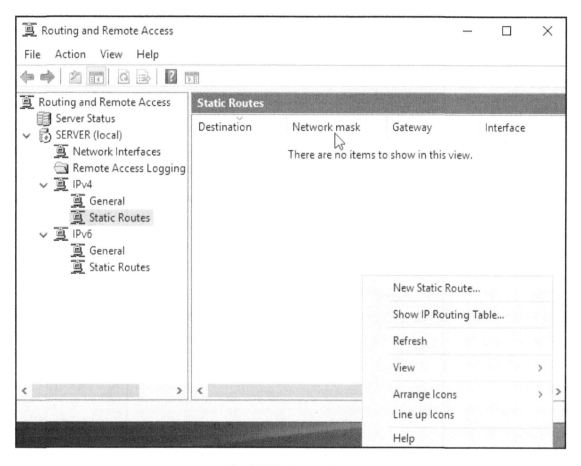

Figure 7.29: Selecting a new static route

3. Configure the various options and click **OK**:

- **Interface**: Which of the available interfaces is the static route being configured on?
- **Destination**: This can be either the network ID of the destination network or, if you are configuring a static route to a specific device, the IP address of the device. In this case, I have chosen a network ID.
- **Network mask**: This is used to identify the IP address range to be covered. It works using a similar principle to subnet masks.
- **Gateway**: This is the default gateway of the network this particular interface is connected to.
- **Metric**: This is the metric value you want to assign to the route. Remember that the lower the value, the more preferred the route is:

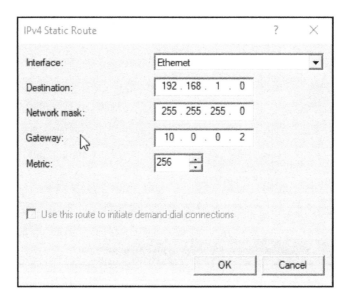

Figure 7.30: Options for a new static route

4. The static route will now appear in the management console:

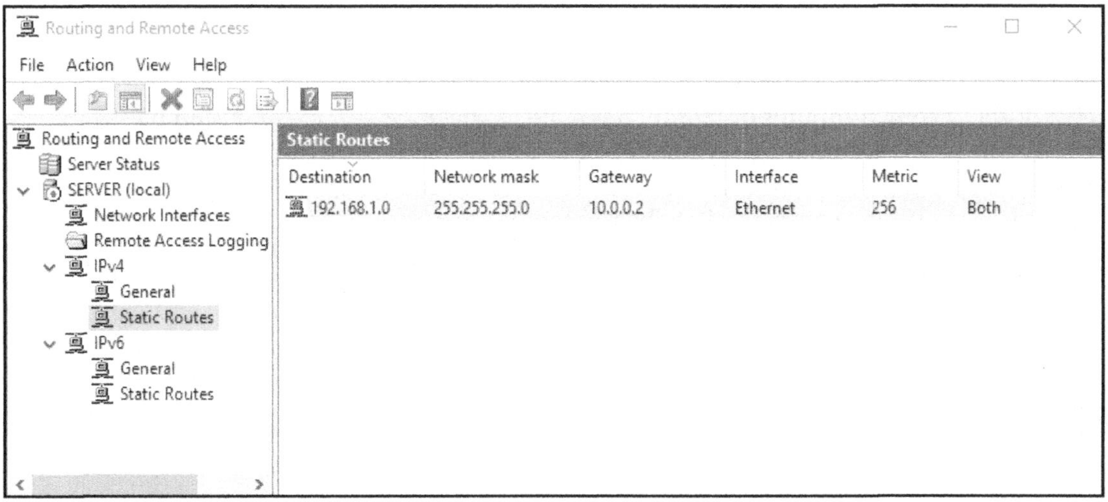

Figure 7.31: Routing and Remote Access console

Note, we could also configure a static route from the command line using the following syntax:

```
route -p ADD <destination_network> MASK <subnet_mask>  <gateway_ip>
<metric_cost>
```

The -p switch tells the system to make this a persistent connection. That is, the static route will be restored even if the system has been rebooted. Using the static route that we configured in the last activity for this example, the command would be as follows:

```
route -p ADD 192.168.1.0 MASK 255.255.255.0  10.0.0.2 256
```

Although we have carried out these activities using a server, I would like to mention the fact that we can also set a static route on a Windows client using the preceding command.

I'm sure this section has provided you with hands-on experience to configure your server to act as a routing device. In the next section, we will walk through NAT to understand its purpose and types.

# Understanding NAT

We're going to start this section with an activity so that you can see NAT in action, and it will help you to better understand its purpose as we go through the section.

**Activity 7**: On your computer or laptop, navigate to www.google.com, and search for What's my IP?. This will display the public IP address of that device. Now, go to a second device that is connected to the same network and do the same. What do you notice about the IP address? They are very likely to be the same.

You may be thinking right now that I had previously said that IP addresses should be unique, and you would be correct. Recall that, in Chapter 2, *Understanding Local Area Networks*, I introduced the idea of private IP addresses being used inside our LAN, and public IP addresses are outside our LAN. If your network is wanting to communicate on the internet, it is going to need a public IP address.

Take a look at *Figure 7.32*, and notice that, in the leftmost and rightmost networks, there is a device with the same IP address. Let's say that PC1 connects to a website: how does it know to send it PC1 and not PC2? Quite simply, it doesn't respond to that IP address; it responds back to the public IP address of the router on the left (126.6.2.3). The router will then send the data to PC1. This is where NAT comes into play:

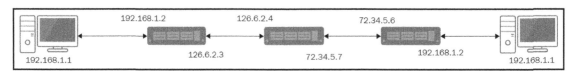

Figure 7.32: Duplicate IP address in different LANs

NAT takes a private IP address and converts it to a public IP address, and vice versa. There are several different ways in which it achieves this, and we will cover these further in the sub-sections.

# Static NAT

Static NAT involves each device having its private IP address mapped to a public IP address that is used solely by that device. This will require an organization to have multiple public IP addresses assigned to them by their ISP. Obviously, this is a costly endeavor.

# Dynamic NAT

With dynamic NAT, an organization has a pool of public IP addresses, and this pool is shared by all of the devices inside the LAN. The mapping of a private IP address to one of the public IP addresses is on a first come, first served basis. If the pool runs out of IP addresses to allocate, then no further devices can communicate outside of the LAN.

# Port Address Translation

**Port Address Translation (PAT)** is a derivative of dynamic NAT, in that there is no static mapping of private IP addresses to a public IP address. With PAT (also referred to as NAT Overload), all devices share a single public IP address.

*Figure 7.33* is the same screenshot as we have just seen. We are going to use that for this explanation:

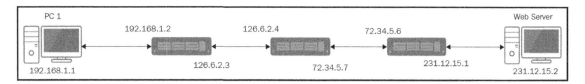

Figure 7.33: Networking with NAT

**PC 1** wants to communicate with a website. The NAT process that is followed is as follows:

1. **PC 1** opens up a network port to communicate to the web server. For this example, it opens port `64001`.
2. **PC 1** sends the data to the router.
3. The router updates its NAT table, which will look something like this:

| Source IP address | Source port | Destination IP address | Destination port |
|---|---|---|---|
| 192.168.1.1 | 64001 | 231.12.15.2 | 80 |

4. The router repackages the data it received from **PC 1**. It removes the private source IP of 192.168.1.1 and replaces it with the public IP address of the 126.6.2.3 network. The port numbers remain the same.

5. The data is routed on to the destination website.

6. The website replies back using its own IP address as the source and puts the public IP address of the destination network, 126.6.2.3, as the destination IP address. It puts the source IP as port 80, and the destination port as 64001.

7. When the destination router receives the data, it looks in its NAT table to see whether any device has communicated with that website source port, 64001, and destination port 80 (the reverse of the ports mentioned in the data transmitted from the website).

8. It sees that 192.168.1.1 meets that criteria, and it repackages the data sent from the website. It removes the public IP address, 231.12.15.1, from the destination IP field, and replaces it with 192.168.1.1. It leaves the source IP and port numbers the same.

9. The repackaged data is then sent to **PC 1**.

Not all of the data transiting across networks is of equal priority. In the next section, we look at a method for prioritizing network traffic.

# Understanding QoS

Routers that support QoS can prioritize network traffic. To be able to do this, the data being sent includes either a **Type of Service (ToS)** or **Differentiated Services (DiffServ)** indicator that allows routers to identify the type of traffic being sent, and hence allow it to be prioritized.

Typical data that would be prioritized over other traffic includes the following:

- Media streaming
- **Voice over IP (VoIP)**
- Teleconferencing
- Safety system traffic

Which data to prioritize will vary from organization to organization, and looking at the preceding examples, it should be fairly obvious why safety system traffic would need to be prioritized over normal non-safety traffic, but what about the first three examples? If we did not prioritize this traffic, we would likely find that we had performance and quality issues, with buffering occurring. This would be annoying when streaming media, but if we want the two-way communication offered by VoIP and teleconferencing, buffering and delay would make these impractical applications.

It should be noted that QoS priorities have to be configured on all routers, and if the data transits a routing device that you do not own, then you may find it as a lower priority than when it is being handled by your own network.

# Summary

In this chapter, we looked at transmitting data outside our subnets. We discussed how routers make their routing decisions to find the most efficient path to the destination. We talked about the use of static and default routes, before moving onto the various routing protocols. We explained some of the characteristics of routers. Finally, we discussed the translation of private into public addresses using NAT and then the prioritization of data with QoS.

You have learned how to identify and interpret the routing table on your Windows device. You have also learned how static and default routes impact how the data is routed. These are key to understanding how your device routes data from it, especially if it has more than one network card. Also, you can now install and configure the routing features on a Windows Server. As an extension of this, you also configured a static IPv4 route on a Windows Server. Finally, you saw how to configure a static route on any Windows system from the command line.

Now that we have seen the various topologies and intermediary devices used within our networks, we need to look at how we can physically connect the devices. In the following chapter, we do just that. We will look at copper cables in the form of coaxial cables and twisted pair cables and fiber optic. For each, we will talk about the key attributes and connectors used.

# Questions

1. Which of these devices has a routing capability?

(A) Hub
(B) Layer 2 switch
(C) Layer 3 switch
(D) Bridge

2. Which of these generic routing protocol types will most likely choose a route that goes through the least number of routers?

(A) Path vector
(B) Link state
(C) Spanning tree
(D) Distance vector

3. Which of these routing protocols is a distance vector protocol?

(A) RIP
(B) OSPF
(C) IS-IS
(D) BGP

4. Which protocol routes between autonomous systems?

(A) OSPF
(B) IS-IS
(C) BGP
(D) IGRP

5. Which of these network addresses would represent the default route on a Windows device?

(A) `127.0.0.0`
(B) `0.0.0.0`
(C) `255.255.255.255`
(D) `10.20.32.0`

6. Which of these IP addresses can be issued to the interface marked with an **X**?

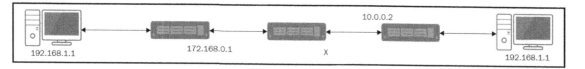

Choose the correct answer:

(A) 192.168.1.2
(B) 172.168.0.2
(C) 10.0.0.1
(D) 192.168.1.1

7. What feature prevents data from flowing between networks forever?

(A) RIP
(B) TTL
(C) STP
(D) OSPF

8. Assuming only the router selected on the right uses NAT, the translation takes place on the interface with the IP address 72.34.5.6. If the web server at 231.12.15.2 sends data to the PC at 192.168.1.1, what would the source IP address be on the data that the PC receives?

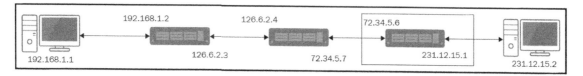

Choose the correct answer:

(A) 231.12.15.2
(B) 231.12.15.1
(C) 72.34.5.6
(D) 192.168.1.2

9. Which function allows for different types of data to be prioritized?

(A) QoS
(B) NAT
(C) DHCP
(D) EIGRP

# Further reading

Visit the following links for more information:

- **Network Address Translation**: https://tools.ietf.org/html/rfc1631
- **Routing Information Protocol**: https://tools.ietf.org/html/rfc1058
- **Bootstrap Protocol**: https://tools.ietf.org/html/rfc1542

# 8
# Media Types - Connecting Everything Together

While you are probably more than aware that most networks are wired, you should note that not every wiring standard is the same. If they were, we would only need the one. As it stands, there are numerous different standards still in operation, from legacy cables running at 10 Mbps to high-speed fiber operating at more than 40 Gbps. As a network engineer, it is imperative that we understand the use cases and limitations of the various different cabling options available to us.

This chapter will follow the progression of cabling from coaxial cables, through to twisted pair cables, to fiber optic cables, all while explaining the characteristics of each, including their connectors and their uses.

The following topics will be covered in this chapter:

- Understanding coaxial cables and their types
- Understanding twisted pair cables and their types
- Understanding fiber optic cables and their types

## Technical requirements

There are no technical requirements for this chapter.

# Understanding coaxial cables and their types

I remember when I was first learning about networking in 2000 and coaxial cables were introduced. I thought to myself, *nobody is going to use that for much longer*. For me, it was dated technology that was being replaced. Yet, it's still here. It has stood the test of time and is used in networking, audio, and video.

A coaxial cable consists of a copper core surrounded by an insulator. This, in turn, is surrounded by a woven copper shield that's encased in an outer plastic jacket. This can be seen in the following diagram:

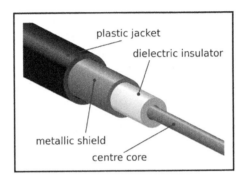

Figure 8.1: Coaxial cable

 The preceding diagram can be found at `https://en.wikipedia.org/wiki/Coaxial_cable#/media/File:Coaxial_cable_cutaway.svg`. It is licensed under Creative Commons CC BY 3.0: `https://creativecommons.org/licenses/by/3.0/deed.en`.

One of the issues with using copper to transmit data is that it gives off an electromagnetic field and can also be impacted by external electromagnetic fields generated by other nearby objects, including other network cables. Put simply, when voltage is applied to a conductive cable, an electromagnetic field is generated, which can affect other electrical systems in close proximity. When it does this, it is referred to as **electromagnetic interference (EMI)**.

EMI can be a major problem with networks using a copper cable, and hence how the cables are placed has to be thought out carefully. Major sources of EMI that can affect your network include fluorescent lights and elevator machinery. The woven copper shield acts to prevent these magnetic fields. It helps to keep the internal data signal within the confines of the cable and provides protection from external electromagnetic fields.

It should be noted that the shield will not protect the cable 100%, and some leakage and interference with the data may take place.

There are two main types of coaxial cable in use in networking. These are 10base5 and 10base2. These names follow a naming convention that roughly follows this syntax:

*<speed><signal type><medium>*

From this, we can see that both have a speed of 10 Mbps and use the baseband signaling type. Baseband utilizes the available bandwidth for one signal. Another term you will hear is broadband. Broadband splits the available bandwidth between multiple signals.

Let's take a closer look at the two coaxial cable types individually.

# 10base5 coaxial cable

10base5 is referred to as thicknet. It utilizes RG-8 cabling and can be a maximum of 500 m in length. If you were to make this any longer, the attenuation, or degradation of the signal, would be so great that it would be unusable. To connect to the cable devices, it uses a vampire tap, as shown in the following picture:

Figure 8.2: Vampire tap with thicknet cable

The preceding image can be found at `https://en.wikipedia.org/wiki/ Vampire_tap#/media/File:ThicknetTransceiver.jpg`. It is under the Creative Commons CC BY-SA 2.5: `https://creativecommons.org/ licenses/by-sa/2.5/`.

The vampire tap literally bites into the cable to make a connection. This is clearly depicted in the following picture:

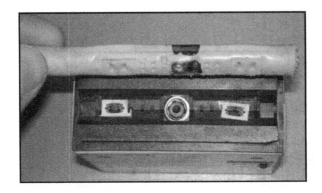

Figure 8.3: Vampire tap showing bite marks

 The preceding image can be found at `https://en.wikipedia.org/wiki/ Vampire_tap#/media/File:VampireTap.jpg`. It is under the Creative Commons CC BY-SA 2.5: `https://creativecommons.org/licenses/by- sa/2.5/`.

An alternative to the vampire tap is the N-connector, as shown in the following picture:

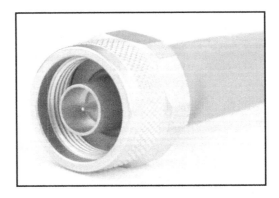

Figure 8.4: A male N-connector

The preceding image can be found at `https://commons.wikimedia.org/wiki/File:Male_type_N_connector.jpg`. It is under the Creative Commons CC BY-SA 3.0: `https://creativecommons.org/licenses/by-sa/3.0/deed.en`.

As its name implies, the thicknet cable is a thick cable, which means it's not very flexible. This makes it difficult to handle, but it is capable of handling up to 100 devices. It should be noted, however, that coaxial cables are usually found in bus topologies (`Chapter 5`, *Network Topologies – Mapping It All Out*) and are half duplex, so the more devices there are, the more contention there will be.

Now, let's learn about the 10base2 coaxial cable.

# 10base2 coaxial cable

In contrast, 10base2 is known as **thinnet**. It utilizes RG-58 cabling and can be a maximum of 185 m in length. For thinnet, we would use a combination of BNC connectors and T-piece connector. The following picture shows a BNC connector:

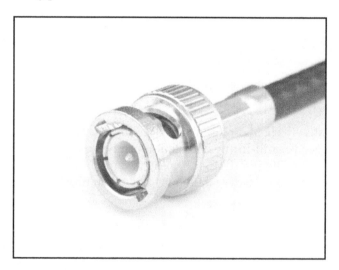

Figure 8.5: BNC connector

The preceding image can be found at `https://en.wikipedia.org/wiki/BNC_connector#/media/File:BNC_connector_50_ohm_male.jpg`. The picture is by Swift.Hg. Licensed under Creative Commons CC BY-SA 3.0: `https://creativecommons.org/licenses/by-sa/3.0/`.

A section of the cable has BNC connectors at either end that connect to the T-piece. The T-piece is connected to either another section of the cable or a terminator (as shown in the following picture) and a network card. The terminator would be placed at the T-piece at either end of the bus topology and would kill the signal to prevent signal bouncing. Since the thinnet is thinner than the thicknet, it is a lot more flexible:

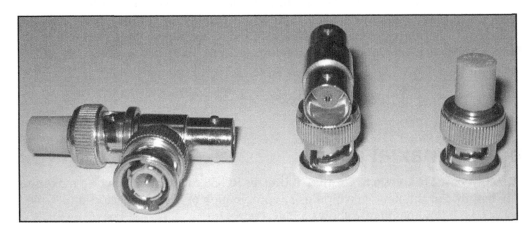

Figure 8.6: T-piece connectors left and center, and [green] terminators

 The preceding picture can be found at `https://en.wikipedia.org/wiki/BNC_connector#/media/File:BNC-Technik.jpg`. The picture is by Romantiker. It is licensed under Creative Commons CC BY-SA 3.0 `https://creativecommons.org/licenses/by-sa/3.0/`.

Coaxial cables are relatively cheap unless you're looking at a large installation. It is simple to install, but a single break or ill-fitting connection can bring the whole network down. Finally, while it is pretty resilient to EMI, it has the potential to be eavesdropped on relatively easily, so protecting sensitive data has to be taken into consideration.

# Understanding twisted pair cables and their types

Perhaps the most common type of network cable in use currently, twisted pair cables are, in my experience, possibly the cables that are mislabeled the most. When showing people a twisted pair cable, I've often heard it being called a Cat 5 cable or an RJ-45 cable. As you will see in this section, the Cat 5 cable is a variant of twisted pair cabling, while RJ-45 refers to the type of connector that's used with a twisted pair cable.

I would like to start off by talking about the characteristics that all twisted pair cables have in common. Firstly, each cable is made of eight inner copper wires that carry a voltage. These eight wires are broken down into four pairs, and the wires in each pair are twisted around their siblings. Each wire in a pair carries an electrical signal that is opposite to other. By twisting the wires of the pairs together, you reduce the electromagnetic field and reduce the prospect of cross talk. Cross talk is when the signal from one wire affects the signal in another. The other characteristic they have in common is the maximum cable length, which is 100 m.

The speed of twisted pair cables is dependent on the physical characteristics of the cable. The following table shows the speed of the common twisted pair categories:

| Category | Nomenclature | Speed |
|----------|-------------|-------|
| Cat 3 | 10baseT | 10 Mbps |
| Cat 5 | 100baseT | 100 Mbps |
| Cat 5e | 1000baseT | 1,000 Mbps/1 Gbps |
| Cat 6 | 1000baseT | 1,000 Mbps/1 Gbps (only to 55 m) |
| Cat 6a | 10GbaseT | 10 Gbps |
| Cat 7 | 10GbaseT | 10 Gbps |
| Cat 7a | 10GbaseT | 10 Gbps |

Regardless of the type of twisted pair cable being used, each of them will be terminated by an RJ-45 connector (as shown in the following picture), also known as an 8P8C modular plug, which would connect to an RJ-45 port:

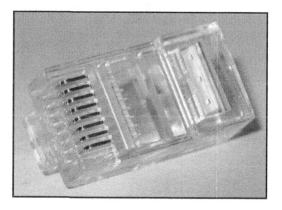

Figure 8.7: RJ-45 connector

The preceding picture can be found at `https://en.wikipedia.org/wiki/Modular_connector#/media/File:Uncrimped_rj-45_connector_close-up.jpg`. This picture is under the public domain.

**Exam tip**: You may see RJ-8 mentioned in the answers to some exam questions. Although this is similar to RJ-45 in design, it is used for telephony/modems and only has four wires (two pairs).

Now, let's take a look at the different types of twisted pair cables.

# Unshielded twisted pair

The **unshielded twisted pair** (UTP) cable consists solely of the wires and their insulators, as well as the outer sheath. This can be seen in the following picture:

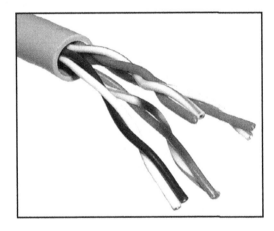

Figure 8.8: UTP cable

The preceding picture can be found at `https://en.wikipedia.org/wiki/Twisted_pair#/media/File:UTP_cable.jpg`. This picture is under the public domain.

Now, let's learn about the **shielded twisted pair** (STP) cable.

# STP

This cable is similar to UTP but the wires and their insulators are surrounded by a foil shield. The foil helps reduce EMI but also reduces flexibility. This can be seen in the following picture:

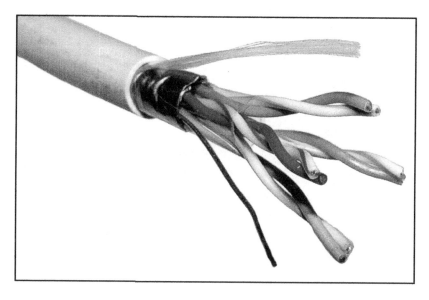

Figure 8.9: STP cable

 The preceding picture can be found at https://en.wikipedia.org/wiki/ Twisted_pair#/media/File:FTP_cable3.jpg. This picture is under the public domain.

Note the grounding wire just below the blue/blue-white pair and the foil shielding surrounding all the inner wires.

# Screened twisted pair

This cable, also known as an ScTP cable, takes the concept of STP and wraps each pair in foil to further improve EMI reduction. This can be seen in the following picture:

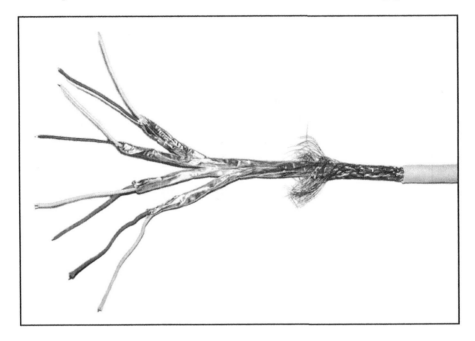

Figure 8.10: ScTP cable

 The preceding picture can be found at https://en.wikipedia.org/wiki/Twisted_pair#/media/File:S-FTP_CAT_7.jpg. This picture is under the public domain.

Now that we have looked at the different types of twisted pair cables, let's learn about the plenum outer coating present in them.

# Understanding the plenum coating

Each of the preceding cables can have a plenum outer coating. The term plenum refers to the floor space the cable is being used in. Plenum cabling runs through **heating, ventilation, and air-conditioning (HVAC)** conduits. This prevents the release of toxic fumes in the event of the cabling being burned.

# Power over Ethernet

I would like to finish off this section by briefly mentioning **Power over Ethernet (PoE)**. Since a twisted pair cable is basically a conduit for electricity to travel through, it can also be used to power devices that are not near a traditional power source. Obviously, there are limitations as to how much power these devices can draw based on how much power can be conducted by the cable, but they have some obvious advantages for low powered devices such as **Voice over IP (VoIP)** phones and **wireless access points (WAP)**.

Moving forward, let's understand the wiring standards that need to be followed while using these cables.

# Following wiring standards

To ensure compatibility when cabling between devices, a set of wiring standards need to be utilized. These are referred to as TIA-568A (see the following diagram) and TIA-568B (see the diagram that follows) and are used with an RJ-45 connector. An RJ-45 connector contains eight pins that bite into one of the wires inside the twisted pair cable. These pins are numbered from 1-8. By following these standards, you are ensuring that a transmitting pin on one device is connected to a receiving pin on the destination device:

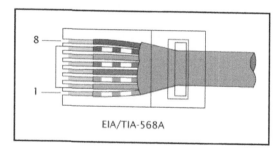

EIA/TIA-568A

Figure 8.11: TIA-568A

 The preceding diagram can be found at https://en.wikipedia.org/wiki/Modular_connector#/media/File:RJ-45_TIA-568A_Left.png. This diagram is under the public domain.

You may find that you use TIA-568A on both ends of the cable or that one end may be wired using TIA-568B:

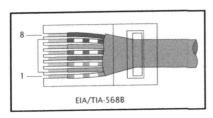

Figure 8.12: TIA-568B

The preceding image can be found at `https://en.wikipedia.org/wiki/Modular_connector#/media/File:RJ-45_TIA-568B_Left.png`. This image is under the public domain.

The following table shows the details of pin/cable pair mapping for the two standards:

| Pin | TIA-568a colors | TIA-568B colors |
|---|---|---|
| 1 | Green/white | Orange/white |
| 2 | Green | Orange |
| 3 | Orange/white | Green/white |
| 4 | Blue | Blue |
| 5 | Blue/white | Blue/white |
| 6 | Orange | Green |
| 7 | Brown/white | Brown/white |
| 8 | Brown | Brown |

There are three different combinations that a twisted pair cable can be wired in. These are straight-through, crossover, and rollover.

## Straight-through cable

A straight-through cable is wired using the TIA-568B standard on both ends. The purpose of a straight-through cable is to connect dissimilar devices, for example, a PC to a switch, a PC to a hub, and a switch to a router. A common misconception is that when we use the term *dissimilar devices*, we are focusing on the device as a whole, while in reality we are focusing on which pins they transmit and receive on. As shown in the following diagram, pin 1 is connected to pin 1, pin 2 is connected to pin 2, and so on:

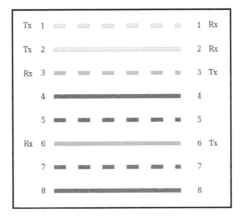

Figure 8.13: Straight-through cable

The next combination is the crossover cable.

# Crossover cable

A crossover cable is used when connecting two similar devices together. Similar devices would be a PC to a PC, a switch to a switch, a router to a router, and a PC to a router. The last one on the list is a good example of how the similarity of devices is based on transmit and receive pins. While crossover cables exist, it is highly unlikely that you will use one. The simple reason for this is that most modern network cards are capable of identifying whether a pin should be used to transmit or receive. As shown in the following diagram, with a crossover cable, pin 1 is connected to pin 3, while pin 2 is connected to pin 6:

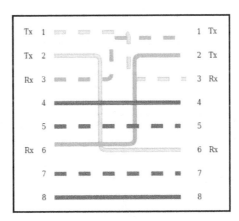

Figure 8.14: Crossover cable

The next combination is the rollover cable.

## Rollover cable

A rollover cable is used to connect to the console port of a device to allow you to manage or configure it. The wiring varies depending on the manufacturer, but for Cisco devices, a crossover cable's pin 1 is connected to pin 8; pin 2 is connected to pin 7, and so on. This can be seen in the following diagram:

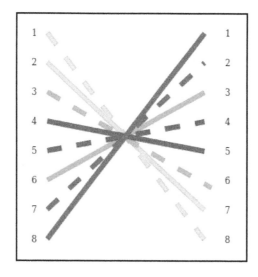

Figure 8.15: Rollover cable

In this section, we have learned about the various types of twisted pair cables and their wiring standards. In the next section, we will introduce you to fiber optic cables.

# Understanding fiber optic cables and their types

As we mentioned previously, both coaxial and twisted pair cables use a copper wire to transmit a signal in the form of voltage. In contrast, fiber optic cables use a signal made up of light. The light is generated by either an LED or a laser. Fiber optic networks provide high speed, long-distance connectivity that is resistant to EMI.

A fiber optic cable consists of either a single glass strand or multiple glass strands surrounded by an outer jacket, as shown in the following diagram. Each glass strand comprises a hollow central core that the light travels down and a glass cladding layer that prevents the light from escaping by reflecting it back into the core:

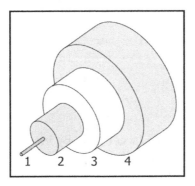

Figure 8.16: Fiber optic cable: 1) Core 2) Cladding 3) Buffer 4) Jacket

 The preceding diagram can be found at `https://commons.wikimedia.org/wiki/File:Singlemode_fibre_structure.svg`. It is under the Creative Commons CC BY-SA 3.0 `https://creativecommons.org/licenses/by-sa/3.0/deed.en`.

Fiber optic cables can be either **single-mode fiber (SMF)** or **multi-mode fiber (MMF)**. Let's go over these now.

# SMF

SMF consists of glass strands with a very thin core that allows only one light signal (from a laser) to be transmitted at a time. SMF is used for high speed, long-distance networks. The following connectors can be used with SMF:

- D4
- Biconic
- E2000
- FC
- LC
- MTP
- MTRJ

- MU
- SC SCapc
- ST

 To see what some of these connectors look like, go to `https://en.` `wikipedia.org/wiki/Optical_fiber_connector#/media/File:LC-` `optical-fiber-connector-hdr-0a.jpg` and `https://commons.` `wikimedia.org/wiki/File:ST-optical-fiber-connector-hdr-0a.jpg.`

# MMF

MMF consists of glass strands with a larger core. By increasing the core size, the cable is capable of transmitting multiple light signals at once through the use of LEDs. The following connectors can be used with MMF:

- FC
- Biconic
- MTP
- SMA
- MTRJ
- SMC
- LC Duplex
- SC
- ST

 To see what some of these connectors look like, go to `https://en.` `wikipedia.org/wiki/Optical_fiber_connector#/media/File:FCPC_002.` `jpg` and `https://en.wikipedia.org/wiki/Optical_fiber_connector#/` `media/File:MMF_optical.jpg.`

The following table shows the speeds of the various forms of fiber optic cabling:

| Type | Speed | Distance | Mode |
|------|-------|----------|------|
| 1000baseLX | 1,000 Mbps/1 Gbps | 5 km | SMF |
| 1000baseSX | 1,000 Mbps/1 Gbps | 550 m | MMF |
| 10GbaseLX4 | 10 Gbps | 10 km | SMF |
| 10GbaseER/EW | 10 Gbps | 22 km | SMF |
| 10GbaseSR/W | 10 Gbps | 550 m | MMF |

| 40GbaseSR | 40 Gbps | 150 m | MMF |
|---|---|---|---|
| 100GbaseLR4 | 100 Gbps | 10 km | SMF |
| 100GbaseER4 | 100 Gbps | 40 km | SMF |
| 100GbaseSR10 | 100 Gbps | 150 m | MMF |
| 100GbaseSR4 | 100 Gbps | 100 m | MMF |

**Exam tip**: You may have noticed that some of the connectors can be used on both SMF and MMF. You may have also noticed there are a lot of connectors with names that are not so easy to remember. The way I treat fiber connectors in terms of the exam is simple. I know the likelihood of having a question that asks me to differentiate between two fiber connectors is low. Therefore, I remember what connectors are used for coaxial and twisted pairs, and whatever is left must be a fiber connector.

# Summary

In this chapter, we concentrated on the physical connections between devices. We began this chapter by looking at what is, arguably, legacy cabling in the form of coaxial. We then moved on to the most common form of cabling in use today, that is, the twisted pair. We finished off this chapter by looking at fiber optic cables. For each of the cable types, we discussed the various different characteristics and connectors they have.

Through this chapter, you have learned how to identify the different cable types that are available to network engineers and the ability to choose the most appropriate cabling for your use. You also learned how to wire twisted pair cables in various formats. While you can obviously acquire this cabling off the shelf, every network engineer will need to make their own network cable at some point during their career.

In the next chapter, we will move on to the OSI model, a set of standards that cover networking from both the software and hardware sides of life. We will walk through the model and discuss the function of each layer of the model, as well as discuss some of the common protocols on each layer.

# Questions

1. Which cable type is most resistant to EMI?

(A) Coaxial
(B) UTP
(C) STP
(D) Fiber optic

2. Which of the following types of connectors would you use with fiber optic?

(A) BNC
(B) ST
(C) RJ-45
(D) 8P8C

3. What is the maximum length of a thinnet (10base2) cable?

(A) 100 m
(B) 185 m
(C) 200 m
(D) 500 m

4. What type of cable would you use to connect a PC to a switch?

(A) Straight-through cable
(B) Crossover cable
(C) Rollover cable
(D) Firewire cable

5. What is the maximum speed of a Cat 5 twisted pair cable?

(A) 10 Mbps
(B) 100 Mbps
(C) 1 Gbps
(D) 10 Gbps

6. What type of cable should be used in HVAC conduits?

(A) Plenum
(B) Coaxial
(C) Firewire
(D) Serial

7. What would you use on a coaxial cable to prevent signal bounce?

(A) BNC
(B) T-connector
(C) Terminator
(D) N-connector

8. What is the maximum distance of a twisted pair cable?
(A) 100 m
(B) 185 m
(C) 200 m
(D) 500 m

9. Degradation of the signal as it travels the length of the cable is known as what?
(A) Fade
(B) Attenuation
(C) Decomposition
(D) Interference

# Further reading

To find out more about the various types of cables, please take a look at the following links:

- *Optical Fiber*: https://www.thefoa.org/tech/ref/basic/fiber.html
- *CAT 5 / 5e / 6 / 6A / 6A / 7 Cable - RJ-45 Connector*: http://www.proav.de/index.html?httpwww.proav.de/data/cables/CAT5.html
- *Coaxial Cable*: https://uk.rs-online.com/web/generalDisplay.html?id=ideas-and-advice/coaxial-cable-guide

# Section 3: Protocols and Services

**3**

In this section, you will learn about the two common network models in use today and gain an understanding of their purpose. You will also gain an understanding of identifying devices through the use of IPv4 and IPv6 addresses. In addition, this section will provide you with the knowledge to explain different name resolution methodologies and various common network services.

This section comprises the following chapters:

- Chapter 9, *Understanding the OSI Model*
- Chapter 10, *Understanding TCP/IP*
- Chapter 11, *Understanding IPv4*
- Chapter 12, *Understanding IPv6*
- Chapter 13, *Understanding Name Resolution*
- Chapter 14, *Network Services*

# Understanding the OSI Model 9

In this chapter, you will be introduced to one of the two main network models in use today: the OSI model. The other TCP/IP model will be covered in the next chapter. These two models form a collection of standards that vendors and developers follow that ensure the compatibility of network devices and software. While both models are important, the OSI model always seems to be the one people talk about. It is beneficial for you, as a network engineer, to understand how this model works and how each layer interacts with the others to help facilitate troubleshooting.

This chapter begins by explaining the rationale behind the concept of network models, which is then followed by an explanation of the functionality of each of the seven layers of the OSI model. As we discuss each layer, protocols and devices will be mapped to each.

The following topics will be covered in this chapter:

- Understanding the purpose of network models
- Application layer
- Presentation layer
- Session layer
- Transport layer
- Network layer
- Data-link layer
- Physical layer

# Technical requirements

To complete the exercises in this chapter, you will require a PC or virtual PC with an internet connection running Windows 7 or later.

# Understanding the purpose of network models

In the early days of networks, most systems utilized proprietary software and protocols that would only allow communication with other devices from the same manufacturer or those manufacturers that had access to those protocols. At the time, this was not much of an issue as organizations would purchase their equipment from the same manufacturer throughout, and there were no real means of communicating outside of your organization. However, over time, this has changed and there's now a need to communicate with systems owned by other organizations. Herein lay an issue.

It was unlikely that the other organization had equipment from the same manufacturer, so there was no way for these devices to talk to each other. To combat this, a request was made for a standard model to be created and to be made publicly available for all to use. The two models that became the standards were as follows:

- **Open Systems Interconnection** (**OSI**) model from the **International Organization for Standards** (**ISO**)
- TCP/IP model

We will cover the OSI model in this chapter, while the TCP/IP model will be covered in the next chapter.

The OSI model is a network model comprising seven individual layers, as shown in the following diagram. Each of these layers communicates to the layers adjacent to it and its equivalent layer on the receiving device:

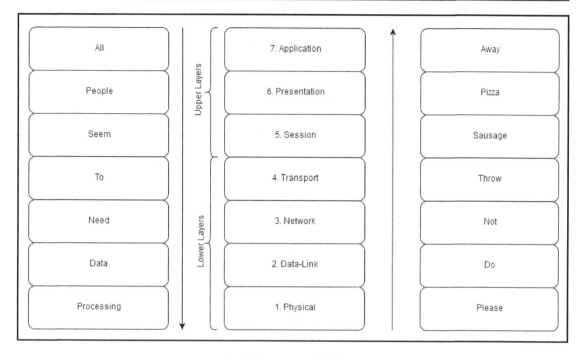

Figure 9.1: The seven layers of the OSI model

The top three layers (**Application, Presentation**, and **Session**) are referred to as the upper layers. The bottom four layers (**Transport, Network, Data-Link, Physical**) are referred to as the lower layers. In the preceding paragraph, I mentioned that the OSI model allows for communication with adjacent layers. This means that the application layer can talk to the presentation layer; the presentation layer can talk to the application layer and the session; the session layer can talk to the presentation layer and transport layer, and so on. This layered approach simplifies the development process. For example, let's say a new type of physical cable is created. Is it that important that protocols that sit on the application layer know about this new type of cable? I would argue that it isn't. Can you imagine if, every time a new cable came out, all the network protocols had to be updated? We would be in a permanent state of development.

Throughout your network career, whenever a question is asked, you will say, *"ahh, the OSI model"* and then rattle off one of two common mnemonics that are used to remember the order of the layers:

- **Layer 1 -> 7**: Please Do Not Throw Sausage Pizza Away
- **Layer 7 -> 1**: All People Seem To Need Data Processing

Obviously, the important thing is remembering which one relates to which, and which way the numbering goes. Think of the numbering similar to the numbering of floors in a tall building.

When we open up a network-enabled application, we are initiating a process that feeds into layer seven and works its way through the layers until it reaches layer one. The data is sent across to the recipient, which processes it back up the model from layer one to layer seven, and then on to the relevant application, file, and so on.

As the data goes through the OSI model on the sending device, it goes through a process called **encapsulation**. Encapsulation is simply taking the data from the previous layer, adding a header (and sometimes a trailer) to it, and passing it on to the next layer where the process is repeated. The header (and trailer) and data that is being passed down to the next layer is referred to as a protocol data unit by the originating layer; on the receiving layer, it is referred to as a service data unit. The following diagram shows encapsulation in process and, on the right, lists the data unit names. There is another mnemonic to remember the data unit titles of the lower layers: Some People Fear Birthdays:

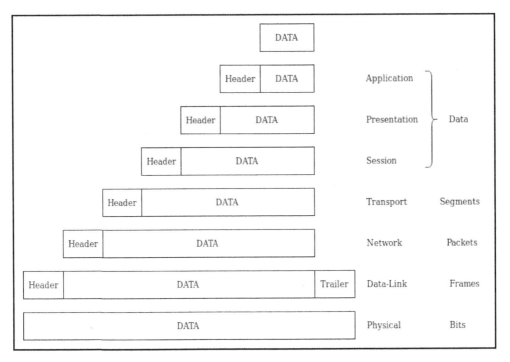

Figure 9.2: Encapsulation

On the receiving device, the headers (and trailer) are stripped away before passing the data up to the next layer. This process is referred to as deencapsulation. Obviously, the headers and the trailer are there for a purpose. They contain key information that allows the data to be processed. As we go through each of the layers, I will call out the important information that is in the header of each. Be aware that each header contains a lot more information than I will cover, but the remainder of it is out of scope for the exam.

Having an understanding of how the OSI model fits together and what talks to what will help you with troubleshooting issues. Finally, talking of troubleshooting, you may hear the term *"layer eight error"* being mentioned by colleagues. Don't worry – I haven't missed a layer out. Layer eight is a tongue-in-cheek way of saying the error is down to the user doing something wrong.

Now that we have understood what an OSI network model is, let's learn about each layer of this model in detail.

# Layer 7 – the application layer

Something important that I would like to clarify from the outset is that applications don't reside on the application layer of the OSI model. In reality, they sit above the OSI model. The application layer acts as an interface between the application and the network model. Any application that supports network communication will be developed using network **application programming interfaces (APIs)**. The API contains code that tells the application how to talk to the application layer.

Rather than the application being at the application layer, there are a number of application layer protocols that the applications will support. Some of these common protocols include the following:

- **Simple Message Transfer Protocol (SMTP)**
- **Post Office Protocol (POP)**
- **Internet Message Access Protocol (IMAP)**
- **Hypertext Transfer Protocol (HTTP)**
- **Domain Name System (DNS)**
- **Secure Shell (SSH)**
- **File Transfer Protocol (FTP)**

We will cover these in more detail in `Chapter 14`, *Network Services*. Now, let's learn about the presentation layer.

# Layer 6 – the presentation layer

The presentation layer takes the data that's passed to it from the application layer and converts it into a generic format or syntax. Some of the data being translated will be very complex and it has to be converted into a flat file, ready for streaming to the recipient. This serialized data stream is received by the recipient device and deserialized and rebuilt into its original format. The reason for this conversion is that the native format of different systems or applications may vary. By converting the data into a generic format, any device receiving the data will understand it, and by extension will be able to take it and convert it into a format the receiving application can understand.

Besides converting the data, the presentation layer also provides data compression and encryption/decryption. Some of the generic standards that are used on this layer include the following:

- JPEG
- ASCII
- TIFF
- GIF

Now, let's learn about the session layer.

# Layer 5 – the session layer

The session layer is responsible for managing sessions between the devices. Management of sessions includes establishing the session, synchronizing the communication between the devices, and terminating the session.

It is on this layer that the devices agree upon the type of communication that's going to take place including the following:

- Simplex
- Half-duplex
- Full-duplex

The protocols that are supported on this layer include the following:

- RPC
- SQL
- NetBIOS
- **Point-to-Point Tunneling Protocol (PPTP)**

Now, let's learn about the transport layer.

# Layer 4 – the transport layer

The transport layer is responsible for host-to-host communication and creating a logical connection between the two devices. It includes initiating the connection between the devices, flow control between the devices, same-order delivery, and multiplex communication.

The two main protocols on the transport layer are as follows:

- **Transmission Control Protocol (TCP)**
- **User Datagram Protocol (UDP)**

I will discuss both of these in more detail in the following sections, but I would like to mention a few areas that they have in common.

First, both protocols include a checksum. This checksum is a means of error detection. When the data is processed for sending, the sending device performs a calculation that generates a value based on the data being sent. The receiving device performs the same calculation. If the value matches, then the data is correct.

Another feature they have in common is the ability to carry out multiplex communications. This is just a sophisticated way of saying that a machine can have multiple conversations with another machine at the same time. A perfect example of this is when you are reading a website and you open a link to another part of the website in another tab.

The other common feature is the use of logical port numbers, which will be discussed in the following section.

# Logical ports

When we discussed switches and routers earlier in this book, we mentioned ports. In that context, we were discussing physical ports. A logical port is one that is defined in software. The purpose of a logical port is to allow the receiving device to identify which application or service the data is destined for.

I always find that an analogy is useful here. Imagine you are calling your bank. You ring their main number (the equivalent of the IP address). When the receptionist answers, you ask to be put through to the mortgage department on extension 253 (the port number).

Both TCP and UDP headers include a source port number and a destination port number. When the data is received by the recipient device, the destination port number is inspected, and the device will pass the data to the relevant application or service.

There are 65,536 logical port numbers available (numbered 0 - 65,535). These numbers are allocated by the **Internet Assigned Numbers Authority (IANA)** and are broken down into ranges:

- **Well-known ports (0- 1,023)**: These are ports that are allocated to commonly used network services.
- **Registered ports (1,024-49,151)**: These port numbers are allocated to applications or services by IANA, following a request by the developers.
- **Dynamic or ephemeral ports (49,152-65,535)**: These ports are not allocated by IANA and are usually used by client machines as the source port.

When a client device wants to communicate with a service on a destination device such as a web page, the originating device opens a port within the dynamic range. This is entered in the header as the source IP. The application will be configured to identify the destination port, and this will be included in the header as the destination IP. For example, a web browser knows that, if it is using HTTP as the destination port, it will be port 80. When the web server sends the requested data back to the client, it will usually reverse the port numbers. So, the source port will be port 80, while the destination port will be the dynamic port that the application opened. I use the term *usually* here since, in some instances, there may be predefined source and destination ports.

The following table provides some of the details of the common ports and their port numbers:

| Port number | Service/Protocol |
| --- | --- |
| 21 | FTP |
| 22 | SSH |
| 23 | Telnet |
| 25 | SMTP |
| 53 | DNS |
| 67, 68 | **Dynamic Host Configuration Protocol (DHCP)** |
| 80 | HTTP |
| 88 | Kerberos |
| 110 | **Post Office Protocol v3 (POP3)** |
| 123 | **Network Time Protocol (NTP)** |
| 137 - 139 | NetBIOS |
| 143 | IMAP |
| 161 | **Simple Network Management Protocol (SNMP)** |
| 389 | **Lightweight Directory Access Protocol (LDAP)** |
| 443 | **Hypertext Transport Protocol Secure (HTTPS)** |
| 3389 | **Remote Desktop Protocol (RDP)** |

**Activity 1**: In this activity, you will identify what ports your PC has open and what port on the destination device it is connected to:

1. Open a Command Prompt.
2. Run the `netstat -a` command (the –a switch shows connected ports and listening ports. Since UDP ports don't establish a connection, you must use this switch to view them).

You should receive an output that's similar to what's shown in the following screenshot:

```
Proto  Local Address          Foreign Address              State
TCP    127.0.0.1:51444        DESKTOP-CTQCANA:51445        ESTABLISHED
TCP    127.0.0.1:51445        DESKTOP-CTQCANA:51444        ESTABLISHED
TCP    127.0.0.1:51446        DESKTOP-CTQCANA:51447        ESTABLISHED
TCP    127.0.0.1:51447        DESKTOP-CTQCANA:51446        ESTABLISHED
TCP    127.0.0.1:51450        DESKTOP-CTQCANA:51451        ESTABLISHED
TCP    127.0.0.1:51451        DESKTOP-CTQCANA:51450        ESTABLISHED
TCP    127.0.0.1:51662        DESKTOP-CTQCANA:51663        ESTABLISHED
TCP    127.0.0.1:51663        DESKTOP-CTQCANA:51662        ESTABLISHED
TCP    127.0.0.1:51691        DESKTOP-CTQCANA:51692        ESTABLISHED
TCP    127.0.0.1:51692        DESKTOP-CTQCANA:51691        ESTABLISHED
TCP    127.0.0.1:51716        DESKTOP-CTQCANA:51717        ESTABLISHED
TCP    127.0.0.1:51717        DESKTOP-CTQCANA:51716        ESTABLISHED
TCP    127.0.0.1:51870        DESKTOP-CTQCANA:51871        ESTABLISHED
TCP    127.0.0.1:51871        DESKTOP-CTQCANA:51870        ESTABLISHED
TCP    127.0.0.1:51896        DESKTOP-CTQCANA:51897        ESTABLISHED
TCP    127.0.0.1:51897        DESKTOP-CTQCANA:51896        ESTABLISHED
TCP    127.0.0.1:52008        DESKTOP-CTQCANA:52009        ESTABLISHED
TCP    127.0.0.1:52009        DESKTOP-CTQCANA:52008        ESTABLISHED
TCP    127.0.0.1:59732        DESKTOP-CTQCANA:59733        ESTABLISHED
TCP    127.0.0.1:59733        DESKTOP-CTQCANA:59732        ESTABLISHED
TCP    192.168.1.3:51427      40.67.251.132:https          ESTABLISHED
TCP    192.168.1.3:51458      ec2-35-163-101-143:https     ESTABLISHED
TCP    192.168.1.3:51627      185-70-40-151:https          ESTABLISHED
TCP    192.168.1.3:52079      stackoverflow:https          ESTABLISHED
TCP    192.168.1.3:52085      ec2-54-194-160-175:https     ESTABLISHED
TCP    192.168.1.3:59802      lhr48s08-in-f10:https        ESTABLISHED
TCP    192.168.1.3:59803      a-0001:https                 ESTABLISHED
TCP    192.168.1.3:59804      204.79.197.222:https         ESTABLISHED
TCP    192.168.1.3:59806      13.107.136.254:https         ESTABLISHED
TCP    192.168.1.3:59807      13.107.246.10:https          ESTABLISHED
TCP    192.168.1.3:59808      51.140.28.150:https          SYN_SENT
```

Figure 9.3: Output for the netstat -a command

The Local Address column details your IP address and states the local port that is open.

3. The Foreign Address column details that the host is connected either by name or IP address and tells us of the port on the destination device.
4. Notice that the port is detailed either as a number or – if it is a well-known port – the name of the service.

Although there are a large number of ports, the ones listed in the preceding table are the ones that are the most likely to be discussed in the exam.

# TCP

TCP is referred to as a connection-orientated protocol. What this means is that, before any data is transferred between devices, a connection needs to be established. By doing this, the sending device is positive that the recipient is ready to receive the data. To form this connection, TCP carries out a process known as a **three-way handshake**, which is depicted in the following diagram. The process is as follows:

1. **SYN**: The sending device sends a synchronization request to the destination computer. This synchronization includes a sequence number. For illustrative purposes, let's say the sequence number is 101.

2. **SYN/ACK**: The receiving device responds with an acknowledgment of the SYN request. This acknowledgment is basically an acknowledgment of what sequence number the recipient is expecting next. In this case, it's 102. It also sends its own synchronization request to the originating device. We will use 201 in this example. At this stage, the devices are agreeing to the parameters that they will use to communicate.

3. **ACK**: The originating device acknowledges the synchronization request from the recipient device. Again, this is the next sequence number that the device is expecting to receive. In this example, this number is 202.

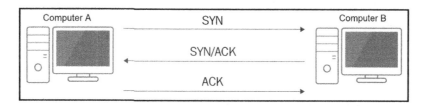

Figure 9.4: TCP three-way handshake

Once the handshake has been completed, data can flow between the two devices. TCP guarantees delivery of the data through a process of using sequence numbers and acknowledgments. The data being transferred is broken down into segments, and each of these includes a sequence number. This allows the recipient to rebuild the data on receipt. In addition, it allows the recipient to identify if it has received all of the data. When the data has been received, the recipient device sends an acknowledgment back to the recipient. This acknowledgment is basically a way of telling the originating device which sequence number the recipient is expecting to receive next. On receipt of the acknowledgment, the originating device sends the next batch of data over.

As part of the synchronization process, the two devices will have agreed on how many segments will be sent across before an acknowledgment is sent back. This helps reduce network overhead by cutting down the number of acknowledgements being sent across. This is a process known as a **sliding window** and is flexible. Let's say, for example, they agree that three segments can be sent across before an acknowledgment is sent in response. If the recipient device doesn't receive all three segments and therefore doesn't send an acknowledgment, the sending device, after a period of time, will realize that it hasn't received the acknowledgment and will resend the data. If this happens a number of times, the two devices will agree to a smaller window to try and reduce the data loss and requirement to resend.

TCP also includes a feature called **flow control**. This is a process that's designed to reduce congestion. If the recipient device is struggling to keep up with the amount of data being received, it can send a "not ready" message to the sender. Once it has cleared the buffer on the network card, the device will send a "ready" message and communication will resume.

When the devices want to cease communicating, they follow a four-way handshake process, which is depicted in the following diagram:

1. **Computer A** no longer needs to send any data to **Computer B**, so it sends a **FIN** packet.
2. **Computer B** receives the **FIN** request and sends back an **ACK** in response.
3. Once **Computer B** has no more data to send its own **FIN** packet to **Computer A**.
4. **Computer A** receives the **FIN** request and sends back an **ACK** in response:

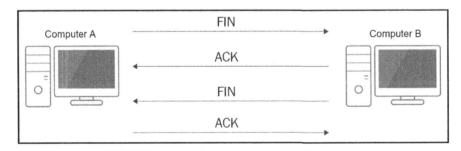

Figure 9.5: TCP four-way handshake

5. Once the four-way handshake has been completed, the devices close down the ports.

Through the use of sequence numbers, flow control, and acknowledgments, the use of TCP provides guaranteed delivery to the destination (as long as the connecting infrastructure is working, of course). This guarantee, however, comes at a price. The TCP header adds an additional 20-60 bytes of data per segment sent, and the acknowledgments add additional bandwidth consumption which, in addition to waiting for the acknowledgments, leads to slower transfer of data. Therefore, TCP is used when it is imperative that data is completely transferred, such as with file sharing or database transactions.

# UDP

While TCP was a connection-orientated protocol, UDP is a connectionless protocol. This means that there is no three-way handshake carried out before data is transmitted. The sending device literally sends the data out on the wire and hopes it is received by the destination device. It is often referred to as a *best-effort* protocol; it doesn't matter if the data gets there or not. This may seem odd because surely you want to receive all of the data every time? Generally, you would be right, but let me give you an example.

You're watching a live football match, streaming over the internet. If you were to use TCP, there would be times when the server is waiting for the acknowledgments before sending the next bit of data. Your viewing would be stuttering. What if there was an issue that caused the data to be delayed 5 minutes? You'd be watching 5 minutes behind everyone else. Wouldn't it be better to just write off those 5 minutes and just carry on with whatever data you have received?

UDP would allow you to do this. It's a faster protocol because it has a smaller header (only 8 bytes) and there are no acknowledgments to add to the bandwidth.

UDP is also used for multicast and broadcast transmissions. It would be impossible to conduct three-way handshakes with so many devices before sending the data on.

There will be occasions where a protocol will use both TCP and UDP, depending on what function it is performing at the time. DNS and DHCP are two perfect examples of this and we will discuss them in more detail in Chapter 14, *Network Services*.

To summarize, when data delivery is critical and time is not a constraint, then TCP should be used; when data delivery is not important and/or time is of the essence, you should use UDP. In reality, most of us won't be the ones deciding which one to use – that will be the developers when they are creating applications.

Now, let's take a look at the network layer.

# Layer 3 – the network layer

We mentioned layer 3 of the OSI model when discussing routers and, conveniently enough, layer 3 switches. The network layer of the OSI model is responsible for the logical addressing of devices through the use of IP addresses. It is also responsible for route selection for the data being transmitted, that is, how it gets from Computer A to Computer B. The process of routing the data has already been discussed in great detail in Chapter 7, *Routers and Routing – Beyond a Single Network*.

In terms of protocols on the network layer, the most common are as follows:

- IP
- **Internetwork Packet Exchange (IPX)**

IP is the most common of the two, and is the core of all networks. IPX is out of scope for this exam since the focus is on IP addressing, which we have already briefly covered but will go into more detail in Chapter 11, *Understanding IPv4*, and Chapter 12, *Understanding IPv6*, where we will discuss IPv4 and IPv6, respectively. At this layer, the protocol data unit is referred to as a packet and its header will include the source and destination IP addresses.

Now, let's learn about the data-link layer.

# Layer 2 – the data-link layer

It could be argued that the data-link layer is only relevant within your own subnet, and, while this is true to an extent, we still require it for transmission of data outside of our subnet. The data-link layer creates a logical connection between nodes on the subnet. If the data is destined for a device within the same subnet, the link will be to that device; if the data is destined for a device outside the subnet, the link will be to the default gateway. The protocol data unit on layer 2 is the frame.

The responsibilities of the data-link layer include placing the data onto physical media, error notifications, and flow control. Error notifications are carried out through the use of a checksum that's included in the trailer that's added to the data. As well as the trailer, a header is added, which will include the source and destination MAC addresses. Recall that switches use these to make forwarding decisions, which is why they are referred to as layer 2 devices.

The layer is split into two sublayers:

- **Logical Link Control (LLC)**: The task of the LLC is to act as an interface with the network layer and identifies what network layer protocol is being used, for example, IP or IPX, and stores that information within the frame header. This happens so that, when the data is received at the other end, the device knows which network layer protocol it needs to send it to.
- **Media Access Control (MAC)**: The MAC sublayer is responsible for controlling how the data is put onto certain media or how we control the data's access to the media. The MAC sublayer can be occupied by a number of protocols; for example, 802.3 and 802.11 reside on this layer. Recall that we already talked about CSMA/CA and CSMA/CD. These are both examples of contention-based media access. All the hosts are contending for access to the media on a first-come, first-served basis. Another method is token passing (802.5), which we discussed previously. If you have a token *in your hand*, you can talk, but if you don't, you can't.

 While **MAC** stands for **Media Access Control** in this context and also when we refer to MAC addresses, that is the only real link between the two uses.

Now, let's learn about the physical layer.

# Layer 1 – the physical layer

The physical transmission of the data in the form of bits takes place on this layer. Depending on the type of media (see the previous chapter) and the network cards in use, the method of sending the data will vary. The important thing is that both ends are using the same method. These signals may be in the form of variations in voltage or patterns in the light being transmitted.

At this layer, there are no protocols per second, but there are sets of standards and criteria that the cabling and network cards will need to adhere to. These standards include the following:

- Voltages
- Speeds
- Wiring

With this, we have covered all the seven layers of the OSI network model.

# Summary

In this chapter, we introduced the concepts of network models while covering the OSI model. We discussed how the seven layers were split into upper and lower layers and covered each of the layers by highlighting the function of each layer and their key attributes. We highlighted the process of encapsulation and deencapsulation as data was passed from one layer to the next.

We included a number of areas that an engineer can utilize in the troubleshooting processes. These included the three-way handshake that's used by TCP. Using this knowledge in conjunction with a tool such as Wireshark will allow you to check to see if a connection is being made to the recipient device. We also covered logical network ports and discussed the common ports. Learning about the allocated ports numbers will allow you to ensure you are making the correct adjustments to firewall rules. In addition, we carried out an activity using `netstat`. This tool is a godsend when troubleshooting network issues and for security purposes. Is the port we are trying to connect to closed? Is there a port open that should be closed?

In the next chapter, we will move on to another common network model, that is, the TCP/IP model. You will see some similarities in the two models in terms of functionality and in the naming of layers, so it will be important to identify which model they are referring to in order to be able to answer exam questions correctly.

# Questions

1. What is layer 4 of the OSI model called?

(A) Session layer
(B) Data-link layer
(C) Transport layer
(D) Application layer

2. What layer of the OSI model is responsible for ensuring data is in the correct syntax?

(A) Presentation layer
(B) Session layer
(C) Network layer
(D) Application layer

3. What means of identifying a device on a local subnet can be found at layer 2 of the OSI model?

(A) IP addresses
(B) MAC addresses
(C) Host names
(D) Port numbers

4. The port number range of 0 - 1024 is referred to as what?

(A) Ephemeral
(B) Well known
(C) Registered
(D) Dynamic

5. What protocol guarantees delivery of data through the use of acknowledgments and sequence numbers?

(A) TCP
(B) UDP
(C) IP
(D) IPX

6. What logical port number is assigned to the NTP?

(A) 23
(B) 123
(C) 443
(D) 3389

7. What is the second step of the three-way handshake?

(A) FIN
(B) ACK
(C) SYN
(D) SYN/ACK

8. What organization assigns port numbers?

(A) IEEE
(B) OSI
(C) IANA
(D) IETF

9. What layer of the OSI model is responsible for the routing of traffic?

(A) Transport layer
(B) Data-link layer
(C) Session layer
(D) Application layer

10. Which of these can be found on the data-link layer? Choose two.

(A) MAC
(B) SMTP
(C) DNS
(D) LLC

# Further reading

To find out more about the OSI model, please go to `https://docs.microsoft.com/en-us/windows-hardware/drivers/network/windows-network-architecture-and-the-osi-model`.

# Understanding TCP/IP

**10**

This chapter discusses the second of the two network models we will be covering in this book: globally the **Transmission Control Protocol/Internet Protocol (TCP/IP)** model. Like the OSI model we discussed in the previous chapter, it is imperative for you, as a network engineer, to understand the constituent components of this model. Nowadays, TCP/IP is ubiquitous in nature. It is on pretty much all network devices. If you can grasp this one model, you will be able to troubleshoot networking issues on a range of devices.

This chapter demonstrates how the TCP/IP model maps against the OSI model and mentions variations of the TCP/IP model, such as the **Department of Defense (DoD)** model.

The following topics will be covered in this chapter:

- Overview of the TCP/IP layers
- Understanding the application layer
- Understanding the transport layer
- Understanding the internet layer
- Understanding the network layer

# Technical requirements

To complete the exercises in this chapter, you will need a computer running a Windows OS with an internet connection.

# Overview of the TCP/IP layers

You will notice as you go through this chapter that the TCP/IP model has many similarities with the OSI model. They both take on a layered approach, with each layer talking to the adjacent layers and their respective layer on the destination device. Like the OSI model, the TCP/IP model is an open or non-proprietary standard, which means any manufacturer can use it. Although most networking courses place a heavy focus on the OSI model, most experts argue that the TCP/IP model is a truer reflection of how networking works:

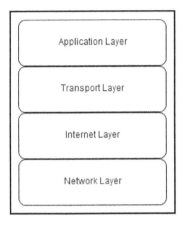

Figure 10.1: The TCP/IP model

As shown in the preceding diagram, the TCP/IP model has only four layers compared to the seven layers of the OSI model. These layers are as follows:

- Application layer
- Transport layer
- Internet layer
- Network layer

We will discuss each of these layers in turn in the following sections, but I'm keen to highlight that some layers in the TCP/IP model have the same names as layers in the OSI model, but are in different positions. In the exam, ensure that you check which model the question is referring to.

> As a general rule of thumb, if they refer to a layer by number, for example, layer 1, layer 2, and so on, as opposed to the first layer, the second layer, and so on, then they are usually referring to the OSI model. The TCP/IP model tends to rely on words rather than numbers.

The TCP/IP model loosely maps against the OSI model in terms of functionality, but there is no defined mapping across the two, and the following diagram should only be used as a guide. This diagram also shows the DoD model. Its name is derived from the fact that the initial funding of the model was provided by the American DoD. It was actually a developmental name for the TCP/IP model. Notice the similarities again. It is unlikely that the DoD model will appear in the exam and it is mentioned here for historical purposes only:

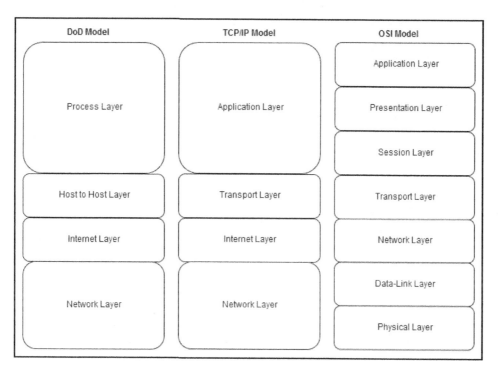

Figure 10.2: Comparison of the OSI and DoD models

Encapsulation and deencapsulation are also in play within the TCP/IP model. Headers and trailers are added to the data as it progresses up and down the model.

The TCP/IP model is sometimes referred to as the **Internet Protocol (IP)** suite as it is a collection of protocols that are used to communicate across the internet. Together, these protocols form a protocol stack. Protocol stacks are collections of protocols that work together to perform a particular overall function: in this case, transmitting data over a network. As we go through the layers, I will flag any particular protocols of note.

Now that we have gained an understanding of models and the positioning of each layer, we will look at each of these layers in turn.

# Understanding the application layer

Similar to its namesake in the OSI model, the application layer of the TCP/IP model acts as an interface between the applications themselves and the network stack, rather than the place the applications actually *sit*. Again, this is through the use of APIs and programming libraries. This layer performs the functionality of the application and the presentation layers of the OSI model, including the formatting, compression, and encryption of data.

There are a number of protocols in use on the application layer, and these can be divided into two areas:

- User protocols
- Support protocols

The user may have some involvement with the initial configuration of these, but then they are usually just left to do their own thing. We will discuss these protocols in more depth in upcoming sections.

# User protocols

User protocols can be generally defined as protocols that are used by the applications the user interacts with. Let's look at some common user protocols.

# Telnet

Telnet is a means of remotely controlling a device from the CLI, which in the case of Windows is the Command Prompt. Telnet works on port 23 and offers a text-based, low-bandwidth means of communicating with other devices. For telnet to work, you need to have a telnet server running on the device you want to send commands to and you must be running a telnet client yourself. Both of these are built into modern versions of Windows.

Now that I've told you about Telnet, I'm going to tell you to never use it, unless as a very last resort or as a means of setting up a more secure connection such as SSH. Telnet works out of the box, while SSH requires configuration. You may be wondering why I would say this. It's simple. Telnet sends all data across in clear text, including your usernames and passwords. Therefore, an attacker can eavesdrop on this information. Because of this, Telnet is not enabled by default in Windows, and alternatives such as **Secure Shell** (**SSH**) should be used. Windows 10 includes SSH natively, but it can be added to earlier versions using third-party applications such as the terminal emulator PuTTY. Most network devices, such as routers and switches, have Telnet enabled by default. Disable it as soon as possible.

**Activity**: If you are a Star Wars fan, you may want to do the following:

1. Download the PuTTY application.
2. Navigate to `towel.blinkenlights.nl`. By default, PuTTY selects SSH.
3. Select the option for Telnet, as shown in the following screenshot.
4. Click **Open**:

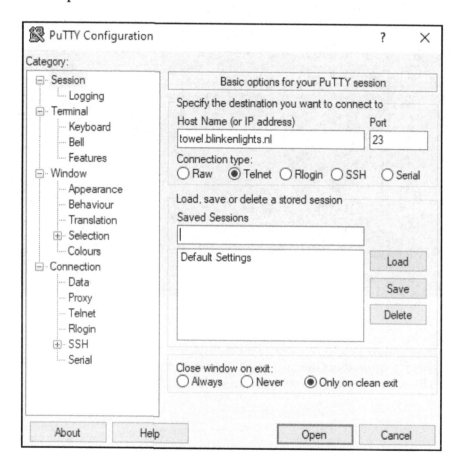

Figure 10.3: PuTTY configuration window

5. If you have configured this correctly, you should see the following screen. Allow the process to run:

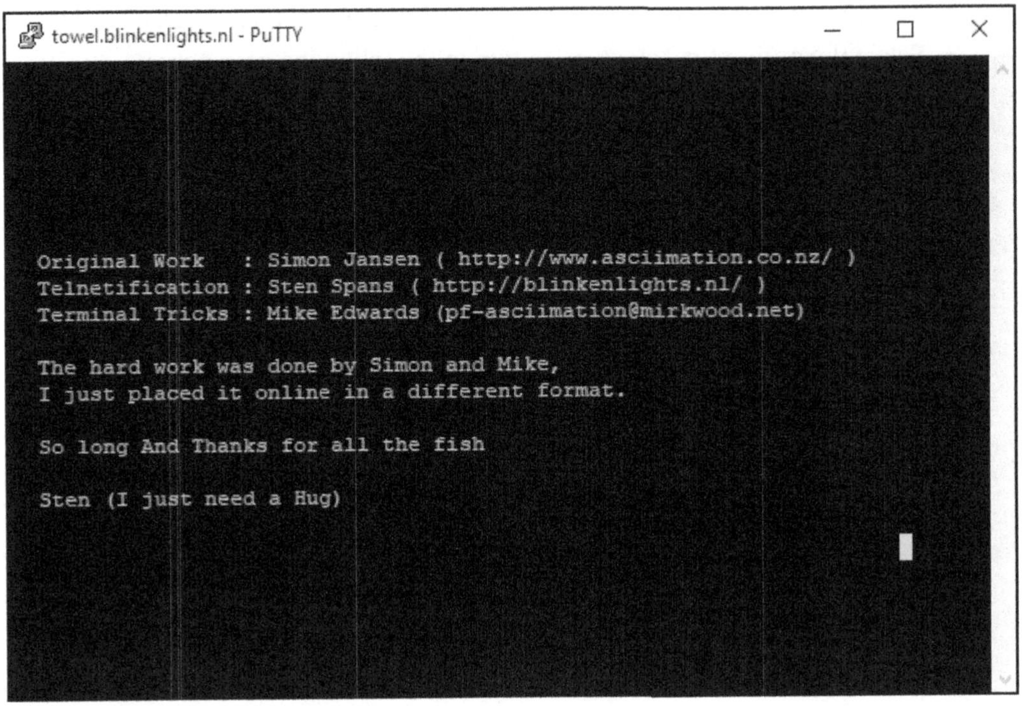

Figure 10.4: towel.blinkenlights.nl credits

While Telnet can allow you to run some commands, it is quite a *jack-of-all-trades* tool. Certain activities require tools that are more specific to their purpose. **File Transfer Protocol (FTP)**, which we discuss next, is one such tool.

# FTP

FTP does exactly what its name implies. It allows you to transfer files from one device to another using ports 20 and 21. Don't mistake this kind of protocol for your organization's network shares system because the latter is more likely to be a **Server Message Block (SMB)**.

To use FTP, we need to have an FTP server application installed on the server hosting the files we wish to access and we must be running an FTP client ourselves. Again, the FTP client is installed on Windows 10 and can be run from the command line either directly or in interactive mode. However, since the commands can be a little daunting at first, a lot of individuals use a third-party application with a GUI. These third-party applications usually have a console window that displays the underlying command being run. FTP runs over TCP which, as you may recall, guarantees delivery of the data.

**Activity**: In this activity, you will use FTP to download a file from a public FTP site:

1. Open your Command Prompt.
2. Type in the `ftp` command and press *Enter* to open FTP in interactive mode. Any commands you type in now are executed by the FTP application. Type in the `help` command and press *Enter* to obtain a list of commands that can be used:

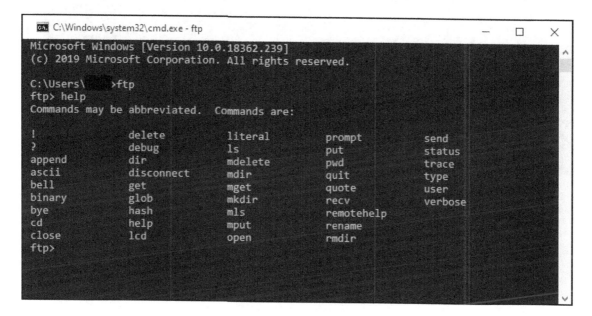

Figure 10.5: List of commands

3. Connect to the public FTP server with the `open speedtest.tele2.net` command and press *Enter*.

4. When prompted for the username, type in `anonymous` and press *Enter*.

5. Leave the password blank and press *Enter*. Note that, if you were to enter a password here, nothing would appear on the screen for security purposes.

6. You should receive a message stating that the logon was successful:

```
C:\Windows\system32\cmd.exe - ftp                                    —   □   ✕
Microsoft Windows [Version 10.0.18362.239]
(c) 2019 Microsoft Corporation. All rights reserved.

C:\Users\    >ftp
ftp> open speedtest.tele2.net
Connected to speedtest.tele2.net.
220 (vsFTPd 3.0.3)
200 Always in UTF8 mode.
User (speedtest.tele2.net:(none)): anonymous
331 Please specify the password.
Password:
230 Login successful.
ftp>
```

Figure 10.6: Login was successful

7. List the files and directories by entering the `ls` command and pressing *Enter*:

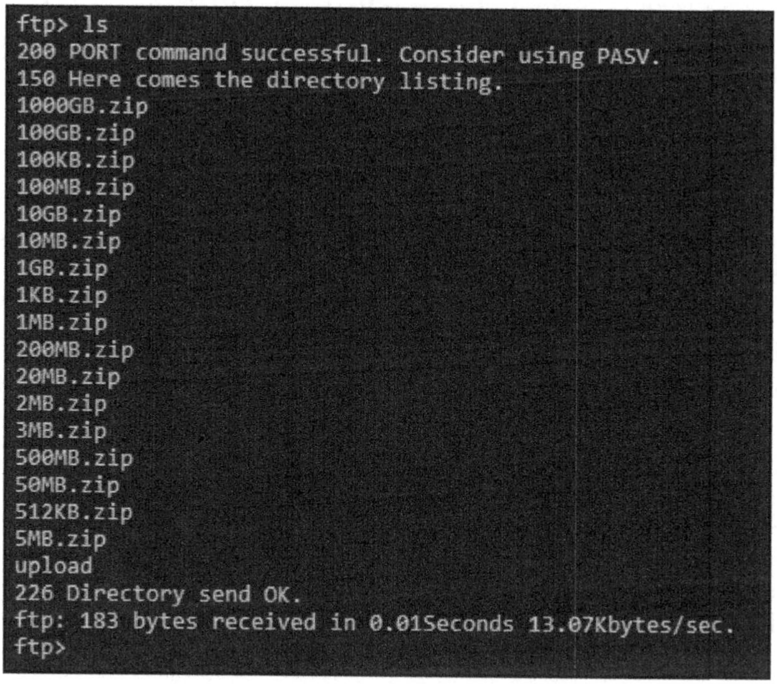

```
ftp> ls
200 PORT command successful. Consider using PASV.
150 Here comes the directory listing.
1000GB.zip
100GB.zip
100KB.zip
100MB.zip
10GB.zip
10MB.zip
1GB.zip
1KB.zip
1MB.zip
200MB.zip
20MB.zip
2MB.zip
3MB.zip
500MB.zip
50MB.zip
512KB.zip
5MB.zip
upload
226 Directory send OK.
ftp: 183 bytes received in 0.01Seconds 13.07Kbytes/sec.
ftp>
```

Figure 10.7: Files and directories list

8. Now, we need to download the `2MB.zip` file. Enter the `get 2MB.zip` command and press *Enter*.
9. The screen will change to advise you that the transfer has been completed.
10. The file should be in the root of your home folder; for example, `C:\users\<yourname>`.
11. Exit FTP interactive mode by typing `quit` and pressing *Enter*.
12. The Command Prompt should return to normal.

Now, you've successfully learned how to download files through FTP. We will look at how FTP works in more detail in `Chapter 14`, *Network Services*.

# Trivial FTP

While FTP runs over TCP, **Trivial File Transfer Protocol (TFTP)** runs over **User Datagram Protocol (UDP)** on port 69, which means it cannot guarantee delivery. While this may seem odd, one of the main reasons for not using TCP is to avoid the three-way handshake and acknowledgment process, thus reducing overhead on potentially low-bandwidth connections. Imagine that you want to reinstall an operating system en masse to a number of devices. Here, you would do the following:

1. Stage the image to be deployed on a deployment server and set the server to transmit the image as a multicast transmission.
2. The server would transmit the image on a loop.
3. Once the server had transmitted everything, it would start again.
4. Because of this, any device you wish to reimage could just be pointed at the deployment server and it would pick up the transmission at its current point.
5. It will obtain anything that it missed (that is, the data is sent prior to it being connected) when the transmission loops round.

It would be inefficient for this process to wait until every device had acknowledged the data before sending the next bit. What if one of the devices hadn't received it but the rest all had? You would end up waiting for it to be retransmitted and acknowledged before the next bit was sent. If the transmission totally fails for one device, so be it. This can be looked at separately.

# Simple Mail Transfer Protocol

**Simple Mail Transfer Protocol (SMTP)** generally provides two functions. It allows you to send emails from your email client, such as Outlook, to your email server. It also allows your email server to transfer mail from your email server to another email server. Both of these functions are performed over port 25.

**Exam tip**: Although the **S** in **SMTP** stands for **Simple**, I quite often say to myself that it stands for **Send** as in **Send Mail**. While not factually correct, it reminds me of its purpose compared to **IMAP** and **POP**, which are used to receive emails.

# Support services

Support protocols can be defined as protocols that are used by the system itself. Generally, support services go beyond the scope of the exam, but I will briefly discuss them here.

## Host initialization

This provides a means for you to boot a computer over a network when it doesn't have its own operating system installed. Booting over the network requires a computer to have a network card that supports a **pre-boot execution environment** (**PXE** – pronounced pixie). Most modern systems will support this, though it may have to be enabled in the system's BIOS.

## Remote management

This service allows managing devices through the use of protocols such as the **Simple Network Management Protocol** (**SNMP**), which runs over port 161. SNMP requires an SNMP agent on the host, which communicates back to an SNMP server. These communications include attributes and their values, such as free disk space, CPU usage, and so on. However, this is not a one-way process and the server can also communicate settings back to the device for remote configuration.

## Domain Name System

The **Domain Name System** (**DNS**) will be discussed in more detail in Chapter 13, *Understanding Name Resolution*, but for now, just be aware that it is classed as a support service and resolves **fully qualified domains** (**FQDNs**) to IP addresses.

Once the application layer has performed its role, it passes the data to the transport layer, which we will discuss next.

# Understanding the transport layer

The transport layer of the TCP/IP model performs the exact same role as its counterpart in the OSI model. Namely, it is responsible for controlling communication between the two hosts. As a brief reminder, recall that the transport layer provides the following features:

- The use of checksums to ensure data integrity
- The use of sequence numbers to ensure data is rebuilt in the correct order
- Flow control to ensure the data that's being received doesn't end up flooding the recipient device
- Multiplexing to allow a host to have multiple connections to another host

The TCP and UDP protocols can be found here again. Think back to the previous chapter. How would you describe each of these two protocols? If you said that TCP was a connection-oriented protocol that uses a system of sequence numbers and acknowledgments, you would be correct. The same applies, if you said that UDP was a connectionless protocol that worked on the principle of best effort.

Again, once the transport layer has completed its task, it passes the data down to the internet layer.

# Understanding the internet layer

The internet layer maps across to the network layer of the OSI. Despite the difference in name, these two layers perform the same functions. They both provide logical addressing through the use of IP addresses. By using IP addresses (and a subnet mask), we can identify whether a host is local to the sending device or on a remote network. If the destination is on a remote network, the IP address is also used in the process of path selection and forwarding of data via routers, routing servers, or layer 3 switches. Note that I use the term layer 3 here, despite the TCP/IP model not using numbering, purely for familiarity since we have referred to them as this previously.

The three main protocols on this layer are as follows:

- IP
- **Internet Control Messaging Protocol (ICMP)**
- **Internet Group Management Protocol (IGMP)**

We already have a basic understanding of the fact that IP provides us with logical addressing, and we will discuss this in more detail in the following chapter. However, it is worth noting that IP also allows for the fragmentation and defragmentation of data being transmitted. The devices that the data is transmitted through may only be able to receive data of a certain size, and this is known as a **Maximum Transmission Unit (MTU)**. Fragmentation breaks the data down into parts to meet the MTU. Defragmentation is where data is combined into an MTU. Let's use some arbitrary values here to illustrate this.

A computer wants to send 5 bytes of data. The first router it transits through has an MTU value of 1 byte. This means that the original data has to be broken down into five parts (fragmentation). The second router the data goes through has an MTU of 3 bytes. If this second router can handle this much, it would be inefficient to keep the data in five parts, so before the data is sent to the second router, it is combined to form two parts (defragmentation).

ICMP is used by devices to send error and control messages to each other. These messages can state that, among other things, a host is unreachable, a host is reachable but the port on the host is unreachable, the network is unreachable, and so on. These control messages are identified in the ICMP data through the use of types and subtypes. Knowing these types goes beyond the requirements of the exam, but for the real world, I would recommend that you have an understanding of what each means. **Request for Comments (RFC)** 792 has an excellent writeup of these. The link to this can be found in the *Further reading* section. ICMP is used by the `ping` and `tracert` command, which we have already covered.

IGMP is used to create logical groups of devices. These logical groups will then be used during multicast transmissions and with IPv4.

Having covered the first three layers of the TCP/IP model, we will now look at the final layer, that is, the network layer.

# Understanding the network layer

The network layer of the TCP/IP model maps against the data-link layer and the physical layer of the OSI model. Because of this, it incorporates the functions of these two OSI layers into this one TCP/IP layer.

While the internet layer is responsible for communications mainly outside the host's network and for routing this data, the network layer is responsible for communications on the link (basically anything within the same subnet). Because of this, the network layer is sometimes referred to as the link layer.

It is on the network layer of the TCP/IP model that media access control is performed, and therefore MAC addresses can be found here. In addition, the attributes of the physical medium, such as modulation and coding, are also here.

There are a number of protocols and standards that are part of the network layer. These include IEEE 802.3 Ethernet, IEEE 802.11, **Point to Point Protocol (PPP)**, **Address Resolution Protocol (ARP)**, and Frame Relay.

# Summary

This chapter provided you with an overview of the TCP/IP model. We went through the four layers: application, transport, internet, and network. We covered the functionality of each layer and some tools found within the model.

In this chapter, you learned how to use a terminal emulator, such as PuTTY, to make a Telnet connection. You also used the FTP tool to transfer files from a remote device. By understanding the TCP/IP model, not only will you have the knowledge required by the exam, but you will also be able to apply what you've learned to real-world scenarios. A firm understanding will provide you with the ability to troubleshoot networks more efficiently and identify points of failure.

In `Chapter 11`, *Understanding IPv4*, we will cover one of the key areas of networking, namely IPv4 addressing. We will discuss classful and classless addressing by highlighting the benefits of each. In addition, we will delve into the realm of subnetting and look at its purpose.

# Questions

1. Which of these is not a layer of the TCP/IP model?

(A) Network layer
(B) Data-link layer
(C) Transport layer
(D) Application layer

2. Which of these is classed as a support service?

(A) DNS
(B) FTP
(C) TFTP
(D) SMTP

3. Which of these standards relates to Ethernet?

(A) IEEE 802.1x
(B) IEEE 802.3
(C) IEEE 802.5
(D) IEEE 802.11

4. Which of these is an internet layer protocol?

(A) PPP
(B) FTP
(C) ICMP
(D) SMTP

5. Which protocol is used to create logical groups of devices?

(A) ARP
(B) ICMP
(C) IGMP
(D) IP

6. Which layer is responsible for controlling communications between hosts?

(A) Transport
(B) Data-link
(C) Application
(D) Network

7. Breaking data into parts to meet MTU requirements is known as what?

(A) Encapsulation
(B) Deencapsulation
(C) Fragmentation
(D) Defragmentation

# Further reading

- To find out more about TCP/IP, visit `https://tools.ietf.org/html/rfc1180`.
- To find out more about the communication layers, visit `https://tools.ietf.org/html/rfc1122`.
- To find out more about the TCP/IP application and its support, visit `https://tools.ietf.org/html/rfc1123`.
- To find out more about ICMP, visit `https://tools.ietf.org/html/rfc792`.

# 11
# Understanding IPv4

An important part of any network communication is addressing. Addressing is a means of identifying a device on a network. Previously, we discussed identifying devices on a network through the use of hostnames, IP addresses, and MAC addresses. Without addressing, how would the data know who it was intended for? And how could it be routed to the destination?

In this chapter, we will discuss IPv4 addresses. Although these are slowly being replaced by IPv6 addresses, this process is being carried out at a glacial pace. IPv4 will still be around for a long time to come. Understanding IPv4 addressing is one of the most important aspects of any networking role, and it is imperative that you are comfortable with it.

The following topics will be covered in this chapter:

- Overview of IPv4
- Understanding classful networks
- Understanding subnet masks
- Understanding **Classless Inter-Domain Routing (CIDR)**
- Assigning IP addresses to hosts

## Technical requirements

To complete the exercises in this chapter, you will need a PC running a Windows OS and a calculator (optional).

# Overview of IPv4

We have already discussed IP in a number of chapters already while touching upon some of the basics. IP addresses provide a hierarchical means of identifying devices on networks. Hierarchical in this context means that we can identify which network an IP address resides on through the use of the IP address and it's subnet mask. Don't worry if the latter term is unfamiliar to you – we will cover it in this chapter.

In this chapter, we will cover arguably one of the primary functions of this ubiquitous protocol: addressing. There are currently two main versions of IP address that are used in everyday networking:

- IPv4
- IPv6

In this chapter, we will focus on IPv4, and in the next chapter, we will cover IPv6.

# Structure of an IPv4 address

An IPv4 address is made up of 32 bits, each with a value of 1 or a value of 0. Because of this, there are 4,294,967,296 possible IP addresses (usually, we just say there are 4.2 billion IP addresses). But how did we get this huge figure? We used a calculation of $2^n$, where $n$ is the number of bits being used. Thus, in the case of an IPv4 address with 32 bits, it would be $2^{32}$.

Each IPv4 address is broken down into four sections that are referred to as octets because they are 8 bits each. Each of those bits can have a value of 1 or a value of 0. Each octet is separated by a dot (.) and therefore an IP address is sometimes referred to as being in a dotted-decimal format:

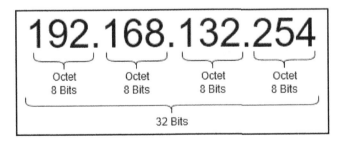

Figure 11.1: Example of an IPv4 address

If you have taken any courses on IT basics, you may be thinking. *I thought 8 bits was a byte,* and you would be right. While each of these sections is a byte of data, when we refer to sections, we call them octets, which refers to a pattern of 8 bits. Each of these octets can have a value of 0 to 255 inclusive. This range is obtained by using $2^n$ again. For each octet, we have 8 bits available, that is, $2^8=256$. Be careful here – there are 256 possible values, but because we count 0 as a valid value, the highest figure we can go to in an octet is 255:

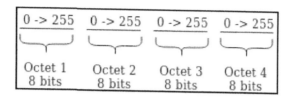

Figure 11.2: Octets in an IPv4 address

An IPv4 address itself represents two elements: the network element and the host element. The network element tells us which network the IP address resides on, while the host element identifies the host on that particular network. The demarcation between the two is dependent on which subnet mask is being used. We will cover this in detail later in this chapter.

So far, we've identified what an IPv4 address looks like and how it is broken down. Now, we will discuss why they need to be unique on a network.

# Need for unique IP addresses

Each IPv4 address has to be unique in its own network, and if it is a public IP address, it has to be unique in the World to prevent issues. To ensure that public IP addresses are unique, the **Internet Assigned Numbers Authority (IANA)** issues blocks of IP addresses to regional registrars for further dissemination. Each of these registrars is responsible for issuing blocks of IP addresses to ISPs, who may in turn issue IP addresses to lower-level ISPs who then issue them to the public or organizations. Some of these registrars are as follows:

- **African Network Information Center (AFRINIC)**: Africa
- **American Registry for Internet Numbers (ARIN)**: Antarctica, Canada, parts of the Caribbean, and the United States
- **Asia-Pacific Network Information Centre (APNIC)**: East Asia, Oceania, South Asia, and Southeast Asia

- **Latin America and Caribbean Network Information Centre (LACNIC):** Most of the Caribbean and all of Latin America
- **Réseaux IP Européens Network Coordination Centre (RIPE NCC):** Europe, Central Asia, Russia, and West Asia

We discussed private IP addresses in Chapter 2, *Understanding Local Area Networks*. While private IP addresses don't have to be unique in the World, they have to be unique within their own subnet. This does give you some leeway, in that a private IP address can be reused within an organization; that is, you could have two subnets containing hosts with the same IP addresses, but this would cause a lot of routing issues. How on earth would a device know which of those versions of an IP address is the correct one?

As a refresher, recall that we discussed how a public IP address is one that is routable across the internet, whereas a private IP address is not routable across the internet. Furthermore, a public IP address has to be issued by an ISP, but a private IP address is managed by you as an individual or as an organization.

When planning your network, you're going to use one of the following addressing:

- Classful IPv4 addressing
- Classless IPv4 addressing

Classful addressing takes the 4.2 billion IPv4 addresses and breaks them down into predefined ranges of IP addresses, with predefined subnet masks, resulting in a predefined number of hosts per network. Using classful addressing, you are simplifying the process of creating and managing IP addresses, but it is not necessarily the most efficient means of using the available IP addresses.

In contrast, classless addressing removes these predefined values and lets network administrators create their own network address ranges and, within certain restrictions, their own subnet masks. Classless addressing is more efficient as you can adjust the number of hosts per network to suit your needs but makes creation and management a lot more taxing.

 As we go through this chapter, I will cover classful addresses first, then talk about subnetting, and then cover classless addressing. You may be wondering why I have split it in this way, and quite simply it is because you need to understand subnetting basics before you can appreciate the use of classless addressing; furthermore, to understand subnetting, it is useful to know classful addressing.

Behind all this sits binary or the base-2 numbering system, which is the underlying system that's used in any form of computing (at least until quantum computing is fully develop(D). I have to admit that I'm always arguing with myself about where to include binary in any IP addressing since it is handy to have an understanding of binary before diving into addressing. For this book, I have decided to talk about it first since you have already had an overview of IP addresses in `Chapter 2`, *Understanding Local Area Networks*.

# Binary math

While discussing the structure of an IPv4 address, I mentioned that a bit can have a value of `0` or a value of `1`. This sums up binary in a simplified nutshell. Using only the numbers 0 and 1, we can make any number we like, and in this section, I'm going to show you how to do this. But first, let me show how I learned decimal at school (back in the 1970s) and then we can apply these principles to binary.

Where binary can only use the numbers 0 and 1, decimal uses the numbers 0-9 to make up any value. When I was at school, my teacher drew a chart on the blackboard that looked a little like this:

| Thousands | Hundreds | Tens | Ones |
|-----------|----------|------|------|
|           |          |      |      |

If she wanted to show the number **1**, she would write the following:

| Thousands | Hundreds | Tens | Ones |
|-----------|----------|------|------|
|           |          |      | 1    |

Likewise, the numbers **2** and **3** would be written like so:

| Thousands | Hundreds | Tens | Ones |
|-----------|----------|------|------|
|           |          |      | 2    |
|           |          |      | 3    |

If I wanted to write the number 10, I would use 1 ten, and 0 ones; if I wanted to write 16, I would use 1 ten, and 6 ones; for the number 349, I would use 3 hundreds, 4 tens, and 9 ones:

| Thousands | Hundreds | Tens | Ones |
|-----------|----------|------|------|
|           |          | 1    | 0    |
|           |          | 1    | 6    |
|           | 3        | 4    | 9    |

As you can see, using these simple principles, we can write any whole number that we like. We will use a similar process for binary. The first difference is that we don't use units, tens, hundreds, and thousands. In binary, we use the following column headings:

| 128 | 64 | 32 | 16 | 8 | 4 | 2 | 1 |
|-----|----|----|----|----|----|----|----|
|     |    |    |    |    |    |    |    |

Note that, when reading from right to left, the numbers double from column to column. I would always recommend learning it from right to left rather than left to right. Trust me – it makes things so much easier. I've stopped at eight columns, mainly because it is quite relevant to this chapter, but we could continue adding columns to the left, for example, 256, 512, 1,024, and so on.

Let's start counting in binary. Remember, we can only use 0 or 1. So, a value of 1 would be written like so:

| 128 | 64 | 32 | 16 | 8 | 4 | 2 | 1 |
|-----|----|----|----|----|----|----|----|
|     |    |    |    |    |    |    | 1  |

Well, that was pretty simple, wasn't it? How about a value of 2? This would be written like so:

| 128 | 64 | 32 | 16 | 8 | 4 | 2 | 1 |
|-----|----|----|----|----|----|----|----|
|     |    |    |    |    |    | 1  | 0  |

To get the value 2, we would need to have 1 from the 2 column and 0 from the 1s from here on column. To get three, we would use **1** from the **2** column, and **1** from the **1** column (*2 + 1 = 3*):

| 128 | 64 | 32 | 16 | 8 | 4 | 2 | 1 |
|-----|----|----|----|----|----|----|----|
|     |    |    |    |    |    | 1  | 1  |

Likewise, if we wanted ten, we would add 1 from the **8** column and 1 from the **2** column; **48** would be **1** from the **32** column and **1** from the **16** column:

| 128 | 64 | 32 | 16 | 8 | 4 | 2 | 1 |
|-----|----|----|----|----|----|----|----|
|     |    |    |    | 1  | 0  | 1  | 0  |
|     |    | 1  | 1  | 0  | 0  | 0  | 0  |

The key here is really as simple as looking at each column. If it has a 1 in it, add the value of the column header to the value of any other column that has a 1 in it.

When we write a number in binary, we can include the leading zeroes, but generally, we drop them. However, we cannot drop any trailing zeroes. So, for example, the decimal value 2 could be written in binary as 00000010 or as 10, but never as 0000001 or 1. Likewise, any zeroes in the middle of the number also have to be included, as we saw with the number 10 in the preceding example. This is to avoid any confusion.

**Activity 1**: In the following activity, I would like you to convert the decimal numbers into binary, and vice versa, using the process you have just seen. Note that *E* to *G* are binary values:

(A) 6
(B) 34
(C) 67
(D) 139
(E) 1101
(F) 11101010
(G) 11111111

Following are the answers to the preceding activity:

(A) 110
(B) 100010
(C) 1000011
(D) 10001011
(E) 13
(F) 234
(G) 255

One thing you may have noticed is that any odd number that's written in binary always ends in a 1. From that, we can assume that any binary number ending in a 0 is an even number. This is always handy to remember when performing a quick check while doing any conversions.

You may be wondering what this has got to do with network addresses. Simply put, a computer uses binary to identify networks and the host elements of an IP address. We will delve into this in more detail later in this chapter when we cover subnet masks. What I would like to draw your attention to now is the answer for *g*) in the preceding activity. Notice that 8 bits, all with the value of 1 (that is, 11111111), gave us a decimal value of 255. Recall that I mentioned that each section of an IP address is 8 bits and called an **octet**. Each octet has a value range of 0 to 255 or 00000000 to 11111111.

If we wanted to convert an IP address into binary, we would look at each octet individually, write down the binary value followed by a dot (.), and then we would do the same for the next octet, like so:

*10.23.56.14 = 00001010.00010111.00111000.00001110*
*198.34.90.210 = 11000110.00100010.01011010.11010010*
*255.0.0.0 = 11111111.00000000.00000000.00000000*
*255.255.0.0 = 11111111.11111111.00000000.00000000*
*255.255.255.0 = 11111111.11111111.11111111.00000000*
*103.45.179.201 = 01100111.00101101.10110011.11001001*
*67.87.14.56 = 01000011.01010111.00001110.00111000*

As we mentioned previously, we will delve more into binary later in this chapter. Now that we have a strong understanding of IPv4 addresses, we will learn about classful networks in detail.

# Understanding classful networks

A network can be regarded as either of the following types:

- Classful networks
- Classless networks

A classful network always has a predefined number of bits allocated to the network element of the IP address, and therefore a predefined subnet mask. Classful networks also allow us to easily identify a network's class from its IP address and are relatively easy to configure. However, the problem with using classful networks, as you will see, is that they do not provide efficient use of IP addresses.

Classless networks do away with the boundaries of predefined network elements and subnets and offer us a degree of flexibility, thus allowing for a more efficient use of IP addresses. Their downside is that they can be difficult to configure in terms of allocating the right number of bits to a network element. This may sound a little confusing, but as we go through each of the classes, it will become easier. I promise.

In terms of classful networks, there are five classes: A, B, C, D, and E. Classes A, B, and C have their own IP address ranges, default subnet masks, a maximum number of hosts, and private address ranges. Classes D and E have their own IP address ranges but do not require the other attributes. First, let's look at classes A, B, and C:

| | Class A: | Class B: | Class C: |
|---|---|---|---|
| Address range: | 0.0.0.0 - 127.255.255.255 | 128.0.0.0 - 192.255.255.255 | 192.0.0.0 - 223.255.255.255 |
| Default subnet mask: | 255.0.0.0 or /8 | 255.255.0.0 or /16 | 255.255.255.0 or /24 |
| IP addresses available: | 16,777,216 or 2^24 | 65,536 or 2^16 | 256 or 2^8 |
| Maximum number of hosts: | 16,777,214 | 65,534 | 254 |
| Private address range: | 10.0.0.0 - 10.255.255.255 | 172.16.0.0 - 172.31.255.255 | 192.168.0.0 - 192.168.255.255 |

Figure 11.3: Classes A, B, and C classful network

Before I move on to classes D and E, I would like to dig a little deeper into some of the preceding attributes.

First, I have written the subnet masks in a dotted-decimal format and as a slash notation, that is, /8, /16, /24. This is often also referred to as CIDR notation. We will cover CIDR in more detail shortly. What this slash notation is telling us is the number of bits that have been allocated to the subnet mask (or network element). Therefore, **Class A** has 8 bits allocated to the network element, **Class B** has 16 bits, and **Class C** has 24 bits.

Recall that I mentioned that an IPv4 address is 32 bits. Well, in a **Class A** network, if 8 bits are for the network, then that leaves 24 bits for the host element (*32 - 8 = 24*); **Class B** networks have 16 bits for the network and 16 bits for the host element (*32 - 16 = 16*); and **Class C** has 24 bits for the network and 8 bits for the host element (*32 - 24 = 8*). The number of bits for the host element tells us how many IP addresses we can have per network. The calculation is $2^n$, where *n* is the number of bits available for the host element. I have included this in the preceding attributes.

Note that the maximum number of hosts is always 2 fewer than the number of IP addresses available. This is because, in each network, the first and last IP address have a special purpose and cannot be issued to hosts. The first IP address in any network is referred to as the Network ID (or address) and the last IP address in a network is referred to as the broadcast ID (or address). We tend to see the Network ID being used in conjunction with a subnet mask in the routing table of any device with an IP address. This is usually to tell the router that the traffic that's destined for the specified network needs to go through a specified interface in the routing table.

As shown in the following screenshot, the **Network ID** is also used on Windows hosts for routing purposes:

```
Active Routes:
Network Destination          Netmask          Gateway      Interface  Metric
          0.0.0.0          0.0.0.0          10.0.0.1       10.0.0.5    281
         10.0.0.0        255.0.0.0           On-link       10.0.0.5    281
         10.0.0.5  255.255.255.255           On-link       10.0.0.5    281
   10.255.255.255  255.255.255.255           On-link       10.0.0.5    281
        127.0.0.0        255.0.0.0           On-link      127.0.0.1    331
        127.0.0.1  255.255.255.255           On-link      127.0.0.1    331
  127.255.255.255  255.255.255.255           On-link      127.0.0.1    331
        224.0.0.0        240.0.0.0           On-link      127.0.0.1    331
        224.0.0.0        240.0.0.0           On-link       10.0.0.5    281
  255.255.255.255  255.255.255.255           On-link      127.0.0.1    331
  255.255.255.255  255.255.255.255           On-link       10.0.0.5    281
===========================================================================
Persistent Routes:
  Network Address          Netmask  Gateway Address  Metric
          0.0.0.0          0.0.0.0         10.0.0.1  Default
===========================================================================
```

Figure 11.4: Route printed with network address highlighted

The broadcast ID is an IP address that is used to communicate to all the devices on that particular network. Rather than listing all the individual IP addresses on a network, or sending out individual transmissions to all the devices on the network, I can use the broadcast IP address to communicate with them all in one go. In a way, it is like putting a label on your transmission that says *FAO: EVERYONE*. If you receive something labelled that way you know it's for you as well as everyone else.

It is important to remember that network and broadcast IDs exist. If you try allocating one of these addresses to a device, it's likely that you will get an error message. This may not happen immediately, but once you have tried applying it in conjunction with a subnet mask, you will get one.

 Be careful if you get an exam question that asks you what constitutes a valid IP address to give a host when presented with an IP address range and a subnet mask. It is too easy to find an IP address that falls within the range but is actually a network or broadcast ID and therefore cannot be allocated to a host.

Now, let's take a look at classes D and E. These two classes contain ranges of IP addresses that cannot be issued to hosts individually since each range is set aside for special purposes. Note that these classes don't have subnet masks, nor do they have public and private address ranges. In fact, no address in these ranges is globally routable.

**Class D** compromises a range of IP addresses that are set aside for multicast transmission purposes, and cannot be assigned specifically to an individual host. The range is 224.0.0.0 − 239.255.255.255.

**Class E** is set aside for mainly experimental purposes, and like **Class D** it cannot be assigned to an individual host. The range is 240.0.0.0 − 255.255.255.255. An important IP address to note is 255.255.255.255. This specific address is used to send broadcast communications to all the devices in network without them having to know any specifics about the IP address range of that network.

In this section, we've seen that classes have fixed address ranges, which stipulates how many hosts are in each subnet. Classful addressing allows you to simplify the process of addressing devices. Simply choose the appropriate class that allows the number of hosts you require.

# Understanding subnet masks

A subnet is a smaller network within a larger network. Let me give you an analogy to reinforce this concept. Imagine you have a huge office complex (the larger network). Now, you could lease out the complex to just one company, or you could put up walls and create a number of smaller separate offices (subnets) that could be used by a number of other companies rather than just one. All of these companies will be identified by which suite number they occupy. The suite number is the equivalent of the network element of the IP address.

 Even if our network is not broken down into smaller networks, we still tend to refer to that one network as a subnet.

Look at the following IP address. Which part of the address is the network element and which part is the host element?

185.23.154.87

Based on the IP address itself, you cannot tell, unless you know that you are using classful networks. This is where subnet masks come into play. A subnet mask tells you which part of the IP address is a network element and which part is the host element. A subnet mask plays an important part in network communications.

At a basic level, when your computer wants to communicate with a remote device, it uses its own subnet mask and IP address to identify its own network element. It runs a similar comparison using its own subnet mask and the destination IP address to identify what it presumes to be the network element of the destination device. If the two network elements match, then it assumes they are on the same network and they will communicate directly. If they do not match, then it assumes they are not on the same network and all the communication is sent via the default gateway. You will notice that I used the term *presumes*. This is because we do not receive the destination devices' subnet mask, so we do not use it in the comparison to identify the network element; hence we use our own. Potentially, but generally unlikely, we might presume a device is on our network when it actually isn't.

 Subnet masks will only contain the values 128, 192, 224, 240, 248, 252, 254, or 255. If you see any other values in octets, then assume it is incorrect. If you are wondering why this is the case, think back to the binary tables we used. Since a subnet mask in binary format consists of continuous 1s starting from the left, it restricts us to these values.

For ease, I will focus on default subnet masks for classful networks initially. First, I'm going to show you the quick-fix way of identifying the network element in classful subnets. Then, I will move on and show you the binary behind it. Once we have done that, we will look at CIDR, although I will make a brief reference to it in these early stages.

## Classful/default subnet masks

We have already identified that the default subnet masks for classes A, B, and C are 255.0.0.0, 255.255.0.0, and 255.255.255.0, respectively. To identify the network element of a classful IP address, we compare it to its subnet mask. If an octet in the subnet mask has a 255 in it, then its respective octet in the IP address is part of the network element. Let's look at each of these in turn.

For class A, we can see that only the first octet of the subnet mask has 255 in it. This means that only the first octet in the IP address is the network element. I tend to write the IP address above the subnet mask and compare them. Look at the following example:

| IP address | 23 . 78 . 23 . 98 |
|---|---|
| Subnet mask | 255 . 0 . 0 . 0 |

From just a quick glance, we can see that the network element is 23.x.x.x; therefore, the remaining part of the IP address, that is, x.78.23.98, must be the host element. Recall that this host element must be unique on the network. What about when we are comparing whether two addresses are in the same network? I can do a similar thing but put the destination IP below the subnet mask:

| IP address | 23 . 78 . 23 . 98 |
|---|---|
| Subnet mask | 225 . 0 . 0 . 0 |
| Destination IP address | 23 . 12 . 232 . 18 |

All we do here is look at the first octet and see if it contains the same value. If they do, they are on the same network; if they do not match, they are not on the same network. Using the preceding process, which of the following destination addresses are on the same network as the source IP address of 120.54.12.78?

(A) 120.23.89.34
(B) 12.54.12.78
(C) 120.54.12.78
(D) 54.40.78.2

The only two that are in the same network are A and C. They both have a first octet containing the value 120. The other two do not. Be careful if you're presented with something like the IP address in B. The first octet is different but the last three octets are identical to the source IP. However, remember it is only the first octet that counts.

For Class B, we can see that only the first two octets of the subnet mask have 255 in them. This means that only the first two octets in the IP address is the network element. Look at the following example:

| IP address | 134 . 67 . 90 . 98 |
|---|---|
| Subnet mask | 255 . 255 . 0 . 0 |

From just a quick glance, we can see that the network element is 134.67.x.x; therefore, the remaining part of the IP address, that is, x.x.90.98, must be the host element. Let's compare two Class B addresses:

| IP address | 134 . 67 . 90 . 98 |
|---|---|
| Subnet Mask | 255 . 255 . 0 . 0 |
| Destination IP address | 134 . 67 . 200 . 43 |

When we are using Class B, both the first and second octets have to match in the two addresses for the devices to be deemed to be on the same network. So, in the preceding example, they are on the same network. If I changed the destination IP address to 134.65.190.7, they would not be on the same network since the second octet is different. Likewise, if I changed the destination IP address to 133.67.2.76, these would not be on the same network since the first octets don't match.

We follow the same *octet matching* principle for Class C. However, we use the first three octets for the network element because the default subnet mask has 255 in these octets. Look at the following example:

| IP address | 197 . 7 . 14 . 200 |
|---|---|
| Subnet mask | 255 . 255 . 255 . 0 |

Here, we can see that the network element is 197.7.14.x and that the host element is x.x.x.200.

**Activity 2**: Compare the following two Class C addresses. Are they on the same network?

| IP address | 197 . 7 . 14 . 200 |
|---|---|
| Subnet mask | 255 . 255 . 255 . 0 |
| Destination IP address | 197 . 7 . 14 . 43 |

Remember that we need to get a match on all of the first three octets for the devices to be deemed to be on the same network. So, in the preceding activity, they are on the same network, and we can see this because both IP addresses are in the 197.7.14.x network. If I changed any of the values in the first three octets of the destination IP address, then they would not be on the same network.

While the preceding method is relatively simple for us as humans to understand, your computer actually uses the binary behind this. Earlier in this chapter, I mentioned that the default subnet masks could also be written in the CIDR or slash notation format, that is, /8, /16, and /24. These numbers refer to the number of bits that are used in the subnet mask. Now, let's look at how this works by converting the subnet masks into binary. Once we have done this, we will look at using binary to find the network element and from this, the network address.

For this example, we'll start with a Class A default subnet mask, `255.0.0.0`. I'm going to break it down into its octets in the following table:

| Octet | Decimal | 128 | 64 | 32 | 16 | 8 | 4 | 2 | 1 |
|---|---|---|---|---|---|---|---|---|---|
| 1 | 255 | | | | | | | | |
| 2 | 0 | | | | | | | | |
| 3 | 0 | | | | | | | | |
| 4 | 0 | | | | | | | | |

Figure 11.5: Breaking Class A's default subnet mask into octets

Then, starting from the left, I'm going to add up the numbers in the column headings until I get the figure in the decimal column. For every column I use, I'm going to put a **1** in the box:

| Octet | Decimal | 128 | 64 | 32 | 16 | 8 | 4 | 2 | 1 |
|---|---|---|---|---|---|---|---|---|---|
| 1 | 255 | 1 | 1 | 1 | 1 | 1 | 1 | 1 | 1 |
| 2 | 0 | 0 | 0 | 0 | 0 | 0 | 0 | 0 | 0 |
| 3 | 0 | 0 | 0 | 0 | 0 | 0 | 0 | 0 | 0 |
| 4 | 0 | 0 | 0 | 0 | 0 | 0 | 0 | 0 | 0 |

Figure 11.6: Adding up the numbers in the column headings

Here, we have *128 + 64 + 32 + 16 + 8 + 4 + 2 + 1 = 255.*

Now, let's add another column on the end and add the ones together:

| Octet | Decimal | 128 | 64 | 32 | 16 | 8 | 4 | 2 | 1 | Total |
|---|---|---|---|---|---|---|---|---|---|---|
| 1 | 255 | 1 | 1 | 1 | 1 | 1 | 1 | 1 | 1 | 8 |
| 2 | 0 | 0 | 0 | 0 | 0 | 0 | 0 | 0 | 0 | 0 |
| 3 | 0 | 0 | 0 | 0 | 0 | 0 | 0 | 0 | 0 | 0 |
| 4 | 0 | 0 | 0 | 0 | 0 | 0 | 0 | 0 | 0 | 0 |
| Grand Total | | | | | | | | | | 8 |

Figure 11.7: Adding up the ones

Here, we have *8 + 0 + 0 + 0 = 8.*

So, a default Class 1 subnet mask could be written in CIDR notation as `/8`.

Let's have a look at the steps for Class B notation without explaining anything and see if you can get it:

| Octet | Decimal | 128 | 64 | 32 | 16 | 8 | 4 | 2 | 1 |
|-------|---------|-----|----|----|----|---|---|---|---|
| 1 | 255 | | | | | | | | |
| 2 | 255 | | | | | | | | |
| 3 | 0 | | | | | | | | |
| 4 | 0 | | | | | | | | |

| Octet | Decimal | 128 | 64 | 32 | 16 | 8 | 4 | 2 | 1 |
|-------|---------|-----|----|----|----|---|---|---|---|
| 1 | 255 | 1 | 1 | 1 | 1 | 1 | 1 | 1 | 1 |
| 2 | 255 | 1 | 1 | 1 | 1 | 1 | 1 | 1 | 1 |
| 3 | 0 | 0 | 0 | 0 | 0 | 0 | 0 | 0 | 0 |
| 4 | 0 | 0 | 0 | 0 | 0 | 0 | 0 | 0 | 0 |

| Octet | Decimal | 128 | 64 | 32 | 16 | 8 | 4 | 2 | 1 | Total |
|-------|---------|-----|----|----|----|---|---|---|---|-------|
| 1 | 255 | 1 | 1 | 1 | 1 | 1 | 1 | 1 | 1 | 8 |
| 2 | 255 | 1 | 1 | 1 | 1 | 1 | 1 | 1 | 1 | 8 |
| 3 | 0 | 0 | 0 | 0 | 0 | 0 | 0 | 0 | 0 | 0 |
| 4 | 0 | 0 | 0 | 0 | 0 | 0 | 0 | 0 | 0 | 0 |

Figure 11.8: Steps for Class B

Here, we have *8 + 8 + 0 + 0 = 16.*

So, a Class B default subnet in CIDR notation looks like: /16.

**Activity 3**: In this activity, I would like you to work out the CIDR notation for a Class C default subnet mask:

| Octet | Decimal | 128 | 64 | 32 | 16 | 8 | 4 | 2 | 1 |
|-------|---------|-----|----|----|----|---|---|---|---|
| 1 | | | | | | | | | |
| 2 | | | | | | | | | |
| 3 | | | | | | | | | |
| 4 | | | | | | | | | |

| Octet | Decimal | 128 | 64 | 32 | 16 | 8 | 4 | 2 | 1 |
|-------|---------|-----|----|----|----|---|---|---|---|
| 1 | | | | | | | | | |
| 2 | | | | | | | | | |
| 3 | | | | | | | | | |
| 4 | | | | | | | | | |

| Octet | Decimal | 128 | 64 | 32 | 16 | 8 | 4 | 2 | 1 | Total |
|-------|---------|-----|----|----|----|---|---|---|---|-------|
| 1 | | | | | | | | | | |
| 2 | | | | | | | | | | |
| 3 | | | | | | | | | | |
| 4 | | | | | | | | | | |
| | | | | Grand Total | | | | | | |

Figure 11.9: Steps for Class C

.... + ..... + ..... + ..... = .....

So, the CIDR notation is ..........

Hopefully, you got *8 + 8 + 8 + 0 = 32*, giving you a CIDR notation of /32. Now that we have looked at the CIDR notation and have had the opportunity to get familiar with some basic binary, we will continue to use binary to identify the network element of an IP address.

# Identifying network elements using binary

Now that you know the binary representations of default subnet masks, we will look at how we can use binary to identify the network element of an IP address. We are going to follow a three-step process:

1. Convert the IP address into binary.
2. Convert the subnet mask into binary.
3. Perform an AND calculation on the two sets of binary values.

For this example, I am going to use a Class A IP address (23 . 78 . 23 . 98) with a default subnet mask:

**Step 1: Convert the IP address into binary**

For this step, we can use the same table we used to convert the subnet mask into binary:

| Octet | Decimal | 128 | 64 | 32 | 16 | 8 | 4 | 2 | 1 |
|-------|---------|-----|----|----|----|----|----|----|----|
| 1 | 23 | 0 | 0 | 0 | 1 | 0 | 1 | 1 | 1 |
| 2 | 78 | 0 | 1 | 0 | 0 | 1 | 1 | 1 | 0 |
| 3 | 23 | 0 | 0 | 0 | 1 | 0 | 1 | 1 | 1 |
| 4 | 98 | 0 | 1 | 1 | 0 | 0 | 0 | 1 | 0 |

Figure 11.10: Converting the IP address into binary

From this, we can see that the binary of the IP address 23 . 78 . 23 . 98 is 00010111.01001110.00010111.01100010.

You may be tempted to remove the leading zeroes here, but we need to keep them in.

**Step 2: Convert the subnet mask into binary**

We have already covered this in the *Classful/default subnet masks* section, and we know that the subnet mask 255.0.0.0 in binary is 11111111.00000000.00000000.00000000.

## Step 3: Perform an AND calculation on the two sets of binary values

For this step, I'm going to use the following table for clarity:

| Host IP | | | | | | | | | | | | | | | | | | | | | | | | | | | | | | | | |
|---|---|---|---|---|---|---|---|---|---|---|---|---|---|---|---|---|---|---|---|---|---|---|---|---|---|---|---|---|---|---|---|---|
| Subnet | | | | | | | | | | | | | | | | | | | | | | | | | | | | | | | | |
| Host (Binary) | | | | | | | | | | | | | | | | | | | | | | | | | | | | | | | | |
| Subnet (Binary) | | | | | | | | | | | | | | | | | | | | | | | | | | | | | | | | |
| Network ID (Binary) | | | | | | | | | | | | | | | | | | | | | | | | | | | | | | | | |
| Network ID | | | | | | | | | | | | | | | | | | | | | | | | | | | | | | | | |

Figure 11.11: Performing an AND calculation

I will complete the first four rows with the information I already know:

| Host IP | 23 | | | | | | | | 78 | | | | | | | | 23 | | | | | | | | 98 | | | | | | | |
|---|---|---|---|---|---|---|---|---|---|---|---|---|---|---|---|---|---|---|---|---|---|---|---|---|---|---|---|---|---|---|---|---|
| Subnet | 255 | | | | | | | | 0 | | | | | | | | 0 | | | | | | | | 0 | | | | | | | |
| Host (Binary) | 0 | 0 | 0 | 1 | 0 | 1 | 1 | 1 | 0 | 1 | 0 | 0 | 1 | 1 | 1 | 0 | 0 | 0 | 0 | 1 | 0 | 1 | 1 | 1 | 0 | 1 | 1 | 0 | 0 | 0 | 1 | 0 |
| Subnet (Binary) | 1 | 1 | 1 | 1 | 1 | 1 | 1 | 1 | 0 | 0 | 0 | 0 | 0 | 0 | 0 | 0 | 0 | 0 | 0 | 0 | 0 | 0 | 0 | 0 | 0 | 0 | 0 | 0 | 0 | 0 | 0 | 0 |
| Network ID (Binary) | | | | | | | | | | | | | | | | | | | | | | | | | | | | | | | | |
| Network ID | | | | | | | | | | | | | | | | | | | | | | | | | | | | | | | | |

Figure 11.12: Filling up the first four rows

Now, we can perform the AND calculation to get the binary representation of the **Network ID**. In this context, the AND calculation is going to look at the condition of each individual bit of the IP address and its counterpart bit in the subnet mask and return a result based on the following table:

| Host bit | 0 | 0 | 1 | 1 |
|---|---|---|---|---|
| Subnet bit | 0 | 1 | 0 | 1 |
| Result | 0 | 0 | 0 | 1 |

I have to admit this table used to confuse me, but have you noticed something that makes it easier for you? There is only one set of conditions that return the result of 1; that is, when the host bit equals 1 and the subnet bit equals 1. So, just remember that, and if that condition is not met, then the result must be a 0.

Let's look at this in action with the first four bits.

The first host bit is a 0 and the first subnet bit is a 1, which gives us a result of 0; the second and third bits are the same, so they also result in 0; the fourth host bit and the fourth subnet bit are both 1, so this gives us a result of 1. So far, the **Network ID** in binary looks as follows:

| Host IP | 23 | | | | | | | | 78 | | | | | | | | 23 | | | | | | | | 98 | | | | | | | |
|---|---|---|---|---|---|---|---|---|---|---|---|---|---|---|---|---|---|---|---|---|---|---|---|---|---|---|---|---|---|---|---|---|
| Subnet | 255 | | | | | | | | 0 | | | | | | | | 0 | | | | | | | | 0 | | | | | | | |
| Host (Binary) | 0 | 0 | 0 | 1 | 0 | 1 | 1 | 1 | 0 | 1 | 0 | 0 | 1 | 1 | 1 | 0 | 0 | 0 | 0 | 1 | 0 | 1 | 1 | 1 | 0 | 1 | 1 | 0 | 0 | 0 | 1 | 0 |
| Subnet (Binary) | 1 | 1 | 1 | 1 | 1 | 1 | 1 | 1 | 0 | 0 | 0 | 0 | 0 | 0 | 0 | 0 | 0 | 0 | 0 | 0 | 0 | 0 | 0 | 0 | 0 | 0 | 0 | 0 | 0 | 0 | 0 | 0 |
| Network ID (Binary) | 0 | 0 | 0 | 1 | | | | | | | | | | | | | | | | | | | | | | | | | | | | |
| Network ID | | | | | | | | | | | | | | | | | | | | | | | | | | | | | | | | |

Figure 11.13: Network ID in binary

Let's complete the table as far as the binary is concerned:

| Host IP | 23 | | | | | | | | 78 | | | | | | | | 23 | | | | | | | | 98 | | | | | | | |
|---|---|---|---|---|---|---|---|---|---|---|---|---|---|---|---|---|---|---|---|---|---|---|---|---|---|---|---|---|---|---|---|---|
| Subnet | 255 | | | | | | | | 0 | | | | | | | | 0 | | | | | | | | 0 | | | | | | | |
| Host (Binary) | 0 | 0 | 0 | 1 | 0 | 1 | 1 | 1 | 0 | 1 | 0 | 0 | 1 | 1 | 1 | 0 | 0 | 0 | 0 | 1 | 0 | 1 | 1 | 1 | 0 | 1 | 1 | 0 | 0 | 0 | 1 | 0 |
| Subnet (Binary) | 1 | 1 | 1 | 1 | 1 | 1 | 1 | 1 | 0 | 0 | 0 | 0 | 0 | 0 | 0 | 0 | 0 | 0 | 0 | 0 | 0 | 0 | 0 | 0 | 0 | 0 | 0 | 0 | 0 | 0 | 0 | 0 |
| Network ID (Binary) | 0 | 0 | 0 | 1 | 0 | 1 | 1 | 1 | 0 | 0 | 0 | 0 | 0 | 0 | 0 | 0 | 0 | 0 | 0 | 0 | 0 | 0 | 0 | 0 | 0 | 0 | 0 | 0 | 0 | 0 | 0 | 0 |
| Network ID | | | | | | | | | | | | | | | | | | | | | | | | | | | | | | | | |

Figure 11.14: Filling up the binary row

Now, we convert the binary of the Network ID into decimal to give us our Network ID in a nice readable format:

| Host IP | 23 | | | | | | | | 78 | | | | | | | | 23 | | | | | | | | 98 | | | | | | | |
|---|---|---|---|---|---|---|---|---|---|---|---|---|---|---|---|---|---|---|---|---|---|---|---|---|---|---|---|---|---|---|---|---|
| Subnet | 255 | | | | | | | | 0 | | | | | | | | 0 | | | | | | | | 0 | | | | | | | |
| Host (Binary) | 0 | 0 | 0 | 1 | 0 | 1 | 1 | 1 | 0 | 1 | 0 | 0 | 1 | 1 | 1 | 0 | 0 | 0 | 0 | 1 | 0 | 1 | 1 | 1 | 0 | 1 | 1 | 0 | 0 | 0 | 1 | 0 |
| Subnet (Binary) | 1 | 1 | 1 | 1 | 1 | 1 | 1 | 1 | 0 | 0 | 0 | 0 | 0 | 0 | 0 | 0 | 0 | 0 | 0 | 0 | 0 | 0 | 0 | 0 | 0 | 0 | 0 | 0 | 0 | 0 | 0 | 0 |
| Network ID (Binary) | 0 | 0 | 0 | 1 | 0 | 1 | 1 | 1 | 0 | 0 | 0 | 0 | 0 | 0 | 0 | 0 | 0 | 0 | 0 | 0 | 0 | 0 | 0 | 0 | 0 | 0 | 0 | 0 | 0 | 0 | 0 | 0 |
| Network ID | 23 | | | | | | | | 0 | | | | | | | | 0 | | | | | | | | 0 | | | | | | | |

Figure 11.15: Converting the binary of the Network ID into decimal

Here, we can see that the network address for this particular host is 23.0.0.0.

Let's have a look at a complete table for a Class B address:

| | | | | | | | | | | | | | | | | | | | | | | | | | | | | | | | | |
|---|---|---|---|---|---|---|---|---|---|---|---|---|---|---|---|---|---|---|---|---|---|---|---|---|---|---|---|---|---|---|---|---|
| Host IP | 182 | | | | | | | | 64 | | | | | | | | 17 | | | | | | | | 2 | | | | | | | |
| Subnet | 255 | | | | | | | | 255 | | | | | | | | 0 | | | | | | | | 0 | | | | | | | |
| Host (Binary) | 1 | 0 | 1 | 1 | 0 | 1 | 1 | 0 | 0 | 1 | 0 | 0 | 0 | 0 | 1 | 0 | 0 | 0 | 0 | 1 | 0 | 0 | 0 | 1 | 0 | 0 | 0 | 0 | 0 | 0 | 1 | 0 |
| Subnet (Binary) | 1 | 1 | 1 | 1 | 1 | 1 | 1 | 1 | 1 | 1 | 1 | 1 | 1 | 1 | 1 | 1 | 0 | 0 | 0 | 0 | 0 | 0 | 0 | 0 | 0 | 0 | 0 | 0 | 0 | 0 | 0 | 0 |
| Network ID (Binary) | 1 | 0 | 1 | 1 | 0 | 1 | 1 | 0 | 0 | 1 | 0 | 0 | 0 | 0 | 1 | 0 | 0 | 0 | 0 | 0 | 0 | 0 | 0 | 0 | 0 | 0 | 0 | 0 | 0 | 0 | 0 | 0 |
| Network ID | 182 | | | | | | | | 64 | | | | | | | | 0 | | | | | | | | 0 | | | | | | | |

Figure 11.16: Network ID for Class B

**Activity 4**: Now, it's over to you. Complete this table for a Class C address:

| | | | | | | | | | | | | | | | | | | | | | | | | | | | | | | | | |
|---|---|---|---|---|---|---|---|---|---|---|---|---|---|---|---|---|---|---|---|---|---|---|---|---|---|---|---|---|---|---|---|---|
| Host IP | 199 | | | | | | | | 87 | | | | | | | | 38 | | | | | | | | 15 | | | | | | | |
| Subnet | | | | | | | | | | | | | | | | | | | | | | | | | | | | | | | | |
| Host (Binary) | | | | | | | | | | | | | | | | | | | | | | | | | | | | | | | | |
| Subnet (Binary) | | | | | | | | | | | | | | | | | | | | | | | | | | | | | | | | |
| Network ID (Binary) | | | | | | | | | | | | | | | | | | | | | | | | | | | | | | | | |
| Network ID | | | | | | | | | | | | | | | | | | | | | | | | | | | | | | | | |

Figure 11.17: Network ID for Class C

If you completed the last activity correctly, you will have got a **Network ID** of 199.87.38.0. Before we move on to CIDR, I would just like to briefly return to talking about the number of hosts per network and how that figure was obtained. Earlier in this chapter, we mentioned that the number of IP addresses in any network is $2^n$, where $n$ is the number of bits allocated to the host element. I'm hoping that, now that we have completed the preceding processes using binary, the number of bits that are allocated to the host element in each class of network is clearer to you.

So far, we've learned how to identify the network element of an IP address, and thus the network address. An understanding of how these can be found is beneficial, particularly when we look at routing. We will look at this in more detail in Chapter 7, *Routers and Routing – Beyond a Single Network*. So far, this chapter has leaned toward classful addressing. In the next section, we will look at a more efficient way of networking with CIDR.

# Understanding CIDR

While classful networks make life simpler, they are not efficient in terms of IP address usage. What if you want a Class C network with only two hosts on it? Well, for that network, you would need to have four IP addresses, that is, two for the hosts, one for the network address, and one for the broadcast address. We would have 252 IP addresses sitting there unused. Admittedly, that does give you scope to grow your network, but it is still not ideal.

CIDR provides us with the means of escaping from default subnet masks, thus allowing us to be more flexible in sizing our networks. Do you only want two hosts? Not a problem – we can create a subnet mask for that. CIDR is a key component in **Variable Length Subnet Masks (VLSMs)**. VLSMs offer you the ability to break your network down into smaller networks of various sizes (as opposed to having multiple smaller networks all of the same size).

> VLSMs are beyond the scope of the exam, and therefore this book; however, I wanted to briefly mention them as I have no doubt you will come across the term in your career.

In the following section, I will show you how to identify the network address from a given IP address, as well as how to determine what subnet mask you need to use based on the number of hosts you require.

# Identifying a network address using CIDR

I'm going to be honest with you here – you pretty much already carried out this task when we were looking at classful addresses. However, because we are moving away from default subnet masks, we need to look at the last step of the process in more detail.

I'm going to use the 13.45.89.1 IP address and the 255.255.255.192 subnet mask for this example. First, we will convert the host IP and subnet mask into binary, like we did previously:

| | | | | | | | | | | | | | | | | | | | | | | | | | | | | | | | | |
|---|---|---|---|---|---|---|---|---|---|---|---|---|---|---|---|---|---|---|---|---|---|---|---|---|---|---|---|---|---|---|---|---|
| Host IP | | | | 13 | | | | | | | | 45 | | | | | | | | 89 | | | | | | | | 1 | | | |
| Subnet | | | | 255 | | | | | | | | 255 | | | | | | | | 255 | | | | | | | | 192 | | | |
| Host (Binary) | 0 | 0 | 0 | 0 | 1 | 1 | 0 | 1 | 0 | 0 | 1 | 0 | 1 | 1 | 0 | 1 | 0 | 1 | 0 | 1 | 1 | 0 | 0 | 1 | 0 | 0 | 0 | 0 | 0 | 0 | 0 | 1 |
| Subnet (Binary) | 1 | 1 | 1 | 1 | 1 | 1 | 1 | 1 | 1 | 1 | 1 | 1 | 1 | 1 | 1 | 1 | 1 | 1 | 1 | 1 | 1 | 1 | 1 | 1 | 1 | 1 | 0 | 0 | 0 | 0 | 0 | 0 |
| Network ID (Binary) | | | | | | | | | | | | | | | | | | | | | | | | | | | | | | | | |
| Network ID | | | | | | | | | | | | | | | | | | | | | | | | | | | | | | | | |

Figure 11.18: Converting the host IP and subnet mask into binary

Then, we calculate the **Network ID** in binary using the AND calculation and convert it into decimal:

| | | | | | | | | | | | | | | | | | | | | | | | | | | | | | | | | |
|---|---|---|---|---|---|---|---|---|---|---|---|---|---|---|---|---|---|---|---|---|---|---|---|---|---|---|---|---|---|---|---|---|
| Host IP | | | | 13 | | | | | | | | 45 | | | | | | | | 89 | | | | | | | | 1 | | | |
| Subnet | | | | 255 | | | | | | | | 255 | | | | | | | | 255 | | | | | | | | 192 | | | |
| Host (Binary) | 0 | 0 | 0 | 0 | 1 | 1 | 0 | 1 | 0 | 0 | 1 | 0 | 1 | 1 | 0 | 1 | 0 | 1 | 0 | 1 | 1 | 0 | 0 | 1 | 0 | 0 | 0 | 0 | 0 | 0 | 0 | 1 |
| Subnet (Binary) | 1 | 1 | 1 | 1 | 1 | 1 | 1 | 1 | 1 | 1 | 1 | 1 | 1 | 1 | 1 | 1 | 1 | 1 | 1 | 1 | 1 | 1 | 1 | 1 | 1 | 1 | 0 | 0 | 0 | 0 | 0 | 0 |
| Network ID (Binary) | 0 | 0 | 0 | 0 | 1 | 1 | 0 | 1 | 0 | 0 | 1 | 0 | 1 | 1 | 0 | 1 | 0 | 1 | 0 | 1 | 1 | 0 | 0 | 1 | 1 | 1 | 0 | 0 | 0 | 0 | 0 | 0 |
| Network ID | | | | 13 | | | | | | | | 45 | | | | | | | | 89 | | | | | | | | 192 | | | |

Figure 11.19: Calculating the Network ID in binary

Now, we have the Network ID/address, you may be wondering why, if this are exactly the same steps we covered previously, I am focusing on it. Have a look at the subnet in binary. In the previous examples, each octet in the subnet mask was either all ones or all zeroes. In this example, the subnet mask only uses two bits of the last octet, so the Network ID doesn't (in this case) end in a zero.

Sometimes, you may not have the subnet mask in decimal – you may be given a CIDR notation instead. Using the subnet from the preceding example, 255.255.255.192, this translates into a /26 CIDR notation. If you are only given the CIDR notation, do not fear, this is actually easier as you don't have to convert the decimal subnet mask into binary. All you have to do is put a 1 in the leftmost column of **Subnet (Binary)**, move to the next column on the right, and put a 1 in there. Repeat this until the number of ones you have equals the number in the CIDR notation. For example, for /26, you need to have put in 26 ones, for /16, you would have to put in 16 ones, and so on.

I have previously stated that the **Network ID** is always the first IP address in a network and that the broadcast address is the last IP address in a network. We've already identified the **Network ID**, so let's look at how to find the broadcast ID.

I have taken the completed table from the preceding example and replicated it here. For clarity, I have put a bold line in the table. Note that this bold line is to the right of the very last bit of the subnet mask:

| | | | | | | | | | | | | | | | | | | | | | | | | | | | | | | | | |
|---|---|---|---|---|---|---|---|---|---|---|---|---|---|---|---|---|---|---|---|---|---|---|---|---|---|---|---|---|---|---|---|---|
| Host IP | 13 | | | | | | | | 45 | | | | | | | | 89 | | | | | | | | 203 | | | | | | | |
| Subnet | 255 | | | | | | | | 255 | | | | | | | | 255 | | | | | | | | 192 | | | | | | | |
| Host (Binary) | 0 | 0 | 0 | 0 | 1 | 1 | 0 | 1 | 0 | 0 | 1 | 0 | 1 | 1 | 0 | 1 | 0 | 1 | 0 | 1 | 1 | 0 | 0 | 1 | 1 | 1 | 0 | 0 | 1 | 0 | 1 | 1 |
| Subnet (Binary) | 1 | 1 | 1 | 1 | 1 | 1 | 1 | 1 | 1 | 1 | 1 | 1 | 1 | 1 | 1 | 1 | 1 | 1 | 1 | 1 | 1 | 1 | 1 | 1 | 1 | 1 | 0 | 0 | 0 | 0 | 0 | 0 |
| Network ID (Binary) | 0 | 0 | 0 | 0 | 1 | 1 | 0 | 1 | 0 | 0 | 1 | 0 | 1 | 1 | 0 | 1 | 0 | 1 | 0 | 1 | 1 | 0 | 0 | 1 | 1 | 1 | 0 | 0 | 0 | 0 | 0 | 0 |
| Network ID | 13 | | | | | | | | 45 | | | | | | | | 89 | | | | | | | | 192 | | | | | | | |

Figure 11.20: Replica of the previous example

What we do here is look at all of the zeroes in the **Network ID (Binary)** that are to the right of that line. I have colored them gray in the following:

| | | | | | | | | | | | | | | | | | | | | | | | | | | | | | | | | |
|---|---|---|---|---|---|---|---|---|---|---|---|---|---|---|---|---|---|---|---|---|---|---|---|---|---|---|---|---|---|---|---|---|
| Host IP | 13 | | | | | | | | 45 | | | | | | | | 89 | | | | | | | | 203 | | | | | | | |
| Subnet | 255 | | | | | | | | 255 | | | | | | | | 255 | | | | | | | | 192 | | | | | | | |
| Host (Binary) | 0 | 0 | 0 | 0 | 1 | 1 | 0 | 1 | 0 | 0 | 1 | 0 | 1 | 1 | 0 | 1 | 0 | 1 | 0 | 1 | 1 | 0 | 0 | 1 | 1 | 1 | 0 | 0 | 1 | 0 | 1 | 1 |
| Subnet (Binary) | 1 | 1 | 1 | 1 | 1 | 1 | 1 | 1 | 1 | 1 | 1 | 1 | 1 | 1 | 1 | 1 | 1 | 1 | 1 | 1 | 1 | 1 | 1 | 1 | 1 | 1 | 0 | 0 | 0 | 0 | 0 | 0 |
| Network ID (Binary) | 0 | 0 | 0 | 0 | 1 | 1 | 0 | 1 | 0 | 0 | 1 | 0 | 1 | 1 | 0 | 1 | 0 | 1 | 0 | 1 | 1 | 0 | 0 | 1 | 1 | 1 | 0 | 0 | 0 | 0 | 0 | 0 |
| Network ID | 13 | | | | | | | | 45 | | | | | | | | 89 | | | | | | | | 192 | | | | | | | |

Figure 11.21: Focusing on the zeroes in the Network ID (Binary)

Then, quite simply, we flip the zeroes into ones. Note that the digits to the right of the line are always going to be zeroes, so flipping them into ones is always going to be the only action you take here. Notice that I have also changed the label of the bottom row to reflect the fact we are talking about the broadcast address now:

| | | | | | | | | | | | | | | | | | | | | | | | | | | | | | | | | |
|---|---|---|---|---|---|---|---|---|---|---|---|---|---|---|---|---|---|---|---|---|---|---|---|---|---|---|---|---|---|---|---|---|
| Host IP | 13 | | | | | | | | 45 | | | | | | | | 89 | | | | | | | | 203 | | | | | | | |
| Subnet | 255 | | | | | | | | 255 | | | | | | | | 255 | | | | | | | | 192 | | | | | | | |
| Host (Binary) | 0 | 0 | 0 | 0 | 1 | 1 | 0 | 1 | 0 | 0 | 1 | 0 | 1 | 1 | 0 | 1 | 0 | 1 | 0 | 1 | 1 | 0 | 0 | 1 | 1 | 1 | 0 | 0 | 1 | 0 | 1 | 1 |
| Subnet (Binary) | 1 | 1 | 1 | 1 | 1 | 1 | 1 | 1 | 1 | 1 | 1 | 1 | 1 | 1 | 1 | 1 | 1 | 1 | 1 | 1 | 1 | 1 | 1 | 1 | 1 | 1 | 0 | 0 | 0 | 0 | 0 | 0 |
| Network ID (Binary) | 0 | 0 | 0 | 0 | 1 | 1 | 0 | 1 | 0 | 0 | 1 | 0 | 1 | 1 | 0 | 1 | 0 | 1 | 0 | 1 | 1 | 0 | 0 | 1 | 1 | 1 | 1 | 1 | 1 | 1 | 1 | 1 |
| Broadcast Address | 13 | | | | | | | | 45 | | | | | | | | 89 | | | | | | | | 255 | | | | | | | |

Figure 11.22: Flipping the zeroes into ones

Once we have done that, we convert this new number into decimal to get the broadcast address. In this example, it is `13.45.89.255`.

In the preceding example, the subnet mask finished in the last octet. In the following example, it finishes in the third octet. This time, we will use `13.45.89.203` and the `255.255.224.0` subnet mask.

We'll do the conversions to binary again and perform the AND calculation:

| | | | | | | | | | | | | | | | | | | | | | | | | | | | | | | | | |
|---|---|---|---|---|---|---|---|---|---|---|---|---|---|---|---|---|---|---|---|---|---|---|---|---|---|---|---|---|---|---|---|---|
| Host IP | 13 | | | | | | | | 45 | | | | | | | | 89 | | | | | | | | 203 | | | | | | | |
| Subnet | 255 | | | | | | | | 255 | | | | | | | | 224 | | | | | | | | 0 | | | | | | | |
| Host (Binary) | 0 | 0 | 0 | 0 | 1 | 1 | 0 | 1 | 0 | 0 | 1 | 0 | 1 | 1 | 0 | 1 | 0 | 1 | 0 | 1 | 1 | 0 | 0 | 1 | 1 | 1 | 0 | 0 | 1 | 0 | 1 | 1 |
| Subnet (Binary) | 1 | 1 | 1 | 1 | 1 | 1 | 1 | 1 | 1 | 1 | 1 | 1 | 1 | 1 | 1 | 1 | 1 | 1 | 1 | 0 | 0 | 0 | 0 | 0 | 0 | 0 | 0 | 0 | 0 | 0 | 0 | 0 |
| Network ID (Binary) | 0 | 0 | 0 | 0 | 1 | 1 | 0 | 1 | 0 | 0 | 1 | 0 | 1 | 1 | 0 | 1 | 0 | 1 | 0 | 0 | 0 | 0 | 0 | 0 | 0 | 0 | 0 | 0 | 0 | 0 | 0 | 0 |
| Network ID | 13 | | | | | | | | 45 | | | | | | | | 64 | | | | | | | | 0 | | | | | | | |

Figure 11.23: Performing the AND calculation

Now, we have the Network ID/address of the network this host belongs to. To calculate the broadcast address, we draw our bold line and flip the zeroes to ones:

| | | | | | | | | | | | | | | | | | | | | | | | | | | | | | | | | |
|---|---|---|---|---|---|---|---|---|---|---|---|---|---|---|---|---|---|---|---|---|---|---|---|---|---|---|---|---|---|---|---|---|
| Host IP | 13 | | | | | | | | 45 | | | | | | | | 89 | | | | | | | | 203 | | | | | | | |
| Subnet | 255 | | | | | | | | 255 | | | | | | | | 224 | | | | | | | | 0 | | | | | | | |
| Host (Binary) | 0 | 0 | 0 | 0 | 1 | 1 | 0 | 1 | 0 | 0 | 1 | 0 | 1 | 1 | 0 | 1 | 0 | 1 | 0 | 1 | 1 | 0 | 0 | 1 | 1 | 1 | 0 | 0 | 1 | 0 | 1 | 1 |
| Subnet (Binary) | 1 | 1 | 1 | 1 | 1 | 1 | 1 | 1 | 1 | 1 | 1 | 1 | 1 | 1 | 1 | 1 | 1 | 1 | 1 | 0 | 0 | 0 | 0 | 0 | 0 | 0 | 0 | 0 | 0 | 0 | 0 | 0 |
| Network ID (Binary) | 0 | 0 | 0 | 0 | 1 | 1 | 0 | 1 | 0 | 0 | 1 | 0 | 1 | 1 | 0 | 1 | 0 | 1 | 0 | 1 | 1 | 1 | 1 | 1 | 1 | 1 | 1 | 1 | 1 | 1 | 1 | 1 |
| Broadcast Address | 13 | | | | | | | | 45 | | | | | | | | 95 | | | | | | | | 255 | | | | | | | |

Figure 11.24: Flipping the zeroes to ones

Converting this into decimal gives us a broadcast address of `13.45.95.255`.

**Activity 5**: Identify the network address and broadcast address of a network that contains a host with the `13.45.89.203` IP address and the `255.240.0.0` subnet mask. Use the online CIDR Calculator located at `http://www.subnet-calculator.com/cidr.php` to check your answers. The first IP in the CIDR address range is the **Network ID**, while the last IP is the **Broadcast Address**.

For the preceding activity, I asked you to use an online subnet calculator. In the real world, you would likely use one of these or an application on your phone; however, for the exam, you will not be able to do so.

Imagine you are at work and your boss tells you that they want you to plan a number of networks that each have *n* amount of hosts and you need to work out what subnet mask to use. Recall that, out of the 32 bits in an IPv4 address, the network element utilizes a number of them, and the remainder are used for the host element. When we have been given a set number of hosts to cater for, we, in a way, reverse that thinking. We work out how many bits are needed for the host element, and whatever is left is used for the subnet mask.

So, let's say your boss has said that they want 66 hosts per network. The important initial thing to remember is that we need to have two addresses put aside for the network address and the broadcast address. Therefore, we actually need a network with the capacity for 68 IP addresses. Recall that the calculation for how many hosts we can get on a network is $2^n$. We just need to find out what *n* needs to be. Well, we could do $2^6 = 64$, but that's too few. How about $2^7$? That gives us 128 IP addresses. This isn't ideal since some IP addresses are being wasted, but it meets our need to support 66 hosts.

 Be careful about the wording of any question that asks you about the number of hosts. Are they asking for a maximum number of hosts or a minimum number?

In the *Further reading* section at the end of this chapter, I have included a link to an excellent site that allows you to test your understanding of subnetting. Having looked at the format and breakdown of IPv4 addresses and subnet masks, it is now time to discuss to assign these addresses to devices.

# Assigning IP addresses to hosts

It is imperative that, when planning your network, you know which IP addresses can be given out to a host. Once you have identified the network address and broadcast address on a network, you can issue an IP address that sits between them to a host device.

Therefore, the first IP address you can issue to a host is the one immediately following the network address. The last IP address you can issue to a host is the one immediately before the broadcast address.

An IP address can either be assigned manually by an administrator or dynamically through **Dynamic Host Configuration Protocol (DHCP)**. We will talk about DHCP in more detail in `Chapter 14`, *Network Services*.

Manually assigning an IP address to a Windows computer involves adjusting the IPv4 properties of the NIC itself. Since a device can have more than one NIC, ensure you are configuring the right one. Let's walk through configuring an IP address manually:

    1.  From **Control Panel**, select **Network and Internet**:

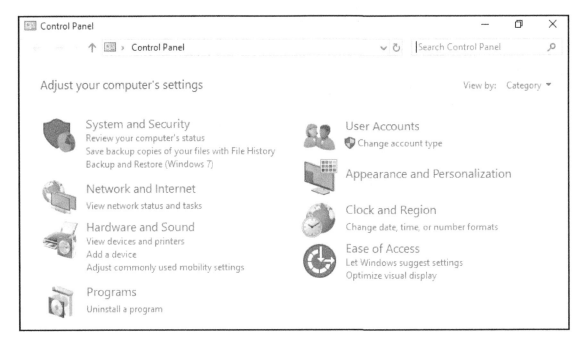

Figure 11.25: Control Panel

2. Then, select **Network and Sharing Center**:

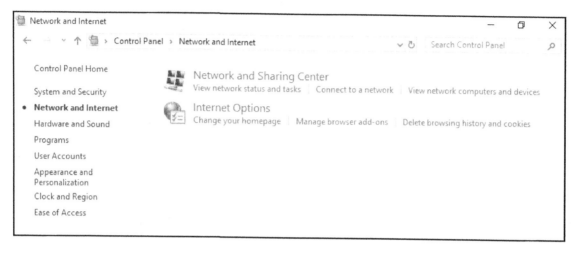

Figure 11.26: Network and Internet tab

3. Select **Change adapter settings** on the left:

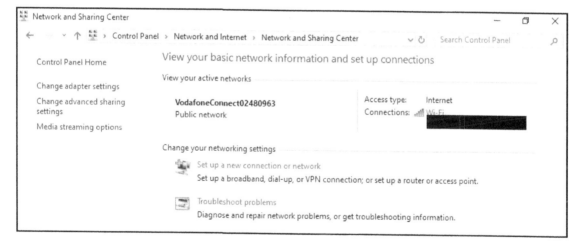

Figure 11.27: Network and Sharing Center

4.  This will present you with adapters you have installed on your device. Note that, on my laptop, I have Bluetooth, a wired connection, and a Wi-Fi connection:

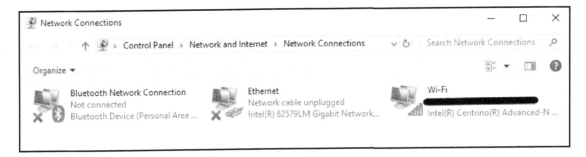

Figure 11.28: Adapters installed on your device

5.  Right-click on the adapter you want to configure and choose **Properties**:

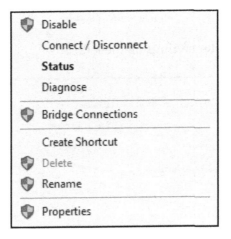

Figure 11.29: Right-clicking the adapter

6. Then, either double-click on **Internet Protocol Version 4 (TCP/IPv4)** or select it and choose **Properties**:

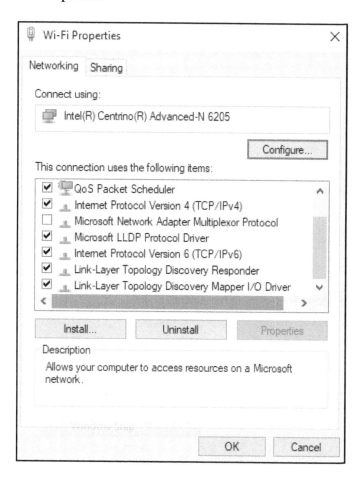

Figure 11.30: Configuration options

7. By default, your adapter will be set to obtain an IP address automatically. Note that not only is it getting the IP address automatically but it will also be given a default gateway and DNS settings automatically:

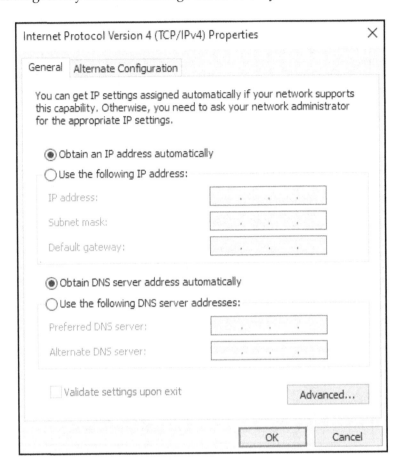

Figure 11.31: IPv4 properties

8. If you prefer, you can configure the adapter so that it has manual DNS settings:

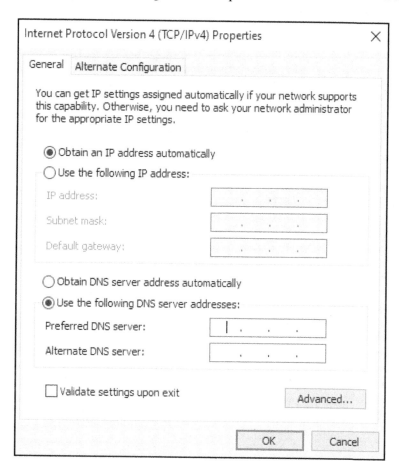

Figure 11.32: Configuring the adapter so that it has manual DNS settings

9. You may have noticed that, while you were obtaining an IP address, there was an **Alternate Configuration** tab. Clicking on it provides us with the option shown in the following screenshot:

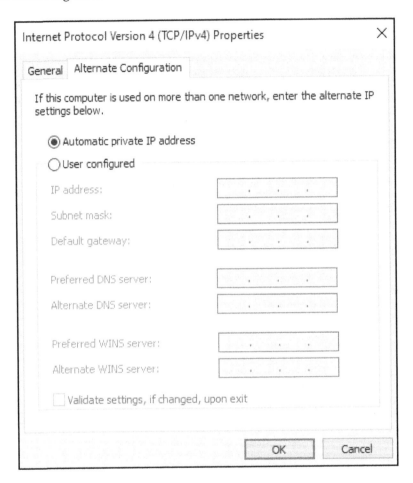

Figure 11.33: Alternate Configuration tab

This tab details what the computer should do if it cannot obtain an IP address automatically. By default, it will be provided with an **Automatic Private IP Addressing (APIPA)** address, which always starts with 169.254.x.x. However, you can choose the **User configured** option to provide it with a static IP address. The latter option is ideal if you use your computer in multiple locations, and in one of those locations you don't have the ability to obtain an IP address automatically. For example, at work, you may want to get an IP address automatically, but at home, you may want a static address.

10. If you want to have a static address, select **Use the following IP address** and enter the required details. Note when doing this that, once you enter the IP address, the subnet mask field auto-populates with a classful subnet mask. Remember to change this as appropriate. Also, the option to obtain DNS server details automatically is no longer available. On selecting this option the **Alternate Configuration** tab will disappear instantly:

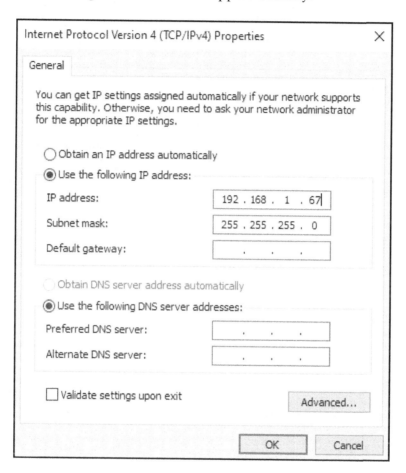

Figure 11.34: Alternate Configuration tab no longer visible

When I first starting configuring IP addresses here, I always had the habit of hitting *Tab* on my keyboard to try to move from one octet to the next. This doesn't work and will take you to the next field in the dialog box. To move from one octet to the next, press **.** after entering the octet value. This will move you to the next octet.

11. Fill in the remainder of the details as appropriate. Note that there is an **Validate settings upon exit** option. This checks whether your settings are correct and will provide an error message if they're not:

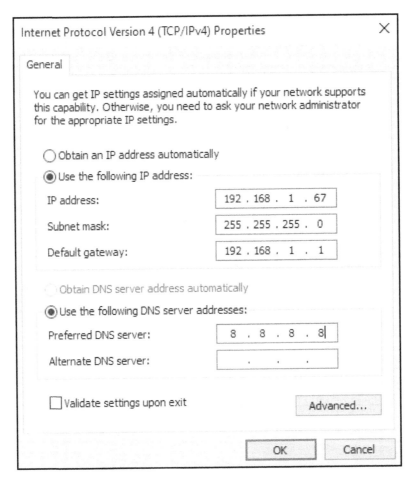

Figure 11.35: Validate settings upon exit option at the bottom

12. By clicking on the **Advanced...** button, you are provided with granular control. From here, you can add additional IP addresses and default gateways, and configure a routing metric value:

Figure 11.36: Advanced TCP/IP Settings

13. Clicking on the **DNS** tab allows us to configure additional DNS settings, including configuring the order DNS servers are queried in. We will discuss DNS in more detail in `Chapter 14`, *Network Services*:

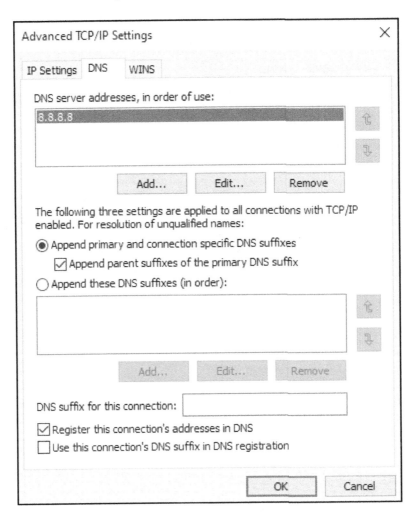

Figure 11.37: DNS tab

14. Clicking on the **WINS** tab will provide us with the option to configure the **Windows Internet Name Service (WINS)** settings. Again, this will be discussed in more detail in Chapter 14, *Network Services*:

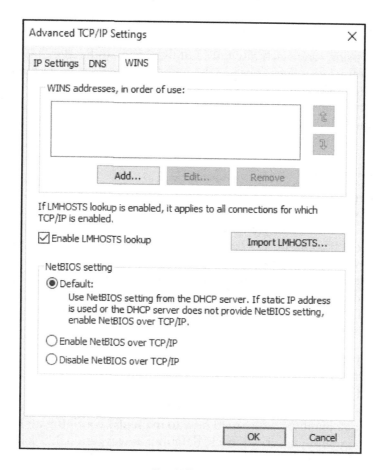

Figure 11.38: WINS tab

15. Once you have configured the IP address either automatically or statically and clicked on **OK**, your computer will send out an ARP request, querying if anyone has that IP address already.

 If a device does have that particular IP address, you will get an error message advising either a duplicate IP or IP address conflict. You will need to investigate this further with your network administrator.

Sometimes, you may find that you have problems with the IP address that's been issued by DHCP. You can ask your computer to either release the IP address or renew the IP address from the command line using `ipconfig /release` and `ipconfig /renew`, respectively. Release gives up the IP address and doesn't attempt to get a new IP address; renew also releases the IP address but attempts to obtain an IP address again.

I sometimes find using renew actually fails, but there is no indication if it has failed when it releases the IP address or when it obtains the new IP address. With that in mind, I tend to run release first and then run renew. Yes, I am releasing twice, but I know that if the first command fails, the problem is likely to be on my device. I just want to reiterate that the two commands are for DHCP addresses only. If you have a static IP address, they will not work.

# Summary

This chapter expanded on what you have learned about IPv4 earlier in this book. We began with an overview of IPv4 addresses before discussing the various attributes of the five classful IPv4 classes, including public and private address ranges and their subnet masks. From there, we delved into subnetting. Following on from this, we introduced the concept of classless inter-domain routing, which is something you will likely come across in all but the smallest of environments. We finished this chapter by discussing the assignment of IP addresses to hosts.

From a practical perspective, you have learned how to identify the class of an IP address and its default subnet based on the IP address itself when using classful addressing. You have also learned how to convert decimal values into binary and vice versa, and how to use this in conjunction with the IP address and subnet when trying to identify network and broadcast addresses. Finally, you learned how to manually configure an IPv4 address on a network card, along with the subnet mask, default gateway, and DNS settings. While most organizations use DHCP, there will inevitably be instances where you will still need to configure a device manually.

In this chapter, we covered IPv4, the most common IP addressing scheme in use currently. However, due to the increased demand for IP addresses, we are exhausting the pool of available addresses. In the next chapter, we look at the *solution* to this: IPv6. Following an overview of IPv6, we will look at the various different address types, understand how addresses can be assigned, and talk about interoperability between IPv4 and IPv6.

# Questions

1. Which of the following is a public IP address?

(A) `126.56.23.0`
(B) `172.16.0.1`
(C) `10.4.2.89`
(D) `172.30.45.23`

2. What is the decimal representation of the binary number 1101010?

(A) 101
(B) 206
(C) 106
(D) 201

3. The last IP address in a network range is known as a what?

(A) APIPA
(B) Network address
(C) Broadcast address
(D) Private address

4. If you need a network with at least 256 hosts on it, how many bits would you need for the host element?

(A) 8
(B) 9
(C) 10
(D) 11

5. What protocol is used to issue an IP address automatically?

(A) APIPA
(B) DHCP
(C) ARP
(D) DNS

6. Which of these is a Class B private IP address?

(A) `10.0.0.1`
(B) `192.168.34.2`
(C) `10.234.56.1`
(D) `172.16.9.90`

7. Which of these is not a valid subnet mask?

(A) `255.124.0.0`
(B) `255.255.128.0`
(C) `255.255.255.192`
(D) `255.255.255.252`

8. You wish to add a new host to a network. One of the hosts that's currently on the network has an IP address of `187.34.23.6` and a subnet mask of `255.255.255.240`. Which of the following IP addresses can I allocate to the new host?

(A) `187.34.23.0`
(B) `187.34.23.6`
(C) `187.34.23.14`
(D) `187.34.23.15`

# Further reading

To test your knowledge on subnetting, visit `http://www.subnettingquestions.com/`.

# 12
# Understanding IPv6

**Internet Protocol version 6 (IPv6)** is becoming more and more prominent. Despite its slow take-up initially, the ever-increasing demand for IP addresses will no doubt make organizations that have been hesitant to implement IPv6 reconsider their stance. I think with the abundance of the **Internet of Things (IoT)** devices that are now available, this demand will continue to increase dramatically and having knowledge of IPv6 will become more important.

This chapter introduces you to IPv6, giving you an overview of how IPv6 addresses are represented in general, before moving on to discuss the various address types. Then, we will cover assigning IPv6 addresses in a Windows environment. We will finish this chapter by briefly talking about intercompatibility between IPv4 and IPv6, which, until we are solely using IPv6, will continue to be an important consideration.

The following topics will be covered in this chapter:

- Overview of IPv6
- Understanding address types
- Understanding assigning IPv6 addresses
- Understanding interoperability with IPv4

# Technical requirements

To complete the exercises in this chapter, you will need an internet-connected PC running Windows 7 or above, preferably Windows 10.

# Overview of IPv6

Let me start this chapter with a question. If IPv4 is so widespread and works well, why has IPv6 been released? Quite simply, we've run out (or are running out) of IPv4 addresses. Yes, you read that right. We have run out of 4.2 billion addresses. You might be wondering how this is possible, so let's have a look at some figures.

As of June 2019, Internet World Stats published figures that stated the world population was 7.7 billion (sourced from the United Nations Population Division), and of those, 4.4 billion people were internet users (sourced from the **International Telecommunications Union (ITU)**). Admittedly, quite a number of those 4.4 billion will be sharing an internet-connected device, such as a home PC, and that will be their only means of connection. But if we flip that, there will be a large number of people who have multiple devices that connect directly to the internet. As an example, I'm currently sitting at the train station typing this up on my internet-connected tablet, with my internet-connected phone next to me. That's two IP addresses gone from me.

We can also add that IPv4 uses IP addresses inefficiently into the mix. Remember, there are certain IPv4 addresses or address ranges that we cannot issue to hosts. This eats into those 4.2 billion addresses. For example, no hosts can be allocated from the following:

- Networks starting with 0: 16,777,216 hosts
- Networks starting with 127: 16,777,216 hosts
- Networks starting with 169.254: 65,536 hosts
- Any Class D network: 268,435,456 hosts
- Any Class E network: 268,435,456 hosts

To combat this, IPv6 was introduced. IPv6 is a 128-bit hexadecimal address that offers a staggering 340 undecillion addresses ($2^{128}$), or to write it in full, 340,282,366,920,938,463,463,374,607,431,768,211,456 addresses.

If you want to know how to read that out loud, I have included a link in the *Further reading* section.

Although the extra addresses that IPv6 provides us are, of course, of massive benefit to us, this is not the only benefit that was brought about by the introduction of this new addressing scheme. When IPv6 was being developed, the developers looked at what was wrong with or missing from IPv4 and, where possible, rectified or included it in IPv6. For example, they changed the header format, not only to support the new address system but also to make it as efficient as possible. They achieved this by creating an IPv6 header that was 40 bytes long, compared to IPv4's header, which was 20 bytes long. This isn't bad when you consider that, by just looking at the address sizes, an IPv4 address is 4 bytes long (32 bits) and an IPv6 address is 16 bytes long (128 bits). Here, the header has to have a source and destination address, and you can see that an IPv6 header has 24 bytes more being used for addressing compared to its IPv4 counterpart. How have they squeezed it in, then? Well, an IPv4 header uses 12 bytes for non-addressing information, whereas an IPv6 header has stripped that back to only 8 bytes of non-addressing information.

I mentioned previously that an IPv6 address is a hexadecimal number, so before we talk about the format of the address, it would be worthwhile to understand what hexadecimal actually is.

# Hexadecimal numbering

The hexadecimal numbering system is also known as base-16. What confuses a lot of people is that it hexadecimal numbers also include letters. Yes, you read that correctly. There are letters in there, but we actually refer to them as **symbols**. Hexadecimal uses the numbers 0-9 and symbols A-F to represent any decimal number that we wish to throw at it. Counting up to and including 15 is relatively straightforward; 0-9 is represented by 0-9 as usual, but 10-15 are represented by symbols, so we would get the following:

| Decimal | Hexadecimal |
|---------|-------------|
| 0 | 0 |
| 1 | 1 |
| 2 | 2 |
| 3 | 3 |
| 4 | 4 |
| 5 | 5 |
| 6 | 6 |
| 7 | 7 |
| 8 | 8 |
| 9 | 9 |
| 10 | A |
| 11 | B |

| 12 | C |
| --- | --- |
| 13 | D |
| 14 | E |
| 15 | F |

When we want to count over 16, we need to combine the characters to continue. Have a look at the following table, where I have continued this:

| Decimal | Hexadecimal |
| --- | --- |
| 16 | 10 |
| 17 | 11 |
| 18 | 12 |
| 19 | 13 |
| 20 | 14 |
| 21 | 15 |
| 22 | 16 |
| 23 | 17 |
| 24 | 18 |
| 25 | 19 |
| 26 | 1A |
| 27 | 1B |
| 28 | 1C |
| 29 | 1D |
| 30 | 1E |
| 31 | 1F |
| 32 | 20 |

While not as simple to read as the decimal and binary tables we have used previously in this book, we could create a similar one for hexadecimal:

| 65536 | 4096 | 256 | 16 | Units |
| --- | --- | --- | --- | --- |
| | | | | |

With just the units column, we cover the range 0-255; by adding the 16 column, we can cover 0-255; the 256 column gives us 0-4,095; the 4,096 column gives us 0-65,535; and finally (in this example, anyway), the 65,536 column gives us 0-1,048,575. The pattern here between the column headings is that each column value is 16 times the column value to the right of it. You'll be pleased to know that, for networking purposes, generally, just having the two right-most columns is enough for us.

I want to finish off this section on hexadecimal with just a quick explanation of how we convert a hexadecimal value into binary. Although it is not part of the exam, having this knowledge forms a good foundation that you can build upon when you continue to upskill your networking knowledge.

# Converting hexadecimal into binary

Each hexadecimal character is made up of 4 bits, so if we have a single character, we can quite simply convert it into its decimal equivalent and then convert that into binary, like we did in the previous chapter. The following table provides a mapping of single hexadecimal characters and their binary and decimal equivalents:

| Decimal | Hexadecimal | Binary |
|---------|-------------|--------|
| 0 | 0 | 0000 |
| 1 | 1 | 0001 |
| 2 | 2 | 0010 |
| 3 | 3 | 0011 |
| 4 | 4 | 0100 |
| 5 | 5 | 0101 |
| 6 | 6 | 0110 |
| 7 | 7 | 0111 |
| 8 | 8 | 1000 |
| 9 | 9 | 1001 |
| 10 | A | 1010 |
| 11 | B | 1011 |
| 12 | C | 1100 |
| 13 | D | 1101 |
| 14 | E | 1110 |
| 15 | F | 1111 |

That is pretty straightforward, but what if you have multiple hexadecimal characters? Would you believe it is as simple as doing each character separately and merging the results? Let's look at a couple of quick examples:

- Hex = A9
- A = 1010
- 9 = 1001

Merging the two gives us `10101001`:

- Hex = AC4
- A = 1010
- C = 1100
- 4 = 0100

Merging the three gives us `101011000100`.

Notice I have kept the leading zero in the binary representation of the hexadecimal value 4. This is important: do not remove leading zeros when converting.

Now, we know how to convert hexadecimal into binary, let's reverse the process and convert binary into hexadecimal. When reversing the process, we need to split the binary into groups of 4 bits. Always split from the right:

- *Binary = 110111001011*
- *Splitting = 1101 1100 1011*
- *1101 = D*
- *1100 = C*
- *1011 = B*

Merging these gives us a hexadecimal value of DCB.

I'm going to give you one last example. In this case, the binary does not split up evenly into groups of 4. We're going to convert the binary value of `1010010111`. If we split that into groups of 4, remembering to start from the right, we get `10 1001 0111`.

Notice that we have a group of only two at the start? All we need to do is pad it out with leading zeroes to make it up to a 4 character number, like this: `0010`.

Once you get familiar with converting between the two, you will most likely stop padding because you know how to interpret it. Let's finish off the conversion:

- *Binary = 1010010111*
- *Splitting = 10 1001 0111*
- *Padding = 0010 1001 0111*
- *0010 = 2*
- *1001 = 9*
- *0111 = 7*

Merging the three gives us a hexadecimal value of *297*.

If you want to practice converting between hexadecimal and binary a bit more, I have included some links to online converters in the *Further reading* section.

I'd like to finish this section by briefly mentioning how we can differentiate between each numbering system. It is quite obvious when we see a number containing symbols, for example, 1C, that this is a hexadecimal number. However, what if we see the number 11? Is this a hexadecimal, binary, or decimal value? We cannot tell just from the number alone. Unfortunately, there is no hard and fast method of doing this, and it can vary depending on what underlying programming language is being used. However, hexadecimal is usually prefixed with 0x. You may see binary prefixed with 0b but this is unusual, and decimal does not have a prefix.

# The format of an IPv6 address

We have already ascertained that IPv6 addresses are 128 bits long and are made up of hexadecimal numbers. In this section, we will look at the format of the address.

An IPv6 address is formed out of 8 groups of 4 hexadecimal numbers, with each group separated by a colon, that is, a : character. Each character in the address is worth 4 bits, so each group of hexadecimal numbers is worth 16 bits or 2 bytes. To round off the math here, 8 groups of 16 bits equals 128 bits.

 Note that, unofficially, these groups are referred to as hextets because they are 16 bits, but this is unlikely to be mentioned in the exam. Also, I have heard people refer to the groups as octets as a throwback to IPv4, but this is 1) not a correct term and 2) will not be in the exam.

Let's look at an example IPv6 address:

```
2001:0034:09FA:F3B2:20E4:1030:0001:4BC2
```

There we go—it just rattles off the tongue, doesn't it? OK, I have to admit, it is quite laborious writing these down. Fortunately, there are some rules we can follow, and we will look at them now.

## Dropping leading zeroes

The one rule that everyone seems to remember is, in each group of numbers, we can drop the leading zeroes. Using our preceding example, I have emboldened the leading zeroes:

2001:**00**34:**0**9FA:F3B2:20E4:1030:**000**1:4BC2

Removing them would give us the following legitimate IPv6 address:

2001:34:9FA:F3B2:20E4:1030:1:4BC2

The important thing to note is that it is only leading zeroes, not intermediate nor trailing zeroes. I'll give you a couple of examples to highlight why we specify only leading. Look at the sixth group of numbers:

1030

If we could remove leading AND trailing zeroes, we would be left with the following:

103

We would have no way to find out whether the original number was 0103 or 1030. This would be even worse if were allowed to removed intermediate zeroes also. We would be left with the following number:

13

Wow; this is much shorter, but what was the original number? All the device would know is there are two zeroes to fit in somewhere. Was it 0013, 0103, 0130, 1300, or 1003?

## Dropping contiguous zeroes once

The first time I heard the term *contiguous*, I thought I had misheard the instructor and they had said *continuous*, but no, contiguous it was. With that in mind, I think it is important to briefly define what the word actually means, although you may still think it the same as continuous. Contiguous means adjacent or being in contact with. This will become clearer when I go through an example.

Take the following IPv6 address:

2001:0034:09FA:0000:0000:1030:0001:4BC2

In the center of it, we can see that it has two groups of numbers made up solely of zeroes, and these two groups are adjacent to each other. They are contiguous, so we can drop them:

2001:0034:09FA:**0000**:**0000**:1030:0001:4BC2

This leaves us with the following:

2001:0034:09FA::1030:0001:4BC2

Notice that, in their place, there is double colon : :; which indicates where in the address the zeroes originally were. Once we have done that, we can also drop the leading zeroes:

2001:**00**34:**0**9FA::1030:**000**1:4BC2

This leaves us with 2001:34:9FA::1030:1:4BC2.

Ahh, that's better. This is much shorter.

I would like to give a further example, to expand on this a little. Let's look at the following address:

2001:0034:0000:0000:0000:1030:0001:4BC2

In this example, we now have three contiguous groups of zeroes, and we can drop all of these:

2001:0034:**0000**:**0000**:**0000**:1030:0001:4BC2

This leaves us with 2001:0034::1030:0001:4BC2.

How many colons did I replace the contiguous zeroes with? Yes, just the two colons again, and this is why I wanted to provide a further example. It does not matter how many groups of contiguous groups of zeroes are removed – they are only replaced with the one set of double colons.

Of course, we can then drop the leading zeroes that remain:

2001:**00**34::1030:**000**1:4BC2

This would leave us with 2001:34::1030:1:4BC2.

Let's look at one final example. Consider the following IPv6 address: 2001:0034:0000:0000:AB76:0000:0000:4BC2. What do you notice about it?

Hopefully, you will have spotted that there are two sets of contiguous groups of zeroes:

`2001:0034:0000:0000:AB76:0000:0000:4BC2`

You might be tempted to shorten it to `2001:0034::AB76::4BC2`.

Unfortunately, you cannot do this, as the device does not know how many sets of zeroes each double colon represents. Was it a group of three and a single group, two groups of two, or a single group and a group of three? Because of this, you can only drop one set of contiguous zeroes. So, either of these would be allowed:

`2001:0034::AB76:0000:0000:4BC2` or `2001:0034:0000:0000:AB76::4BC2`.

OK, this doesn't look too amazing, but remember we can drop leading zeroes, including the leading zeroes in the groups that consist solely of
zeroes: `2001:0034::AB76:0000:0000:4BC2`.

This gives us `2001:34::AB76:0:0:4BC2` or `2001:0034:0000:0000:AB76::4BC2`, and finally, this gives us `2001:34:0:0:AB76::4BC2`.

We have just seen the format an IPv6 address can take and have looked at the various methods of shortening the addresses to make them a little more user-friendly. As you can see, the address format is vastly different to that of IPv4. Likewise, the method of displaying subnets is different, as you will see in the next section.

# Subnets and prefixes

Just like IPv4, IPv6 addresses use a similar concept of subnetting. However, we do not use the dotted decimal notation. Instead, we use the slash notation we used in CIDR, and this is referred to as a prefix. Like CIDR, the notation refers to how many bits of an IPv6 address the network element uses. The remainder, like IPv4, is set aside for the host element.

The term prefix is used here as it refers to the bits at the start of the IP address indicating the network element. Fortunately, the MTA exam does not interrogate you much on IPv6 subnets and prefixes—at least not to the same degree as it does for IPv4. As we go through the various addresses, it will be sufficient just to know what prefixes go with what address type.

# Transmission types

With IPv4, we had three types of transmissions: unicast, multicast, and broadcast. IPv6 has similar transmission types, but drops broadcast and introduces anycast transmissions.

The easiest way to understand anycast is with an analogy. Imagine you have seen a crime being committed. Do you have to tell every police officer (broadcast)? Do you have to tell a particular police officer (unicast)? Or do you have to tell the first police officer that you see (anycast)? Anycast transmissions are sent to the nearest device from a predefined group of devices. Usually, anycast addresses are allocated to routers only.

Before we move on to the next section, I would just like to reiterate how important it is for you to understand the format of an IPv6 address. Given the length of the addresses, it is very easy for a *typo* to creep in, so knowing how the address is written in its various formats, and which characters are valid, will be beneficial not only in the exam but also in real life. While each address follows the same format, just like IPv4, there are various address types. We will discuss them in the next section.

# Understanding address types

For the exam, it is important to be able to identify each of the various address types and understand their purpose. In this section, we will discuss each of them in turn.

# Global unicast address

An IPv6 global unicast address is similar to a public IP address in IPv4, in that it is routable across the internet. Because there are so many available IPv6 addresses, it is feasible that every device can have its own global unicast address. This means that **Network Address Translation (NAT)** is not required, although this has not been well-received by all network administrators who appreciate the added security NAT provides.

Global unicast addresses all begin with $2000::/3$, and the address is broken down into parts:

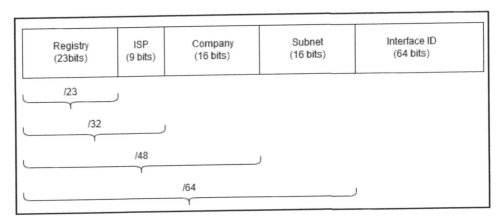

Figure 12.1: Breakdown of a global unicast address

The first 23 bits identify the registry that controls the IPv6 address; the next 9 bits identify the ISP that has been granted the IP address. The ISPs issue an IPv6 address to an organization, and this organization is identified in the next 16 bits. Finally, the organization subnet this with the next 16 bits. This leaves the final 64 bits for the interface ID. An interface ID is the same as the host element we have seen in IPv4.

# Link-local addresses

A link-local address is similar to an IPv4 APIPA address. They are not designed to be routable across the internet. A Windows device is automatically assigned one of these addresses, but unlike IPv4, a Windows device can have a link-local address, as well as a unicast address. In *Figure 12.2*, we can see a link-local address in use:

```
Wireless LAN adapter Wi-Fi:

   Connection-specific DNS Suffix  . : broadband
   Link-local IPv6 Address . . . . . : fe80::8968:12c2:4895:9665%13
   IPv4 Address. . . . . . . . . . . : 192.168.1.12
   Subnet Mask . . . . . . . . . . . : 255.255.255.0
   Default Gateway . . . . . . . . . : 192.168.1.1
```

Figure 12.2: Link-local address

Link-local addresses all begin with FE80::/10. While it is not Windows-specific, a lot of network administrators will allocate the same link-local address to each interface on a router. As you may recall, each interface on a router connects to a different network. Therefore, allocating the same link-local address to each interface is permitted because they are all on different interfaces.

The presence of a % number at the end of the line, for example, %13, as seen in the preceding screenshot, is another indication that this is a link-local address. This number is an identifier of the reachability scope of the address. Reachability scopes are beyond the exam objectives, but as the number is showing in the screenshot, I felt it important to just mention it here. There is a link to a Microsoft article in the *Further reading* section that goes into a little more detail about these if you wish to read it.

One last point I would like to make about link-local addresses is that a network card can have a link-local address AND one of the other address types simultaneously.

# Unique local addresses

Unique local addresses are the IPv6 equivalent of private IPv4 addresses and begin with FC00::/7. Like their IPv4 counterparts, these are not routable across the internet.

# Multicast addresses

Like their IPv4 counterpart, IPv6 multicast addresses are used to transmit data to devices within a specified group. Multicast IPv6 addresses begin with FF00::/8.

As a sort of replacement for broadcast, there is a multicast group called **all nodes**, which sends data to all the devices on the network. The all nodes multicast address is FF02::1.

# Loopback address

Despite having so many IP addresses available, the IPv6 developers realized that the loopback address range used in IPv4 wasted so many IP addresses. Therefore, in IPv6, there is only one loopback IP address and that is ::1. This is obviously the shortened version of the address, and all the preceding hexadecimal characters are zeroes.

By understanding the various address types, you will be able to not only identify what an address is used for, but you will also be able to identify whether it has been applied correctly. For example, you may see a link-local address in use when you were anticipating a global unicast address.

Now, we have discussed the address formats and types, let's move on to actually assigning an IPv6 address to a host.

# Assigning IPv6 addresses

Like IPv4, IPv6 addresses can be assigned manually or dynamically. However, to obtain an IP address automatically, we can use either stateless auto-configuration or DHCPv6.

# Manual configuration

Manually assigning an IP address to a Windows computer involves adjusting the IPv6 properties of the NIC itself. As a device can have more than one NIC, ensure you are configuring the right one. Let's quickly walk through this process:

1. From the Control Panel, select **Network and Internet**:

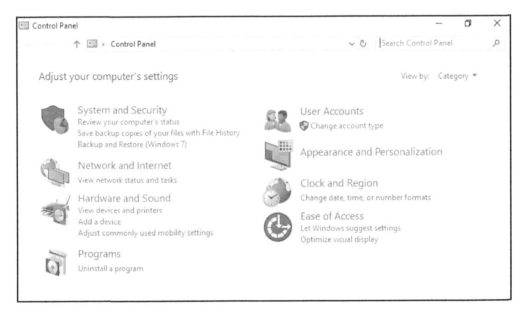

Figure 12.3: Control Panel

2. Then, select **Network and Sharing Center**:

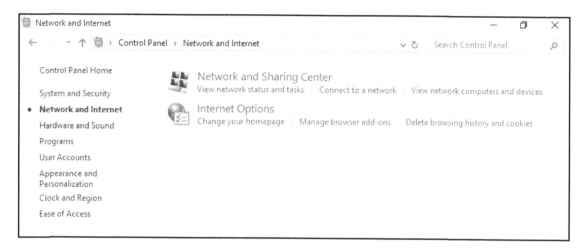

Figure 12.4: Network and Internet tab

3. Select **Change adapter settings** on the left:

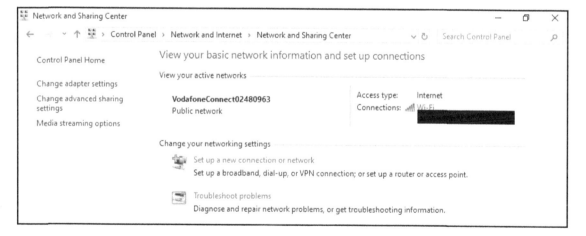

Figure 12.5: Adapter settings

4. This will present you with the adapters you have installed on your device. Note that, on my laptop, I have Bluetooth, a wired connection, and a Wi-Fi connection:

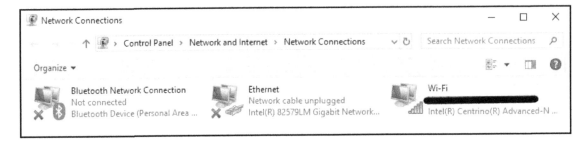

Figure 12.6: List of adapters installed

5. Right-click on the adapter you want to configure and choose **Properties**:

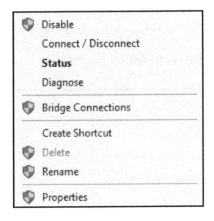

Figure 12.7: Right-clicking the adapter

6. Then, either double-click on **Internet Protocol Version 6 (TCP/IPv6)** or select it and choose **Properties**:

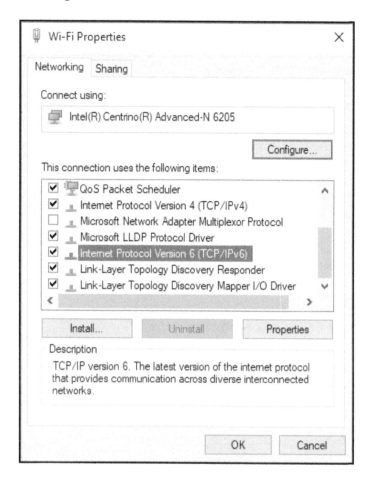

Figure 12.8: Configuration options

7. By default, your adapter will be set to obtain an IP address automatically. Note that not only is it getting the IP address automatically, but it will also be given a default gateway and DNS settings automatically. Notice that, unlike IPv4, there is no **Alternative Configuration** tab:

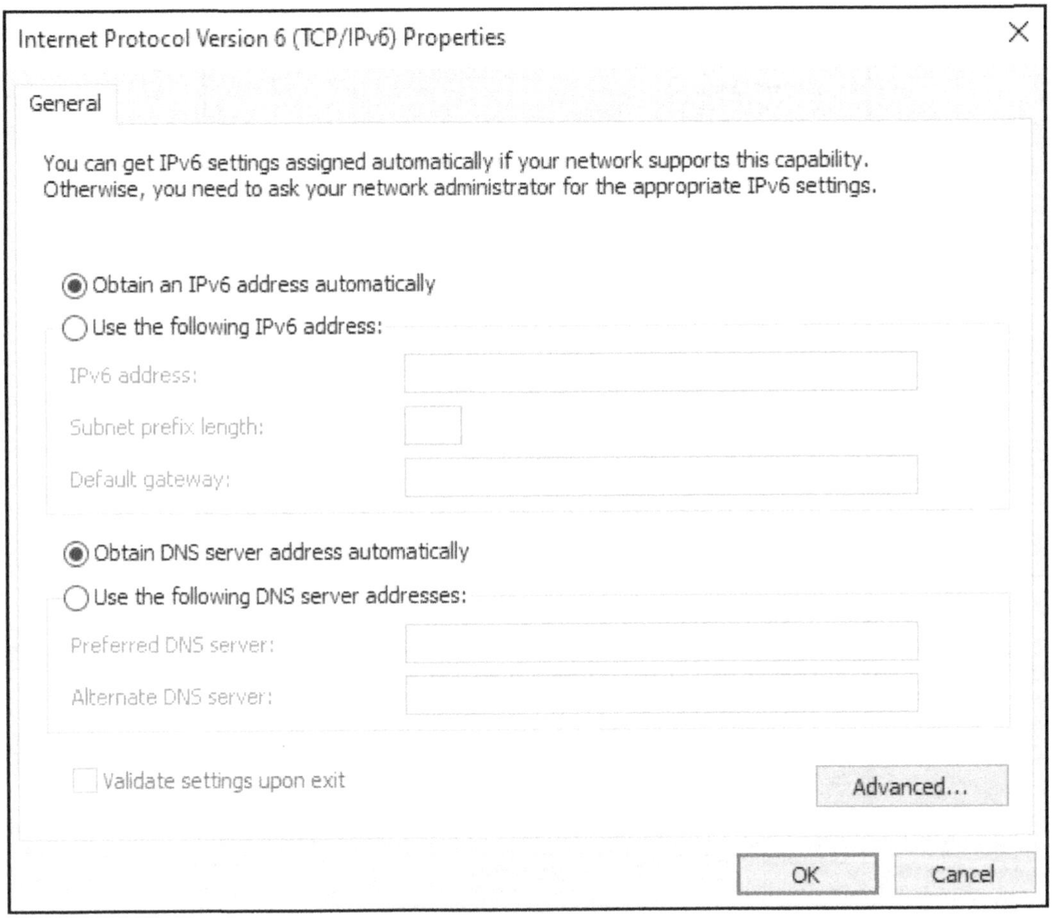

Figure 12.9: IPv6 properties

8. If you want to set the IP address manually, you can choose the option to **Use the following IPv6 address:** and enter the address there. Note that this can be the full address or a shortened version, as shown in the following example:

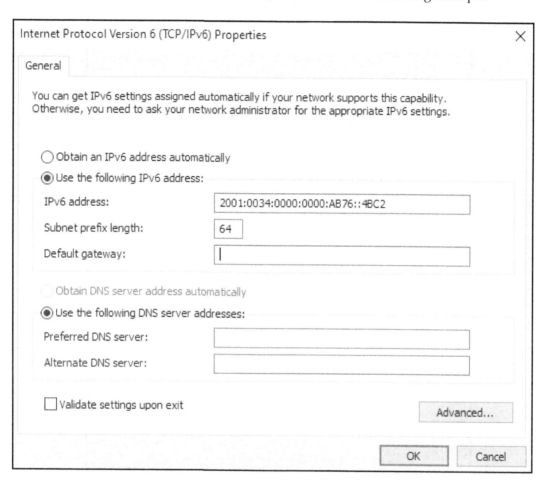

Figure 12.10: Setting the IP address manually

9. The advanced options are similar to IPv4, except that the WINS tab has been removed:

Figure 12.11: Advanced options

10. Once you have configured everything, click **OK**.

As you can see, the preceding process is similar in parts to the process for applying an IPv4 address manually, and generally, the information that's being configured is the same. I'm sure this activity has also provided you with insight into how laborious typing out IPv6 addresses can be and the benefits of being able to shorten them.

# Stateless Address Auto-Configuration (SLAAC)

Stateless auto-configuration uses a concept called **Extended Unique Identifier (EUI-64)** to generate a unique IP address in conjunction with information that's been obtained from a router and the device's own MAC address. The 64 part of the label refers to the address being 64 bits long in total. For most IPv6 devices, SLAAC is the default option, and this became available in Windows 10.

As a high-level overview of this process, the device requests the network prefix information, pads out and adjusts its own MAC address, and combines the two to form a unique address. Digging deeper into this, the process is as follows:

1. The device sends an ICMP packet to all the routers on the network using a multicast address of FF02::2. This is known as a **Router Solicitation (RS)** message and is requesting the network prefix information.
2. The router replies using an ICMP packet called **Router Advertisement (RA)**, which contains the prefix information only. Normally, the router sends out RAs regularly, but on receipt of an RS, it will send one out immediately to speed the process up. Note that RS and RA messages are part of an overall function called neighbor discovery, which we will discuss a little later in this chapter.
3. The device takes its own MAC address and splits it in two. In-between the two sections, it inserts an additional 16 bits with the value FFFE. Recall that MAC addresses are 48 bits long, so adding padding of 16 bits takes it to the required 64 bits in length.
4. The device then needs to use some form of *flag* to identify whether this is a universally unique address or just locally unique. Given that MAC addresses should be unique in the world, this will usually always be a universally unique address, unless someone has manually changed the MAC address. The flag in question is the 7th bit in the underlying binary. If the address is universally unique, it holds a value of 1; if it is locally unique, it holds a value of 0. Because of this, you may find that the value of the second hexadecimal number in the EUI-64 address is different from its original value in the MAC address.

You only need an overview of this process for the exam and will not be asked to convert a MAC address into an EUI-64 address.

Notice that, throughout this process, no information is returned to the router or any servers on the network. Therefore, there is no central listing of which device has which IP address, and to be honest, there doesn't need to be. Because of this lack of tracking, this is referred to as being stateless.

Whilst these addresses should be unique, because of the lack of a centralized listing, we need some way of double-checking no-one else has the IP address on the network, although this is extremely unlikely. In IPv4, we used ARP to perform this check; in IPv6, we use **Neighbor Discovery (NDP)** to do this. More specifically, we use a feature called **Duplicate Address Detection (DAD)**.

DAD uses a process known as **Neighbor Solicitation (NS)** and **Neighbor Advertisement (NA)**. This works similarly to ARP. Once the device has been configured with an IP address, it sends out a DAD request in the form of an NS, asking if any of its neighbors have the same address. They respond using an NA message, confirming whether they have the address or not.

# Stateful configuration using DHCPv6

DHCP is as relatively similar in IPv6 as it is in IPv4, although there is a precursor that takes place before any requests are sent to a DHCP server. That precursor is that the device waits until it hears a router advertisement message before contacting a DHCP server. We mentioned previously that these are sent out regularly, and part of the information that is included in the advertisement is details of any DHCP servers or relay agents in use. If no RA is heard after a period of time, the device sends out multicast transmission addresses to all the DCHP servers and relay agents. The process that follows is this:

1. The host device sends a DHCP solicit message to the multicast address, `FF02::1:2`.
2. The DHCP server responds with a DHCP advertisement that offers the host an IP address. Note that the source and destination address of the advertisement is the respective link-local addresses of the host and DHCP server. This is also the case for the remaining steps.
3. The host sends a request message to the DHCP server, asking for the offered IP address.
4. The DHCP server sends a reply, confirming the IP address, assignment.

Unlike SLAAC, the DHCPv6 server DOES keep track of the address assignments and therefore knows the state of the devices, which means DHCPv6 is classed as stateful.

There may be occasions when you want to force your device to obtain a new IPv6 address. This can be done in the same way as in IPv4, that is, using the `ipconfig` command but with the `/renew6` and `/release6` switches.

# ICMPv6

I have mentioned neighbor discovery several times in this chapter. This functionality is part of the ICMPv6 protocol. You should recall that ICMP is the underlying protocol that provides us with tools such as `ping`, `tracert`, and `pathping`. We can tell these commands to specifically use either IPv4 or IPv6 by adding the `-4` or `-6` switches. *Figure 12.12* shows the help option of the `ping` command, and we can see the two switches listed at the bottom:

```
Usage: ping [-t] [-a] [-n count] [-l size] [-f] [-i TTL] [-v TOS]
            [-r count] [-s count] [[-j host-list] | [-k host-list]]
            [-w timeout] [-R] [-S srcaddr] [-c compartment] [-p]
            [-4] [-6] target_name

Options:
    -t             Ping the specified host until stopped.
                   To see statistics and continue - type Control-Break;
                   To stop - type Control-C.
    -a             Resolve addresses to hostnames.
    -n count       Number of echo requests to send.
    -l size        Send buffer size.
    -f             Set Don't Fragment flag in packet (IPv4-only).
    -i TTL         Time To Live.
    -v TOS         Type Of Service (IPv4-only. This setting has been deprecated
                   and has no effect on the type of service field in the IP
                   Header).
    -r count       Record route for count hops (IPv4-only).
    -s count       Timestamp for count hops (IPv4-only).
    -j host-list   Loose source route along host-list (IPv4-only).
    -k host-list   Strict source route along host-list (IPv4-only).
    -w timeout     Timeout in milliseconds to wait for each reply.
    -R             Use routing header to test reverse route also (IPv6-only).
                   Per RFC 5095 the use of this routing header has been
                   deprecated. Some systems may drop echo requests if
                   this header is used.
    -S srcaddr     Source address to use.
    -c compartment Routing compartment identifier.
    -p             Ping a Hyper-V Network Virtualization provider address.
    -4             Force using IPv4.
    -6             Force using IPv6.
```

Figure 12.12: ping help options

The neighbor discovery portion of ICMPv6 allows for the following to take place:

- RS
- RA
- NS (including DAD)
- NA

Solicitation is the method of querying or requesting information from either a neighbor or router. Advertisement can be either a response to that solicitation or information that is *announced* at regular intervals onto the network.

Correctly assigning IPv6 addresses to a host is of utmost importance. If the assignment is incorrect, it can have a major impact on the ability to communicate and possibly on security. Ideally, you would want to use some form of automatic assignment to avoid errors, but there will likely be instances when IPv6 will need to be assigned manually.

# Understanding interoperability with IPv4

Because IPv6 has not yet fully replaced IPv4, there needs to be a means of using the two protocols together to allow communication to take place. What if you are using IPv6 and the recipient is using IPv4? What if you are both using IPv6 but the data needs to transit through an IPv4 network or vice versa? Let's find out.

 The MTA exam only requires you to have overview knowledge of the technologies we are going to cover.

# Dual stack

Dual stack is a means for a network interface card to support and process IPv4 and IPv6 traffic simultaneously. To be able to do this, the NIC needs to have both protocols enabled and configured to have an IP address from each version, whether that is an address that's assigned automatically or manually. This has been part of the Windows OS since Windows Vista. It could be enabled in Windows XP, but it needed some changes to be made to fully support it.

You can check whether your ISP supports dual stack by using this website: `https://whatismyipaddress.com/ds-check`.

# Intra-Site Automatic Tunnel Addressing Prot

The **Intra-Site Automatic Tunnel Addressing Protocol (ISATAP)** takes advantage
stack capabilities to allow for the transmission of IPv6 data across an IPv4 network
essence, what ISATAP does is take the IPv4 address of the NIC that wishes to tran
IPv6 data and adds it to one of two IPv6 prefixes:

- **Globally unique**: FE80::0200:5EFE
- **Locally unique**: FE80::0000:5EFE

You may see this modified address as a mixture of both hexadecimal and decimal,
may see it as purely hexadecimal; for example, FE80::0200:5EFE:129.90.32.7
or FE80::0200:5EFE:81:5A:20:4C.

One easy way of identifying whether an IPv6 address is an ISATAP address is by
for the 5EFE in it. Any ISATAP-enabled device will be able to interpret the traffic

# 6to4

6to4 allows devices on separate IPv6 networks to communicate with each other ac
IPv4 network. It does this by encapsulating the IPv6 data packet as the payload of
packet. 6to4 addresses always begin with the prefix 2002::/16. When communic
across an IPv4 network, an IPv4 source and destination address must be used. Th
obtained by the transmitting device by looking at the next 32 bits that follow the 2
prefix in the IPv6 addresses being used.

While the preceding sounds reasonably straightforward, we have to bear in mind
needs to be a supporting infrastructure in place including 6to4 routers, as well as
IPv4 address for each endpoint. Also, it does not work for devices that are sitting
network using NAT.

# Teredo tunneling

Teredo tunneling is very similar to 6to4 but allows IPv6 communication between
sitting on a network that use NAT. To do this, the endpoint encapsulates the IPv6
an IPv4 UDP packet. This system works because NAT devices can usually proces
appropriately and forward the traffic to the specified endpoint device. Because o
endpoint does not require its own dedicated public IPv4 address.

# Summary

There is an ever-increasing demand for IP addresses, and IPv6 is really the only method available to keep up with this demand. This chapter provided you with an introduction to IPv6 and talked about some of the underlying concepts related to it, such as hexadecimal numbering, transmission types, and different IPv6 addresses. We also learned how to assign IPv6 addresses and configure them on a Windows device. We finished off this chapter by discussing the methods available to us so that we can use IPv6 alongside IPv4.

Although IPv6 addresses can look intimidating, this chapter has taught you how to write an address in both the long and shortened formats, as well as how to interpret a shortened address to obtain its long representation. By gaining an understanding of the different address types, you will be able to effectively configure and troubleshoot your network by knowing the use cases each of these represent. By configuring IPv6 on a Windows device, you now know what options are available to you on the client and where to go to check the settings. Understanding the systems that are available to us so that we can use the IPv4 and IPv6 protocols together is critical for pretty much any network engineer.

In this chapter and the previous one, we have seen how IPv4 provides us with addresses that are reasonably easy to read and remember and how IPv6 provides us with addresses that are not so easy to remember. In the next chapter, we will look into a method of making this easier, by remembering names rather than numbers in a process referred to as name resolution.

# Questions

1. How many bits are in an IPv6 address?

A) 6
B) 32
C) 64
D) 128

2. Which of these is a valid IPv6 address?

A) `2001:AG10:0256:7623:ABCD:1FA8:22EE:1908`
B) `2001:87F6:1234`
C) `2001:AC10:0256:7623:ABCD:1FA8:22EE:1908`
D) `2001:AC10:0256:7623:ABCD:::22EE:1908`

3. What is the prefix for a global unicast address?

(A) `2000::/3`
(B) `FE80::/10`
(C) `FC00::/7`
(D) `FF00::/8`

4. What is the IPv6 loopback address?

(A) `127.0.0.1`
(B) `127::1`
(C) `::1`
(D) `127::127`

5. Which method of configuring IPv6 addresses uses RS?

(A) DHCPv6
(B) Manual
(C) SLAAC
(D) None of the methods use RS

6. Which of these is the full representation of the following shortened IPv6 address: `2001:34:0:0:AB76::4BC2`?

(A) `2001:3400:0000:0000:AB76:0000:0000:4BC2`
(B) `2001:0034:0000:0000:AB76:0000:0000:4BC2`
(C) `2001:0034:0000:AB76:0000:0000:0000:4BC2`
(D) `2001:0034:0:0:AB76:0:0:4BC2`

7. Which type of transmission sends data to only one device out of a predefined group of devices?

(A) Anycast
(B) Unicast
(C) Broadcast
(D) Multicast

8. Which service allows IPv6 communication between devices on NAT-enabled networks and uses UDP for encapsulation?

(A) 6to4
(B) ISATAP
(C) Dual stack
(D) Teredo

# Further reading

To learn more about IPv6 addressing, take a look at the following links:

- *Tongue twister: The number of possible IPv6 addresses read out loud*: `https://royal.pingdom.com/the-number-of-possible-ipv6-addresses-read-out-loud/`
- *IPv6 Addressing*: `https://docs.microsoft.com/en-us/previous-versions/aa917150(v=msdn.10)`
- *Connection of IPv6 Domains via IPv4 Clouds*: `https://www.ietf.org/rfc/rfc3056.txt`

# 13
# Understanding Name Resolution

As humans, we generally find it easier to remember names rather than numbers. Can you remember everybody's number in your phone's contact list? The use of names not only makes things easier to remember but also makes things a lot more user-friendly when configuring devices and services. This is similar in the case of a complex IP address. Hence, rather than us having to recall an IP address, we use name resolution, which we will learn about in this chapter.

In this chapter, we will look at the four main means of performing name resolution, that is DNS, hosts files, **Windows Internet Name Service (WINS)**, and LMHOSTS files. As a network technician, you will definitely need to understand these systems, as well as how they are configured at the host level, since this will be part of your day-to-day workload.

The following topics will be covered in this chapter:

- **Domain Name Service (DNS)**
- Hosts file
- WINS

## Technical requirements

To complete the exercises in this chapter, you will need a computer running a recent Windows OS (preferably Windows 10) with administrator rights.

# Exploring DNS

The DNS is the most common form of name resolution that's currently in use. This vendor-agnostic system is used by all modern-day networked operating systems, including Windows, Linux, macOS, Android, iOS, and Cisco IOS. DNS provides a hierarchical means of resolving a hostname to an IP address – more specifically, a **fully qualified domain name (FQDN)**. Because of its hierarchical nature, DNS can be used within local networks and across the internet. When resolving an FQDN to an IP address, we use what is known as a forward lookup zone. When we are resolving an IP address to an FQDN, we use a reverse lookup zone.

 A lot of people seem to confuse DNS and DHCP. This is probably because they think of both as providers of IP addresses. DHCP provides an IP address, while DNS provides an IP address for an FQDN. Because of this, I would urge you to think of DHCP as *issuing* an IP address and DNS as *resolving* an IP address (from an FQDN).

To fully understand how DNS works, we need to understand how an FQDN is formed. Once we understand that, we can look at the different types of DNS records, and then how name resolution takes place using DNS.

# FQDN

You have used an FQDN without realizing it every time you have put a URL into the address bar. Suppose I wanted to visit the website of this book's publisher. I would open up my browser, type `https://www.packtpub.com` into the address bar, and hit the *Enter* key. Everything I've entered after `https://` in this particular example forms the **FQDN**. Here, the FQDN is `www.packtpub.com`. Just for clarification, if I used the URL `https://www.packtpub.com/index.html`, the FQDN would still only be `www.packtpub.com`. It is only the data between the second and third / that forms the FQDN. I've used a URL in my example here, but we can and do use FQDNs in lots of different ways.

Let's look at how an FQDN is broken down:

Figure 13.1: Breakdown of an FQDN

Working from left to right, in the upcoming sections, we will discuss each of these elements in turn.

# Host

This is the hostname of the particular device. This could be anything within reason. It may be something that reflects the owner, for example, `gordons_laptop`; something that reflects the device's role, for example, `www` for a web server; or something totally random, for example, `win789658221`.

I have worked for some organizations that named their servers after characters or locations from movies or books. One company had all the domain controllers named after Star Wars and all the file servers named after Star Trek. Whatever the naming convention, the host element is always the leftmost part of the FQDN. The hostname is controlled by the organization themselves.

I previously mentioned that the host is the hostname of the particular device; however, it may also be the **Canonical Name (CNAME)** linked to the host. This concept will be discussed in more detail when we cover DNS record types.

# Domain

The domain element relates to the domain that the organization has registered with a domain name registrar. There is a caveat, though: if the domain is restricted to internal use, we don't need to register the domain name. For example, when I'm studying, I often create my own virtual network, which is inaccessible from outside. I set up and run my own domain controller and create a domain with amazingly creative names, such as `gordon.local`.

It is feasible to create subdomains and include them in the FQDN. A lot of global organizations do this to differentiate between regions. For example, let's imagine that my publisher uses separate subdomains for its presence in Europe and in the United States, and each region has its own web server, that is, `www.europe.packtpub.com` and `www.us.packtpub.com`.

In turn, each of these may have a subdomain for accounting and another for marketing. Just focusing on the Europe subdomain, this may give us `www.marketing.europe.packtpub.com` and `www.accounting.europe.packtpub.com`.

Although the first domain needs to be registered with a domain registrar (with the exception stated), the subdomains do not need to be registered and are controlled by the organization themselves:

# www.accounting.europe.packtpub.com.

Controlled by the Organisation Itself | Needs to be Registered

Figure 13.2: FQDN registration

The preceding diagram is a visual breakdown of which FQDN elements need to be registered.

## Top-level domain (TLD)

The TLD is usually the rightmost part of an FQDN that we normally see. In our example, `com` is the TLD. The management of these top-level domains is controlled by the **Internet Corporation for Assigned Names and Numbers (ICANN)**.

TLDs fall under one of three main categories:

- **Country-code TLD**: This is a two-letter domain name that reflects the country of origin, for example, `.uk` and `.au`. Usually, you will see these paired with a second-level domain, such as `.co`, giving us `.co.uk` or `.co.au`.
- **Sponsored TLD**: These TLDs reflect the community that they represent. Let's look at some examples: `.edu` is for post-secondary education organizations, while `.gov` is for the US government. What about `.museum`? Well, I think you can guess that one.

- **Unsponsored TLD**: These TLDs don't represent any form of community as such, and include examples such as .com and .org.

There are more categories, but they are not as common as the three we listed previously. In the *Further reading* section, I have linked an article that provides further information about these other TLD types.

# Root domain

In our original example of www.packtpub.com, I mentioned that there was a missing element. This was the root domain. However, I included this when we broke down an FQDN. The root domain is represented by a period . at the end of the FQDN. The root domain generally refers to the 13 root domain servers on the internet. We tend not to add the . at the end when using an FQDN as the application/service usually assumes it is required and puts it in for us.

# Hierarchical view

By breaking down an FQDN in this way, we can form a hierarchical structure. The following diagram is a graphical representation of the hierarchical DNS structure:

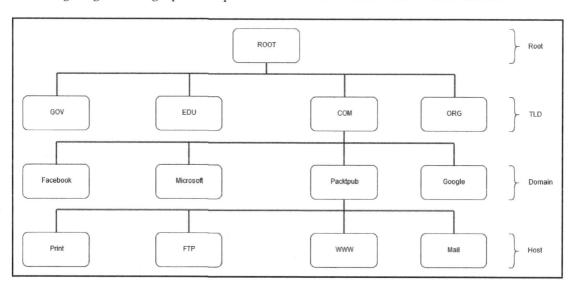

Figure 13.3: DNS hierarchy

It should be noted that this is not a complete representation. The huge volume of hosts, domains, TLDs, and so on means that a full image would not fit in this book.

For DNS to work, the servers need to be aware of the IP address that is linked to the FQDN. Let's discuss which DNS records allow us to do this.

# DNS records

We have already ascertained that DNS resolves an IP address from a given FQDN. To be able to do this, DNS needs to populated with the relevant information in the form of DNS records. A DNS server can obtain records in one of three main ways:

- Manual entry
- Dynamic entry
- Zone transfer

With manual entry, a network administrator enters the details in themselves. This is useful when you don't want the record entry to be overwritten or when the device the IP address is linked to doesn't support updating DNS automatically.

 As a word of caution, setting a manual entry is not the wisest decision if the endpoint doesn't have a static IP address since you will be continually updating the DNS every time it gets a new IP address.

Dynamic entry requires an operating system that can register its IP address and hostname automatically. Windows is one such OS.

Most organizations will have numerous DNS servers. These servers will exchange information between each other in what are referred to as zone transfers. The main DNS server is the one that replicates all the DNS information. It is referred to as the primary zone and replicates to secondary zones. This main DNS server is also likely to be classed as the authoritative server for the domain. These zone transfers connect to port 53 and use TCP at the transport layer so as to guarantee delivery of the transfer. In contrast, although they still use port 53, DNS queries use UDP at the transport layer. This is to reduce performance overhead on the DNS server due to the number of requests it is likely to receive.

# Configuring client DNS settings

**Activity 1**: The following activity details how you can configure a device to update DNS with its IP properties. Let's get started:

1. From the **Control Panel**, select **Network and Internet**:

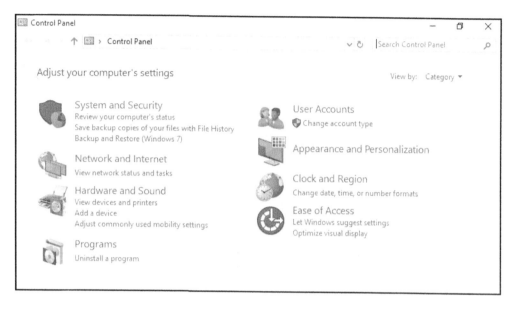

Figure 13.4: Control Panel

2. Then, select **Network and Sharing Center**:

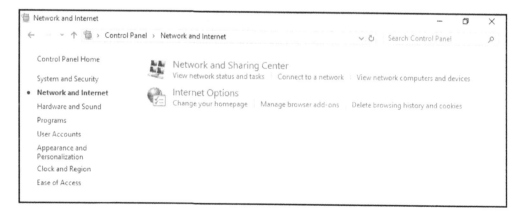

Figure 13.5: Network and Internet tab

3. Select **Change adapter settings** on the left:

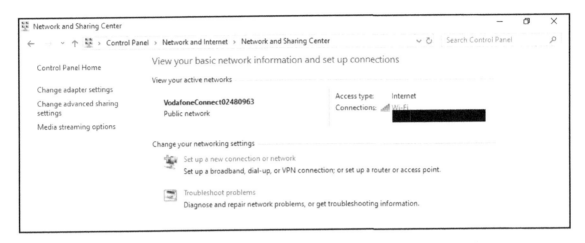

Figure 13.6: Network and Sharing Center

4. This will present you with the adapters you have installed on your device. Note that, on my laptop, I have Bluetooth, a wired connection, and a Wi-Fi connection:

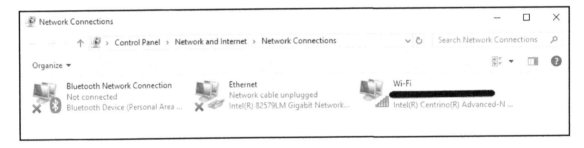

Figure 13.7: List of installed adapters

5. Right-click on the adapter you want to configure and choose **Properties**:

Figure 13.8: Right-clicking your network adapter

6. Then, either double-click on **Internet Protocol Version 4 (TCP/IPv4)** or select it and choose **Properties**:

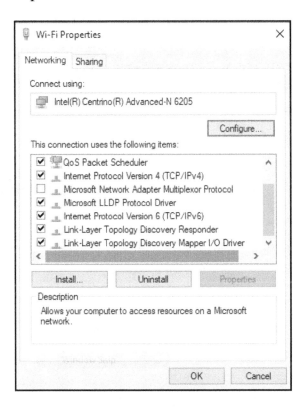

Figure 13.9: Configuration options

7. By default, your adapter will be set to obtain an IP address, a default gateway, and DNS settings automatically:

Figure 13.10: IPv4 properties

8. If you prefer, you can configure the adapter so that it has manual DNS settings:

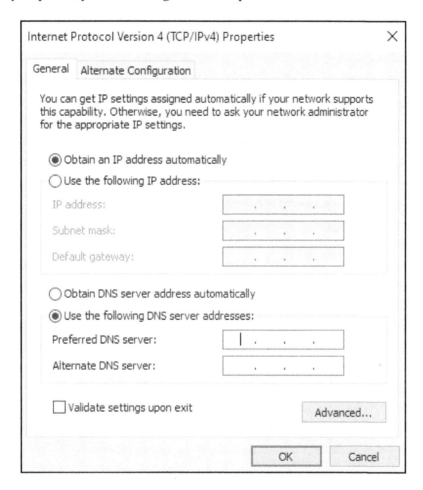

Figure 13.11: Manual DNS settings

9. If you are setting an IP address manually, you must set the DNS server details manually as well:

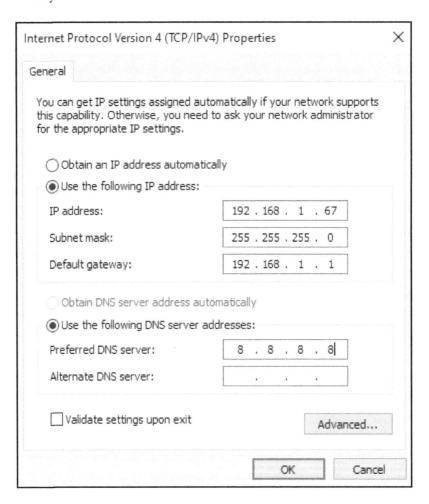

Figure 13.12: Setting the DNS server details

10. By clicking on the **Advanced...** button, you are provided with more granular control. Clicking on the **DNS** tab allows us to configure additional DNS settings, including configuring the order the DNS servers need to be in.

11. To ensure your device registers with the DNS server, check the **Register this connection's address in DNS** option:

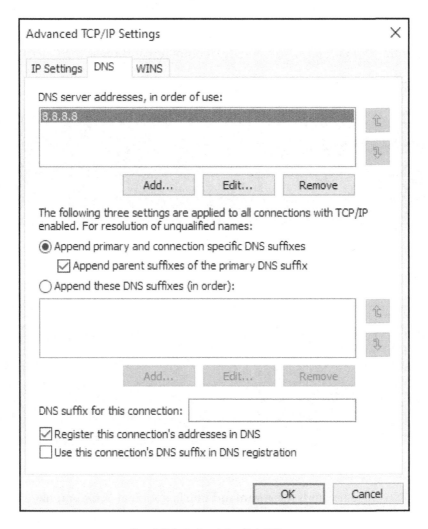

Figure 13.13: Registering a device with the DNS server

It should be noted that these settings are interface-specific, and if you have more than one interface, you will need to check the configuration on the others as well.

You can also force a Windows device to register its IP address through the command line. We'll learn how to do this in the next section.

# Registering a DNS from the command line

**Activity 2**: To register a DNS from the command line, follow these steps:

1. Open Command Prompt as an administrator.
2. Enter the `ipconfig /registerdns` command and press the *Enter* key:

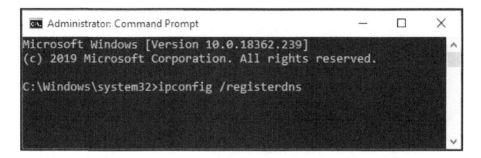

Figure 13.14: Entering the command

3. You will receive the following message:

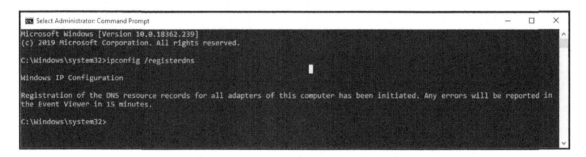

Figure 13.15: Command output

Registering a DNS entry through the command line is not ideal since you have to run it on all machines. However, I have used it when troubleshooting DNS issues.

# DNS record types

When a DNS query takes place, the information can be directly from the authoritative server or from a server that has been provided from elsewhere. The latter servers are referred to as non-authoritative servers. As a general rule of thumb, the authoritative server will be a DNS server belonging to the domain itself. A non-authoritative server will be one that holds a copy of some or all of the information that's held by the authoritative server. For example, a lot of organizations have Google's public DNS server at 8.8.8.8 specified as one of the servers to perform DNS queries against. Any queries this server responds to would be classed as non-authoritative.

A basic DNS server will be broken down into a forward lookup zone, which resolves FQDN to IP addresses, and a reverse lookup zone, which resolves IP addresses to FQDN:

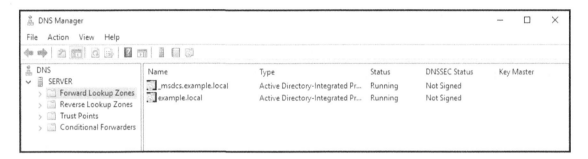

Figure 13.16: DNS zones

Each zone on a DNS server consists of a number of different records that take an FQDN and point it toward an IP address. These records fall under different categories, with the main ones being as follows:

- **A records**: Resolves FQDNs to IPv4 addresses.
- **AAAA records**: Referred to as *quad A* records, they resolve FQDNs to IPv6 addresses.
- **NS records**: These records detail the name servers in a domain.
- **MX records**: These records detail mail servers in a domain.
- **SRV records**: These records detail devices that offer a service, such as a domain controller. As an aside, I found that, when trying to connect a device to a domain, if there is no DNS configured or no SRV record listed, it will not connect.
- **SOA records**: The **Start of Authority (SOA)** record only appears once in a zone and holds information such as the name of the primary DNS server and a serial number. The serial number changes following each update and is a means of secondary servers identifying whether they have the latest version or not.

- **PTR record**: These records are found in reverse lookup zones and are used to identify an FQDN from an IP address.
- **CNAME/alias records**: These two record types perform a similar function. They take an FQDN and point it to another hostname rather than an IP address. In turn, that hostname can be resolved to an IP address using an A record or a AAAA record. Let's look at this in practice to gain a better understanding.

The following diagram shows a server on the right-hand side called **WinServices.example.local** on IP address **192.168.23.78**. This particular server hosts an FTP element, a web server element, and a mail server element. While this is not an issue, the name of the server is not that user-friendly in that it gives quite a generic impression of what function it performs. Note that all the clients are communicating to it using this generic name. To be honest, this example isn't too bad. I have seen some hosts with some very random names:

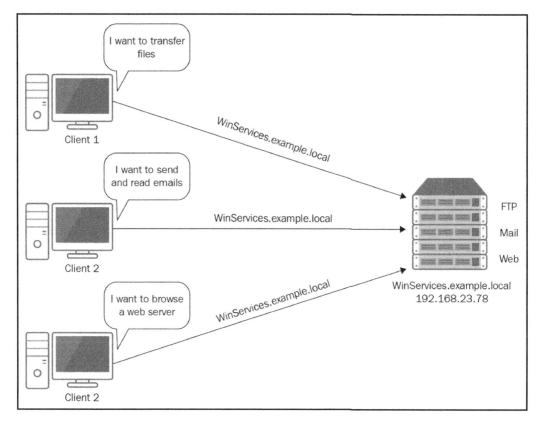

Figure 13.17: Multiple services on a server without CNAMEs being used

To make this a little more user-friendly, we can create CNAMEs/alias records in DNS, such as the following:

- `ftp.example.local`
- `www.example.local`
- `mail.example.local`

When creating each of these, we wouldn't point these toward the IP address of **192.168.23.78**; instead, we would point them to the name **WinServices.example.local**. Whenever a query came in for one of the CNAME/alias records, the DNS server would see the query, notice that it points to the **WinServices.example.local** hostname, and then do a further query to identify the IP address for that name rather than the CNAME/alias that was originally queried. We can see this process flow in the following diagram:

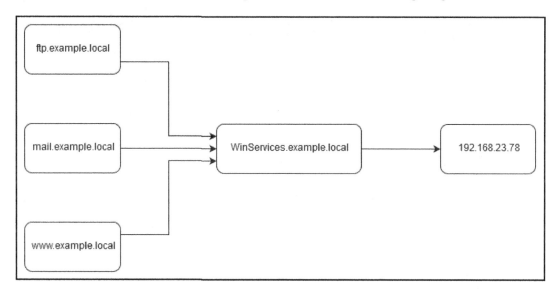

Figure 13.18: Resolving CNAMEs to IP addresses

In the following diagram, we can see how the clients now communicate via the server's aliases:

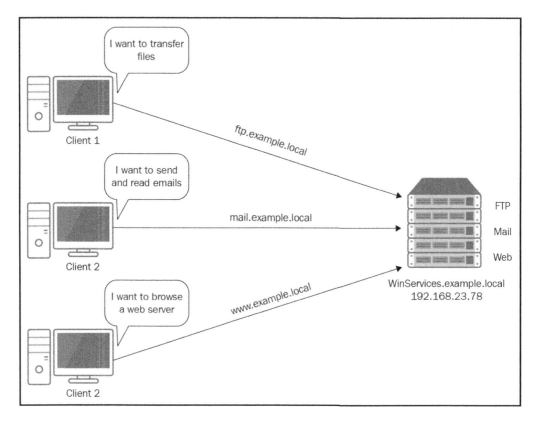

Figure 13.19: Hosts communicating using CNAMEs

When the host wants to communicate with a particular service on **WinServices.example.local**, we can see that they still use the CNAMEs, such as **ftp.example.local**, **mail.example.local**, and **www.example.local**. Then, through the magic of CNAME/alias in DNS, the data is sent to the correct server.

# Manually creating a DNS record

The following process can be used to create a manual DNS A record. If you have a server virtual machine available, you can follow along:

1. Right-click in the white space and choose **New Host (A or AAAA)...**:

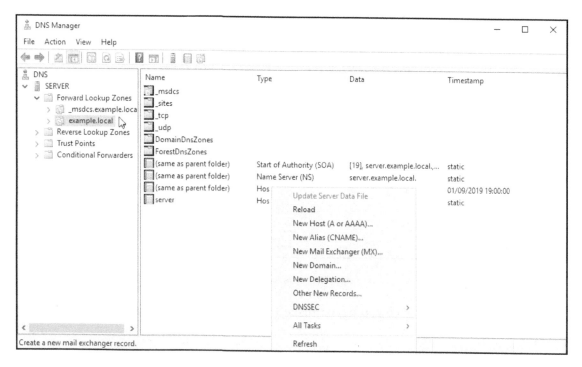

Figure 13.20: DNS Manager window

2. Enter the FQDN and specify the IP address (IPv4 or IPv6). Optionally, you can choose the option to create a PTR record, but it should be noted that unless a reverse lookup zone has been configured, this will not work:

Figure 13.21: Entering your details

3. Click **Add Host** once you have finished. Now, you will be able to see the created entry at the bottom:

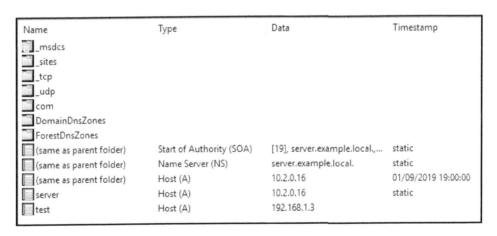

Figure 13.22: New host visible

Now, let's walk through the process of creating a CNAME that points an alternative FQDN (ftp.example.local) to test.example.local:

1. Right-click in the white space and choose **New Alias (CNAME)...**:

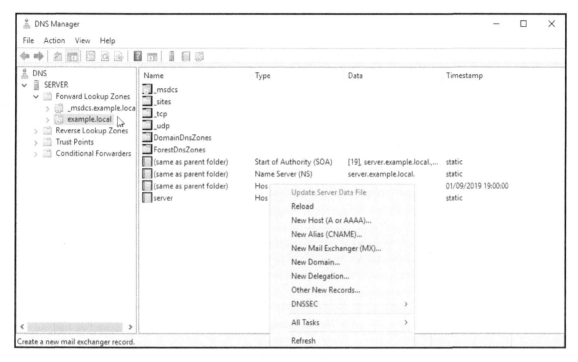

Figure 13.23: DNS Manager

2. Only enter the host element of the CNAME. Then, point the record to the appropriate host:

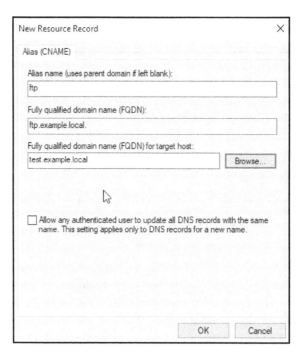

Figure 13.24: New Resource record tab

3. You will see the entry listed at the bottom:

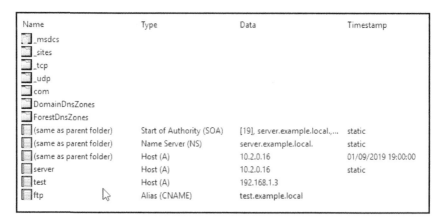

Figure 13.25: New entry visible

In this final walkthrough, we will look at creating a PTR record. To configure a PTR record, you need to have a reverse lookup zone configured. Let's get started:

1. Select the appropriate reverse lookup.
2. Right-click in the white space and choose **New Pointer (PTR)...**:

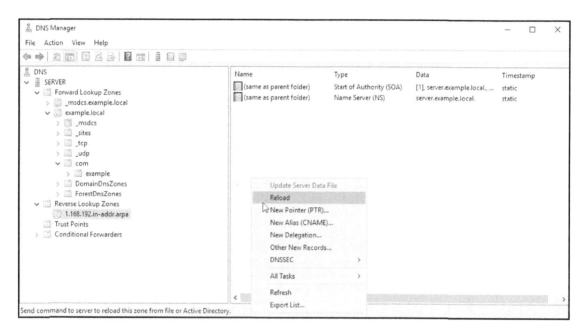

Figure 13.26: DNS Manager window

3. Enter the IP address (this will have been part-populated) and the FQDN of the host:

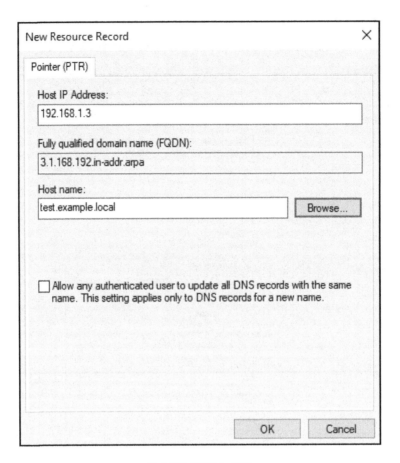

Figure 13.27: Entering the details

4. The entry will now appear as follows:

| Name | Type | Data | Timestamp |
|------|------|------|-----------|
| _sites | | | |
| _tcp | | | |
| (same as parent folder) | Host (A) | 10.2.0.16 | 01/09/2019 19:00:00 |

Figure 13.28: New entry visible

In this section, we have walked through configuring a number of different record types. The remaining types are all configured in a similar sort of way.

Now that we know how these records are created, we need to know how our PC obtains the IP address that the DNS holds for a FQDN. We will look at this in the next section.

# Performing DNS queries

For a limited time, Windows devices store the results of any previous DNS queries in an area called the **DNS cache**. Results that are stored here are removed after a period of time has passed, that is, since they were last queried or when the device is shut down. In addition to this being populated by the results of queries, which are dynamic, it also contains static entries that have been populated by the HOSTS file, which we will talk about in more detail later in this chapter. Unlike the query results, the information that's obtained from the hosts file is not removed after a period of time.

We can view the DNS cache information by running the `ipconfig /displaydns` command from the command line. Sometimes, we may need to clear out the DNS cache if we suspect that it holds outdated information. We can do this by running the `ipconfig /flushdns` command. In the following activity, we look at using both of these commands.

**Activity 3**: Execute the following steps to perform DNS queries:

1. Open a Command Prompt as an administrator. We will see what the DNS cache looks like when a device has been booted up for the first time.

2. Enter the `ipconfig /flushdns` command and press the *Enter* key:

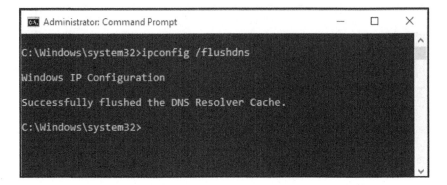

Figure 13.29: Command output

3. Now, we will look at the current state of the DNS cache. Enter the `ipconfig /displaydns` command. This shouldn't return any results:

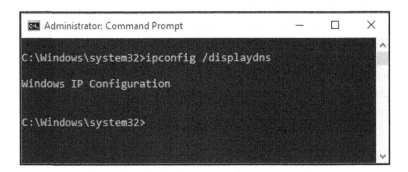

Figure 13.30: No results visible

4. Open a web browser of your choice and navigate to `https://news.bbc.co.uk`.

5. Once the page has loaded, return to Command Prompt and run the `ipconfig /displaydns` command again.

You will see that you have a number of entries in the DNS cache rather than just the one entry. This is because, when you load up most web pages, they pull in data such as images, music, and so on from other locations, and your device has to perform DNS queries for those other locations:

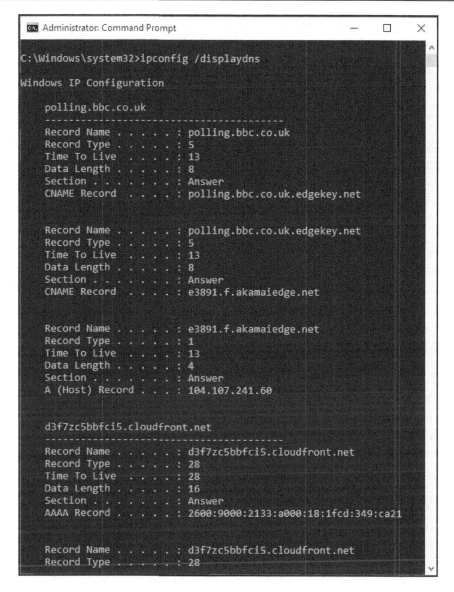

Figure 13.31: DNS cache now visible

The preceding screenshot shows us that there are three entries. Let's look at the top host entry, that is, `polling.bbc.co.uk`. It contains the following information:

- Name of the record.
- A numerical representation of the record type.

- **Time to Live** (TTL) is the time in seconds that this entry will stay in the cache.
- Data length relates to the length in bytes of the IP address being returned. Four bytes is an IPv4 address, sixteen bytes is an IPv6 address, and eight bytes is a CNAME or PTR record.
- `Section` shows that it has come from the `Answer` section.
- Below this line is the actual response.

Notice that, with `polling.bbc.co.uk`, the first answer points to a CNAME called `polling.bbc.co.uk.edgekey.net`. The next set of values relates to `polling.bbc.co.uk.edgekey.net`. This resolves to another CNAME called `e3891.f.akamaiedge.net`. The third set of values relates to `e3891.f.akamaiedge.net` and finally resolves to an IPv4 address, that is, `104.107.241.60`.

Finally, at the bottom of the screenshot, we can see an entry that resolves to an IPv6 address.

There are two types of DNS queries that we need to focus on for the MTA exam. These are iterative and recursive. I will explain each of these in turn and then provide a common scenario that you are likely to see in a lot of organizations.

# Iterative DNS queries

With an iterative DNS query, the client sends its query to the DNS server that it is configured to use. The DNS server will check its own cache and records and will either respond with the IP address in question or tell you that it doesn't know the IP address for the FQDN being queried.

# Recursive DNS queries

When a recursive DNS query takes place, the client sends its query to the relevant DNS server. Like an iterative query, the DNS server checks its records and cache, and if it can resolve the FQDN to an IP address, it will respond to the client accordingly. If it cannot resolve the FQDN, it becomes quite helpful. Rather than just responding with an *I don't know* message, it actually says *I don't know, but here's the IP address of the root domain server. They'll be able to point you in the right direction.* The client sends the query to the root domain server, who will then point the client in the direction of the TLD DNS server. In turn, the TLD DNS server points it to the relevant domain DNS server, which will provide the client with an IP address or point you to the relevant subdomain DNS server.

# Example DNS query

In a lot of cases, the client performs an iterative DNS query, and if the DNS server doesn't know the IP address, it performs a recursive query on behalf of the client. This can be seen in the following diagram:

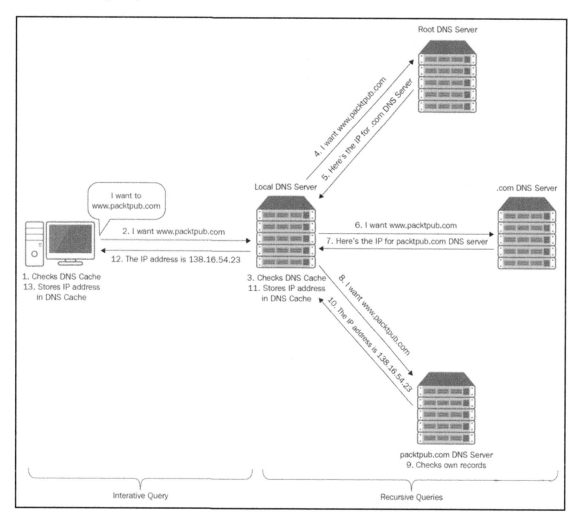

Figure 13.32: DNS name resolution

The client on the left-hand side wants to communicate with **www.packtpub.com**, and follows the following process:

1. It checks its own DNS cache but finds no entry.
2. It sends a query to the DNS server specified in the host's configuration.
3. The DNS server checks its own DNS cache but finds no entry. Rather than replying negatively to the host, it undertakes recursive queries.
4. It sends the query to the root DNS server.
5. The root DNS server doesn't know the IP address for the queried FQDN, so it replies to the local DNS server, advising the IP address of the `.com` DNS server.
6. The local DNS server sends the query to the `.com` DNS server.
7. The `.com` DNS server doesn't know the IP address for the queried FQDN, so it replies to the local DNS server, advising the IP address of the `packtpub.com` DNS server.
8. The local DNS server sends the query to the `packtpub.com` DNS server.
9. The `packtpub.com` DNS server checks its records for `www.packtpub.com`.
10. Upon finding an entry, it replies to the local DNS server by providing the IP address.
11. The local DNS server updates its own DNS cache with the entry.
12. Then, it replies to the original host, advising it of the IP address for `www.packtpub.com`.
13. On receipt of the IP address, the client updates its own DNS cache.

Once the client has been given the IP address, it can start communicating with `www.packtpub.com`.

# nslookup

nslookup is a command-line tool that allows you to perform manual DNS queries. It is a handy tool that can be used for troubleshooting. The tool can be used in two modes:

- Non-interactive mode
- Interactive mode

Non-interactive mode means you perform the query by typing in the command, whereas interactive mode allows you to configure more in-depth parameters in your query. The easiest way to understand how nslookup works is by using it, so we will carry out two activities: one in non-interactive mode and the other in interactive mode.

# Non-interactive mode

**Activity 4**: In this activity, we will perform a simple nslookup in non-interactive mode. Let's get started:

1. Open a Command Prompt.
2. First, we will look at the help options. Enter the `nslookup /?` command and read through the output:

```
Administrator: Command Prompt                                    —    □    ×

C:\Windows\system32>nslookup /?
Usage:
   nslookup [-opt ...]            # interactive mode using default server
   nslookup [-opt ...] - server   # interactive mode using 'server'
   nslookup [-opt ...] host       # just look up 'host' using default server
   nslookup [-opt ...] host server # just look up 'host' using 'server'

C:\Windows\system32>
```

Figure 13.33: Command output

3. Enter the `nslookup www.packtpub.com` command and press the *Enter* key. Your output will look similar to this:

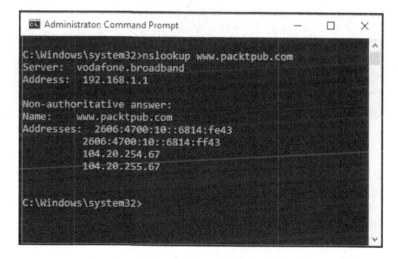

Figure 13.34: Command output

Looking at the preceding output, the top two lines provide information about the DNS server that has provided the response. In this case, the DNS server is my ISP provided router on `192.168.1.1`. The next line tells us whether the response has come from an authoritative server or a non-authoritative server. You will only get an authoritative response if your DNS server is responsible for the domain that the queried FQDN is in. The remaining lines detail the IPv4 and IPv6 addresses that were resolved from the FQDN.

**Activity 5**: In this activity, we will continue to use non-interactive mode, but also configure some additional parameters. Let's get started:

1. Open a Command Prompt.
2. Enter the `nslookup -type=mx packtpub.com 8.8.8.8` command and press the *Enter* key. Some things to note here are as follows:
   - `-type=mx` tells nslookup to search for mail exchange servers.
   - For `packtpub.com`, we are specifying the domain and not an individual host.
   - For `8.8.8.8`, we are asking it to perform the DNS query using the DNS server located at `8.8.8.8`.
3. Your output will look similar to this:

Figure 13.35: Command output

4. The top two lines of this output are as per the previous activity and tell us which DNS server has provided the result. Since we specified `8.8.8.8` in our command, the server is no longer my ISP's router. Again, we can see this is a non-authoritative answer. The last line provides us with details of the MX records for `packt.pub`. In this case, there is only one. MX preference is a numerical value that tells us which MX server to use in the case of multiple mail servers being present. The preferred server will have a lower number. Then, we see the FQDN of the mail exchanger.

# Interactive mode

**Activity 6**: In this activity, we are going to repeat the previous activity but we are going to carry it out in interactive mode. Let's get started:

1. Open a Command Prompt.
2. Enter the `nslookup` command and press the *Enter* key.
3. Note that Command Prompt has turned to a >. This indicates that you are now in interactive mode. Any commands you enter here are only used by `nslookup`.
4. Let's view the help options. Enter the `help` command and press the *Enter* key. You will see a lot more options than were displayed in non-interactive mode:

```
Select Administrator: Command Prompt - nslookup                        —    □    ×

C:\Windows\system32>nslookup
Default Server:  vodafone.broadband
Address:  192.168.1.1

> help
Commands:   (identifiers are shown in uppercase, [] means optional)
NAME            - print info about the host/domain NAME using default server
NAME1 NAME2     - as above, but use NAME2 as server
help or ?       - print info on common commands
set OPTION      - set an option
    all              - print options, current server and host
    [no]debug        - print debugging information
    [no]d2           - print exhaustive debugging information
    [no]defname      - append domain name to each query
    [no]recurse      - ask for recursive answer to query
    [no]search       - use domain search list
    [no]vc           - always use a virtual circuit
    domain=NAME      - set default domain name to NAME
    srchlist=N1[/N2/.../N6] - set domain to N1 and search list to N1,N2, etc.
    root=NAME        - set root server to NAME
    retry=X          - set number of retries to X
    timeout=X        - set initial time-out interval to X seconds
    type=X           - set query type (ex. A,AAAA,A+AAAA,ANY,CNAME,MX,NS,PTR,SOA,SRV)
    querytype=X      - same as type
    class=X          - set query class (ex. IN (Internet), ANY)
    [no]msxfr        - use MS fast zone transfer
    ixfrver=X        - current version to use in IXFR transfer request
server NAME     - set default server to NAME, using current default server
lserver NAME    - set default server to NAME, using initial server
root            - set current default server to the root
ls [opt] DOMAIN [> FILE] - list addresses in DOMAIN (optional: output to FILE)
    -a           - list canonical names and aliases
    -d           - list all records
    -t TYPE      - list records of the given RFC record type (ex. A,CNAME,MX,NS,PTR etc.)
view FILE          - sort an 'ls' output file and view it with pg
exit            - exit the program

>
```

Figure 13.36: Command output

5. We will configure `nslookup` to search for MX records by entering the `set type=mx` command and hitting the *Enter* key. Note that no confirmation is provided. Unless you get an error message, assume that you have entered it correctly.

6. Now, we will set the DNS server that we will run the query against with the `server 8.8.8.8` command and hit *Enter*.

7. Finally, we will tell it what domain we are querying. Type in `packtpub.com` and hit *Enter*. You will see that we get a similar output to before (note that I have removed the help output here for clarity):

```
Select Administrator: Command Prompt - nslookup                    —    □    ×

C:\Windows\system32>nslookup
Default Server:   vodafone.broadband
Address:   192.168.1.1

> set type=mx
> server 8.8.8.8
Default Server:   dns.google
Address:   8.8.8.8

> packtpub.com
Server:   dns.google
Address:   8.8.8.8

Non-authoritative answer:
packtpub.com     MX preference = 5, mail exchanger = packtpub-com.mail.protection.outlook.com
>
```

Figure 13.37: Command output

One thing to note if you're troubleshooting a network connectivity issue to a host is that if you can connect to it by IP address but not by name, then the issue is usually DNS-related. This may be because the DNS cache has an incorrect entry. Running the `ipconfig /flushdns` command may resolve the issue, but there may be a static or possibly old record on the DNS server that needs amending, or it may be that you have or the application you are using has the wrong name for the destination device and it is resolving incorrectly.

Although DNS is the most commonplace name resolution method, we occasionally use the hosts file for more localized name resolution.

# The hosts file

The hosts file is a text file that can be used to provide a static form of name resolution that only impacts the host that the hosts file is stored on. On a Windows device, the file is stored at `%systemroot%\System32\drivers\etc\`:

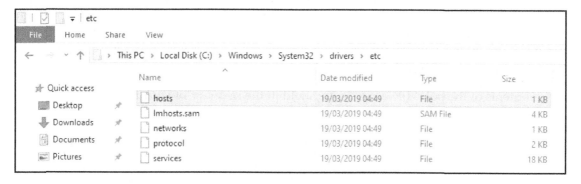

Figure 13.38: Location of the hosts file

Since this is a straightforward text file, it can be edited using any standard text editor, such as Notepad; however, to be able to edit it, you need to run Notepad as an administrator. Once we have the file open, we can configure it accordingly.

The file contains a number of comments and examples of how to configure the file. Each of these is *commented out* by using a #. Any text that follows a # is treated as a comment and not actioned. From the preceding examples, we can see that the IP address is on the left-hand side and the FQDN is on the right-hand side.

The concept of hosts files goes back to the early days of networking, before we had name resolution servers of any description, and the only devices you would be communicating to would be internal to the organization, so the network administrator would be responsible for populating and maintaining the file. They would put all the hostnames and IP addresses manually into this file and add it to each system. Despite this, the hosts file is still used today and does have use cases.

One common scenario is when you are testing a new service or server that you need to communicate with by name, but because you are only testing, you don't want to create a DNS record on the server. Another scenario that I have seen is when the device you are wanting to communicate with is on another domain, and the DNS server of that domain does not share its DNS records. Just create a manual entry in the hosts file and this will resolve the issue. While there are various other uses, a great use of the hosts file is to point known malicious FQDNs to `127.0.0.1` or some DNS black hole. That way, if a user or an application attempts to contact them, they can't. Now, you can manually add these yourself, download a pre-populated one from the internet, or copy and paste the contents of an online one into your existing hosts file.

The contents of the hosts file are read and held in the memory of your PC and are not flushed when the DNS cache is flushed.

**Activity 7**: In this activity, we are going to edit the hosts file and look at the outcome of this change. Let's get started:

1. First, we are going to prove that the FQDN we are going to use doesn't exist. Open a Command Prompt, enter `ping www.obscurewebsite.com`, and press *Enter*:

Figure 13.39: Command output

2. Now, let's make the necessary changes. Open up Notepad as an administrator.
3. Click **File** | **Open**, change the file type to **All files**, navigate to `C:\Windows\System32\drivers\etc\`, select the hosts file, and click **OK**:

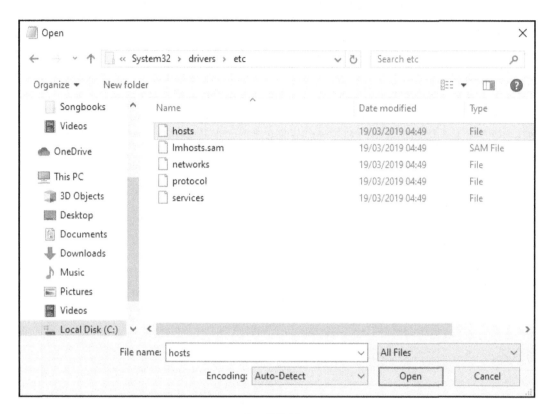

Figure 13.40: Drivers

4. At the bottom of the existing text, add the following line, which points the FQDN to your local device: `127.0.0.1 www.obscurewebsite.com`:

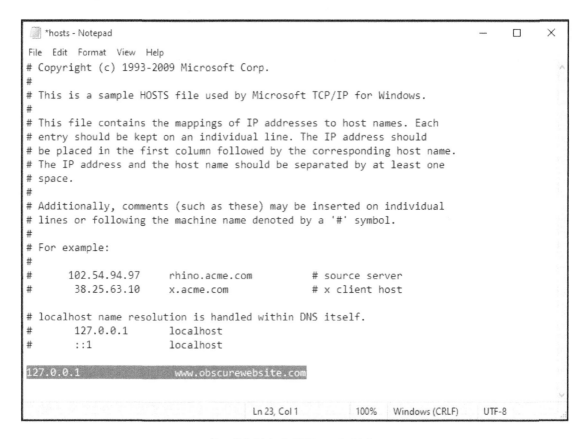

Figure 13.41: Pointing the FQDN to your local device

5. Click **Save**. You don't need to close the file down.

6. Return to Command Prompt and attempt to ping the address again. Now, you should get a response:

```
Administrator: Command Prompt                           —    □    ×

C:\Windows\system32>ping www.obscurewebsite.com

Pinging www.obscurewebsite.com [127.0.0.1] with 32 bytes of data:
Reply from 127.0.0.1: bytes=32 time<1ms TTL=128
Reply from 127.0.0.1: bytes=32 time<1ms TTL=128
Reply from 127.0.0.1: bytes=32 time<1ms TTL=128
Reply from 127.0.0.1: bytes=32 time<1ms TTL=128

Ping statistics for 127.0.0.1:
    Packets: Sent = 4, Received = 4, Lost = 0 (0% loss),
Approximate round trip times in milli-seconds:
    Minimum = 0ms, Maximum = 0ms, Average = 0ms

C:\Windows\system32>
```

Figure 13.42: Command output

7. Optional step: run the `ipconfig /displaydns` command. Can you see an entry for this website?
8. Now, we will return the file to its original state by removing the line we just added and clicking **Save**.
9. Close the file.

As you can see, it is fairly simple to configure, but you can imagine how laborious it would be to make multiple entries by hand compared to the automation offered by DNS. In addition, the hosts file is only beneficial if the IP addresses it contains are static; otherwise, you would have to change it every time a device was issued a new IP address by DHCP.

 I would like to finish off this section by giving you a tip. Often, I have edited the hosts file, clicked **Save**, and received an access denied message because I had forgotten to open Notepad as an administrator. If you do this, my tip is to copy the text you have entered, close the file, reopen it as an administrator, and then paste the text back in.

# WINS

I need to make two things abundantly clear from the outset. First, despite its name, the WINS does not work over the internet; it only works internally. Secondly, do not deploy WINS if you have DNS. Even Microsoft recommends this course of action. This is because WINS is a legacy service. However, it is one of the exam objectives, so we need to discuss it.

WINS is similar to DNS in that it resolves names to IP addresses; however, it deals with NetBIOS names, rather than an FQDN. The NetBIOS is, in essence, the hostname on its own, that is, without a domain, TLD, or root. This format is known as a single-label, unqualified domain name. Like DNS, a server that's called a WINS server needs to be available.

There are certain steps that need to be performed to configure a host to use WINS. We will discuss this in the upcoming sections.

# Registering a client's IP address in DNS

**Activity 8**: The following activity details how you can configure a device to update DNS with its IP properties. Let's get started:

1. From the **Control Panel**, select **Network and Internet**:

Figure 13.43: Control Panel

2. Then, select **Network and Sharing Center**:

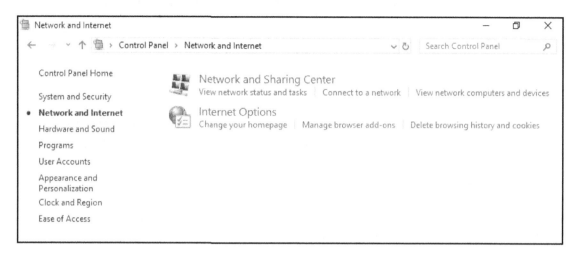

Figure 13.44: Network and Internet tab

3. Select **Change adapter settings** on the left:

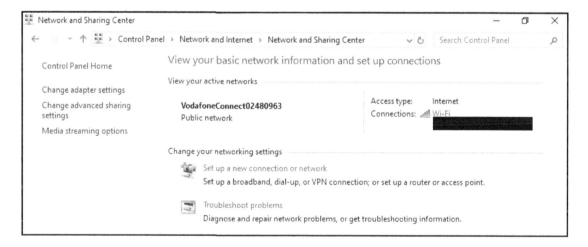

Figure 13.45: Network Sharing Center

4. This will present you with the adapters you have installed on your device. Note that on my laptop, I have Bluetooth, a wired connection, and a Wi-Fi connection:

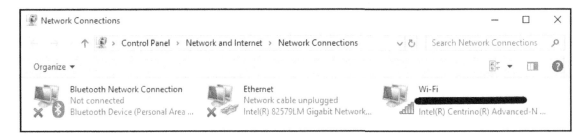

Figure 13.46: List of adapters

5. Right-click on the adapter you want to configure and choose **Properties**:

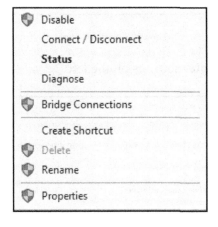

Figure 13.47: Right-clicking on the adapter you want to configure

6. Then, either double-click on **Internet Protocol Version 4 (TCP/IPv4)** or select it and choose **Properties**:

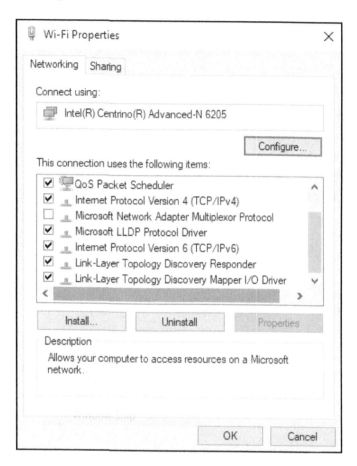

Figure 13.48: Configuration options

7. If your system is set to obtain an IP address automatically, you may already be provided with WINS settings automatically. If you are setting an IP address manually, you must set the WINS server details manually as well:

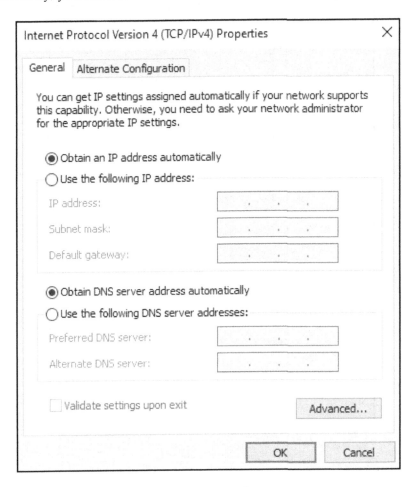

Figure 13.49: IPv4 properties

8. By clicking on the **Advanced...** button, you are provided with more granular control. Clicking on the **WINS** tab allows us to configure additional WINS settings, including configuring the order in which the WINS servers are queried and whether we want to use the locally configured LMHOSTS or not. It also allows us to specify whether or not NetBIOS is used in name resolution:

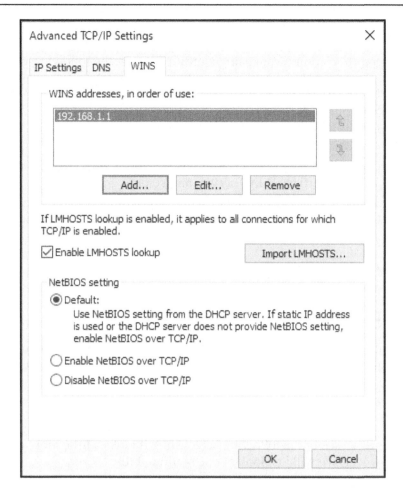

Figure 13.50: Advanced settings

When a WINS-enabled host is powered up, it registers its NetBIOS name with a WINS server. The WINS server checks to see if the name already exists in its database. If there is a duplicate, the server sends a query to the owner of the existing entry. If a reply is received, a message is sent to the new device, telling it that it is trying to register a duplicate name. If no reply is received, the server confirms its acceptance to the new device and updates its records accordingly. If no duplicate is found, the server confirms acceptance to the device and provides a TTL. Before the TTL expires, the device will attempt to renew the name registration.

# WINS query

When a device needs to communicate using NetBIOS names, the following process occurs:

1. The client device checks its NetBIOS name cache (similar to DNS cache).
2. If no result is found, it sends a query to the primary WINS server.
3. If the primary server has the necessary information, it responds accordingly.
4. If the primary WINS server does not know the IP address, or it fails to respond to three requests, the client device attempts the query with the secondary WINS server, then the tertiary WINS server, and so on.
5. If no resolution is made, the device will attempt to resolve the name using a file called LMHOSTS, checking its own name, checking the DNS cache, and querying DNS.

In the last step, I mentioned the LMHOSTS file. Let's look at that now.

# LMHOSTS

The LMHOSTS file is the NetBIOS names equivalent to the hosts files that are used by FQDN and is stored in the same location. It is unlikely that you will ever need to configure one of these files, and the exam doesn't go into in-depth details. It is safe for you to just know what it does.

Windows provides a sample file called `Lmhosts.sam` that you can edit and save as LMHOSTS. As you can see in the following screenshot, it looks a little more complex than the hosts file. However, we will just look at one section of it:

```
# The following example illustrates all of these extensions:
#
# 102.54.94.97     rhino                  #PRE #DOM:networking  #PDC: DC1  #net group's DC
# 102.54.94.102    "appname  \0x14"                    #special app server
# 102.54.94.123    popular              #PRE            #source server
# 102.54.94.117    localsrv             #PRE            #needed for the include
#
```

Figure 13.51: LMHOSTS sample

The top entry is broken down into the following components:

- IP address.
- NetBIOS name.
- `#PRE` indicates it is preloaded into cache.
- `DOM` is the name of the domain.
- `PDC` is the primary domain controller for that domain (note that PDC is a depreciated role).

# Summary

In this chapter, we looked at the four ways to perform name resolution on a system. Both DNS and WINS required servers and provided centralized administration of IP address resolution. In contrast, both the hosts file and LMHOSTS file provide name resolution restricted to the localhost only.

You learned how to configure both DNS and WINS settings on a client device, as well as how to manually configure a client to register its details on a DNS server from the command line. While the configuration of a DNS server is out of scope for the exam and therefore this book, we looked at common DNS record types and the uses of each of them. You also gained knowledge of how DNS and WINS queries are performed, starting with a check on the cache of the local machine. By understanding how each of these queries is performed, especially DNS queries, you will also be able to ensure the use of FQDN in your own environment. Finally, you have also learned about a number of command-line tools that you can use to configure and troubleshoot name resolution. Despite being on the command line, you will use these tools on a fairly regular basis.

DNS is one of the most common network services we use. In the next chapter, we will look into some additional common network services, some of which we have briefly touched upon already.

# Questions

1. What type of DNS record is used for IPv6 addresses?
   (A) A record
   (B) NS record
   (C) AAAA record
   (D) Av6 record

2. What port and transport layer protocol do DNS zone transfers use?
   (A) TCP, port 53
   (B) UDP, port 53
   (C) TCP, port 23
   (D) UDP, port 23

3. Looking at the following FQDN, what is the domain? For example,
   `www.example.com`.
   (A) `www`
   (B) `example`
   (C) `com`
   (D) `.`

4. If you wanted to manually configure a static name resolution of an FQDN that would only be used by a single client, what would you use?
   (A) DNS
   (B) The hosts file
   (C) WINS
   (D) LMHOSTS

5. Which of these allow you to resolve a device's IP address, even if it is across the internet? Choose two.
   (A) DNS
   (B) The hosts file
   (C) WINS
   (D) LMHOSTS

6. What type of DNS query will attempt to redirect you to the root domain name servers if it cannot resolve the IP address?
   (A) Iterative
   (B) Recursive
   (C) WINS
   (D) Hosts

7. If you wanted to clear your device's DNS cache, what command would you use?
   (A) `ipconfig /dnsclear`
   (B) `ipconfig /cleandns`
   (C) `ipconfig /dnsflush`
   (D) `ipconfig /flushdns`

8. What name resolution requires a server to resolve a NetBIOS name?
   (A) DNS
   (B) The hosts file
   (C) WINS
   (D) LMHOSTS

9. Which of these prefixes would you include in an LMHOSTS file to instruct the system to preload the address/name mapping into its cache?
   (A) PRE
   (B) PLD
   (C) PDC
   (D) IPPRE

10. When using `nslookup` in interactive mode, what command would you use to configure the details of the DNS you would like it to query?
    (A) `set server =<IPaddress>`
    (B) `server set=<IPaddress>`
    (C) `set server <IPaddress>`
    (D) `server <IPaddress>`

# Further reading

You can learn more about registries at `https://www.icann.org/resources/pages/registries/registries-agreements-en`.

# 14
# Network Services

One of the main reasons for networking to evolve was the ability to access resources and services not locally available on devices. In this chapter, we will look at these network services. We have already touched upon a number of network services in earlier chapters and we will go into more detail regarding them here, as well as introduce a number of other services not yet mentioned. The network services covered here do not involve an exhaustive list, and others do exist. In fact, we covered DNS, another common network service, in the previous chapter.

All of the services detailed in this chapter are ones that you will have involvement with on a regular basis. Depending on your organization, this involvement could be anything from supporting an already configured network to being the individual configuring the services. Therefore, having a good understanding of these services at this early stage in your career will give you a good foundation for your career.

The following topics will be covered in this chapter:

- **Dynamic Host Configuration Protocol (DHCP)**
- Firewalls
- Proxy servers
- Remote desktop
- **File Transfer Protocol (FTP)**
- File servers
- Print servers
- Domain controllers

# Technical requirements

To complete the exercises in this chapter, you will require a PC running a Windows operating system (preferably Windows 10).

# DHCP

I'd like to start this section by recapping what we already know about DHCP. You should recall that DHCP is used to issue an IP address automatically to any host that requests it. To do this, the process of DORA is followed:

- **Discover**: The client sends a broadcast packet to discover the DHCP server.
- **Offer**: The DHCP server offers an IP address and other information to the host.
- **Request**: The client, on receipt of the offer, requests the IP address and other details provided by the server.
- **Acknowledge**: The server sends an acknowledgement that the IP address has been issued to that client.

*Figure 14.1* shows a Wireshark capture of the DHCP process. Note that on the first line, the source IP address is 0.0.0.0, as the requesting device does not have an IP address as of yet; and the destination address is the general broadcast address of 255.255.255.255. On the second line, we see the source IP address is a unicast IP address of 192.168.1.1, which is the address of the DHCP server making the offer. What may strike you as odd is that this line also contains a destination IP address, yet the device requesting the IP address does not have one. This address is the address that is being offered to the device:

| No. | Time | Source | Destination | Protocol | Length | Info |
|---|---|---|---|---|---|---|
| 688 | 134.535039 | 0.0.0.0 | 255.255.255.255 | DHCP | 344 | DHCP Discover - Transaction ID 0x77ec88a6 |
| 707 | 136.095521 | 192.168.1.1 | 192.168.1.15 | DHCP | 342 | DHCP Offer - Transaction ID 0x77ec88a6 |
| 708 | 136.097044 | 0.0.0.0 | 255.255.255.255 | DHCP | 370 | DHCP Request - Transaction ID 0x77ec88a6 |
| 710 | 136.398745 | 192.168.1.1 | 192.168.1.15 | DHCP | 342 | DHCP ACK - Transaction ID 0x77ec88a6 |

Figure 14.1: Wireshark capture of a DHCP request

You may be wondering how the device knows that it is being offered the IP address and that the address isn't being offered to another device. Quite simply, the data being transmitted from the DHCP server will include a destination MAC address that reflects that of the requesting device.

The third line again shows a source IP address of 0.0.0.0 because, until the process is complete, the IP address is technically not allocated; the destination address is still a broadcast address. This allows a device to request an IP address from a DHCP server, and ensures any other DHCP servers that may have offered IP addresses know that their IP address is not required. The final line is the DHCP server acknowledging that the original device can have that address.

We have covered how to configure DHCP on the client already.

# Configuring a DHCP server

In this section, I would like us to focus more on the server side of DHCP. Although DHCP is not solely a Microsoft product, and is used on various different devices and operating systems, I will be discussing configuring DHCP on a Microsoft Server.

Once we have identified the server we wish to install DHCP on, we need to add the DHCP role to the machine. On completion of the role installation, we then need to configure the server settings. As a DHCP server can have multiple DHCP scopes, we may have settings that are common across all scopes. These can be configured in **Server Options** (*Figure 14.2*):

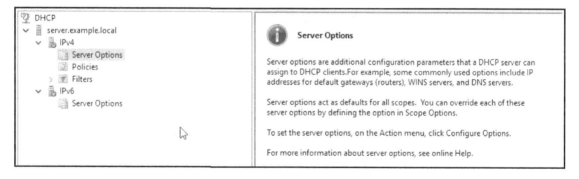

Figure 14.2: Server Options

We then move on to configuring the DHCP scopes. A DHCP scope tells the DHCP server what pool of IP addresses it has to lease out to client machines. Also included in the scope is settings for subnet masks, default gateways, DNS servers, reservations, exclusions, and an array of other information.

The IP address range (*Figure 14.3*) tells the DHCP server what IP addresses it has available to lease out to hosts. This can be as small or as big as you want it, and it does not have to use up the whole of your subnet. In fact, it is recommended that you do not do this. When planning your network, you will have identified a number of critical devices that need to have static IP addresses. To make life easier for you, I would suggest having all the static IP addresses be at the start or at the end of your subnet, and creating a scope of IP addresses in between, rather than have to do more in-depth configuration to work round any static IP addresses stuck in the middle of the range:

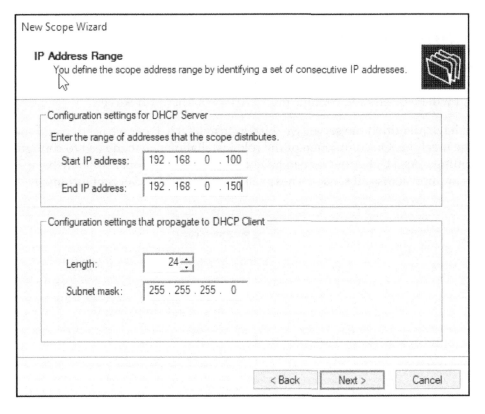

Figure 14.3: IP Address Range

I would also suggest future-proofing your DHCP setup. By this, I mean think beyond the current network, and plan for growth. Will there be more devices added in the future? I say this not just about the size of the pool, but also think about the static IP addresses. Imagine you have a 192.168.0.0/24 network, with 10 static hosts. We could set aside the first 10 host IP addresses (192.168.0.1 - 192.168.0.10) to these and start our DHCP scope at 192.168.0.11. That might be okay for now, but what static IP addresses can you give to any future devices that may need them?

# DHCP exclusions

What if there are static addresses slap bang in the middle of the IP address range we wanted to create? Do we need to create one scope that goes up to that address, and then another scope after? It's possible, but not generally practical. Instead, what we can do is set an exclusion within the IP address range we want to use. As you can, no doubt, guess from its name, an exclusion excludes a specified IP address from within a pool being issued to hosts (*Figure 14.4*):

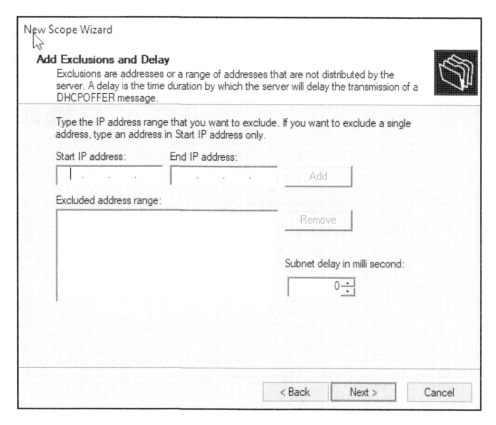

Figure 14.4: Setting exclusions

We see that we can specify the range by adding the start and end IP addresses. We can also provide a subnet delay. This is useful for when you have multiple DHCP servers on the network and you want one to only provide an IP address if one hadn't been obtained from another DHCP server.

# DHCP leases

Once all the IP addresses have been issued from the pool to the hosts, no more devices can be serviced by the DHCP server for that particular scope. This is known as IP address exhaustion. To try and reduce this, each IP address is leased to a host for a set period of time known as a lease duration (*Figure 14.5*). For wired devices, this is usually set to about 7 days; for wireless devices, this is usually set to 8 hours only. The reason for this disparity is that it is generally assumed that wireless devices are more likely to be guests visiting for a short period of time, and there may be a heavy rotation of guests. Wi-Fi in a coffee shop is a perfect example of where this may happen:

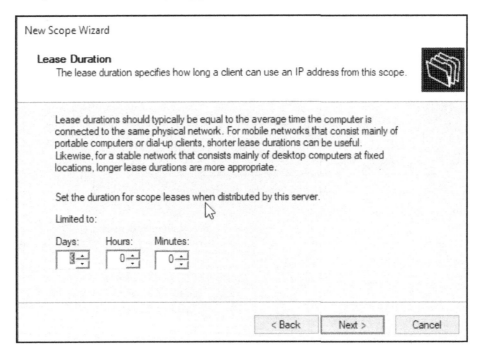

Figure 14.5: Setting Lease Duration

On being issued an IP address, the host retains that address for the duration of the lease. However, halfway through the lease, the host will attempt to renew the lease with the DHCP server. If the DHCP server hears the request, it will renew the lease for the full duration again. If the DHCP server does not respond, the client waits half of the remaining lease time, and requests again. It will repeat this process of waiting half the remaining time and keep requesting, until such time that it either renews the lease or the lease expires. If the lease expires, then the host reverts to an **Automatic Private IP Addressing (APIPA)** address. Recall that an APIPA address always starts with 169.254.x.x.

# DHCP reservations

There may be instances when we have a device on our network that cannot be issued a static IP address, but needs to have the same IP address each time from the DHCP server. In this case, we can set up a reservation (*Figure 14.6*). A reservation links the device's MAC address to a specified IP address. Every time the DHCP server receives a request from that MAC address, it knows to issue out the specific IP address. An important thing to note is that if you change the NIC in that device, its MAC address will also change. If this happens, the reservation will not work, so you need to ensure you update the DHCP entry also. Reservations can be preconfigured or created after a device has connected and been issued an IP address:

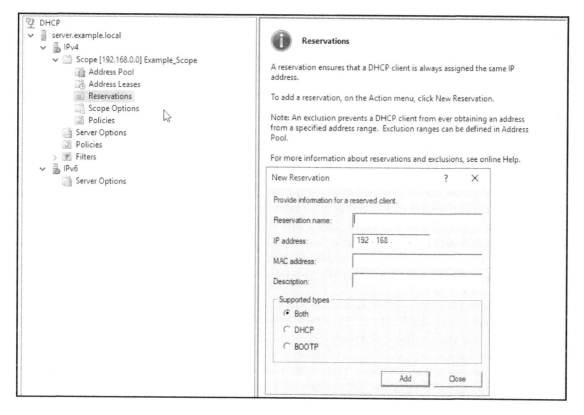

Figure 14.6: Setting reservations

It is easy to confuse exclusions and reservations as it sometimes feels like they do the same job, just from a different angle. Remember, exclusions prevent an IP address being issued; reservations issue an IP address to a specific host.

DHCP is something you will come across quite frequently in any network engineering role, so a good understanding of it is important. Another service that plays an important role on a network is a firewall. How much exposure you have to these will vary between organizations. We will look at these now.

# Firewalls

We have already introduced the concept of firewalls in Chapter 1, *Differentiating between Internets, Intranets, and Extranets*. Recall that a firewall can either block or deny network traffic based upon certain criteria. In this section, we will look at the common forms of firewall.

## Packet-filtering firewalls

Packet-filtering firewalls are the most basic of firewalls. They are able to block or allow network traffic based on source or destination IP address, ports, or protocols within the header of the traffic. Because only the header is inspected and no analysis of the actual payload of the network traffic is carried out, this is quite a fast process. The downside to this is that it is not very secure, as traffic may be allowed because it meets the criteria specified; however, what if there is a malicious payload? Quite simply, it is allowed in. Packet-filtering firewalls operate at layers 3 and 4 of the OSI model.

What I have described previously is what is known as stateless packet-filtering, and, in essence, is an **access-control list (ACL)**, which just specifies what is or is not allowed based on the criteria that we mentioned. However, another form of packet-filtering is stateful inspection. Stateful inspection still allows or blocks traffic based on the criteria, but it also factors in the state of the connection. To be able to do this, a firewall capable of stateful inspection keeps track of all communications that are being made and records them in a state table. Let's look at some examples to see how this works. In each case, the firewall has received some inbound HTTP traffic from a website, coming from a source port of 80.

**Example 1**: A stateless firewall with a rule allowing inbound traffic from port 80:

1. Traffic is received by the firewall from port 80.
2. The firewall compares the header to its rules and sees that inbound traffic on port 80 is allowed.
3. The firewall allows the traffic through.

**Example 2**: A Stateful firewall with a rule allowing inbound traffic from port 80. The user has requested the data (solicited):

1. Traffic is received by the firewall from port 80.
2. The firewall compares the header to its rules and sees that inbound traffic on port 80 is allowed.
3. The firewall then checks the state table to see whether HTTP traffic has been requested by the device listed as the destination IP. In this example, it has been requested.
4. The firewall allows the traffic through.

**Example 3**: A Stateful firewall with a rule allowing inbound traffic from port 80. The user has not requested the data (unsolicited):

1. Traffic is received by the firewall from port 80.
2. The firewall compares the header to its rules and sees that inbound traffic on port 80 is allowed.
3. The firewall then checks the state table to see whether HTTP traffic has been requested by the device listed as the destination IP. In this example, it has not been requested.
4. The firewall does not allow the traffic through.

 In the aforementioned examples, I have used the terms **solicited** and **unsolicited**. Solicited means that the data has been requested by a device or user, such as a web page. Unsolicited means that it has not been requested by a device or user but has been sent anyway. This could be an indication of something malicious.

# Circuit-level gateways

A circuit-level gateway is a type of firewall that only checks that the initial connection between the two devices is permitted. Once that connection has been made, no further checks are carried out, and all subsequent data flowing between the devices for that specific connection are allowed to pass through uninhibited. This has the benefit of improving performance but also has the obvious concern that malicious data could be transmitted after that initial connection has been made.

# Application-level gateways

An application-level gateway goes further than the other firewall types mentioned previously. They can actually perform deep-packet inspection and analyze the data within the payload besides identifying what application is in use. This means you can block or allow traffic specifically based on the application rather than a port. This is especially useful when attackers are trying to send data on a port that is used for something else. Let's look at an example of this.

A firewall has been set up to allow inbound traffic from port 53 (DNS). An attacker is aware of this and forges a packet with a malicious payload, and sends it from port 53 on their machine to a destination on the other side of the firewall. The data is received by the firewall, which inspects the data. The firewall observes that the data does not match the DNS format expected on port 53, thus discards the data, and logs the event as a port mismatch (or something similar).

Firewall technology improves on a regular basis, and it is important that you keep up to date with the developments to ensure your organization is suitably protected. In addition to firewalls, a number of organizations will use a proxy server to add some more control.

# Proxy servers

Quite simply, a proxy server is a device that forwards requests from one device to the intended recipient, and does the reverse for any response. Let's talk through *Figure 14.7*, where we can see this operation:

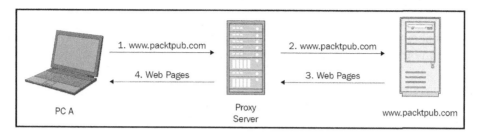

Figure 14.7: Communicating via a proxy server

1. **PC A** wants to look at the website www.packtpub.com and sends its request to the proxy server.
2. The proxy server forwards the request on to www.packtpub.com.
3. The web server at www.packtpub.com receives the request and sends the requested web pages to the proxy server.
4. The proxy server forwards the web pages to **PC A**.

It should be noted that between *step 3* and *step 4*, the proxy server may cache the requested web pages locally for use by other devices. *Figure 14.8* continues on the preceding steps to show this:

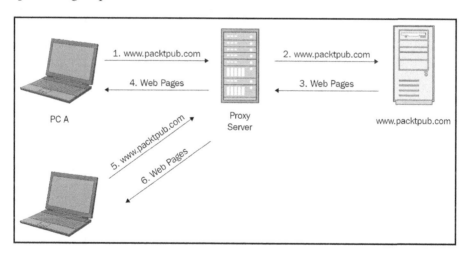

Figure 14.8: Retrieving web pages from a proxy server cache

5. **PC B** wants to look at the website www.packtpub.com and sends its request to the proxy server.
6. The proxy server knows it has these pages in its cache, so replies to **PC B** with the stored copies.

This caching of data that we have just seen is beneficial for organizations that pay by the amount of data being received. By caching the data on the proxy server, we have pulled it down once from our ISP but have it available to all our clients.

In the preceding steps, we learned a simplified version of how this process works. To go any more in-depth would be beyond the scope of this book. It is not unusual for organizations to specify a proxy server on port 8080 in the LAN settings configuration.

**Activity**: In this activity, we will configure a device's internet options to use a proxy server:

1. Open up **Internet Options** in the Control Panel.
2. Click on **LAN settings**, as shown in the following screenshot:

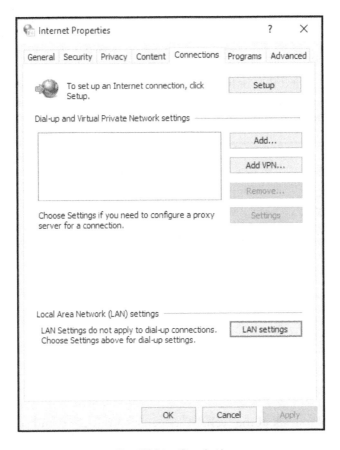

Figure 14.9: Internet Properties tab

3. Check the **Use a proxy server for your LAN** checkbox and enter the IP address of your proxy server and the relevant port:

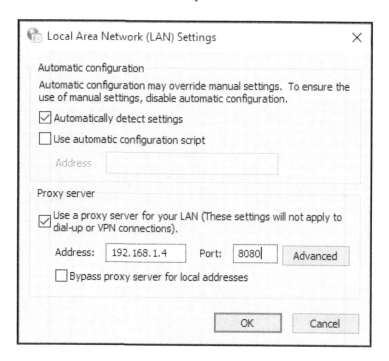

Figure 14.10: LAN settings

 You can also select whether local addresses are routed via a Proxy server or not.

4. You have now configured a basic setup, however, I would like you to click on the **Advanced** button.

5. Here, you can set up proxy configuration for individual protocols, and exceptions. The **Exceptions** section is useful for external addresses that you do not route via the proxy server, potentially due to the sensitive nature of the data being transferred:

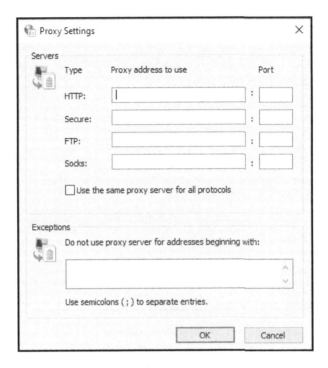

Figure 14.11: Proxy Settings

6. Click **OK** on both screens to exit.

We will now look at another use of proxy servers, namely using whitelists and blacklists.

# Whitelisting and blacklisting

A number of organizations will also use a proxy server in conjunction with either a whitelist or a blacklist to allow or deny traffic:

- **Whitelists**: Only destinations/applications listed on the whitelist are permitted through the proxy. Anything not on the list is not permitted.
- **Blacklists**: All destinations/applications are permitted through unless they are on the blacklist.

Whether your organization uses a whitelist or a blacklist will be dependent on the nature of the organization. For example, a school would likely use a whitelist so they have control over what the students are accessing; an insurance company may use a blacklist allowing staff to access anything on the internet with the exception of adult-themed sites.

 Before applying either list, get input from your users so they don't come in and find they cannot access anything business-critical. I recall working for a health organization that blacklisted any website containing the word **sex**. Needless to say, the staff in the **sexual health department** could not do any work until this was rectified.

It is unlikely that you go through your networking career without working for an organization that utilizes proxy servers at some point. Being aware of how they work and whether your organization uses them will greatly assist in troubleshooting access issues. We will now look at remotely accessing a system using remote desktop.

# Remote desktop

The use of remote desktop/terminal services is very commonplace in larger organizations, and is also known as terminal services, **Remote Desktop Protocol (RDP)**, or **Windows Based Terminal (WBT)**. This service allows you to connect to a suitably configured remote device on port 3389 and have a **graphical user interface (GUI)** frontend.

To connect to a remote desktop, you need to have a remote desktop client application installed on your device. Fortunately, Windows comes with one preinstalled.

**Activity**: In the following activity, we will look at configuring this client:

1. Open up a **Run** command using Windows + *R*.
2. Type in mstsc and hit *Enter*:

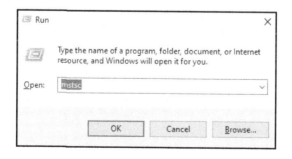

Figure 14.12: Command prompt

3. The following dialog box opens. Note, I have expanded this by clicking on **Show Options**. This tab allows me to enter the IP address or hostname of the remote device. It also offers the option to save the configuration, which I would highly recommend if you are accessing the device regularly or have multiple devices to connect to:

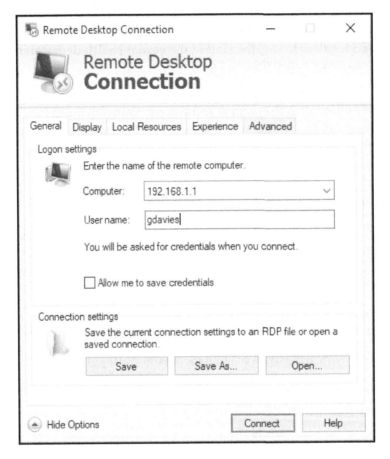

Figure 14.13: Remote Desktop Connection window

4. Click on the **Display** tab. Here, you can configure the screen size and the colors. You may find you need to adjust these depending on the resolution of the remote desktop you are connecting to:

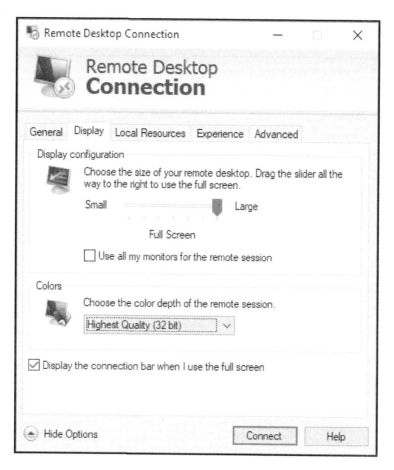

Figure 14.14: Display tab

5. Click on **Local Resources**. This tab allows you to configure sound—whether you want the remote audio to be played on your system; keyboard shortcuts—if you press a keyboard shortcut, whether it will be actioned on your machine or the remote machine; and **Local devices and resources**—whether you want to share printers, drives, and so on with the remote machine:

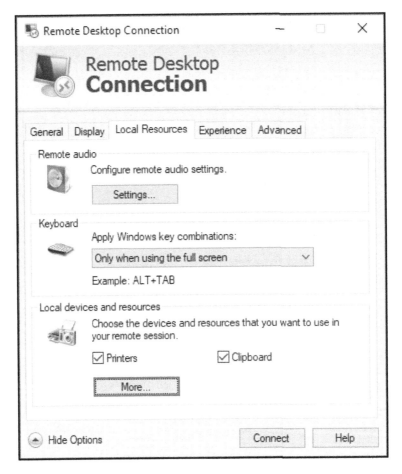

Figure 14.15: Local Resources tab

6. Click on the **More...** button. This allows you to specify more local resources to share. I usually allow access to one of my local drives as it makes transferring files easier. Any drives shared this way will appear as network drives on the remote system. Click **OK** to exit the following screen:

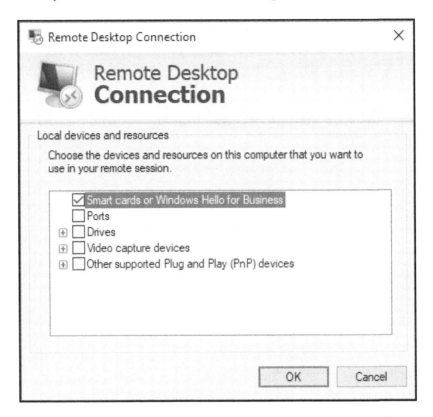

Figure 14.16: More local resources

7. Click on the **Experience** tab. This tab allows you to specify your user experience in regard to the GUI based upon the speed of your connection. It defaults to **Detect connection quality automatically**, but you can adjust this if you experience any issues. You can also specify whether you want any dropped connections to reconnect automatically. If you do not select this option, you are required to manually reconnect each time:

Figure 14.17: Experience tab

8. Click on **Advanced**. This tab allows you to specify whether the server you are connecting to requires authenticating itself or not, and also allows you to configure settings if you are trying to connect to a remote desktop outside of your network:

Figure 14.18: Advanced tab

Remote desktop is a great tool and is used by network engineers on a daily basis. Familiarize yourself with its use as soon as you can. We mentioned in the activity about transferring files by mapping the remote desktop connection to local drives. We will now look at another method of transferring files.

# FTP

We have introduced FTP previously, and we mentioned that it is a means of transferring files across different operating systems, and requires an FTP server and an FTP client. Recall that it uses port 20 for data and 21 for commands. There are two types of FTP mode in use:

- Active FTP
- Passive FTP (sometimes written PASV)

Let's discuss these one by one.

# Active FTP

With active FTP, the client will open a random port and connect to the FTP server on port 21. For the purposes of this explanation, we will use port 2031 as the port opened on the FTP client. Therefore, command communication is taking place between port 2031 on the client and port 21 on the server. Once the initial connection has been made, the client opens up the next port, in this case, 2032, to listen for the data communications coming from the server. All data communications will take place between ports 20 and 2031. You can see this in *Figure 14.19*:

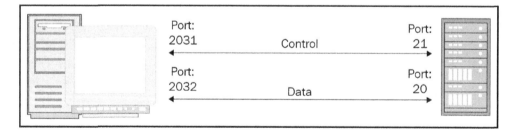

Figure 14.19: Active FTP

The problem with this mode is that the firewall on the client's side sees the data communication as an externally initiated connection, and may block it.

# Passive FTP

To avoid the potential firewall issues experienced, we can use passive FTP. In passive FTP, the client opens a random port, and the port immediately after it. For this example, let's use 2031 and 2032 again. The client connects to the FTP server on port 21 from port 2031. This connection is used for command traffic, and one of the first things the client sends is a message telling the server that it is running in passive mode. The server responds back to port 2031 on the client and provides the number of a port that the server has made available to the client. For this example, the server has stipulated port 2879. Continuing our example, on receipt of this port number, the client connects from port 2032 to port 2879 on the server. All data communication is transferred between these two ports. As the client has initiated this connection, the firewall is less likely to block the traffic.

# File server

We have already discussed one method of accessing files across a network in the previous section about FTP. However, while FTP is of great benefit when communicating between devices with disparate operating systems, the requirement to use some form of FTP client as well as installing FTP server software doesn't always make this the best choice. Likewise, we could just make folders available across the network using shares. Again, this is not an ideal solution in larger organizations. A better alternative is to create a file server.

Quite simply, a file server is a server where an organization's files are stored and made available to users with the appropriate permissions to access the files. This is a similar concept to file sharing on a local device, but with the added benefit of centralized storage and administration. This will also make configuring backups, and other forms of redundancy, a lot simpler. Organizations implementing file servers will usually apply group policies, and administrative policies which mean all user files are stored on the file server rather than locally. Undoubtedly, you will still have users that save files to their desktop and accidentally delete them, or their device fails on them, and the data is lost as the file will not have been backed up.

To facilitate the use of a file server and ensure only authorized individuals are accessing the data, we usually place users into groups based upon some form of attribute, for example, where they are based, their job role, and so on. Users are not restricted to just one group, and it is very common to see them in multiple groups. For example, let's look at Billy. Billy is a manager in the sales department. Therefore, it is likely that he may be a member of the sales group, and also a member of the managers group. Once a member of a group, that group will be allocated certain permissions on the folder that they are accessing. Let's look at some of those permissions now.

# Share permissions

Applying a share permission means setting the permissions for a user to access a folder across the network from a remote device. Share permissions only apply across a network, and can only be applied to folders. If a user is sat at the device, the permissions do not apply. To apply local restrictions, we have to apply NTFS permissions.

Creating a local share is relatively straightforward. In the following process, we will walk through the steps of sharing a folder:

1. Create a folder called `Top` on your desktop.
2. Right-click on it and choose **Properties**.
3. Choose **Sharing**.
4. Click on **Advanced Sharing...**, as shown in the following screenshot:

Figure 14.20: Advanced haring options

5. Check the **Share this folder** box and give the shared folder a name:

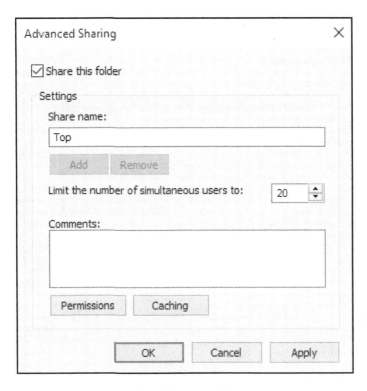

Figure 14.21: Naming the folder

6. Click on **Permissions**.

7. Notice the `Everyone` group has **Read** permissions by default:

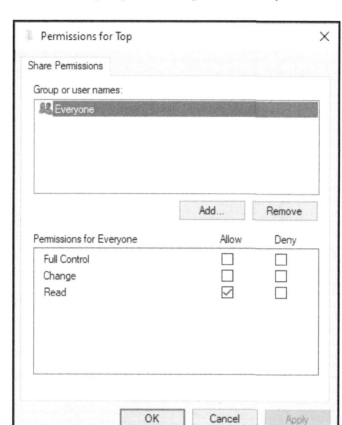

Figure 14.22: Share permissions

8. We will add the `Users` group to this share. Click **Add**.

 I have chosen this group purely for ease, and it is unlikely that you would add this group to a share if the `Everyone` group is still being used.

9. Type in `Users` and click **Check Names**.
10. If the group exists, it will be underlined. Click **OK**:

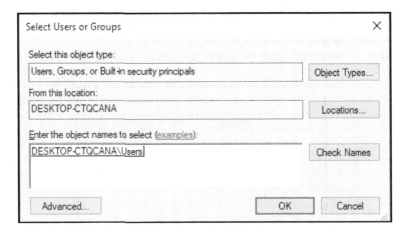

Figure 14.23: Selecting users or groups

11. Give the `Users` group the change permission, and click **OK**:

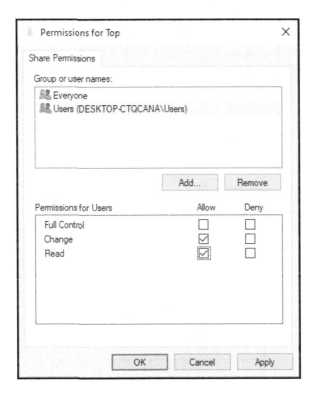

Figure 14.24: Providing change permission

12. Click **OK** again and you will return to the original **Sharing** tab.

13. Note that **Share...** now has a **Network Path:** displayed. This is in the **universal naming convention (UNC)** format of `\\<server_name>\<share_name>`:

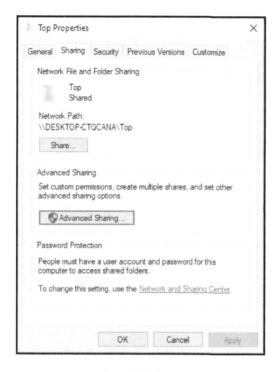

Figure 14.25: Sharing tab

14. Now you have created the share, we will add a document to the folder. Double-click the folder to explore it. You will see it is empty.

15. Right-click in the white space, and choose **New | Text Document**. Call the file `Top.txt`:

Figure 14.25: Top.txt file

16. Now, close down and reopen the **File Explorer** window.

17. In the address bar, type in \\<hostname>\top, replacing <hostname> with the hostname of your device. In my case, I would write \\DESKTOP-CTQCANA\Top, then hit *Enter*.

18. You should now see the Top.txt file listed. Also, note the address bar indicates that it is a network address:

Figure 14.26: Top.txt file

We will continue on from the preceding process to demonstrate the usefulness of the UNC method. In the previous example, we looked at a folder that was shared relatively high up in the system's directories. What if the folder being shared is many levels below? Let's look at this in the following example:

1. Open up the Top folder you have created.

2. Create a new folder called Second.

3. Open up this new folder and create a further folder called Third.

4. Open up this new folder and create a further folder called Fourth.

5. Open up this new folder, create a new text document as you did before, and call it Fourth.txt. Your folder structure should look like this:

Figure 14.27: Fourth.txt file

6. Share this folder, in the same way as we did on the previous activity.

7. Now, close down and reopen the **File Explorer** window.

8. In the address bar, type in \\<hostname>\fourth, replacing <hostname> with the hostname of your device, then hit *Enter*. You should now see the Fourth.txt file listed, as shown in the following screenshot:

> Network > DESKTOP-CTQCANA > Fourth

| Name | Date modified | Type | Size |
|---|---|---|---|
| Fourth | 22/09/2019 11:40 | Text Document | 0 KB |

Figure 14.28: Fourth.txt file

Notice we only had to use the share name Fourth, and did not have use a full folder path. We have basically jumped the intermediary folders.

It should be noted that unless hidden, the share will be visible to all who navigate to the device over the network. To avoid this, you can create a hidden or admin share quite simply by suffixing the share name with a $ sign. This hides the share, and to access it, you need to actually know the name of the share. A lot of organizations use this technique to hide shares containing installation files or other sensitive information that certain individuals may need access to.

If a user is more than one group, the least restricted permission applies. This throws people a little bit because, from a security perspective, we tend to talk about restricting things a lot. Let's return to our example of Billy. Recall he is a member of the Sales group and the Managers group. For this example, Billy needs to access a folder on a remote computer. The Sales group has **Read** access; the Managers group has **Change** access. If we made this so the most restrictive applies, then Billy would only have the read permission and wouldn't be able to change anything. Well, that's no good. Billy is a manager and needs to change things in that folder. This is why we use the rule of least restrictive. Billy is still only being granted the permissions he needs to do his job properly. To reinforce this, let's do one more example.

Billy is a member of the groups shown in the following table, with the permissions given. What is his effective share permission?

| Group | Share permission |
|---|---|
| Sales | **Full Control** |
| Managers | **Read** |
| H_and_S | **Read** |

In this example, the least restrictive permission is **Full Control**, and this is, therefore, Billy's effective permission.

A lot of organizations follow this process:

1.  Create a user.
2.  Add the user to a group that reflects their job role (as we saw with the example of Billy).
3.  Add that group to another group that is named to reflect the folder and permissions it will be applied to.
4.  Apply the folder permissions to that last group.

That may sound a little confusing, so an example would be of benefit here. Let's use another user here to avoid any confusion. Summer is a user in the writing department, and all members of the writing department have the **Read** permission to a folder called New Marketing. This is what we would do:

1.  Create a user account called Summer.
2.  Add Summer's user account to a group called Writing.
3.  Add the Writing group to a new group called Writing_READ.
4.  On the New Marketing folder, give the read permission to the Writing_READ group.

As I mentioned, **share folders** only apply over the network, and for local permissions we need to use NTFS permissions. Because NTFS permissions also apply restrictions across the network, we will look at them now. One thing to bear in mind is that should an explicit deny permission be applied, this overrules any other permission that has been applied. Because of this, system administrators try to avoid using the **Deny** permission as much as possible, and use appropriate allow permissions instead.

# NTFS permissions

NTFS permissions apply to both files and folders, and apply regardless of whether you are accessing locally or across the network. Again, the process for configuring the permissions is relatively simple and we will demonstrate this in the following example:

1.  Create a new folder on your desktop and call it NTFS.
2.  Right-click on the folder and choose **Properties**.
3.  Click on the **Security** tab.

If this tab is not present, it means the underlying filesystem on the device is not NTFS.

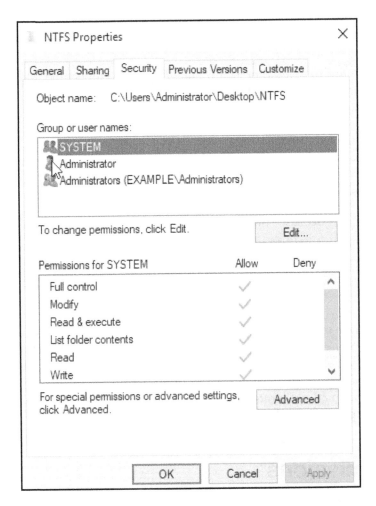

Figure 14.29: Security tab

4. This screen shows the existing users and groups with NTFS permissions to this folder. Selecting a user or group in the top frame will display their permissions in the bottom frame.

5. Clicking on the **Edit** button allows you to change the selected user/group's permissions or allows you to add permissions for a new user or group. Adding new permissions is the same as for share permissions:

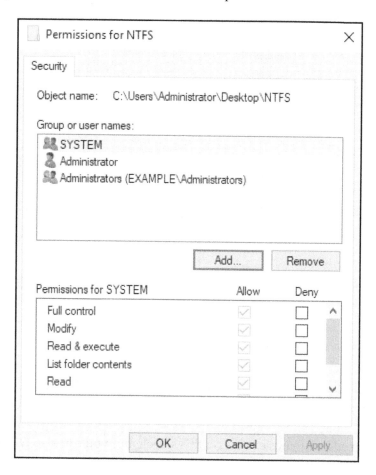

Figure 14.30: NTFS permissions

Notice that some of the boxes are grayed out. This means they cannot be changed as this folder is inheriting the permissions from a parent folder.

6. Click **OK** here to go back to the previous tab, and click **Advanced**. You can see where these permissions are inherited from:

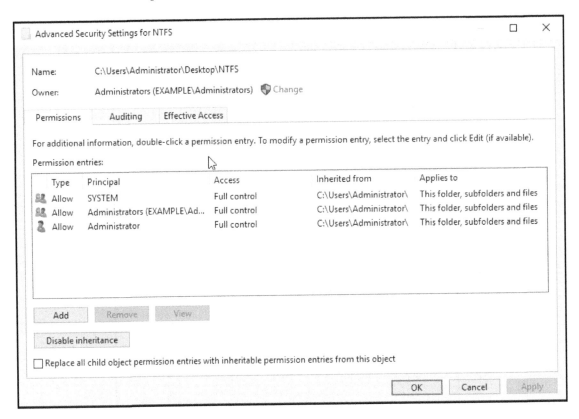

Figure 14.31: Advanced NTFS settings

You can add or remove users on this screen, but you can also **Disable inheritance**.

7. Select the `Administrators` group and click **Disable inheritance**. You will be presented with the following choice:

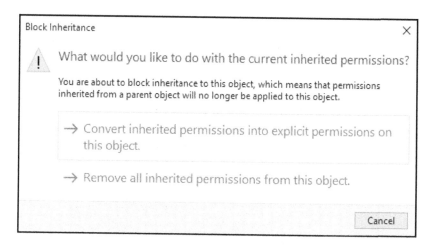

Figure 14.32: Disabling Inheritance

 When presented with this prompt, I always choose to convert the inherited permissions into explicit permissions. This removes the inheritance but leaves the permissions that were granted through inheritance in place. I then manually remove any permissions no longer required. I do this because I have found that choosing the **Remove** option takes all the permissions away and has left me with issues in the past.

8. Click **Cancel** to return back to the previous screen.

9. Click on the **Effective Access** tab. This tab allows us to check what a user's overall permissions are on this object:

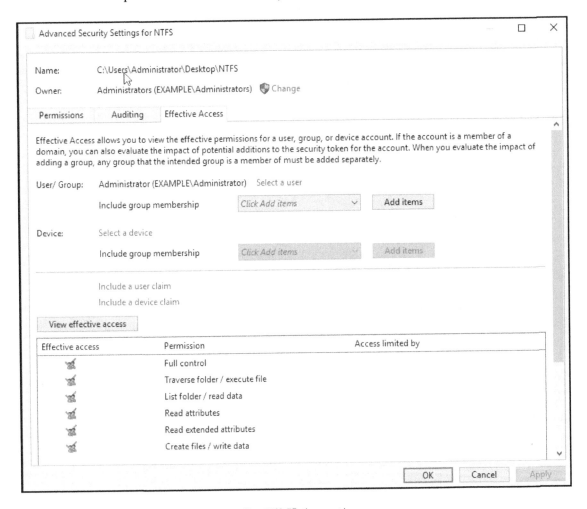

Figure 14.33: Effective access tab

10. Click **Cancel** until the **Properties** dialog box closes.
11. Open the folder and create a new text document called NTFS.txt.

12. View the NTFS properties of this file compared to those of the folder:

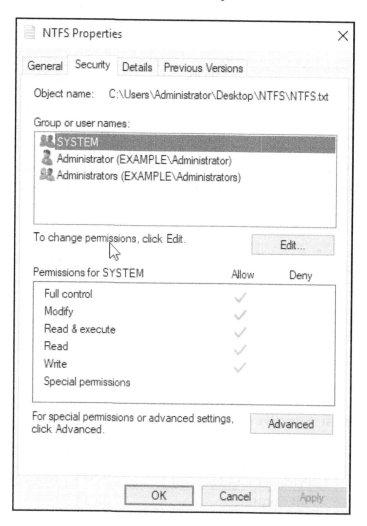

Figure 14.34: File properties

As with share permissions, if a user is in more than one group that have permissions applied to a file or folder, then the least restrictive one is applied. Let me give you an example of this in action. Billy is a member of the groups shown with the following permissions allocated:

| Group | NTFS permission |
|-------|-----------------|
| Sales | Modify |
| Managers | Write |
| H_and_S | Read |

Comparing the permissions provided, we can see that the least restrictive permission is **Modify**. As a tip, the permissions are usually listed in decreasing order, with the least restrictive at the top, and the most restrictive at the bottom.

# Combining share and NTFS permissions

We have already identified that NTFS permissions are effective both locally and over the network. Therefore, what if a user tries accessing a resource where the two sets of permissions conflict with each other? We perform a three-step process to identify the effective permission:

1. Look at the share permissions and take the least restrictive.
2. Look at the NTFS permissions and take the least restrictive.
3. Compare the two least restrictive permissions you identified at *step 1* and *step 2*, and the **most restrictive** of these applies.

I'm going to give an example here to reinforce this. A user is in the groups listed:

| Group | Share permission | NTFS permission |
|-------|------------------|-----------------|
| Sales | Full Control | Read |
| Managers | Read | Modify |
| H_and_S | Read | Read |

1. First, we look for the least restrictive share permission. This is **Full Control**.
2. Then, we look at the least restrictive NTFS permission. This is **Modify**.
3. We then compare the two, and choose the *most* restrictive. Comparing **Full Control** against **Modify**, we can see that the most restrictive is **Modify**. Therefore, the user's effective permission is **Modify**.

Because of this process, a lot of organizations tend to give groups **Full Control** as a share permission, and use the NTFS permission to restrict access. It may seem odd, but certainly makes administration simple yet effective.

# Print server

Organizations have moved away from the idea of everyone having a printer on their desk, and have moved more toward having a large printing device that is shared by everyone. The computer that controls this is referred to as a print server. This could be a local computer sharing its printer or a server controlling a network-enabled printer. It is imperative that when you are creating a print server, you ensure it has drivers installed for all possible clients that may use the printer.

# Domain controllers

I'd like to finish off this chapter by briefly discussing domain controllers. While these are not tested on the exam, I feel it worthwhile including them here for completeness as we have been discussing groups in the earlier sections.

A **domain controller** is a device that manages the devices on a network. In the world of Microsoft, this is a device that will be running Active Directory. **Active Directory** is a logical database of all users, groups, and computers in the Microsoft domain, and allows for central administration of these.

Active Directory is broken down into the following:

- Containers
- **Organizational Units (OUs)**

Network administrators will create OUs in a way that usually reflects the organization's structure, and you may find that an OU has sub-OUs within it. In *Figure 14.35*, we see that the `Manchester` OU, has a `Sales` sub-OU, which in turn has two sub-OUs called `Computers,` and `Users`:

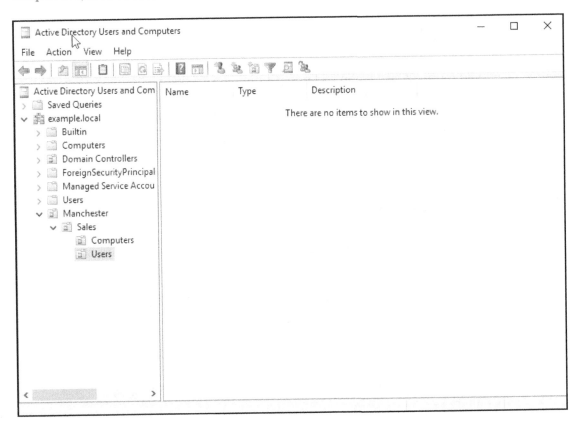

Figure 14.35: OU structure in Active Directory

Users, groups, and computers are then added to their respective OU. It should be noted that they can only be a member of one OU. Once these are set up, we can administer them using group policies applied to the OU.

When a user logs on to a permitted device anywhere in the domain, they are authenticated on a domain controller, as are computers when they power up. Because this can take up a lot of resources, you will find a lot of larger organizations will have multiple domain controllers that help share the workload.

# Summary

In this chapter, we wrapped up the main part of this book by discussing some of the common network services available. We covered the DHCP process and how it was configured, before moving on to covering various types of firewalls available. From there, we highlighted the purpose of proxy servers in terms of acting as an intermediary device to cache data and add a level of security. Next, we talked about remote desktop connections and FTP. We rounded off this chapter by talking about file servers, print servers, and domain controllers.

As we went through this chapter, you learned about the DHCP process and how DHCP is configured. This knowledge will be beneficial when troubleshooting APIPA issues. You also learned how to configure a Windows client to use a proxy server, which is a common occurrence in organizations. You then gained the knowledge of connecting to a remote desktop using mstsc, an activity you will perform repeatedly throughout your career. You also saw how to configure share and NTFS permissions, and how to calculate a user's effective permission.

With the conclusion of this chapter, we have now covered all the materials required for the exam. The following two chapters present you with mock exams to test your knowledge. However, before going through these, I would encourage you to revisit each of the chapters, and try to identify and address any gaps in your knowledge.

# Questions

1. Stephen wants to use FTP on his network. Which pair of ports should he have open on his firewall to allow this traffic through?

(A) 20 and 21
(B) 21 and 22
(C) 22 and 23
(D) 23 and 25

2. What happens when a device cannot renew its IP address lease?

(A) It retains the IP address it was originally issued.
(B) It receives a 169.254.x.x address.
(C) It receives a 127.0.0.1 address.
(D) It receives a 0.0.0.0 address.

3. Dani needs to ensure that a DHCP-enabled device receives the same IP address from the DHCP server each time. What should she configure?

(A) Reservation.
(B) Exclusion.
(C) MAC filtering.
(D) It is not possible to do this with DHCP.

4. In the following UNC example, what is the server name? Here is an example:
`\\mail\finance`

(A) \\
(B) mail
(C) \
(D) Finance

5. Steve is a member of the following groups: Sales, Marketing, Managers. Each of these groups has been allocated the following share permissions on a folder:
Sales: Read
Marketing: Change
Managers: Read
What is Steve's effective permission?

(A) Read
(B) Read and Change
(C) Change
(D) Full

6. When looking at a user's NTFS permissions, you see a number of checkboxes are grayed out. What is the most likely cause of this?

(A) The user is not an administrator.
(B) The permissions are inherited.
(C) You are not an administrator.
(D) Permissions can only be changed by the user themselves.

7. You want to change the NTFS permissions on a file and right-click and choose **Properties**. You notice that the **Security** tab is not visible. What is the most likely reason for this?

(A) The underlying filesystem is FAT.
(B) You are not an administrator.
(C) The Security tab is not normally visible in the file properties dialog box.
(D) The file is encrypted.

8. You want to create a hidden share called `Marketing`. What would you use as the share name?

(A) `Marketing*`
(B) `Marketing!`
(C) `Marketing%`
(D) `Marketing$`

# Further reading

To know more about NTFS and share permissions, visit the following links:

- *Windows 101: Know the basics about NTFS permissions*: `https://www.techrepublic.com/article/windows-101-know-the-basics-about-ntfs-permissions/`
- *Share Permissions*: `http://techgenix.com/Share-Permissions/`

# Section 4: Mock Exams

**4**

In this section, you will undertake two mock exams designed to imitate the actual exam experience. Each exam will provide you with 40 multiple choice questions covering various exam objectives. It is recommended that you achieve a score of 32 at least on each exam before contemplating taking the exam for real.

This section comprises the following chapters:

# Mock Exam 1

1. Which of these devices uses a MAC address to make forwarding decisions?

(A) Hub
(B) Switch
(C) Router
(D) Bridge

2. IP addresses can be found at which layer of the OSI model?

(A) Network layer
(B) Data-link layer
(C) Application layer
(D) Session layer

3. What type of transmission is sent to all devices on a subnet?

(A) Broadcast
(B) AllCast
(C) Anycast
(D) Unicast

4. The ability to transmit data in both directions but only in one direction at a time is known as what?

(A) Simplex
(B) Full duplex
(C) Uniplex
(D) Half-duplex

5. What type of network could be described as an internal internet?

(A) Perimeter network
(B) Extranet
(C) Intranet
(D) DMZ

6. What type of network allows trusted partners to have access to limited internal resources?

(A) Perimeter network
(B) Extranet
(C) Intranet
(D) DMZ

7. What term describes a network that covers a small geographical area?

(A) LAN
(B) MAN
(C) CAN
(D) SAN

8. Which of these is a private Class B IP address?

(A) `172.15.56.23`
(B) `172.31.56.23`
(C) `172.33.56.23`
(D) `192.168.56.23`

9. Which of these is a valid MAC address?

(A) `A6:8G:EE:12:C6:89`
(B) `B9:DA:00:12:78:34:09:EE:D2`
(C) `A698::0976:AD5B:F78A`
(D) `AA:6F:7A:BB:C3:9D`

10. Which of these is a WAN technology that breaks data down into smaller *chunks* and does not use a fixed path to the destination network?

(A) Packet switching
(B) Frame Relay
(C) ISDN
(D) ADSL

11. The point where services from your service provider interface with your own services is known as what?

(A) Hub
(B) POTS
(C) Demarcation point
(D) ISDN

12. Which Windows command-line tool will output a list of routers that your data traverses?

(A) `ping`
(B) `ipconfig`
(C) `traceroute`
(D) `tracert`

13. Which of the following provides a dedicated connection between your premises and another location?

(A) POTS
(B) ADSL
(C) Leased line
(D) ISDN

14. Which of these IEEE standards covers Wi-Fi?

(A) 802.3
(B) 802.5
(C) 802.11
(D) 802.16

15. What access methodology is used by Wi-Fi?

(A) CSMA/CA
(B) CSMA/CD
(C) Token ring
(D) STP

16. What is the third step of the DHCP process?

(A) Acknowledge
(B) Request
(C) Discover
(D) Offer

17. Which of these Wi-Fi standards use MIMO?

(A) 802.11a
(B) 802.11b
(C) 802.11g
(D) 802.11n

18. Which network topology provides the greatest redundancy?

(A) Mesh
(B) Bus
(C) Star
(D) Ring

19. Look at the topology in the following diagram:

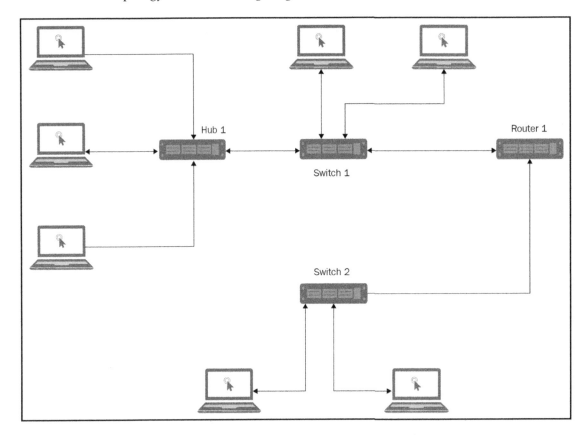

How many broadcast domains and how many collision domains are there?

(A) 1 x Broadcast domains and 7 x collision domains
(B) 2 x Broadcast domains and 7 x collision domains
(C) 1 x Broadcast domains and 10 x collision domains
(D) 2 x Broadcast domains and 10 x collision domains

20. What is the maximum length of a Cat 5 cable?

(A) 100 m
(B) 185 m
(C) 200 m
(D) 500 m

21. What type of cable should be used in HVAC?

(A) Unshielded twisted pair
(B) Plenum
(C) Fiber optic
(D) Shielded twisted pair

22. Look at the simple topology in the following diagram and the accompanying screenshot of the MAC table on the switch:

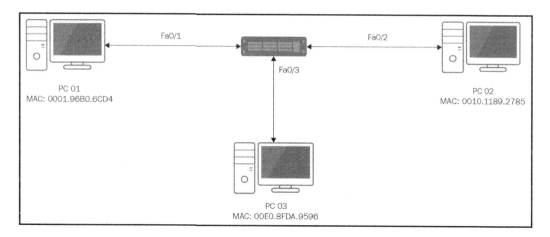

```
Switch>show mac-address-table
          Mac Address Table
-------------------------------------------------

Vlan      Mac Address       Type        Ports
----      -----------       --------    -----

  10      0001.96b0.6cd4    DYNAMIC     Fa0/1
Switch>
```

PC 02 sends some data destined for PC 01. What would the switch do after receiving the data from PC 02?

(A) Forward the data through port Fa0/1 to PC 01.
(B) Forward the data out of ports FA0/1 and Fa0/3.
(C) Update the MAC table with the MAC address and port number for PC 02.
(D) Discard the data.
(E) Sends it out to all ports

23. What can be used to avoid broadcast storms?

(A) RIP
(B) OSPF
(C) STP
(D) IS-IS

24. What does a router look at to determine the correct interface to forward data through?

(A) Hop count
(B) Bandwidth
(C) Jitter value
(D) Metric

25. RIP is an example of what type of routing vector?

(A) Link-state vector
(B) Distance vector
(C) Hybrid vector
(D) Shortest path vector

26. Thicknet cable is also referred to as what?

(A) 10baseT
(B) 10base2
(C) 10base5
(D) 10baseTx

27. To avoid network bounce, what should be used with a bus topology?

(A) BNC
(B) Terminator
(C) RJ-45
(D) Vampire tap

28. Which layer of the OSI model is responsible for encryption?

(A) Application layer
(B) Presentation layer
(C) Session layer
(D) Transport layer

29. Which of these protocols would you find at the transport layer of the OSI model?

(A) HTTP
(B) POP3
(C) IMAP
(D) UDP

30. Port number 1400 falls under what range of ports?

(A) Registered ports
(B) Well known ports
(C) Ephemeral ports
(D) Dynamic ports

31. You need to allow SMTP traffic through your firewall. What port should you open?

(A) 21
(B) 22
(C) 23
(D) 25

32. Which of these is NOT a layer of the TCP/IP model?

(A) Application
(B) Presentation
(C) Network
(D) Transport

33. Which of these services runs on port 23?

(A) Telnet
(B) FTP
(C) POP3
(D) DNS

34. Which of these is the IPv6 loopback address?

(A) 127.0.0.1
(B) ::1
(C) 127::1
(D) FE80::1

35. Which of these is a valid IPv6 address?

(A) 2001:0db8:85a3:0000:0000:8a2e:0370:7334
(B) 20:01:0d:b8:85:a3
(C) ae03:0d2c:15b3::8a2g:0370:7334
(D) 2001::85a3::8a2e:0370:7334

36. What type of transmission sends data to the nearest device providing a particular service?

(A) Nearcast
(B) Unicast
(C) Anycast
(D) Broadcast

37. Which of these a link-local IPv6 address?

(A) 2000::/3
(B) ff00::/8
(C) fe80::/10
(D) ::1

38. A user complains their device cannot connect to a resource using a fully qualified domain name but can access it using an IP address. What service should you investigate?

(A) ARP
(B) DNS
(C) DHCP
(D) WINS

39. Billy is a member of the following security groups: Marketing, Finance, Management, and Manchester. Each group has the following share permissions applied to a folder:
Marketing: Read
Finance: Full control
Management: Read
Manchester: Change
What is Billy's effective share permission?

(A) Read
(B) Change
(C) Read and change
(D) Full control

40. When a user logs on to a device on a domain, where are their credentials sent for authentication?
(A) Domain controller
(B) DNS server
(C) DHCP server
(D) ARP

# 16
# Mock Exam 2

1. Which of these devices uses IP addresses for forwarding decisions?

(A) Switch
(B) Hub
(C) Router
(D) Bridge

2. Which of these devices is classed as a layer 1 device?

(A) Switch
(B) Hub
(C) Router
(D) Bridge

3. What type of transmission is sent to a predefined group of devices on a network?

(A) Anycast
(B) Multicast
(C) Broadcast
(D) Unicast

4. The ability to transmit data in only one direction is known as what?

(A) Simplex
(B) Half-duplex
(C) Full duplex
(D) Simple duplex

5. A perimeter network is also known as what?

(A) Intranet
(B) DMZ
(C) Extranet
(D) Internet

6. Which of these is a Class D address?

(A) 10.34.56.12
(B) 129.87.98.87
(C) 192.15.8.223
(D) 224.45.34.23

7. Which of these IEEE standards covers Ethernet?

(A) 802.3
(B) 802.5
(C) 802.11
(D) 802.15

8. Which of these IEEE standards covers a token ring?

(A) 802.3
(B) 802.5
(C) 802.11
(D) 802.15

9. At what point during a dynamic IP address lease does the client first attempt to renew the address?

(A) 25% of the lease used
(B) 50% of the lease used
(C) 75% of the lease used
(D) Once the lease expires

10. OSPF is an example of what sort of routing protocol?

(A) Link-state vector
(B) Distance vector
(C) Hybrid vector
(D) Shortest path vector

11. What is the maximum segment length of a thinnet cable?

(A) 100 m
(B) 185 m
(C) 200 m
(D) 500 m

12. You wish to connect to a device to control it via a secure command-line connection. Which service would you use?

(A) Telnet
(B) HTTPS
(C) SSH
(D) SFTP

13. Which of these services resolves NetBIOS names to IP addresses?

(A) DNS
(B) DHCP
(C) ARP
(D) WINS

14. When a computer first sends a discover packet to a DHCP server, what IP address is used as the source IP?

(A) `127.0.0.1`
(B) `192.168.0.1`
(C) `0.0.0.0`
(D) `255.255.255.255`

15. You wish to configure a static route from the command line. What switch would you use to ensure the route remained after a system reboot?

(A) `-p`
(B) `-persistent`
(C) `-remain`
(D) `-r`

16. What is the transmission rate of OC-3?

(A) 10 Mbps
(B) 51.84 Mbps
(C) 155.52 Mbps
(D) 622.08 Mbps

17. Which technology does the term POTS refer to?

(A) Dial-up
(B) Fiber optic networking
(C) Satellite networking
(D) PAN networking

18. You are testing a server and need to communicate to it by its FQDN, but want to restrict the name resolution to just one device. What would you do?

(A) Configure a PTR record on the DNS server.
(B) Configure the LMHOSTS file.
(C) Configure an alias on the DNS server.
(D) Configure the HOSTS file.

19. Rather than pointing to an IP address, a DNS record points to another FQDN. What type of record is this?

(A) PTR
(B) CNAME
(C) SRV
(D) NS

20. What type of DNS record would you find in a reverse lookup zone?

(A) PTR
(B) CNAME
(C) SRV
(D) NS

21. Which of these is NOT an alternative representation of the following IPv6 address?
`2001:0000:3238:DFE1:0063:0000:0000:FEFB`

(A) `2001:0:3238:DFE1:063::FEFB`
(B) `2001::3238:DFE1:63:0:0:FEFB`
(C) `2001::3238:DFE1:0063::FEFB`
(D) `2001:0:3238:DFE1:63:0:0:FEFB`

22. The first six characters of a MAC address represent what?

(A) Network ID
(B) OUI
(C) CPU type
(D) Maximum bandwidth

23. A client opens up port 2031 and connects to an FTP server on port 21. The client then informs the FTP server it is running in PASV mode. What port would the server open to receive the data being transferred?

(A) 20
(B) 2032
(C) 21
(D) A random port selected by the server itself

24. You have a wireless access point that supports IEEE802.11b and IEEE 802.11g. What would happen if you added an 802.11b device to this network?

(A) The speed of the 802.11b device would increase to 54 Mbps.
(B) The speed of the network would drop down to 11 Mbps.
(C) The 802.11b device would still communicate at 11 Mbps, and the 802.11g devices would still communicate at 54 Mbps.
(D) The access type would change to CSMA/C(D)

25. What command would you run to show the MAC address of a network interface?

(A) ipconfig /all
(B) ipconfig
(C) ipconfig /getmac
(D) ipconfig /displaymac

26. Which of these technologies uses 2 x B channels and 1 x D channel?

(A) PRI
(B) Satellite
(C) Dial-up
(D) BRI

27. How long is an IPv6 address?

(A) 32 bits
(B) 48 bits
(C) 128 bits
(D) 256 bits

28. Which of these Wi-Fi encryption standards requires the use of a RADIUS server?

(A) WEP
(B) WPA
(C) WPA2-PSK
(D) WPA2-enterprise

29. At which layer of the OSI model would you find frames?

(A) Transport layer
(B) Data-link layer
(C) Application layer
(D) Session layer

30. Which network topology requires a central hub or device?

(A) Mesh
(B) Ring
(C) Bus
(D) Star

31. You wish to configure NTFS permissions on a folder but the security tab is not visible in the properties. What is the most likely reason for this?

(A) The folder is on a FAT partition.
(B) You do not have the appropriate permissions.
(C) NTFS permissions can only be applied to files.
(D) The folder is encrypted.

32. You wish to create a hidden share. Which of these would you suffix to the share name to create this?

(A) %
(B) *
(C) $
(D) !

33. What is the MAC table on a switch also referred to as?

(A) CAM table
(B) ARP table
(C) RARP table
(D) NAT table

34. The `ping` command is part of which suite of tools?

(A) HTTP
(B) TLS
(C) ICMP
(D) ARP

35. You believe your PC has cached an old IP to name resolution. What command would you run as part of this process to alleviate this issue?

(A) `ipconfig /releasedns`
(B) `ipconfig /flushdns`
(C) `ipconfig /cleardnscache`
(D) `ipconfig /cleandns`

36. When creating a cross over cable, which pins would you need to rewire compared to a straight-through cable?

(A) 1, 2, 3, 4
(B) 4, 5, 6, 7
(C) 3, 5, 7, 8
(D) 1, 2, 3, 6

37. What connector would you use with a telephone line?

(A) RJ-45
(B) RJ-11
(C) BNC
(D) Vampire tap

38. The process of connecting two adjacent channels on a Wi-Fi device is known as what?

(A) NIC teaming
(B) Channel bonding
(C) NIC bonding
(D) MIMO

39. What Windows command would you run to identify all of the routers that your data transits through to reach its final destination?

(A) `route print`
(B) `ping`
(C) `tracert`
(D) `show route`

40. A firewall that keeps track of all outgoing connections, hence blocking unsolicited traffic, is known as what type of firewall?

(A) Stateful
(B) Stateless
(C) Dynamic
(D) Heuristic

# Assessments

## Answers to end of chapter questions

### Chapter 1, Differentiating between Internets, Intranets, and Extranets

1. (C) Internet
2. (A) Virtual port number
3. (C) Firewall
4. (D) VPN
5. (D) Web server
6. (D) High
7. (B) ICMP
8. (C) When a branch office is connecting to the head office
9. (A) Extranet

### Chapter 2, Understanding Local Area Networks

1. (D) ARP
2. (C) `AB:12:12:CA:1F`
3. (D) Full-duplex
4. (C) MAN
5. (B) Private IP address
6. (A) `ipconfig /all`
7. (C) Destination MAC address
8. (B) LAN
9. (B) `ff:ff:ff:ff:ff:ff`
10. (A) 2

# Chapter 3, Understanding Wide Area Networks

1. (D) Optical
2. (C) 34.368 Mb/s
3. (A) Modem
4. (C) Router
5. (B) 2
6. (C) ATM
7. (A) CRC
8. (D) 320 Kb/s
9. (A) PSE

# Chapter 4, Understanding Wireless Networking

1. (D) CSMA/CA
2. (C) 2.4 GHz
3. (C) 802.11n
4. (B) Ad-hoc mode
5. (D) WPA2-Enterprise
6. (B) 802.11a
7. (D) You have an 802.11b device on the network
8. (B) 802.1x

# Chapter 5, Network Topologies - Mapping It All Out

1. (A) MAU
2. (D) CSMA/CD
3. (C) Switch
4. (B) Ring
5. (D) 20
6. (A) Full mesh
7. (C) 802.5
8. (D) Hybrid

# Chapter 6, Switches and Switching - Forwarding Traffic on a Local Network

1.(C) Layer 3
2. (C) Send it to `Fa0/2` and `Fa0/3` only
3. (B) Store and forward
4.(A) Unmanaged switch
5.(C) 4
6.(D) STP
7. (A) Broadcast storm
8. (B) Backplane Speed
9. (B) Full-Duplex
10. (B) One

# Chapter 7, Routers and Routing - Beyond a Single Network

1.(C) Layer 3 switch
2.(D) Distance vector
3.(A) RIP
4.(C) BGP
5. (B) 0.0.0.0
6. (C) 10.0.0.1
7. (B) TTL
8. (C) 72.34.5.6
9. (A) QoS

# Chapter 8, Media Types - Connecting Everything Together

1. (D) Fiber optic
2. (B) ST
3. (B) 185 m
4. (A) Straight-through cable
5. (B) 100 Mbps
6. (A) Plenum

7.  (C) Terminator
8.  (A) 100 m
9.  (B) Attenuation

# Chapter 9, Understanding the OSI Model

1.  (C) Transport layer
2.  (A) Presentation layer
3.  (B) MAC addresses
4.  (B) Well known
5.  (A) TCP
6.  (B) 123
7.  (D) SYN/ACK
8.  (C) IANA
9.  (A) Transport layer
10. (A) MAC and (D) LLC

# Chapter 10, Understanding TCP/IP

1.  (B) Data-link layer
2.  (A) DNS
3.  (B) IEEE 802.3
4.  (C) ICMP
5.  (C) IGMP
6.  (A) Transport
7.  (C) Fragmentation

# Chapter 11, Understanding IPv4

1.  (A) 126.56.23.0
2.  (C) 106
3.  (C) Broadcast address
4.  (B) 9

5. (B) DHCP
6. (D) 172.16.9.90
7. (A) 255.124.0.0
8. (C) 187.34.23.14

# Chapter 12, Understanding IPv6

1. (D) 128
2. (C) `2001:AC10:0256:7623:ABCD:1FA8:22EE:1908`
3. (A) `2000::/3`
4. (C) `::1`
5. (C) SLAAC
6. (B) `2001:0034:0000:0000:AB76:0000:0000:4BC2`
7. (A) Anycast
8. (D) Teredo

# Chapter 13, Understanding Name Resolution

1. (C) AAAA record
2. (C) TCP, port `23`
3. (B) `example`
4. (B) The hosts file
5. (A) DNS and (B) The hosts file
6. (B) Recursive
7. (D) `ipconfig /flushdns`
8. (C) WINS
9. (A) PRE
10. (D) `server <IPaddress>`

# Chapter 14, Network Services

1. (A) 20 and 21
2. (B) It receives a `169.254.x.x` address
3. (A) Reservation

4. (B) `mail`
5. (C) Change
6. (B) The permissions are inherited
7. (A) The underlying file system is FAT
8. (D) Marketing$

# Answers to mock exam questions

## Chapter 15, Mock Exam 1

1. (B) Switch
2. (A) Network layer
3. (A) Broadcast
4. (D) Half-duplex
5. (C) Intranet
6. (B) Extranet
7. (A) LAN
8. (B) `172.31.56.23`
9. (D) `AA:6F:7A:BB:C3:9D`
10. (A) Packet switching
11. (C) Demarcation point
12. (D) `tracert`
13. (C) Leased line
14. (C) 802.11
15. (A) CSMA/CA
16. (B) Request
17. (D) 802.11n
18. (A) Mesh
19. (B) 2 x Broadcast domains and 7 x collision domains
20. (A) 100 m
21. (B) Plenum
22. (C) Update the MAC table with the MAC address and port number for PC 02
23. (C) STP
24. (D) Metric

25. (B) Distance vector
26. (C) 10base5
27. (B) Terminator
28. (B) Presentation layer
29. (D) UDP
30. (A) Registered ports
31. (D) 25
32. (B) Presentation
33. (A) Telnet
34. (B) `::1`
35. (A) `2001:0db8:85a3:0000:0000:8a2e:0370:7334`
36. (C) Anycast
37. (C) `fe80::/10`
38. (B) DNS
39. (D) Full control
40. (A) Domain controller

# Chapter 16, Mock Exam 2

1. (C) Router
2. (B) Hub
3. (B) Multicast
4. (A) Simplex
5. (B) DMZ
6. (D) `224.45.34.23`
7. (A) 802.3
8. (B) 802.5
9. (B) 50% of the lease used
10. (A) Link-state vector
11. (B) 185 m
12. (C) SSH
13. (D) WINS
14. (C) `0.0.0.0`
15. (A) `-p`

16. (C) 155.52 Mbps
17. (A) Dial-up
18. (D) Configure the hosts file.
19. (B) CNAME
20. (A) PTR
21. (C) `2001::3238:DFE1:0063::FEFB`
22. (B) OUI
23. (D) A random port selected by the server itself
24. (B) The speed of the network would drop down to 11 Mbps
25. (A) `ipconfig /all`
26. (D) BRI
27. (C) 128 bits
28. (D) WPA2-enterprise
29. (B) Data-link layer
30. (D) Star
31. (A) The folder is on a FAT partition
32. (C) $
33. (A) CAM table
34. (C) ICMP
35. (B) `ipconfig /flushdns`
36. (D) 1, 2, 3, 6
37. (B) RJ-11
38. (B) Channel bonding
39. (C) `tracert`
40. (A) Stateful

# Other Books You May Enjoy

If you enjoyed this book, you may be interested in these other books by Packt:

**Azure Networking Cookbook**
Mustafa Toroman

ISBN: 978-1-78980-022-7

- Learn to create Azure networking services
- Understand how to create and work on hybrid connections
- Configure and manage Azure network services
- Learn ways to design high availability network solutions in Azure
- Discover how to monitor and troubleshoot Azure network resources
- Learn different methods of connecting local networks to Azure virtual networks

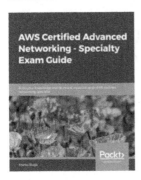

## AWS Certified Advanced Networking - Specialty Exam Guide
Marko Sluga

ISBN: 978-1-78995-231-5

- Formulate solution plans and provide guidance on AWS architecture best practices
- Design and deploy scalable, highly available, and fault-tolerant systems on AWS
- Identify the tools required to replicate an on-premises network in AWS
- Analyze the access and egress of data to and from AWS
- Select the appropriate AWS service based on data, compute, database, or security requirements
- Estimate AWS costs and identify cost control mechanisms

# Leave a review - let other readers know what you think

Please share your thoughts on this book with others by leaving a review on the site that you bought it from. If you purchased the book from Amazon, please leave us an honest review on this book's Amazon page. This is vital so that other potential readers can see and use your unbiased opinion to make purchasing decisions, we can understand what our customers think about our products, and our authors can see your feedback on the title that they have worked with Packt to create. It will only take a few minutes of your time, but is valuable to other potential customers, our authors, and Packt. Thank you!

# Index

## G

Generic Routing Encapsulation (GRE) 31
Global System for Mobile (GSM) 109
global unicast address 341, 342
graphical user interface (GUI) 423

## H

heating, ventilation, and air-conditioning (HVAC)
  244
hertz (Hz) 116
hexadecimal numbering
  about 333, 334, 335
  converting, into binary 335, 336, 337
host initialization 285
hostnames 46, 47, 48
hosts file 393, 394, 395, 396, 397
hosts
  IP addresses, assigning 315, 317, 318, 319,
    320, 321, 322, 323, 324, 325, 326, 327
hybrid protocols 206
hybrid topology 158, 159
Hypertext Transfer Protocol (HTTP) 261
Hypertext Transport Protocol Secure (HTTPS) 265

## I

ICMPv6 353, 354
IEEE 802.11a 120
IEEE 802.11ac 123
IEEE 802.11b 121
IEEE 802.11g 122
IEEE 802.11n 122
IMAP 284
Independent Basic Service Set (IBSS) 124
Initialization Vector (IV) 130
Institute of Electrical and Electronics Engineers
    (IEEE) 114
Integrated Services Digital Network (ISDN) 104
Interior Gateway Protocol (IGP) 207
  versus EGP 207
International Organization for Standards (ISO) 258
International Telecommunications Union (ITU) 332
internet 11, 12
Internet Assigned Numbers Authority (IANA) 207,
    264, 293

Internet Control Messaging Protocol (ICMP) 286
Internet Corporation for Assigned Names and
    Numbers (ICANN) 362
Internet Group Management Protocol (IGMP) 286
Internet Key Exchange (IKE) 32
internet layer 286, 287
  protocols 286
Internet Message Access Protocol (IMAP) 261
Internet of Things (IoT) 10, 331
Internet Protocol (IP) 277
Internet Protocol Security (IPSec) 32
Internet Protocol version 6 (IPv6)
  about 331
  hexadecimal numbering 333, 334, 335
  overview 332, 333
  prefixes 340
  subnets 340
  transmission, types 341
Internet Service Providers (ISPs) 65
Internetwork Packet Exchange (IPX) 270
interoperability, with IPv4
  6to4 355
  about 354
  dual stack 354
  Intra-Site Automatic Tunnel Addressing Protocol
    (ISATAP) 355
  teredo tunneling 355
Intra-Site Automatic Tunnel Addressing Protocol
    (ISATAP) 355
intranets 12
IP addresses
  about 48, 49, 50, 51, 52
  assigning, to host 315, 317, 318, 319, 320,
    321, 322, 323, 324, 325, 326, 327, 328
  need for 293, 294, 295
IPv4 address
  binary math 295, 296, 297, 298
  structure 292, 293
IPv4
  overview 292
IPv6 address
  assigning 344
  configuring, manually 344, 345, 346, 347, 348,
    349, 350
  contiguous zeroes, dropping 338, 339, 340

# X

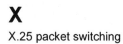

X.25 packet switching